Lawyers Professional Development

THE LEGAL EMPLOYER'S COMPREHENSIVE GUIDE

Strategies for effective leadership & design of all aspects of professional development

- **WORK ASSIGNMENTS**
- **MENTORING**
- **EVALUATIONS**
- **TRAINING**
- **AND MORE...**

by Ida O. Abbott, Esq.

© 2002 National Association for Law Placement, Inc. (NALP)
All rights reserved.

1025 Connecticut Avenue NW, Suite 1110
Washington, DC 20036-5413
(202) 835-1001 — Fax (202) 835-1112
Email: info@nalp.org
Web: www.nalp.org

ISBN: 1-55733-033-6

Contents

Introduction 9

Acknowledgments 12

Part I — Establishing the Foundations for Effective Professional Development 13

Chapter 1. The Professional Development Imperative 14

   Today's Practice Environment 17

      • Changes in Law Practice 17

      • Changes in the Industry 19

      • Changes in Attitudes about Legal Careers 23

   Why Professional Development Is Essential 24

      Table 1. Benefits of Professional Development 25

   What Goes into a Professional Development Program? 33

      Figure 1. Components of Professional Development 34

      Table 2. Missing Professional Development Components: Their Manifestations and Consequences 35

Chapter 2. Designing a Professional Development Program 36

      Table 1. Designing a Professional Development Program: Ten Steps to Creating a Strategy and Plan 37

   Approaching Professional Development Strategically 38

   Leading the Strategy Development Process 38

      • Who will be in charge of the process? 39

      • Who will gather the information? 39

      • Who will make the final decision? 40

   Developing a Strategy 41

      • The Present State 41

      Table 2. Information-Gathering Questions 42

      Table 3. Examining the Firm's Culture 44

      • The Ideal Program 46

      Table 4. Hypothetical Ideal Action Plan to Help Lawyers Develop "Superior Real Estate Knowledge and Skills" 48

      • Bridging the Gaps 49

      Table 5. Assessing Professional Development Systems: Deciding Whether to Keep, Modify, or Replace 50

      Figure 1. Force Field Analysis 53

      Figure 2. SLOT Analysis 54

   How Will the Parts Fit Together? 55

   Continuous Reassessment 60

      Table 6. Examples of Information Found on Professional Development Intranet Pages 60

Chapter 3. Leading the Professional Development Program 62

    Table 1. Why Law Firms Need Professional Development Specialists 62

The Training Partner 64

Professional Development Committee 65

Professional Development Specialists: Responsibilities 66

    Sidebar. Professional Development Specialists: Titles and Functions 66

    Table 2. Various Responsibilities of Professional Development Specialists 69

    Table 3. Twelve Core Areas of Responsibility for Professional Development Specialists 70

Professional Development Specialists: Qualifications 73

Finding Professional Development Specialists 76

Reporting Relationship of Professional Development Specialists 79

- Professional Development and the Human Resources Department 80

    Table 4. Examples of Firms with Executive Level Professional Development Directors 81

- Professional Development Committees and the Specialist 82

Practical Suggestions for Professional Development Specialists 83

Appendix 3. Two Sample Job Descriptions for the Position of Director of Professional Development 88

Chapter 4. How Legal Employers Help Lawyers Learn and Develop 91

Adult Learning 92

    Figure 1. Kolb's Experiential Learning Model 93

    Table 1. Principles of Adult Learning 94

How Lawyers Learn 96

- What Lawyers Need to Learn 96
- Emotional Intelligence 100

Informal and Formal Learning 101

    Table 2. Activities That Provide Informal Learning Opportunities 102

Creating a Learning Environment 104

    Table 3. Indicators of a Strong Learning Environment 105

    Table 4. Action Steps for a Learning Environment 111

References Related to How Professionals Learn 111

Part II — Four Essential Components of a Professional Development Program 113

Chapter 5. Work Assignments: The Core of Learning 114

Developmental Work Assignments 116

    Table 1. Work-Based Learning Outcomes and Examples of How They Are Learned 118

    Table 2. Development Potential of Assignments: Elements 118

    Table 3. Attributes of Good Supervisors 121

Allocating Work Assignments 130

- Work Allocation Systems vs. Laissez Faire 131

Monitoring Associates' Work: Productivity, Progress, and Human Resource Management 135

Contents

Figure 1. Fenwick & West LLP Skills Assessment and Self-Inventory Application 138

Components of an Effective Work Allocation System 140

Specialization and Practice Group Assignments 145

Creating Learning Opportunities 149

Pro Bono Assignments as Learning Opportunities 150

Chapter 6. Mentoring: Promoting Development Through Relationships 154

The Influence of Mentors 157

Enhancing Informal Mentoring 158

Establishing a Mentoring Program 160

Sidebar. Group Mentoring 161

Mentoring Program Elements 163

Sidebar. Coaching and Mentoring 165

Table 1. Responsibilities of Two Types of Assigned Mentors 166

Table 2. Contents of Mentoring Program Guidelines 168

Appendix 6-A. Establishing a Mentoring Program: Checklist 177

Appendix 6-B. Sample Mentoring Agreement 180

Appendix 6-C. Mentoring: Core Training Curriculum 181

Chapter 7. Using Evaluations to Promote Lawyers' Development 182

Informal Feedback and Formal Evaluations 183

Table 1. How Feedback Influences Performance and Development 184

- A Culture Conducive to Feedback 185

Basing Evaluations on Explicit Performance Standards 186

Table 2. How Performance Standards Enhance Evaluations, Performance, and Development 187

- Two Types of Performance Standards: Benchmarks and Competencies 189

Sidebar. Blackwell Sanders' Level System 191

Table 3. Example: One of the Colgate-Palmolive Company's Competencies for Lawyers 195

Adopting and Implementing an Evaluation System 196

- Making the Case: Why Conduct Performance Evaluations? 196

Table 4. Comparison of Features in Evaluation Systems Used for Results and Development 197

- Selecting and Articulating Performance Standards 202

Table 5. Examples of Performance Standards 207

- Establish Procedures for Evaluations 208

- Allocating Sufficient Personnel and Resources 227

Table 6. Key Questions to Answer in Setting Up an Evaluation System 228

Appendix 7. Associate Practice and Development Goals for 20___ 229

Chapter 8. Training **231**

    Needs Analysis..**235**

    Curriculum Considerations **242**

        Table 1. Subject Areas Customarily Included in Law Firm Training Curricula 243

        Table 2. Potential Topics for Inclusion in Core Curricula for First-Year Associates.......... 245

        Table 3. Cost-Efficient Training Approaches and Techniques for Small Firms..................... 246

    In-House Training or Outside CLE? **247**

        Table 4. Reasons to Conduct Training In-House 248

        Table 5. Factors to Consider in Deciding Between In-House and Outside CLE Courses 250

    Technology in Training **251**

    Course Design for In-House Programs........**257**

        Table 6. Teaching Methods 260

    Faculty **262**

      • Inside Faculty.. 262

        Table 7. Topics to Discuss with Instructors..... 265

      • Outside Faculty 266

    Instructional Materials............................**270**

    Time and Place **272**

      • Choosing the Time 272

      • Choosing the Place....................................... 273

    Administrative Support............................**274**

        Table 8. Representative Training Responsibilities of Professional Development/Training Directors 274

    Technology **275**

    Program Costs **275**

    Evaluating Training Programs **275**

    Measuring Investment in Training **277**

    The Law Firm as an Accredited CLE Provider **278**

    Multi-Office Firms: Special Training Considerations..**281**

    Common Training Questions....................**284**

    Appendix 8-A. Four Sample Law Firm Curricula **289**

    Appendix 8-B. Questions to Ask When Choosing Online CLE Providers **299**

    Appendix 8-C. Annual In-House Survey to Identify Future Training Topics and Faculty: Sample Form **302**

    Appendix 8-D. 2001-2002 Cooley College Faculty Guidelines **303**

Part III — Knowledge Management **307**

Chapter 9. Knowledge Management: Harnessing Information and Expertise **308**

    How Does Knowledge Management Work? **310**

        Table 1. Terminology..................................... 311

      • *Sidebar.* Advantages of Web-Based Knowledge Management Systems................ 312

    How Does Knowledge Management Benefit Lawyers and Firms?......................**314**

    Knowledge Management and Professional Development..**315**

    Obstacles to Knowledge Management **316**

    Making Knowledge Management Work to Support Learning **319**

Part IV — Budgeting 327

Chapter 10. Budgeting for a Professional Development Program 328

The Budgeting Process 330

Table 1. Monthly Working Plan for Training Budget..331

Table 2. Monthly Operating Expense Worksheet..332

Table 3. Breakdown of Cost Categories for Budgeting 334

Special Budgeting Issues for the Professional Development Director 335

Part V — Coordinating Professional Development Efforts with Recruiting, Summer Programs, and Orientation............339

Chapter 11. Associate Recruiting and Summer Programs 340

Associate Recruiting 341

Summer Programs 342

Table 1. Elements of a Summer Program 343

- Orientation 343
- Work Assignments 344
- Effective Supervision 345
- Feedback and Evaluations 345
- Learning 347
- Personal Attention...348
- Social Events..349
- Program Evaluation 350

Chapter 12. Orientation Programs 351

- *Sidebar.* Administrative Orientation 352

Content and Format of Orientation Programs..353

- New Associate Orientation 354

  Table 1. Potential Topics to Include in New Associate Orientation Programs............357

- Orientation for Laterals.................................358
- Orientation for Newly Elevated Partners........362

  Table 2. Orientation Topics for Newly Elevated Partners 363

Organizing an Orientation Program 366

- Timing and Frequency 366
- Personnel 367
- Location..369
- Social Events..370

Appendix 12-A. Shook Hardy & Bacon LLP Partner Orientation Program 372

Appendix 12-B. Pillsbury Winthrop LLP Orientation for New and Lateral Partners 374

Part VI — Special Issues Related to Professional Development 377

Chapter 13. Women and Minority Lawyers 378

Diversity Training 379

Training for Practice Development 379

Work Assignments.......................................380

Evaluations 380

Mentoring 381

Culture Change 381

Useful References on Diversity and Work-Life Balance 382

Chapter 14. Associate Participation on Committees 383

   Table 1. Committees on Which Law Firm Associates Serve 384

  Associate Committees 386

  Associate Selection for Firm Committees .. 387

Chapter 15. Career Guidance 388

Chapter 16. Succession Planning 392

Chapter 17. The Role of the Ombudsperson 396

Part VII — Professional Development in Corporate and Government Settings 399

Chapter 18. Corporate Law Departments ... 400

  Career Advancement and Development ... 401

  Orientation 402

  Work Assignments 403

  Evaluations 404

  Mentoring 405

  Training 406

- *Sidebar.* Outside Mentoring and Coaching Services 407

- *Sidebar.* Training Program at Oracle Corporation 408

- Corporate Training Resources 409

- Outside Resources 409

- Knowledge Management Technologies 410

Chapter 19. Lawyers in the Public Sector ... 411

Index 415

Introduction

Legal employers today are focusing more seriously on the development needs of lawyers. Until very recently, only a few large law firms in the United States approached lawyers' professional development in a considered and systematic way. The last few years have seen a sudden and significant rise in the number of law firms, corporations, and government agencies devoting substantial resources to training, mentoring, and other aspects of professional development. One key indicator of this trend is the increase in membership in the Professional Development Consortium (PDC), the only association in the United States comprised solely of in-house legal training and professional development personnel. The PDC, which was formed in 1990, had a relatively stable membership for its first decade. Since January 2000, however, PDC membership has more than doubled. The surging numbers of dedicated professional development personnel illustrate that legal employers now consider the training and development of lawyers to be a wise and necessary investment.

Research on lawyers' careers by The NALP Foundation for Law Career Research and Education anticipated — and perhaps even contributed to — this movement. The Foundation's studies have consistently documented that lawyers ardently desire and expect to learn and grow in the workplace — and that talented lawyers will leave their jobs if employers fail to provide training, mentoring, good work, and opportunities for development.

Recognizing the importance of this area, NALP has expanded the association's focus to embrace and champion professional development in the legal workplace. This book is NALP's latest entry in that campaign. Because professional development is a relatively new enterprise for law firms, there are few resources to guide the employers and professional development personnel who are entering the field. NALP has taken the lead in publishing this book as a resource to help fill this need. In addition, NALP and ALI-ABA will launch a new annual Professional Development Institute in December 2002.

Lawyers' Professional Development: The Legal Employer's Comprehensive Guide presents a new way of looking at employers' professional development endeavors. It presents professional development as a strategic management function that is inextricably bound to an organization's business goals — and tied to its bottom line. Effective professional development, as described in these pages, requires a firm to have a vision and plan for the future and then to design professional development activities to fulfill that vision and achieve the goals set out in that plan. To do this, a firm must have leaders committed to professional development, an expansive point of view, careful preparation, and sensible program design. Creating a strategic professional development program is essentially a search for the answers to three basic questions:

1. **Where is our organization headed?**

2. **What skills, knowledge, and experience do our lawyers need to get there?**

3. **How will we provide what our lawyers need?**

A comprehensive approach to lawyers' development integrates all of the major elements needed to achieve the answers to those questions: interesting and challenging work assignments, access to mentors, regular evaluations, and a good training program. Each of these elements has inherent value. But the positive influence of each component is substantially greater when all are planned and carried out in concert. Maximum impact is achieved when those components are combined into a complete, well-coordinated system that fosters lawyers' learning and growth while advancing a firm's strategic goals.

This book is written for legal employers, professional development directors, and all individuals interested or involved in lawyers' learning and development. It is intended to be a comprehensive and practical reference for those who are starting, expanding, revising, or restructuring a professional development program. While readers with extensive experience in professional development may find more detail than they want or need, those who are new to the field should find enough information to help them create and run an effective and successful program. It is my hope that all readers will find information that is useful, valuable, and responsive to their needs.

A few additional points should be made about the focus of this book. First, this book is written for and about lawyers. Although paralegals, secretaries, and other legal personnel also need professional development activities and programs, those needs are beyond the scope of this book. However, many of the activities discussed in the following pages, such as training and evaluations, can be adapted for paralegals and staff. I encourage you to include all legal personnel in your firm's professional development efforts whenever suitable.

Second, although this book speaks primarily in terms of lawyers in law firms, the principles and suggestions presented here apply equally to lawyers in any workplace setting, including corporate and government practice. Nonetheless, because lawyers who work in corporations or in the public sector do face some different issues than lawyers in private practice, Chapters 18 and 19 are devoted to their unique professional development concerns.

Third, to make the language consistent and easy to follow, I have elected to use traditional law firm categories when discussing lawyers: Lawyers are generally referred to as *partners* or *associates*. Law firms today place lawyers in other categories as well, e.g., non-equity partners, staff associates, and counsel. Corporations and government agencies give lawyers completely different titles. Rather than attempt to encompass all of these variations in terminology, this book speaks principally of partners and associates. Your firm or organization may use different position titles or terms for lawyers, but it should be very easy to adapt the lessons and ideas in the text for them.

As the enthusiasm for professional development continues to build, it sounds a hopeful note in a profession beset by discontent, high turnover, and public criticism. This is an area where the best interests of lawyers, firms, and society coincide. By committing resources to the development and advancement of lawyers, your organization is taking steps to improve the success of its practice and the quality of the legal profession.

Acknowledgments

Many colleagues and friends helped me in researching this book, and I greatly appreciate their support and assistance. I want to thank Erika Abner, Sharon Abrahams, Chris Abramson, Diane Allen, Tess Amato, Gina Anderson, Steve Armstrong, Leslie Belasco, Laura Blumenfeld, Ward Bower, Kathleen Brady, Kelly Brown, Vince Caminiti, Martha Capper, Randy Christison, Dan Cooperman, Jim Cotterman, Mark Cowing, Rachel Cramer, Gail Crawford, Jacqueline Daunt, Teresea Dufort, Jane Eiselein, Valerie Fitch, Marshall Fletcher, Josie Ganek, Deborah Graham, Megan Greenberg, Jim Hargarten, Janet Herman, Sheri Howard, Marie Huxter, Peter Kalis, Judy Zeprun Kalman, Karen Kennard, Betty Koltis, Dick Lee, Carl Leonard, Sharon Litsky, Sandra Magliozzi, Carol Mapes, Gaye Mara, Ray Marshall, Michele Coleman Mayes, Irena McGrath, Judith McKenna, Katya Miller, John Mola, Deirdre Mullen, Mara Nickerson, Elaine Pascal, Mark Petersen, Brett Pletcher, Barbara Portnoy, Nicole Rodney, Lonny Rose, Andrew Rossner, Jeff Rovner, David Sanders, George Sape, Peter Sloan, Deidra Sparks, Jeanne Svikhart, Andrew Talpash, Katharine Tsakalakis, Helena Twist, Christine White, Bryn Vaaler, Pamela Winthrop, Lane Vanderslice, Zack Wasserman, Linda Blackwell Williams, and Amy Zinman.

Special thanks go to Paula Patton, formerly Executive Director of NALP and now President and CEO of The NALP Foundation, and to NALP for having the foresight to propose this book and faith in my ability to write it, and to Janet Smith for her invaluable assistance.

Once again, my most heartfelt thanks go to my husband and ace editor, Myles Abbott, who made this book happen. Although I have known him most of my life, he still amazes me with the range of his talents, the depth of his patience, and the warmth of his love.

PART I

Establishing the Foundations for Effective Professional Development

CHAPTER 1

The Professional Development Imperative

- *How do your new lawyers learn to be great legal practitioners?*
- *How do your experienced lawyers keep their skills and talents in top form?*
- *How can you increase your lawyers' productivity, career satisfaction, and profitability?*
- *How do you ensure that your lawyers are committed to the firm and to serving its clients?*

The answers to these questions lie in a comprehensive professional development program. For all but the smallest law firms and legal departments, a systematic approach to professional development is no longer optional. It must be the highest priority. In the 1990s, competition and globalization forced firms to devote attention and resources to technology and marketing. In the years ahead, the action and emphasis will be in professional development.

The reason is simple. Lawyers are your law firm's most valuable — and only indispensable — resource. You depend exclusively on your lawyers for your existence. Their individual and collective knowledge, experience, abilities, judgment, and energy are the means by which your clients are served and your profits are earned. Your firm's success requires that your lawyers be as good as they can possibly be in every aspect of practice.

Any firm that hopes to survive in the competitive world of legal services must be clear about its values, purpose, and direction, and convert them into a strategic vision for the future. The process involves making careful choices about what is most important to the firm over the long term. This requires that the firm set specific priorities and goals and agree on what it will do to achieve them.

Whatever the strategic vision for the future of your firm, it undoubtedly presumes that you will have a sufficient number of lawyers with the abilities, attitudes, and values to make the vision a reality. But without a conscientious, systematic effort to promote professional development, this presumption will not hold true. In particular, firms that have been expanding nationally and internationally face a scarcity of lawyers able to work on transactions and cases that are increasingly sophisticated and complex. To find and hold onto those lawyers, a firm must make a substantial and ongoing commitment to professional development.

Every organization invests in its people, if only by paying their salaries. Lawyers require a far greater investment. They are high-priced professionals who undertake complicated and difficult work, often conducted under great pressure and for high stakes. Their value to the firm and to clients comes not just from what they know but from their judgment and from what they can do that others cannot: diagnose clients' legal issues and needs, secure a client's trust and confidence, counsel clients, solve legal problems, try cases, and structure transactions. To become fully competent and responsible professionals, lawyers have to know far more than case law, legal principles, and reasoned analysis — far more, in other words, than what they learn in law school. Successful lawyers also need to be leaders, managers, business people, rainmakers, and trusted advisers — traits that are, to a great extent, developed on the job. A firm cannot assume its lawyers will naturally acquire the skills essential to achieve the firm's strategic goals. Instead, a firm has to be a place where "the individual's knowledge is skillfully acquired and collective knowledge is freely transferred."[1] This can only happen when learning is purposeful and focused, tied to the firm's strategic business objectives, and supported with sufficient incentives and resources.

The question for your firm is not *if* you should invest in nurturing and developing lawyers' abilities, but *how* to do it most effectively. The competition for talented lawyers is fierce and continues to escalate. Today and in the future, your firm's principal challenge will be attracting, developing, and retaining top talent. To meet this challenge, your firm must treat professional development as a strategic imperative.

Making professional development *strategic* means linking learning and development directly to the firm's critical business objectives. Tying professional development to business objectives requires visualizing and articulating the future direction of the firm, defining the abilities that all lawyers should have to drive the firm toward that future, and providing the training, experience, and support to ensure that partners and associates develop those abilities.

---

[1] Kathy M. Morris and Stephen V. Armstrong, "Market Demands a Shift in Professional Development," *The National Law Journal*, June 3, 1996.

Let's say that one of your firm's objectives is to deliver "superior client service." The problem is that "superior client service" means different things to different firms. Before your firm's lawyers can deliver "superior client service," the firm needs to define what this means. What does "superior client service" look like in your firm and for your clients? What substantive, management, business, and interpersonal capabilities must lawyers have in order to deliver such service? Once these questions have been answered, the next step is to decide how lawyers will acquire the skills, knowledge, and experience they need in order to carry out this goal effectively. Only then can your firm integrate the various types of learning and development activities (e.g., training, mentoring, work assignments) that enable lawyers to learn what they need to know and do. When lawyers understand their firm's expectations and enjoy their firm's support in learning how to meet those expectations, what they learn is aligned with their firm's institutional interests. This learning has special value because it furthers the firm's strategic business goals. What's more, as lawyers are able to demonstrably add value to the firm, their opportunities for advancement improve, which in turn increases their motivation and satisfaction.

Much is made about the generational differences between young lawyers today and in the past. While there are many notable generational differences in expectations and attitudes, the basic needs and desires of today's young lawyers have not really changed much. Young lawyers may be less patient and expect results more quickly, but what they want are the same fundamental things that lawyers have always desired: interesting and intellectually challenging work, financial security, responsibility, autonomy, a collegial and respectful work environment, and a feeling that they are included in and contributing to the mission and future of the firm. These needs have always been addressed in large part through professional development.

Chances are that your firm already has some professional development activities in place, such as an orientation program for new associates and annual performance reviews. However, while many firms engage in these and similar activities, far fewer firms create an overall professional development scheme and synchronize its various components. Instead, the activities usually proceed along separate tracks, with little coordination or common purpose. Information is gathered but then nothing is shared collectively. Committees with complementary agendas fail to communicate with one another, leading to redundant or conflicting efforts. In one example, a law firm's Training Committee and its Human Resources Director both decided to undertake diversity initiatives and separately hired different consultants to conduct similar diversity training. In addition, without a well-thought-out strategy, individual professional development activities are apt to be misconceived, poorly designed, or inefficiently run. Consider one firm that decided to start a mentoring program in order to stem associate attrition. The firm did not provide training for mentors, nor did it do anything to stop the pervasive rudeness and arrogance of partners toward associates. Predictably, the program failed and associates continued to leave. This firm wasted a lot of time and money and produced no positive results.

Today's Practice Environment

As you undertake formal professional development efforts in your firm, you may encounter resistance from partners who believe that "cream rises to the top" and that good lawyers don't need special help. Some partners forget the help they received as they climbed the ladder to partnership. They may also take too lightly the new realities of a world that is increasingly more competitive and oppressive, especially for new associates. You may have to point out to those partners how law practice has changed, how the legal industry has changed, and how attitudes about legal careers have changed since they entered practice.

Changes in Law Practice

Lawyers in practice today face a different, more difficult work environment than their predecessors did. Law practice is relentless in its professional demands and takes an enormous toll on lawyers' personal lives. Let's look at some specific examples.

■ More Pressure at Work

Associates today are burdened by more onerous work requirements than lawyers faced in the past. Historically, associates were paid and advanced solely on the basis of their entering class year. Each class was paid the same salary and promoted at the same rate. Many firms are replacing this "lockstep" system with a compensation scheme featuring a standard base pay plus a bonus based on "merit." While a few firms determine "merit" by looking at an associate's contributions to the firm (e.g., through committee work) or the community (e.g., through pro bono work), in most firms it is defined by the number of billable hours in excess of the minimum required.[2] Meanwhile, hourly expectations have risen. In the 1980s,

---

[2] ABA Commission on Billable Hours Report, August, 2002. Also see the ABA web site on issues and suggestions related to the billable hour system (http://www.abanet.org/careercounsel/billable.html).

billable hour *targets* for associates in large law firms were generally in the 1,600 to 1,800 hour range. Today, the ABA Commission on Billable Hours reports that 80 percent of law firms have a minimum *requirement* between 1,750 and 2,050 billable hours, 1.4 percent of firms require between 2,050 and 2,150 hours, and 1.9 percent of firms require 2,151 hours or more.[3] As for the actual hours billed, the median for associates was 1,823 hours in 1995; by 2000, the median had risen to 1,842, and 10 percent of associates billed 2,250 hours or more.[4] In particular, associates in large firms are working at the high end of the billable hour scale,[5] with many billing over 3,000 hours a year.

■ More Work, But Less Opportunity to Learn

The crush of work and the pressure to bill leave little time for training and mentoring associates. Consequently, inexperienced lawyers are given responsibilities they are unprepared to handle and are expected to exercise professional judgment before they have the experience to base it on. Junior lawyers used to cut their teeth on simple cases or projects they could handle alone or with modest supervision. They were able to learn by observing and conversing with more experienced lawyers at meetings or legal proceedings, or in the course of the day as they worked together. The opportunities to handle small matters have virtually disappeared because most corporate clients refuse to underwrite associate training and refer more basic work to their in-house lawyers or to less expensive service providers (e.g., legal research services). This means that associates have to learn the basics while doing highly complicated legal work with little guidance, training, or time to observe or reflect.

■ More Speed, Less Down Time

Law firms now put a premium on speed, and lawyers are beset by a constant sense of urgency. They are expected to turn work around faster and to be available to clients and partners around the clock. Global offices and international transactions add to the burden as projects extend across all time zones. The technology that makes many aspects of law practice easier and more efficient also makes it more intrusive on lawyers' personal lives. Even vacations fail to offer an escape unless one goes somewhere unreachable by e-mail or cell phone. Because work now

---

[3] ABA Commission on Billable Hours Report.
[4] *Altman Weil.*
[5] ABA Commission on Billable Hours Report.

consumes so much of a lawyer's life, the time available for family, personal pursuits, enjoyment, and relaxation has shrunk to practically nothing.

■ Less Career Certainty

While partnership was never assured, the path toward partnership used to be clearly drawn, with few variations and detours. Today the road to partnership is longer and fraught with more obstacles. In most firms the partnership track has been extended to eight or nine years or even longer, and few associates are tapped to become partners. The current competitive environment also demands that associates generate their own business before they can be considered for partnership. Even if they become partners, they have no promise of job security. The pressure on partners to generate high revenues is brutal, and there is little tolerance for underperformance. Partners move in and out of law firms, sometimes on their own initiative but often because their partners have asked them to go. As a result, partnership has become both less obtainable and less desirable. Instead, associates prefer to choose their own career paths, which may or may not include law firm partnership.

■ Less Loyalty and Cohesion

The collegial, mutually supportive environment that once characterized law practice is gone, replaced by a business model that prizes financial gain above all. Law firm compensation places a premium on client origination, creating an "eat what you kill" reward system, so lawyers vie with their own partners for business and fight with them over origination credit. While this system generates more business and higher revenues, it also causes partners to compete with one another for greater individual gain at the expense of trust and collegiality. In fact, it seems odd to talk of "loyalty" at all today, when partners steal clients away from other partners and have no qualms about expelling or "de-equitizing" partners to increase their own profits. Is it any wonder that associates, partners, and whole practice groups move from one employer to another without hesitation?

Changes in the Industry

The institutions of law practice are also undergoing revolutionary changes. Growth, consolidation, and a tight labor market are exerting tremendous forces on the legal industry.

■ Growth and Consolidation

Law firms are getting bigger, and the biggest firms are becoming giants. The legal industry is consolidating into a smaller number of larger firms. In 1975, if you spoke about a large law firm, you were probably referring to a firm with 50 or more lawyers. Most lawyers worked in solo practice or small firms and served a local clientele. In the mid-1980s, law firms started to expand; a decade later the growth became exponential. Firms began to hire lawyers by the dozens (and in a few cases by the hundreds) and to open offices throughout the country and around the world. Before long, a firm with 50 lawyers was considered mid-sized. As firms continued to grow, these mid-size firms began to disappear, either by merging with others or by closing their doors. The large firms that emerged from all this activity now have hundreds and even thousands of lawyers.

The rate of growth in large firms dwarfed the expansion of the profession as a whole. Between 1980 and 1995, the entire legal profession grew 58 percent. During this period the number of lawyers in firms of more than 50 lawyers grew 287 percent, while firms of five or fewer lawyers grew only 49 percent.[6] This was *before* the most intense upsurge in law firm growth, which occurred after 1995. In 1995, the Am Law 100 (i.e., the largest grossing firms in the United States) listed three law firms with more than 500 lawyers; five years later, there were 45 such firms.[7] Today, the AmLaw 100 firms have an average of 621 lawyers,[8] and more than 15 global law firms have more than 1,000 lawyers.[9]

One of the forces driving law firm growth is the consolidation of the corporate world, which is creating fewer but larger clients. As clients grow, so do their legal needs. To meet those growing needs, law firms have to provide a broader range of services in more geographic locations, which requires more lawyers in more practice areas and in more cities. While these clients want more services, they also want to cut costs and streamline legal department operations. One way they do this is to limit the number of law firms they hire. Increasing client needs from fewer clients place intense competitive pressures on law firms. To get the work and do the job, law firms have to expand both their capabilities and their presence.

---

[6] Herbert M. Kritzer, "The Professions Are Dead, Long Live the Professions: Legal Practice in a Postprofessional World," *Law & Society Review*, Vol. 33, No. 3 (1999), fn.1. If we go back to 1960, the growth of large firms from 1960 to 1991 was 3,592 percent!

[7] Douglas McCollam, "Life on the Bubble," *American Lawyer*, July 3, 2001.

[8] Jim Schroeder, "The AmLaw 100: An Overview," *American Lawyer*, July 1, 2002.

[9] It is noteworthy that some of the largest concentrations of lawyers work not in private law firms at all, but in multi-disciplinary practices and Big Four accounting firms. For example, Landwell Legal Services, the legal practice of PricewaterhouseCoopers, has more than 2,700 lawyers in 40 countries.

■ Tight Labor Market

With demand and competition rising, large law firms are having trouble finding the qualified lawyers they need to serve their clients. While we may joke about America being overrun by lawyers, in fact, the supply of lawyers who are able to handle sophisticated, complex, and highly demanding legal work is not increasing fast enough to meet demand.

The total number of lawyers in the United States increased 142 percent from 1975 to 1999,[10] but law school enrollment began to decline during the recession in 1991, and since 1994 the number of new lawyers admitted to the Bar has steadily decreased each year.[11] Compounding this situation is the fact that new lawyers are choosing to go into fields other than private practice. During the decade of the 1990s, the number of new graduates who went into business and industry doubled, while the number of graduates going to private law firms declined by 6 percent.[12]

When the economy rebounded in the mid-1990s, law firms experienced a surge in legal work that continued through the end of the decade. The economic boom, new technologies, and emerging new markets produced an unprecedented demand for lawyers in fields such as intellectual property, biotechnology, capital markets, and cyber law. Firms also needed associates to handle the rising demand in traditional transactional practice areas like real estate and finance. Law firms clamored for more associates to handle the work that was pouring in, but their demand for associates was at times significantly greater than the supply in many major markets.[13]

Unable to find enough new associates to keep up with client service demands, firms began to recruit lawyers from other firms or organizations. This quickly became a preferred source of new hires, and the rate of lateral hiring soon outpaced entry-level hiring. Since 1997, lateral hiring has outpaced entry-level hiring each year.[14]

The tight supply and high demand for lawyers fueled attrition. Every lateral a law firm hired was another employer's turnover statistic. According to The NALP Foundation's studies of associate employment patterns, one in seven associates changes jobs each year.[15] 8.3 percent of associates now leave by the end of their first

---

[10] Kritzer, "The Professions Are Dead, Long Live the Professions: Legal Practice in a Postprofessional World."
[11] ABA, http://www.abanet.org/legaled/statistics/LE_BAstats.html.
[12] *The Lateral Lawyer: Why They Leave & What May Make Them Stay*, The NALP Foundation for Law Career Research and Education, Washington, DC, 2001, p. 9 ("*Laterals*").
[13] *Laterals*, p. 9.
[14] *Patterns & Practices: Measures of Law Firm Hiring, Leverage & Billable Hours*, NALP, Washington, DC, 1997–2001.
[15] *Laterals*, p. 8.

year in practice, and more than half (50.5 percent) leave within four years.[16] More than 40 percent of associates who leave move to other law firms of the same or larger size, usually in the same city.[17]

These conditions make it harder and more costly for legal employers to find the lawyers they need. Big firms require a steady supply of new lawyers and typically hire large classes of new associates every year. They expect those associates to work hard and do well, and hope that some will advance through the ranks to partnership. But firms cannot be sure that the associates they hire will stay long enough to become profitable, much less to become partners. Associates who start practice with large firms typically do not intend to stay for long. They join big firms for money, prestige, exciting work, and good training. Few expect to remain there more than a year.[18] Associates in larger firms are significantly more likely to be contemplating a move from their current employer. One study of young lawyers revealed that 80.7 percent of associates in firms of over 200 lawyers stated they would be open to such a change.[19]

This problem is not limited to private law firms. Corporations and government agencies face the same supply-demand issues. Corporate lawyers and those in the public sector are also apt to move from one type of practice and employer to another. Working conditions in corporate departments have become subject to many of the same time and performance pressures as in law firms, and limited advancement opportunities often lead to work dissatisfaction, especially for women.[20] Corporate counsel are highly sought after by private law firms because of their credentials, experience, and contacts. Government agencies, which draw good lawyers by promising interesting work and good work-life conditions, frequently lose these lawyers to the better paying private sector.

A slowdown in the legal marketplace has relieved some of this labor-related stress on legal employers and will continue to do so until the market recovers. The stability of government work, for example, attracts more lawyers to government positions in an economic downturn.[21] Layoffs and hiring reductions in private firms and corporate law departments allow these employers to be more selective in hiring and promoting associates. A shaky job market has sent law school applications for

---

[16] *Beyond the Bidding Wars: A Survey of Associate Attrition, Departure Destinations, & Workplace Incentives*, The NALP Foundation for Law Career Research and Education, Washington, DC, 2000 ("*Bidding Wars*"); *Keeping the Keepers: Strategies for Associate Retention in Times of Attrition*, The NALP Foundation for Law Career Research and Education, Washington, DC, 1998 ("*Keepers*").
[17] *Bidding Wars*, p. 17; *Laterals*, p. 21.
[18] *Keepers*, p.14.
[19] *Young Lawyers Division Survey: Career Satisfaction*, American Bar Association, 2000, p. 30.
[20] *Women in the Law: Making the Case*, Catalyst, New York, 2001, p. 47.
[21] Jennifer Myers, "The Lure of Uncle Sam," *Legal Times*, July 30, 2002.

2002-03 to their highest levels in 20 years, as college graduates find fewer alternative options. While this is good news for employers, it is only temporary. Competition for the best and brightest lawyers will continue. Coupled with lawyers' readiness to switch firms, this will make unwanted attrition — among partners as well as associates — an ongoing concern. What's more, an economic rebound will once again increase pressure on employers and perhaps even repeat the labor shortages of the 1990s.

Changes in Attitudes About Legal Careers

Another major change in the legal profession is a striking shift in how lawyers view their employers and their careers. In the past, a lawyer's relationship with the firm had an aura of permanence about it. Lawyers joined firms and stayed there for their entire career unless they went into business or politics, became a judge, or were passed over for partnership. As firms have become more competitive and business-like, they no longer hold out the promise of job security or even of long-term career opportunities. In response, lawyers no longer feel bound to their firms by a promise of future ownership, a paternalistic affiliation, or blind loyalty. Lawyers now view their employment relationship as "temporary, negotiable, and market-driven."[22]

Today's lawyers do not need to identify with or feel dependent on any particular employer for career success. They put themselves in charge of their careers, and many consider partnership neither desirable nor accessible.[23] Relatively few young lawyers think of their first employer as their permanent employer. Instead, they prefer to change jobs from time to time in order to get different kinds of work experience. Many associates consider each firm they join as one step on a long career path that may take many twists and turns along the way. Others merely see their first firm as a ticket to escape law school debt more quickly, get useful training, and develop some relationships that might be beneficial later in their careers — wherever they end up.

Associates perceive that diversity in types of employers and experience will enrich their development and improve their career prospects. They make ongoing professional development a personal priority and place tremendous importance on remaining marketable and keeping their options open. A study conducted by polling giant Harris Interactive Inc. on behalf of Spherion Corporation, found that the majority of lawyers (57 percent) felt their prospects for growth would improve

---

[22] *Laterals*, p. 7.
[23] *Perceptions of Partnership: The Allure and Accessibility of the Brass Ring,* The NALP Foundation for Law Career Research and Education, Washington, DC, 1999 ("*Perceptions*").

if they left their current employer.[24] What's more, many lawyers do not contemplate a lifetime career in law practice. The Spherion survey found that one-quarter (24 percent) of the lawyers surveyed do not intend to remain in the legal profession for their entire career.

The perception that employment relationships are temporary is not restricted to associates. Partners no longer feel bound by loyalty or partnership agreements; they move from one firm to another almost as readily as do associates. In the year between October 1999 and September 2000, 1,859 partners in the Am Law 200 firms — representing about 6 percent of all the partners in those 200 firms — moved to another firm or organization.[25]

These attitudes reflect the changing bargaining relationship between lawyers and firms. Employment relationships between lawyers and employers have traditionally been one-sided, with the employer holding most of the bargaining power. Today, individual lawyers have a better bargaining position and are willing to flex their negotiating muscles. The scarce supply of highly qualified practitioners and the high demand for them has given lawyers more clout. Lawyers see themselves as "owners and investors" of their human capital, that is, their individual abilities (e.g., knowledge, talents, skills), behaviors (e.g., work habits, approaches to problems), and attitudes (e.g., motivation, drive). They bring these abilities, behaviors, and attitudes to the job. They decide how much effort and time they will devote to work. They choose where they will invest themselves, how much they will contribute, and how long they will stay in any given position. They are willing to invest their human capital in a firm or organization only as long as they continue to receive a high return on their investment. Although financial rewards are very important, a high return is not limited to compensation. It also includes sound firm management, a respectful workplace, and ongoing professional development. For most associates, high-return professional development means training, mentoring, challenging work, and advancement opportunities. For partners, growth prospects and practice support are key.

Why Professional Development Is Essential

To meet the challenges of the new practice environment, your firm needs a cohesive professional development strategy. The best way for your firm to distinguish itself as a premier legal employer is by providing training, development, and

---

[24] "2000 Spherion Legal Workforce Study," Spherion Corporation, 2001.

[25] Paul Braverman, "In Motion," *American Lawyer*, February 2001. This is apparently the first time the number of lateral moves by law firm partners was counted.

> **TABLE 1. Benefits of Professional Development**
>
> - Improve the firm's bottom line.
> - Increase recruitment, promotion, and retention of talented people.
> - Promote professional satisfaction among lawyers.
> - Promote client satisfaction and loyalty.
> - Promote professional responsibility.
> - Protect the firm from professional liability.
> - Facilitate succession planning and institutional stability.
> - Promote lawyers' compliance with CLE requirements.

advancement opportunities that demonstrably profit the lawyers it hires. That is how you can beat the competition and ensure your firm's success.

Studies repeatedly identify the importance of learning and development as one of the top factors in lawyers' job decisions. Law students rank a firm's strong commitment to professional development as one of the top three factors they consider in choosing an employer.[26] Associates place even greater emphasis on professional development. In the Spherion study, 99 percent of lawyers felt that on-the-job training was the best way to learn what they need to know to practice law, and 80 percent believed that their law firm is responsible for providing the necessary training and development. In a NALP Foundation study, three-quarters of all lateral associates cited professional development as their number one reason for moving to another employer.[27] This held true for associates regardless of age, gender, race, or practice area.

The importance of ongoing development opportunities for both individual lawyers and a firm as a whole cannot be overstated. The benefits produced are real and vital. (See Table 1.) Professional development will improve:

- Bottom line profitability,
- Recruitment, promotion, and retention of talented people,
- Professional satisfaction, and
- Client satisfaction.

---

[26] *Keepers*, p. 22.
[27] *Laterals*, p. 24.

It also promotes professional responsibility, protects the firm from professional liability, facilitates institutional stability, and promotes compliance with continuing legal education (CLE) requirements. Let's take a look at how these benefits can be achieved.

Bottom Line Profitability

Professional development is a bottom-line issue. Your firm's financial success is directly tied to the performance of the firm's lawyers. It's really very straightforward: The better your lawyers perform, the more profitable your firm will be. Because the tight labor market forces your firm to pay more for good lawyers, it behooves you to increase the value of their work. A professional development program can provide the guidance, training, and support that help new lawyers become productive and efficient quickly and help experienced lawyers maintain high levels of performance.

But high productivity does not happen without effort, no matter how smart your lawyers are. Even brilliant lawyers need to learn how to be efficient; they have to learn how to make the right choices, deliver high-quality work, and manage themselves and others wisely. It has been noted that, "[a] busy firm is not always an efficiently busy firm."[28] To perform the best they can, all lawyers need tools, skills, and work conditions that foster productivity. They need guidance, support, and positive reinforcement. By making all of these elements available, professional development translates into sustained law firm profitability.

Some of the reasons that professional development leads to favorable economic outcomes include the following:

- Formal training courses teach lawyers the skills, substantive knowledge, and professional values they need to practice effectively and efficiently. Well-trained associates mean better work product and fewer write-offs.

- Informal training creates an environment where experienced lawyers share their knowledge and wisdom with colleagues. Colleagues spend less time tracking down information or reinventing wheels and more time billing.

- Mentoring builds trust and commitment through personal and professional relationships. Those relationships disseminate knowledge and create strong bonds to the firm. This improves retention, which saves lawyer replacement costs.

---

[28] Werner L. Polak and Stephen V. Armstrong, "Why Law Firms Should Adopt In-House CLE and What They Can Expect to Do," from *CLE and the Lawyer's Responsibilities in an Evolving Profession: The Report on the Arden House III Conference, November 13th to 16th, 1987*, ALI-ABA, 1988, p. 443.

- When associates' assignments provide challenging, interesting, and meaningful work experience, lawyers are more engaged and perform better. Clients are more willing to pay when they see associates add value.

- Attention to development strengths and needs results in appropriate delegation of work assignments. This increases productivity and cost-effective staffing.

- Performance evaluations communicate and maintain standards. Lawyers strive to achieve or surpass those standards, which ensures higher levels of productivity and profit.

Recruiting, Promotion, and Retention

There is abundant evidence that professional development is one of the most important factors for lawyers in deciding whether to go to or stay with an employer. Having a reputation as a good professional development firm will help with your recruiting efforts; making professional development a reality will help you promote and keep your best lawyers. Norman Letalik, Managing Director, Professional Excellence at the Canadian firm Borden Ladner Gervais LLP, explains it this way:

> "It's a win-win strategy…It is both a development strategy and a recruitment strategy. We believe that the process of earning the leading reputation for professional development will lead us to develop better lawyers faster. Good lawyers attract good clients. Good clients provide good work. And good work — and good training — attracts the best lawyers and students."[29]

▪ Recruitment

Recruiting is the first hurdle in the competition for talent. Firms spend a fortune trying to woo the best and brightest associates. You want to be sure that every associate you hire will be a good fit and a valuable addition to the firm. This requires that you have a well-designed plan to target and recruit the right candidates. Who are the right candidates? They are the law students and lawyers whose substantive knowledge, personal characteristics, and motivation make them most likely to succeed in your firm. To identify who they are, you first need to understand the firm's culture, strengths, and performance expectations. Then you can establish

---

[29] Quoted in Tim Leishman, "Accelerating Professional Development," *Lexpert*, September 2001.

hiring criteria that correspond to those characteristics. This process also helps you articulate what your firm has to offer recruits so that you can emphasize those points in your marketing efforts. As research and experience show, one of the strongest selling points your firm can put forward is a fervent commitment to professional development.

■ Promotion

How does your firm decide which lawyers should be promoted? Performance standards, evaluations, and clearly defined career possibilities let associates know what their options are and what they have to do to remain a valued lawyer in the firm. By making standards for promotion explicit, the firm can be specific about what each associate must do to be promoted. With the firm's guidance and support, associates can set short-term development goals and make long-term career plans.

By incorporating performance standards into a regular evaluation process, the firm can identify the associates who are "stars" or have the potential for stardom. These associates have the most opportunities to go elsewhere, even in a down market. Once identified as stars, they should be counseled about their opportunities for promotion and given the support that will keep them advancing steadily. They must know they are valued and that the firm wants them to stay.

Promotion standards are also important for associates who are not stars. All of your firm's associates were hired because the firm believed they had the potential to succeed and advance within the firm. Some associates need more time to shine, and some will be good, solid lawyers who never set the world on fire. With sufficient time and support, a few of these lawyers may become partners. For those who never become partnership material but whose contributions are valuable, the firm may offer alternative long-term career opportunities (e.g., permanent associate, counsel, or non-equity partnership positions). By outlining the standards for promotion to these positions, you give productive lawyers other options that may be professionally satisfying — and you keep them at the firm.

■ Retention

Perhaps the most important reason for a comprehensive professional development program is to retain talented lawyers. Professional development is a proven remedy for attrition. Firms that do not make it a priority do so at their peril. As most law firms are well aware, turnover is very expensive and disruptive. The out-of-pocket cost of replacing a single associate is hundreds of thousands of dollars. Many turnover-related costs can be more damaging to the firm although they are not easily quantified into dollars and cents: discontinuity of client service, loss of client confidence, and demoralization of lawyers and staff.

One of the arguments often raised against professional development efforts for associates is that they are self-defeating. The argument goes like this: "If we train our associates, they will become more skilled and therefore more marketable. Other firms will recruit them actively, and we will lose both the associates and our investment. Why should we 'pay the tuition' when it is the associate's next employer who will enjoy the benefit of our training?" Research conducted by The NALP Foundation and others clearly shows that this argument has little merit and that, to the contrary, professional development actually increases retention. Paula Patton, President and CEO of The NALP Foundation, points out, "The simplicity of this fact is stunning: associates have reported that when they perceive that their firms are adequately 'investing' in them by providing training and giving attention to their development as attorneys, they are less likely, not more likely, to leave their firm."[30] Moreover, this argument ignores the fact that law firms really have no choice. Without professional development, good lawyers will leave. What's more important, those who stay will lack the skills they need to serve the firm's clients and keep the firm competitive.

An effective professional development program will also help firms retain valued partners. Even in a weak market, law firms actively recruit experienced lawyers with substantial books of business. These partners will be less tempted to leave when they know they can rely on the firm to provide what they need for continued success: excellent client and practice support from high quality, well trained, and enthusiastic lawyers.

Professional Satisfaction

Professional satisfaction is no small thing for a legal employer. Dissatisfaction is widespread and turnover is high throughout the profession. Lawyers want to find fulfillment and meaning in the work they do. They want to feel they are being intellectually challenged and encouraged to achieve their potential. They value excellence and set high standards for themselves and their co-workers. A workplace where professionals uniformly strive for excellence requires ongoing training and support that enable lawyers to expand their knowledge and hone their skills. This is the purpose of professional development.

---

[30] Paula A. Patton, *Beyond the Bidding Wars*, The NALP Foundation for Law Career Research and Education, Washington, DC, 2000, p. 42.

For the firm, job satisfaction translates into higher retention, greater organizational stability, and higher productivity. Lawyers who are well trained and experienced feel more satisfied about their work; they are confident about their own abilities and the firm's career support. Their satisfaction has a strong and positive impact on the firm's bottom line. Studies prove that firms with the most satisfied employees are measurably more profitable.[31]

Strong Client Relationships

Serving clients is the fundamental purpose of law practice. Pleasing clients is essential to the continued success of a law firm. Only if clients are completely satisfied can the firm be assured that they will remain clients.[32] Professional development teaches lawyers how to identify and meet client needs in a timely, responsive, cost-effective, and supportive manner. Clients will eagerly send work your firm's way when the firm offers them excellent service — using the right number of lawyers with the right knowledge and abilities. Clients will be less prone to question hourly rates for associates when those associates are demonstrably capable and efficient. A commitment to lawyer development builds your reputation as a firm that produces high-quality lawyers who deliver superior client service. What better reputation could you ask for?

Professional Responsibility

Law is a profession that demands constant study and learning in order to maintain an acceptable level of competence. Lawyers are ethically obligated to provide competent legal representation. Some would argue that they also have a duty to improve the competence of lawyers new to practice.

The first requirement of professional responsibility is competent representation:

> "A lawyer shall provide competent representation to a client. Competent representation requires the legal knowledge, skill, thoroughness and preparation reasonably necessary for the representation."
> (Rule 1.1, ABA Model Rules of Professional Conduct, 2001)

Under this ABA Model Rule and its counterparts in the various state codes of conduct, lawyers are required to attain and maintain the appropriate level of

---

[31] David H. Maister, *Practice What You Preach*, The Free Press, New York, 2001.
[32] Thomas Jones and W. Earl Sasser, "Why Satisfied Clients Defect," *Harvard Business Review*, December, 1995.

proficiency for their practice. At no time has this been as challenging as today, when there is so much to know and so little time to learn. The speed and quantity of the changes affecting lawyers are overwhelming. The impact of technological advances and financial pressures on every aspect of law practice is profound. Lawyers have an obligation — to themselves and their clients — to continue refining their lawyering skills and to expand their knowledge in all fields relevant to their practice.[33] Through professional development programs, law firms keep their lawyers informed and equipped to deal with these changes.

Arguably, lawyers also have a broader duty to educate the profession. While this is not a mandated duty, it lends additional support for the implementation of professional development efforts in law firms. In 1992, the American Bar Association published the MacCrate Report, which assessed the education of lawyers in law school and after graduation. The Report stressed that while law school familiarizes students with lawyering skills and values, it is only through practice and ongoing learning that they attain a level of competence. It concluded that members of the legal profession have a responsibility to "assist in the training and preparation of new lawyers and the continuing education of the Bar."[34]

Protection from Liability

A professional development program has an added benefit: It protects the firm from malpractice and mismanagement. Especially as law firms get larger, the need for such protection takes on greater urgency. With lawyers in multiple offices, it is difficult but critical to monitor the quality of their work. For risk management purposes, a firm must ensure that its lawyers act in accordance with applicable rules of professional responsibility. Your firm has to have procedures in place to promote compliance with these rules and to clarify practice standards, especially in ambiguous areas (e.g., for offices in foreign jurisdictions). Law firms — often with the assistance of their liability insurance carriers — can teach lawyers the rules of professional responsibility and the firm's risk management procedures as part of professional development.

Succession Planning and Institutional Stability

In the corporate world, leaders spend a great deal of time and energy engaging in succession planning. Jack Welch, the celebrated former CEO of General Electric

---

[33] ABA Model Rules of Professional Conduct, Comments to Rule 1.1.
[34] *Report of the Task Force on Law Schools and the Profession: Narrowing the Gap,* ABA, 1992, p. 216.

Co., was known for his extensive hands-on involvement in leadership development. He personally spent several weeks each year in formal development efforts, grooming the high performers who were tapped to become the company's future leaders. His emphasis on training and development extended to the legal department, where the work experience has been likened to "being in a graduate business program."[35] The outcome is an extensive corps of superb in-house counsel that is the envy of the legal profession.

The concepts of succession planning and leadership development are still in their infancy in law firms. When firms were small, they didn't worry about leadership development. Few of them had a formal management structure, a collection of practice groups, or multiple offices. Firms operated as partnerships and made decisions by consensus. The leaders were well known and leadership transitions were not a concern until those leaders retired or died.

Law firm growth is changing all of this. Succession planning and leadership development must be taken seriously as firms become organized and managed like corporate entities. Law firms need vigorous leadership at every level, from the lawyers in charge of case teams up to the Chair of the firm. It is a responsibility of current leaders to train the firm's future leaders. In a turbulent marketplace that threatens not just law firms' success but their very survival, leaders have to maintain institutional stability and continuity. They have to be sure that, when their watch is over, others will be ready to take the helm. A professional development program can help a firm select and prepare its future leaders.

CLE Compliance

More than 40 states now have mandatory continuing legal education (CLE). Each state's CLE requirements are unique, and lawyers who are members of the bars of more than one state must comply with the requirements of each one. Because most lawyers are busy practicing law and pay scant attention to either CLE requirements or deadlines, the tracking, reminder, and resource functions of a firm's professional development program can help lawyers comply with state rules. In addition, most states permit law firms to become qualified providers of CLE programs. By conducting your own training courses, you can present programs that meet the specific needs of your firm and its practice groups, making CLE more relevant for your firm's lawyers. This is also cost-effective because it helps lawyers comply with CLE requirements without leaving the office.

---

[35] Catherine Aman, "GE's General Counsel Incubator," *Corporate Counsel*, September 20, 2002.

What Goes into a Professional Development Program?

Professional development is an ongoing and dynamic process of learning and improvement that occurs within the context of legal practice. It begins where law school leaves off and continues throughout a lawyer's career. Law school is the means for students to acquire basic legal knowledge through study and discourse. Professional development is the process by which lawyers extract wisdom from knowledge and experience. The ability to discern lessons and draw deeper understanding from what they learn and experience is one of the most valuable skills lawyers can have in confronting the challenges of modern practice.

A *professional development program* is a systematic effort to present and coordinate learning opportunities that will help a firm's lawyers reach their highest potential in the areas needed for the firm to achieve its strategic business goals. What exactly should go into your firm's professional development program? The answer, of course, depends on the needs of the firm's lawyers, the size and culture of the organization, and the strategic goals that have been set. Your law firm probably sponsors some professional development activities already. The key to an effective professional development program is to integrate those activities, and any others that are added, into a comprehensive, purposeful, coordinated plan that encourages and enables continuous learning and improvement.

Lawyers learn all the time. In the course of practice, they refine and expand their knowledge and skills in order to maintain their competence and adapt to rapidly changing conditions. In the process of doing their work, they have to constantly evaluate, interpret, and manage information and ideas that affect their work. The more they do it, the more adept they become. Lawyers get better at trying cases by handling more trials; better at doing deals by negotiating more transactions. Experience makes their intuition sharper and their judgment clearer. What they learn from books, courses, and advance sheets is enriched by what they learn through everyday work, by interacting with others, through committee assignments, and from new and challenging job-related problems.

Lawyers learn *informally* through work assignments and encounters with experts, supervisors, and mentors; *formally* through training courses; and *incidentally* through unexpected discoveries. An effective professional development program sponsors and promotes these kinds of learning through three principal components: work experience, mentoring, and training. (See Figure 1.) Each of these professional development components offers different kinds of opportunities for learning.

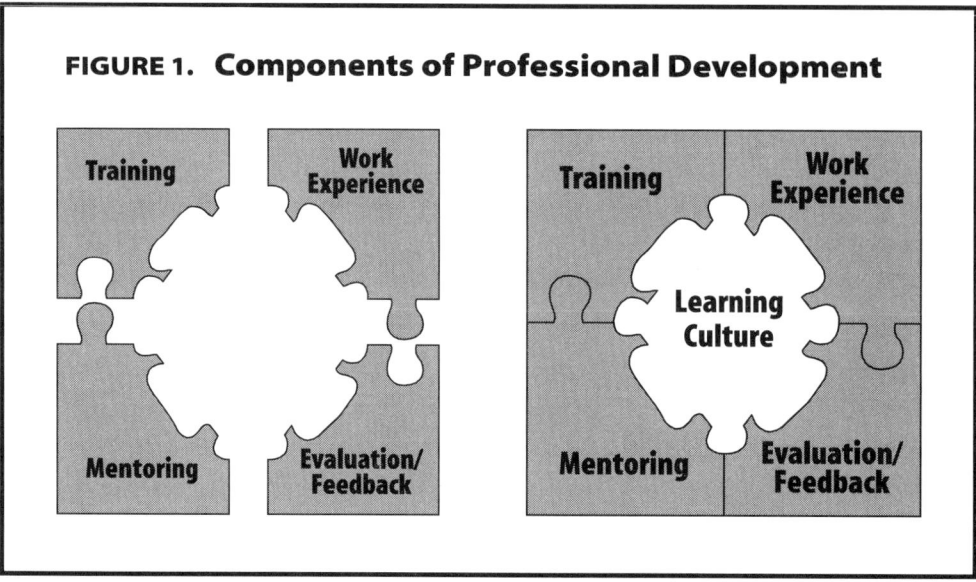

FIGURE 1. Components of Professional Development

- **Work experience** encompasses billable and pro bono work assignments and committee participation. This component provides an opportunity for informal, formal, and incidental learning.

- **Mentoring** is a relationship in which learning occurs through interaction between mentor and mentee. It is primarily an informal and incidental learning process, but a structured mentoring program can also provide formal learning activities.

- **Training** is a planned and structured means of transferring information, knowledge, and skills. Training courses are the most common settings for formal learning. Training also offers opportunities for incidental learning, especially when the format is interactive or experiential and participants have a chance to practice what they learn.

In addition, **feedback** in all three components serves as a catalyst for learning. Both everyday feedback and scheduled performance reviews give lawyers the perspective and insight that allow them to gauge their performance, progress, and learning needs. When all of these components are present, a learning culture can take hold. If any of these components is absent, professional development is impaired. (See Table 2.)

Many other law firm activities also have an impact on professional development or provide learning opportunities for a firm's lawyers. They include: recruiting, summer associate programs, orientation, knowledge management, transition to partnership, leadership development, business development, and even outplacement services. Whether or not you include these activities in your program, they should be aligned with other professional development efforts to avoid redundancy and inconsistency, and to maintain the program's objectives.

The chapters that follow will provide guidance about creating, coordinating, and implementing a professional development program that most appropriately suits the needs and goals of your firm.

TABLE 2. Missing Professional Development Components: Their Manifestations and Consequences

Missing Component	Manifestations	Consequences
Experience	Undeveloped skills and judgment	Lack of competence; frustration, boredom, stagnation
Mentoring	Lack of guidance, reality checks, support; isolation	Delayed development of identity, leadership, wisdom; attrition
Training	Insufficient knowledge and preparation; greater likelihood of mistakes	Impaired competence; Lower productivity; more write-offs; risk of malpractice
Feedback	No perspective or insight about performance; no guidance about learning needs	Inadequate performance; bad habits; failure to achieve potential; dissatisfaction

Designing a Professional Development Program

Professional development programs arise in many ways. Some are a deliberate response to perceived organizational needs. A managing partner decrees that the firm must produce lawyers who are fully trained and prepared to carry out his or her vision for the future, or the firm decides to make professional development a top priority to increase associate retention. More often, however, programs evolve without a plan, as when a partner who sees a need or has an interest in training initiates a training course that inspires additional programming. No matter how they arise, professional development initiatives involve multiple law firm functions unified by a common purpose: to attract, develop, and retain outstanding lawyers. To achieve that purpose in an optimal manner requires integrating these various functions into a cohesive and comprehensive professional development program.

Translated into practical terms, a successful professional development program furthers the interests of the organization in keeping productivity and profits high and turnover low. An effective program ensures that the firm has lawyers with the skills and abilities necessary to serve its clients and continue its professional success. Such a program also advances the personal interests of individual lawyers

> **Clarification of Terms.** A professional development program provides the infrastructure through which firms make available the resources and activities that support lawyers' learning and professional maturation. The core components of a professional development program are systems for managing work assignments, evaluations, mentoring, and training. Although law firms often use "professional development" and "training" interchangeably, training is only one of many professional development activities. Related activities such as orientation, diversity initiatives, and committee participation also contribute to the development of lawyers, as do the resources of the firm, such as ombudspersons and knowledge management. These and other related subjects are discussed in later chapters of this book.

in continuous professional learning and development. In this regard, the interests of the lawyers and the interests of the firm are not just compatible: They are completely intertwined. Lawyers who continually improve their capabilities benefit the organization's profitability; a profitable firm that supports lawyers' development will be able to recruit and keep better lawyers.

Before designing such a program, the firm must determine its strategic long-term business goals. No comprehensive professional development program can be developed without those goals clearly delineated. The goals describe how the firm views its future: the practice areas it will maintain, build up, or phase out; plans for growth or expansion; markets it hopes to penetrate; anticipated financial performance; or expected changes in its organizational structure. Understanding where the firm is going enables the people responsible for directing professional development to design a program that will move the firm toward the desired destination. This chapter explains how to create a strategy and plan for a comprehensive, well-coordinated professional development program. (See Table 1.)

TABLE 1. Designing a Professional Development Program: Ten Steps to Creating a Strategy and Plan

1. Identify business objectives.
2. Ensure firm leaders' commitment.
3. Decide who will participate in the design process.
4. Inventory current professional development activities, programs, and processes.
5. Envision the ideal professional development program for your firm.
6. Determine the capabilities lawyers will need to achieve the firm's goals.
7. Analyze potential future program components.
8. Set realistic and achievable priorities.
9. Design an action plan to institute the new program components.
10. Show how program components will be coordinated and communicated.

Approaching Professional Development Strategically

Whether you are trying to advance existing systems or taking a fresh look at professional development in its entirety, you need to approach the task strategically. Strategy development is about *thinking*; it seeks to understand the present and envision the future. Thinking strategically is critical because no professional development effort will work unless the people responsible for the professional development program can clearly explain to everyone affected why it is important and how it will benefit them. Strategy lays out the *why* and the *what*: Why your firm needs a professional development program and what kind of program will best suit the firm's needs. After articulating a strategy, you can move on to the *how*: designing a plan for making the strategy happen.

Although strategy development is an analytical process, it is also highly creative. The first step is to look at the firm's long-term business objectives and compare them to where the firm is now. Then conceptualize how to build a bridge between the present and the future by asking "What capabilities do our lawyers need in order to best serve our clients, improve and sustain the firm's profitability, and carry out the firm's vision for the future?" With this question as your guide, the strategy becomes the foundation from which all major planning decisions will be made.

Leading the Strategy Development Process

Shaping the strategy for the firm's professional development program requires extensive input and strong leadership. Before embarking on this endeavor, the leaders of the firm must be committed to the project. With their backing, people can be selected to participate in the strategy development process. Deciding who will be involved in planning the firm's professional development strategy includes three main considerations:

1. Who will be in charge of the process?

2. Who will gather the information?

3. Who will make the final decisions?

Who will be in charge of the process?

The strategy development process must have a designated leader. This leader might be the head of existing professional development efforts (e.g., a full-time professional development director or, in a smaller firm, someone whose job description encompasses this role on a part-time basis), the partner responsible for training, or a new professional development director brought on board to develop and lead a new program. If the firm expects to hire a new professional development director from outside the firm, then firm managers must decide whether to create a strategy first and hire someone to execute it, or hire someone first and have that person spearhead the strategy development process.

There are advantages to developing a strategy before hiring a new professional director. People familiar with the firm will be leading the process, and current employees know the firm's culture and needs. People will be less threatened or resistant to change when those who propose new initiatives are colleagues they already know and trust. In addition, the strategy development process may help the firm decide what the role of a professional development director will be and what qualifications will be needed to carry out the job.

On the other hand, having the new director conduct the strategy development process also has advantages. Most obvious is that the new director will bring expertise to the design of a professional development program and will also be the person responsible for implementing the program. The process will introduce the person to the firm and help to establish contacts, relationships, and credibility that will be essential for success in the job. Being a participant in the process gives the director a real sense of the people in the firm and the environment they work in. It also opens lines of communication between the director and the individuals whose ongoing support will be needed for the program to succeed.

Who will gather the information?

Obtaining pertinent information is a time-intensive project. It requires meeting with constituents throughout the firm, individually and in groups, in all offices and all departments. It requires collecting and reviewing extensive documentation, and may involve producing and analyzing surveys. Many firms leave data collection to the individual or committee in charge of professional development; some firms appoint a special committee or task force. Whether the job is delegated to one person or to a committee, it is important to seek creative ideas, concrete suggestions, and buy-in from individuals and groups throughout the firm. Involving as many people as possible expands understanding of the goals of professional development and shows people that the firm values their ideas. It also yields additional benefits:

- People think about the future as well as the present. They consider both the capabilities needed to carry out the firm's long-term strategic vision and the specific short-term steps necessary to develop those capabilities.

- Participation encourages cross-functional planning and communication. People see how their own activities, practices, and policies affect those of other departments and groups, and how purposeful interaction and coordination can achieve better results.

- The firm can make better decisions about where to invest its resources. As various activities and operations are examined and compared, investment priorities emerge. In particular, the priority given to professional development is increased when the organization realizes how professional development efforts contribute to productivity and profitability by reducing attrition and by equipping lawyers with skills that enhance efficiency.

- Managers, who often get bogged down in details, learn to take a "big picture" approach to planning as they listen to what people throughout the firm have to say.

- Those involved become committed to making the desired future a reality. When participants contribute to a shared vision for professional development, they are more likely to take ownership of the plan that is produced.

Who will make the final decisions?

While the data collecting task force can accommodate a large number of people, the body that decides a firm's ultimate strategy should be relatively small. A small, well-chosen group should be able to act efficiently. The size and make-up of the decision-making group will vary, but key members of the firm's management team, some practice group leaders, and partners with particular interest, involvement, or expertise in professional development should be included. It is beneficial to include a senior associate or junior partner in the group to add the perspective of those who will be most affected by professional development efforts. Some members of the data gathering task force may also participate in the decision-making group.

There may be a temptation to delegate strategy development to one person (e.g., the professional development director) or to a few interested partners. While data gathering may be left to one person, creating a program strategy is too complex and too important to delegate the whole project to one individual or to a select few. A cross-section of the firm needs to be involved, especially people affected by professional development activities and people whose buy-in is key to the program's success. Even in small firms, more than one person should be involved.

As Goldilocks discovered, finding the composition and size that is "just right" takes careful consideration. If only those with the greatest interest in the professional development program participate, the few who are involved may become convinced that they can best define the purpose and appropriate course of action for everyone. Their conviction about unity of purpose or course of action can become dogmatic, which can alienate, neglect, or anger those who are not represented or who disagree. However, there is also a risk if too many people are involved in deciding strategy. If you hear from too many voices, you can get caught up in competing agendas, personality conflicts, information overload, and gridlock. So it is important to go deep and wide when soliciting input, but to keep the decision-making process and the number of participants under tighter control. This offers the benefit of diverse viewpoints and broad participation while avoiding the risk of the group being too large and unwieldy to operate effectively.

Developing a Strategy

Strategy development is a three-part process:

1. Taking inventory of the present state of professional development in your firm;

2. Determining the ideal program — the "desired future" — that will enable the firm to achieve its strategic goals; and

3. Finding ways to bridge the gap between the present and the future.

Although most firms approach this process in the order listed, step two can precede step one, or both can proceed simultaneously.

The Present State

Information about the current state of professional development within your firm is a prerequisite for any plan. This means taking an inventory of what is currently being done, what's working well and what isn't, which needs are being met and which ones are not. This is a basic information gathering effort and requires considerable data collection. Begin by deciding the kind of information to be obtained and identifying the sources of that information.

Information to Be Gathered

Assuming your firm's program is expected to apply to all lawyers, you must investigate current conditions in all offices, departments, and practice groups. Table 2 contains some questions you might ask to expedite the information gathering process. You cannot ask these questions of just one department or group. In most law firms, "sampling" will not work because professional development activities are amazingly variable from one group to the next within the same office and even within the same department. Likewise, even if the program being developed is expected to have a more limited application (e.g., to only one office or department),

---

TABLE 2. Information-Gathering Questions

- **Why do we need a professional development program?**
    - What do we hope to accomplish?
    - How will a professional development program advance the firm's strategic business objectives?
- **What do we have now?**
    - What's working? What isn't? What's missing?
    - What opportunities and threats do we face?
    - What are our internal strengths and limitations?
- **What would our ideal program look like?**
    - What would the components be?
    - How would it be structured?
    - How would it be coordinated?
- **What can we realistically implement?**
    - How can we close the gap between the ideal and the real?
    - What resources do we need to close the gap?
    - What program components must we have to achieve our objectives?
    - How will we structure and coordinate the program components?
    - How will we get people to support our plan and participate?
    - What can we afford, given our budget?

it is still important to know what is happening in other parts of the firm. This knowledge will help those developing a strategy to be more efficient by enabling them to identify what works well, avoid duplication of efforts, and adopt or adapt successful existing projects.

Start with the firm's strategic goals. If your firm has written a strategic plan, mission statement, or statement of core values, those should be reviewed. But don't stop with the written words; take a close look at the firm's culture (Table 3) and whether it will really support a professional development program. What the firm values and stands for will ultimately determine what you can successfully create. All firms say that they value training and mentoring, but for many the words ring hollow. You must look at the actual development activities, work processes, compensation system, attitudes, and behaviors of lawyers toward each other to determine how much real support there is for lawyers to learn and grow.

It is also useful to ascertain:

- What the firm's present professional development needs are and how they are determined.

- How professional development activities, procedures, and policies are currently decided and administered.

- Which professional development efforts are working successfully and how success is measured.

- How various professional development activities are coordinated and any operating inefficiencies or redundancies that need to be remedied.

- How technology supports professional development, what current technological capabilities are, and what plans there are for future expansion and enhancement of technological resources.

- What the budget is for professional development activities, which activities fall within each budget, and how budget allocation decisions are made, both firm wide and by office, department, and practice group.

- What other professions, industries, and firms are doing. Do not limit this search to similar law firms. Successful programs from a broad spectrum of law firms, corporations, and other organizations can provide ideas and benchmarks against which to measure your firm.

TABLE 3. Examining the Firm's Culture

- What are the activities that the firm values the most?
- What are the firm's major sources of pride?
- Who are the lawyers most admired within the firm?
- What is the firm's reputation in the marketplace?
- How would you rank the following factors in order of their value to the firm?
    — Quality of work
    — Hours worked
    — Client relationship management
    — Bringing in new clients
    — Training and mentoring
    — Community and pro bono service
    — Management activities
- What draws lawyers to the firm?
    — Why did lawyers choose the firm?
    — Why do they stay there?
    — Why did others leave?
- Who are the five or ten most highly compensated lawyers in the firm?
    — What are they compensated for?
    — Are they the same lawyers as those who are most admired?
    — If not, what accounts for the difference?

Sources of Information

In gathering information, cast a wide net. While lawyers will be your primary sources of information, virtually everyone in the firm is affected by how much and how well the lawyers learn and manage — and most people will be happy to tell you where improvement is needed. Clients, secretaries, and mailroom personnel, for example, can all provide very valuable information about lawyers' management abilities. Useful sources of information include:

Program managers. Lawyers and administrators in charge of firm-wide training and other professional development efforts can provide information about how current programs are implemented and where improvement is needed.

Practice group leaders. These leaders are responsible for many professional development efforts in their groups. Find out what they're thinking and what they want a professional development program to include. What obstacles do they see? How much are they willing to do? To what extent can you count on them to persuade others to participate?

Marketing director. The individual heading the firm's marketing effort can explain how the firm is positioning itself in the marketplace, how it distinguishes itself from the competition, and what is expected of lawyers in terms of marketing skills and activities.

Information systems/technology department. The people involved in technology on a daily basis are indispensable sources of information on the firm's technological and information systems capabilities. For example, could the firm's video conferencing technology be used to let lawyers at branch offices participate in a seminar hosted by the main office? Could technology currently available within the firm streamline management of the professional development program?

Associate committees. Since most of the professional development efforts in the firm are directed at associates, it is essential to know what they want and need to develop their skills and advance their careers.

Associate evaluations. Associate evaluations are important sources of information about where to focus training and development. Your firm's programs will be more relevant and effective if they are targeted to needs or deficiencies highlighted in evaluations.

Core competencies. Many organizations identify the "core competencies" that their lawyers should demonstrate. Organizations use these core competencies in conjunction with training, evaluation, coaching, and counseling processes to help lawyers measure their performance and gauge their progress. If your firm has articulated core competencies, they should be carefully scrutinized. Because these competencies describe what lawyers in the organization need to know and do, they have obvious relevance to decisions regarding professional development.

Upward evaluations. Some firms have "upward" reviews in which associates evaluate the partners and more senior associates who supervise them. A few firms conduct 360° reviews, in which associates, staff, peers, and clients evaluate partners. If your firm conducts those kinds of evaluations, the information they contain will reveal areas where partners and senior associates would benefit from training and coaching. Because of privacy concerns, you may not be able to see information about individual lawyers, but you may have access to summary data or to evaluations with identifying information redacted.

Clients. Clients commonly perceive lawyers differently than the way lawyers perceive themselves. If your firm conducts client satisfaction surveys, or if you obtain feedback from clients about how client service could be improved, utilize this information.

Staff and administrators. The people who work with lawyers will offer invaluable insights into what your lawyers need, especially with respect to management and interpersonal skills.

Exit interviews. Review the reasons why lawyers leave your firm and where professional development systems could be improved or changed to reduce turnover.

Employee satisfaction surveys. If you survey lawyers and employees about their satisfaction with the firm, the results usually reveal professional development areas where attention or changes are needed.

Surveys of other firms. Contacting firms that provide professional services, including other law firms, is an effective way to find out what they are doing to train and develop their professionals. Although they will probably not disclose proprietary data or sensitive details, most firms will provide enough information about their professional development activities to provide good ideas and enable those developing your firm's strategy to set some benchmarks.

Literature searches. There is a wealth of information available from publications in the fields of human resources, organization development, and corporate training and development. Legal journals, magazines, and newsletters often report about innovative professional development initiatives in law firms. A search of the literature for these activities can be a rich source of good ideas and practical suggestions.

The Ideal Program

Taking an inventory of your firm's present state is relatively easy and straightforward. The data gathering process will elicit a great deal of information about the firm's current needs and future direction. It is a far greater challenge to determine what capabilities your firm's lawyers will need in order to achieve the firm's goals for the future and to decide how lawyers will acquire those capabilities. This challenge is at the heart of every firm's professional development program.

To determine future needs, look at the firm's strategic goals and decide what skills, mindsets, and experiences are necessary or desirable to carry out each of those goals. Brainstorm how the firm might achieve those goals through training, mentoring, evaluations, or work experience. This is the time for you and for everyone else involved in formulating the strategy to let your imaginations run free! Visualize what an ideal professional development program would look like. Stretch your creative muscles and try to envision a comprehensive program that would allow the firm to provide all the training, mentoring, work experience, and related activities that lawyers and the firm might possibly want. Think about professional development for lawyers in every kind of practice and at every experience level or career stage. Assume that there are no constraints — that the firm can allocate all the money, time, technology, and people the ideal professional development program requires. In the absence of any limits, what would your firm's ideal program look like?

Let's say your firm has a thriving local real estate practice and intends to become the premier real estate law firm in the Southwestern United States. What must your lawyers do in order to achieve and sustain that leadership position? What capabilities will your firm's lawyers need to have that your competitors can't match? How will your lawyers acquire the expertise and reputation to achieve the firm's goal? As you and others involved in this strategy development process ponder these questions and brainstorm answers, countless possibilities will emerge. Out of these possibilities, identify key factors that are essential to achieve your firm's objective. For example, to become "the premier real estate law firm in the Southwestern United States," lawyers will need to have superior real estate knowledge and skills; the firm must effectively market its unique capabilities to targeted existing and potential clients; and the firm must have a work environment that attracts and keeps outstanding real estate lawyers. Having identified these factors, you can then begin to formulate specific action plans that will help move your firm toward its goal.

Table 4 provides an example of envisioning an ideal program to ensure that a firm's lawyers have "superior real estate knowledge and skills." Some of the ideas listed in Table 4 are far-fetched and unrealistic, and the firm that brainstormed these ideas would not expect to implement all of them. Similarly, your own firm's ideal plan should be far-reaching and may include some unconventional, controversial, and radical ideas. This step is intended to move you beyond conventional thinking toward the best possible program you can imagine. The next step will bring you back to reality.

TABLE 4. *Hypothetical Ideal* **Action Plan to Help Lawyers Develop "Superior Real Estate Knowledge and Skills"**

- Develop a comprehensive real estate training program; require all partners to teach and all associates to attend.

- Articulate core competencies, i.e., the substantive knowledge, legal and management skills, and real estate experience that lawyers must have.

- Assign each associate a partner-supervisor who will be personally responsible for ensuring that the associate develops the required knowledge and skills and gets the required work experience.

- Have all associates "shadow" partners, at no charge to the client, to observe site inspections, negotiations, and closings.

- Place all junior associates in six-month internships with developers, brokers, bankers, and others in real estate-related fields.

- Hire a law school professor specializing in real estate law as a private consultant and educator for the firm.

- Invite clients and outside experts (including developers, brokers, bankers, and management company executives) to talk to the firm's lawyers about real estate issues.

- Have weekly meetings for all real estate lawyers to discuss real estate topics.

- Send all lawyers to the week-long National Real Estate Conference.

- Order subscriptions to *Real Estate Weekly* for all lawyers.

- Retain a coach to work with real estate lawyers individually to improve communication and business development skills.

Bridging the Gaps

Now comes the real challenge: finding ways to bridge the gaps between your firm's existing state and the desired future. Comparing what you have learned about the present and what you have envisioned for the future will reveal where professional development gaps exist. To bridge the gaps, assess the possible options and decide which ones will best help your firm reach its objectives. Those will be the components of your firm's professional development program. Once you decide what the discrete components will be, you can begin to design an integrated plan.

The ideal program you have been contemplating can be your planning guide, but it is likely to be more expansive — and expensive — than your firm will agree to. This is the time to do a reality check:

- What will it take to get the support you need for your ideal vision to become a reality? Will you be able to get lawyers to participate? What will it take to motivate them?

- Which elements of the firm's desired future are most important and/or urgent? What will the firm commit in terms of time, money, personnel, and physical resources (including space and technology)?

The answers to these questions will point out the most significant constraints you face. Assume that most limitations can be overcome in the long term and set targets for the firm to move toward over a number of years. The plan you design should be realistic, practical, and achievable, but it should also stretch the firm beyond its current capabilities and resources. The plan may seem unattainable in the short run but possible to reach over time. Throughout this process be sure to involve everyone who is part of the strategy development team; the more that key firm leaders are involved, the more likely they will be to identify creative new possibilities you may not have considered — and the more committed they will be to the resulting plan.

Unless you really do have *carte blanche*, you will need to make some choices. To ascertain the options you can choose from, the easiest place to start is with your current professional development efforts. It will usually cost less in time, money, and aggravation to work with existing activities and practices as a foundation. Occasionally a firm may choose to institute something entirely new and different in order to meet new overall objectives or to reinvigorate a program that has grown stale. But in most cases, retaining or improving existing systems that are working well is easier than starting anew. So take a look at the professional development activities, programs, and processes that are now in place. What is the firm presently doing that can stay the same? What will have to be changed? What needs to be eliminated? Table 5 presents some specific questions that will help you determine whether an existing system should be included as it is, whether it needs to be modified, or whether it should be replaced.

TABLE 5. Assessing Professional Development Systems: Deciding Whether to Keep, Modify, or Replace

1. **Operation**
   - What does this system encompass? How does it work?
   - Is it working efficiently?
   - Is it achieving its current objectives?
   - As the system currently operates, will it be able to achieve the firm's new objectives?
   - How could this system be improved?
   - Would a new system be better?

2. **Participants**
   - Who are the beneficiaries (e.g., mentoring for first-years or all associates)?
   - Who are the faculty, mentors, and supervisors?
   - How do we use the assistance of outside providers (e.g., consultants, trainers)?
   - How are lawyers encouraged to participate? How are lawyers rewarded for participating?
   - What encouragement and rewards will be necessary to make a new system succeed?

3. **Firm-wide vs. local considerations**
   - How much discretion and authority do local offices and practice groups have?
   - Is the system the same in all offices? In all practice groups?
   - If not, how does it differ from office to office and group to group? What accounts for the differences? Would the system work in other offices and practice groups?
   - Should the system be the same in all offices? In all practice groups?
   - How much latitude should offices and practice groups have to do things differently?
   - What special considerations affect overseas offices?

4. **Coordination**
    - What are we now doing to coordinate this system?
    - What other professional development-related systems are linked to this one? How are they linked?
    - What other systems should be linked to it? How can they be linked?

5. **Administration**
    - How is the system being administered? How many layers of administration are involved?
    - Is it being managed effectively?
    - Is it currently administered from a central office? If not, what aspects are managed by different offices or practice groups?
    - What personnel will be needed to implement a new system? Will current personnel be able to administer a new system?
    - Where will administrators be needed? What special training will they need?

6. **Technology**
    - How are we currently using technology to support professional development?
    - How can technology be used to support a new system and achieve its objectives?
    - Do we have adequate capability to support a new system?
    - What additional capacity and support will we need?
    - Will the firm be able and willing to acquire and maintain the needed support?
    - What special training will be required for users of new technology?
    - Will the firm be able to provide such training?

7. **Facilities**
    - What facilities do we now use?
    - Do we have the space to implement new systems?
    - Can we do this in the office? Will we need to go off-site?
    - Are off-site facilities available?

8. **Financial considerations**
    - What is the cost of the current system?
    - What is the estimated cost of a new system?
    - How will the difference, if any, impact our budget?
    - How will we justify the amount?

Examine how effectively the various current professional development efforts operate together as well as independently. Consider what makes successful programs work well in your firm, and whether they could become even more effective and efficient if coordinated with other activities. Look for particular problem areas and try to determine what is causing the problem or obstructing possible solutions. Find redundancies, inefficiencies, and areas of neglect that could be remedied by better coordination or communication. For example, you may find that one of your firm's offices has an excellent orientation for new associates while another office has none at all, and that no offices provide orientation for lateral associates. You might want to make orientation a part of your new professional development program and, using the well-run orientation as a model, institute a standard orientation program for all new lawyers in all firm offices.

You also have to decide which professional development pieces are missing and will have to be created. If your firm does no formal mentoring, for example, do you want to propose that the firm institute a mentoring program? Whatever choices you contemplate, whether starting new efforts or revamping current ones, think through the implications of the different options you might propose. Weigh the factors working for and against each option, choose options that are most important, and then decide upon a direction that is realistic and achievable. Two techniques that may help you make decisions at this stage of the process are "force field analysis" and "SLOT assessment." Using these techniques to examine your various options will help you make more thoughtful selections.

■ Force Field Analysis

A new professional development strategy will likely require the firm to make changes, either to do something differently or to try something new. Change is usually met with resistance. You will have to be prepared to overcome that resistance. Force field analysis examines the forces that drive and restrain change. With that understanding, you can select and introduce new proposals more wisely.

Based upon the work of social scientist Karl Lewin, force field analysis views change as a struggle between forces seeking to maintain and upset the status quo. Lewin explained that "driving forces" move a situation toward change, while "restraining forces" block that movement. When the opposing forces are equal, or the restraining forces are too strong to allow movement, no change occurs. A desired change occurs only when the driving forces are more powerful than those restraining them. In order to effect change, therefore, it is necessary to either strengthen the driving forces or reduce the restraining forces. Reducing or eliminating the restraining forces is usually more effective than strengthening the driving forces; pushing too hard for a proposed change often has the unexpected result of *increasing* resistance.

Figure 1 shows an example of how a force field analysis might be used to examine the question of whether the real estate group in our earlier example should have a mentoring program. In deciding the question, you would weigh the relative priorities of the information in both columns. How important are the driving forces? How powerful are the restraining forces? After you analyze the forces, explore whether and how you can strengthen the driving forces; whether and how you can eliminate or diminish the restraining forces; and the repercussions of doing either. Then decide how to move ahead.

FIGURE 1. Force Field Analysis

Should We Have a Mentoring Program for Real Estate Lawyers?

DRIVING FORCES →	CHANGE	← RESTRAINING FORCES
Improves associate performance		Lack of time
Higher commitment, retention		Lack of interest
Raise morale		Inadequate mentoring skills
Competitive recruiting advantage		Time not billable
More collegiality		No proven benefit

■ "SLOT" Analysis

A SLOT analysis is a strategic planning tool that analyzes the firm's **S**trengths, **L**imitations, **O**pportunities, and **T**hreats.[1] (See Figure 2.) It helps you make more intelligent strategic decisions by analyzing the issues behind a proposal, problem, or choice. The analysis entails examining all of the factors — favorable and unfa-

---

[1] This "SLOT" analysis is a variation of the commonly used "SWOT" analysis, substituting *Limitations* in place of *Weaknesses*. See George L. Morrisey, *Morrisey on Planning: A Guide to Long-Range Planning*, Jossey-Bass, San Francisco, 1996.

FIGURE 2. SLOT Analysis

Internal	**S**trengths	**L**imitations
External	**O**pportunities	**T**hreats

vorable, internal and external — that potentially impact any decision made. Studying these factors enables you to identify and weigh alternatives, determine which alternatives have the highest potential for success, and clarify and set priorities. The conclusions you draw from a SLOT assessment give you the grounding necessary to make smart decisions about how to proceed.

A firm's internal *strengths* are characteristics and factors that work to its advantage, e.g., a longstanding commitment to training, sound leadership, or wise financial management. Internal *limitations*, on the other hand, are foreseeable barriers or stumbling blocks that impede professional development in the firm, e.g., dissension among partners, declining profits, or a compensation system that fails to reward (or even penalizes) informal training and mentoring.

External forces and trends in the marketplace are also analyzed. *Opportunities* are the external forces and trends that have the potential to work to the firm's benefit, while *threats* have the potential for harm. Analyzing those external factors helps you plan how to take advantage of the opportunities and avoid the threats. It also helps you convert perceived threats into opportunities, or at least to minimize those threats. If, for example, the firm anticipates a declining demand for legal services in one of its practice areas, it can transition lawyers from that group into an area where demand is on the upswing. This turns a perceived practice threat in one service area into a promising opportunity for growth in another.

How Will the Parts Fit Together?

In developing a strategy for your firm's professional development program, you decided what was needed; now the challenge is to decide how to make it happen. You have identified the parts you want to include in your program; now you have to determine how they will take shape and how they will fit together. All the parts need to be woven into a whole, integrated system. This requires an organizational infrastructure, i.e., the basic facilities, resources, personnel, and network of reporting relationships necessary for the system to function.

A professional development program needs enough structure and organization to ensure efficient and cost-effective ongoing implementation but not so much that it inhibits action or decision-making. The point is not to centralize or control all professional development functions but to facilitate learning, enhance accountability, and ensure that all aspects of professional development operate together to realize the firm's objectives. Sometimes, a whole new organizational framework must be created to make the system function, but most often, you will be able to reach your objectives by just refining and synchronizing existing systems. By synchronizing development efforts, you will be able to ensure firm-wide consistency, prevent redundancies, and use available resources and professional development dollars efficiently.

There are many ways to configure an organizational framework for professional development. However you structure your firm's program, you will need to create a proposed plan. For that plan to work efficiently and achieve the defined strategic objectives, the various elements need to be coordinated to produce a coherent approach and avoid unwanted duplication. To ensure that implementation can be sustained effectively, your plan also must set up channels for ongoing communication.

■ Planning

Professional development planning never ends. You will continually be faced with new lawyers, new needs, and new ideas that demand new policies, procedures, and programs — all of which have to be integrated into and coordinated with the rest of the program. To propose a professional development program to the firm, and to implement the program once it is approved, you have to create a plan. This plan is like a blueprint that lays out the individual components that will be involved, how they will interact, who will be in charge, and what the estimated costs will be. It should include a timeline for implementation, indicating the order in which the components will be introduced and the target dates to have them up and running.

It should also indicate any special facilities, resources, or preliminary steps that are prerequisites to implementation (e.g., a needs analysis, certain computer systems, a conference room large enough for training programs).

You do not need to go into great detail about each program component at the start; those details can be filled in later, but your blueprint should include some or all of the following:

- **Program purpose**
    - The business case for the proposed program
    - Long-term goals to be achieved over time
    - Short-term objectives
- **Program components (i.e., activities, practices, processes)**
    - Components that will be uniform throughout the firm
    - Components that will be managed and implemented centrally
    - Office, practice group, or department-led components
    - Targeted lawyers (e.g., all lawyers, senior associates, particular departments)
- **Organizational framework**
    - Individuals or groups in charge
    - Firm personnel involved in implementation and management
    - Channels of communication and coordination
- **Timetable**
    - Time frame for implementing the entire plan and each component
    - Preparatory steps to be undertaken (e.g., surveys)
    - Order in which steps will be undertaken and components will be implemented
- **Resources**
    - Resources and facilities needed
    - Prerequisites to implementation
    - Estimated budget and budget allocation

■ Coordination

A comprehensive professional development program is not simply a collection of assorted programs and policies. A framework is required to coordinate the various elements into an integrated program with a common purpose. Unity of purpose can be achieved by establishing links between the program elements and the way they are administered. The focus in a coordinated program is not just on the individual elements but also on how they function together to further the learning and growth of the lawyers being served. For a lawyer's development, it is important — but not enough — to have good stand-alone program elements. A first-rate system for evaluating associate performance is not beneficial unless it is tied to a firm's training, mentoring, and work allocation systems. Telling an associate in an evaluation that he should improve the way he organizes and manages work is not sufficient if the associate does not understand how to make the necessary changes. To help him improve those behaviors, the associate needs an in-house or outside training program, one-on-one coaching from a mentor, or a work assignment with a supervisor who will help him sharpen his work management skills. A well-coordinated program can assemble the resources necessary to get the associate the help he needs.

In planning how to coordinate and administer your firm's program, one of the questions to decide is which measures and policies should be standardized across the firm and which should not. This is especially problematic when the firm has offices in different states and countries. As a general rule, basic performance standards should be uniform. Mandatory risk management training and the number of times a new lawyer may fail the bar exam before being dismissed are examples of measures and policies that should apply in the same way to all lawyers in the firm. On the other hand, some issues are purely local and do not require a uniform approach. Dress codes may be very different in Honolulu and Boston, and training programs are governed in large part by each state's MCLE requirements. Most of the time, the result will be a hybrid: uniform standards with local variations. As an example, firms may set minimum performance standards against which all associates will be evaluated but expect each practice group to supervise the evaluations of its own associates and to supplement those standards with others that are practice-specific.

A professional development plan should specify who is responsible for program administration. In multi-office firms, it is not uncommon to have programs administered at all management levels. Ultimately, management responsibility rests with the director or with the committee in charge of the firm-wide professional development program. This ensures that firm-wide policies and systems are consistent and efficiently run. But day-to-day operations can be handled either centrally or locally. Many firms have a centralized administration, with personnel in one office in charge of the entire program. In other firms, a de-centralized structure allows administration at the levels of a local office, department, or practice group. Even when the program is centralized, implementation is usually best managed at the local level. Similarly, policy-making and program development can occur locally as well as centrally. Policies and programs can be established locally so long as they fit into the firm's overall scheme, values, and goals.

■ Communication

Regardless of the structure chosen, good coordination can only be achieved through good communication. Coordination of a professional development program requires information sharing, both within the management team and with the firm at large. People who are managing the program, making policies, and implementing the various program elements, must keep each other apprised of new issues and needs. They have to stay informed about how things are going and what could be improved.

Professional development management teams should schedule meetings so that information and ideas can be exchanged on a regular basis. A firm-wide professional development leader should meet in person, or at least communicate, weekly with local professional development managers. It is especially important for the firm-wide professional development leader to personally visit and stay in touch with all of the firm's offices to consult with leaders in those offices; to get to know department and practice group heads and members of local professional development committees; and to meet with associates. This personal involvement helps the professional development leader monitor the implementation and effectiveness of ongoing projects; solicit ideas for new projects; advertise the scope and availability of education and career development services and resources; and maintain a position of visibility as the central person for professional development in the firm.

Committees usually play an integral role in professional development efforts, even when there is a professional development director. Different committees often deal with hiring, summer programs, evaluations, training, and associate affairs, as well as other activities related to lawyer development. Communication among these committees is essential. Professional development leaders and committee chairs have to stay informed about what the various committees are doing. Firms can facilitate communication among committees in several ways:

1. **Professional development director acts as a link:** The professional development director serves on all committees that deal with professional development issues and attends meetings and retreats of the firm's management committee, departments, and practice groups.

2. **Overlapping committee membership:** In this type of scheme, individual partners sit on more than one committee. These few partners meet together from time to time to compare notes and discuss the professional development issues that each committee is dealing with.

3. **Reporting by an administrator:** An office administrator, paralegal, or secretary attends committee meetings and takes minutes, which are distributed to all committee chairs.

Communication at all levels can be advanced through the use of technology. Communication technology makes regular meetings easy to hold, even for law firms with offices around the world. Teleconferencing, videoconferencing, and webcasts allow members in all offices to participate live and in person. Technology also assists in implementing discrete professional development functions (e.g., organizing recruiting efforts, tracking work assignments, executing evaluation procedures).[2] It helps professional development programs run easily and efficiently and allows in-house programs to be delivered to all firm offices and departments at the same time. It also provides methods to disseminate information throughout the firm about available education and career information.

One of the most useful technology resources for coordinating professional development is your firm's intranet. The intranet can serve as a central, easily accessible source of information about anything and everything that relates to professional development. A dedicated professional development home page on the intranet can be a repository for training and development information, materials, resources, and services. It can also be a portal to training programs available online, both those presented in-house and those available from outside providers. A typical professional development home page provides access to the information noted in Table 6, although the possibilities for entries, links, and services are virtually endless.

---

[2] The uses of technology for training and knowledge management are addressed separately in Chapters 8 and 9, respectively.

Continuous Reassessment

You have now completed a blueprint for professional development in your firm. Your plan grows out of the firm's strategic business objectives and is based on your best assessment of the future. As we all know, predicting the future is a shaky proposition. Conditions, needs, and priorities will undoubtedly change over time. Your plan should permit as much flexibility as possible to accommodate those changes. Regular assessment (at least once or twice a year, more often in the first two or three years) is important to make sure that your plan remains aligned with the firm's objectives, to confirm that you are getting the results you want, and to allow for revisions or additions if priorities or expectations have changed.

TABLE 6. Examples of Information Found on Professional Development Intranet Pages

- **Training Calendar**
    - Program announcements
    - Procedures for attending a teleconference or videoconference

- **Training programs and materials**
    - Registration procedures and forms
    - Video streaming, videotapes
    - Program materials
    - Archive of programs and materials
    - Index of audiotapes and videotapes

- **CLE information**
    - State-by-state requirements
    - Compliance periods
    - Reporting procedures
    - Self-study procedures and forms

- **How to plan a CLE program**
    - Program requirements
    - How to obtain CLE certification
    - Checklists
    - How to obtain administrative assistance

- **Vendors of CLE programs**
    - Program calendar
    - Procedure for obtaining approval to attend
    - Information about firm-negotiated discounts
    - Direct links to vendors' web sites
- **Professional development resources**
    - "Self-guided tour" of professional development services, activities, resources, and opportunities available in the firm
    - What the professional development director or committee does
    - Who to call with questions
- **Associate evaluations**
    - Benchmarks and performance criteria
    - Evaluation procedures and forms
- **Mentoring program**
    - Program design and objectives
    - Program guidelines
    - How to participate
    - Mentoring materials
- **Legal writing assistance**
    - Internal resources, references, examples
    - Procedure for obtaining assistance
- **Timekeeping information**
    - Activities that can be recorded as professional development time
    - Timekeeping numbers
- **Employment policy and procedure manuals**
- **Bulletin Board**
- **Frequently asked professional development questions**

CHAPTER 3

Leading the Professional Development Program

Law firms have come to appreciate the value of delegating many management functions to professional managers rather than leaving them in the hands of practicing lawyers. Professional development is one of the management functions better left to specialists. Every firm that intends to have a professional development program should designate a specialist to plan, coordinate, and manage lawyers' learning, training, and development. (See Table 1.) The ever-increasing complexity of law practice requires more extensive and frequent training and development efforts. Many different efforts related to professional development — ranging from summer associate programs to knowledge management — need to be coordinated to maximize efficiency, consistency, and fairness. Most firms have partners or committees that oversee professional development activities, but it is more practical and efficient to delegate day-to-day responsibility for professional development to a specialist dedicated to the task.

TABLE 1. Why Law Firms Need Professional Development Specialists

- **Profitability.** Professional development contributes directly to your firm's bottom line. A professional development specialist helps optimize revenues by maximizing the competence and profitability of lawyers.
- **Cost-effectiveness.** Lawyers are experts at practicing law; professional development specialists are experts in the training and development of lawyers. Leaving professional development up to a specialist is more efficient and cost effective than having practicing lawyers run the program.

- **Productivity.** Having a specialist in charge of running the professional development program relieves lawyers of administrative burdens and frees them to serve clients and spend more time on billable work.
- **Participation.** Leaving program design and administration to a specialist means that lawyers have more time to participate in — and benefit from — professional development activities such as training and mentoring.
- **Better programming.** Specialists understand principles of adult education and program design. They know about the wide variety of educational and development options available to law firms. This expertise translates to higher quality programming.
- **Higher overall quality.** A specialist dedicated to a firm's professional development program can ensure that resources and activities are regularly planned, implemented, monitored, assessed, and improved. This increases the overall quality of professional development efforts.
- **Coordination.** Having a specialist coordinate your firm's program prevents duplicative activities and procedures, which can be expensive and embarrassing.
- **Consistency.** Policies and activities are consistent, and conflicts are avoided, when a specialist oversees a professional development program.
- **Accountability.** Lack of accountability for professional development can be a frustration both for lawyers and administrators. When a specialist is in charge, especially if that person is known to be a decision-maker, people know where to go with their questions, interests, needs, proposals, and complaints.
- **Smooth delivery.** Having a specialist ensures that professional development functions are carried out systematically, competently, and completely. Organization and communication are enhanced, and the overall approach to professional development is more orderly.
- **Continuity.** A professional development specialist promotes continuity and stability. In planning for professional development, a specialist takes a broad, long-term perspective and plans accordingly.

Today's more systematic and multi-faceted approach to professional development requires a greater commitment and focus than any practicing lawyer can give. In large firms, hundreds of associates in different practice groups, working out of several offices, make it impossible for one partner or even a small group of partners to carry on a practice and take charge of professional development at the same time. Even in a small firm, practicing lawyers simply do not have the time, skills, or incentives necessary to manage a comprehensive professional development program. It is better to delegate these responsibilities to a part-time or full-time specialist.

With a specialist in charge of professional development, lawyers are free to do what they do best (practice law, develop business, and maintain client relations) and handle the issues they cannot delegate (ownership decisions and strategic planning). Placing a professional development specialist in charge of a firm's program does not eliminate the role of the partner or committee of lawyers who guide professional development efforts. To the contrary, it enhances their work and lessens their burdens. Specialists typically work with a partner or committee to plan professional programs and policies, but they are the people who see to it that those programs and policies are correctly designed and successfully implemented. The need for a specialist to manage professional development will become even more essential as law firms grow and expand, assume more corporate organizational structures, and become more multi-disciplinary. Let's examine how "training partners" and professional development committees operate, and how a professional development specialist can assist them.

The Training Partner

Until very recently, few law firms devoted anyone to professional development full-time. It is still far more common to have a practicing lawyer — usually called the "Training Partner" — decide the subjects to be taught, schedule training programs, recruit faculty, and teach some courses. Training partners are committed to their task, but most do not have the time to coordinate a comprehensive and integrated professional development scheme. Consequently, different partners handle associate hiring, evaluations, and mentoring. This fragmentation of responsibilities hinders the effective coordination of a professional development program.

In small firms where partners and associates work together closely and know each other well, a Training Partner model can work well. Small firms need less organizational structure for professional development activities and have less need for a dedicated specialist. Teaching and mentoring occur routinely and informally, and formal training, if needed, is usually provided by an occasional in-house program or by sending lawyers to outside CLE vendors. Work assignments, learning needs, and performance can be addressed directly. While their programs can be quite sophisticated, small firms have fewer resources for professional development. Just as in large firms, small firm Training Partners face considerable client and business constraints. A dedicated professional development specialist — even on a part-time basis — can spare these partners the burdens of planning, organizing, and implementing professional development efforts.

Professional Development Committee

Another prevalent model places responsibility for professional development in committees of practicing lawyers. Committee membership may be limited to partners or may include associates. Representatives from the firm's major departments and offices often participate as well. Most commonly, firms have a central committee that sets policies, plans programs, and oversees professional development processes and activities. Some firms do not have a central committee, but instead delegate separate professional development functions to multiple committees.

Large, multi-office firms that use a central committee model sometimes augment their firm-wide committee with local or regional committees. The national committee establishes programs, policies, and procedures with firm-wide application, such as core curricula for all first-year associates, performance criteria, and standards for in-house CLE program certification. Local committees implement these, but also have the freedom to undertake locally relevant or desired professional development efforts. For example, the national committee may determine the basic content for new associate orientation, but local committees can add topics and activities pertinent to the associates in a particular office, department, or practice group.

In firms where multiple committees handle different aspects of professional development, there may be one committee for mentoring, another for training, and still others for recruitment, work assignments, evaluations, and associate affairs. This system can be successfully integrated if a mechanism is in place to ensure that the different committees work in sync with each other and do not duplicate efforts, e.g., if the committees have overlapping membership.

Regardless of how they are structured, expecting committees of lawyers to run professional development efforts burdens lawyers and impedes long-term planning. Lawyers have to attend multiple meetings that require a considerable commitment of time. In making decisions, committees tend to focus on immediate rather than long-term needs. A system that employs multiple committees is especially problematic. It makes coordination more difficult, slows down decision-making, and risks redundancy, inconsistency, and conflict. Involving a professional development specialist in the committee system lessens the lawyers' burden and ensures robust and ongoing planning. The specialist assumes both the long-term and day-to-day responsibility for the program. By participating on all relevant committees, the specialist provides consistency and continuity, and maintains a global perspective over the entire program. Specialists do the groundwork, present background information, and clarify issues. Committees continue to meet, but not as often and with a better defined focus and purpose. They may even decide to assume more of an advisory or policy-making role, leaving most professional development matters to the specialist.

Professional Development Specialists: Responsibilities

Both the title and function of the professional development specialist are still being defined. (See sidebar.) The role of the specialist is relatively new and still evolving. The specialist's position was virtually unknown in the early 1990s except

---

Professional Development Specialists: Titles and Functions

A professional development "specialist" refers to the person in the firm with primary responsibility for lawyers' professional development, regardless of where that person appears in the firm's organization chart. Firms assign professional development specialists different titles, including *Director, Coordinator,* or *Manager*. These titles are often misleading, as they do not necessarily reflect the person's role or level of authority. Because of these wide variations, it may be helpful to categorize professional development specialists according to their respective positions within the firm's management hierarchy. These distinctions can define more clearly the professional development specialist's responsibilities, authority, qualifications, compensation, and place in the firm's governance structure.

- A **Professional Development Director** is a member of the firm's executive management team and reports directly to the top leadership of the firm (e.g., Chair, Managing Partner, Executive Committee). A Director may be a partner in the firm who transitions into this role and relinquishes law practice. Alternatively, it is someone who may or may not be a lawyer, who has considerable law firm experience, and who is hired or promoted specifically to take charge of firm-wide professional development functions. A Director usually consults with a Professional Development Committee to plan programs and initiatives but is the person responsible for developing and overseeing policies, procedures, and programs affecting most or all aspects of lawyer development throughout the firm (subject to partnership approval on major propositions).

- A **Professional Development Coordinator** is a senior manager-level employee whose responsibilities are firm-wide, encompassing training and development for lawyers in all offices in the firm. Unlike the Director, who reports directly to top management, a Coordinator is at least one management step removed, usually reporting to a member of the firm's executive management team (often the Director of Legal Personnel or Chief Operating Officer). A Coordinator may or may not be a lawyer. Coordinators support and work in concert with a professional development partner or committee to create, carry out, and generally oversee the firm's professional development procedures and activities. While Coordinators participate in policy decisions, the ultimate responsibility for policy-making usually lies with the professional development partner or committee.

- A **Professional Development Manager** supervises implementation of firm-wide professional development activities in one or more offices, manages and supports locally initiated professional development efforts, and acts as liaison between local or regional offices and the firm-wide professional development leadership. A Manager may be a lawyer but often is not. A Manager reports to a Professional Development Director or Coordinator, or to a professional development partner or committee. As back-up for the local professional development partner or committee, the role of Manager may parallel on an office level the role that the Professional Development Coordinator holds firm-wide.

In addition to specialists, firms also need personnel to provide administrative assistance and support. These individuals often hold the title of Professional Development Assistant. They handle the logistics involved in implementing training and development activities, procedures, and policies that are planned by the specialist or by committees of the firm. They also take care of the administrative details, such as monitoring work assignments, collating evaluations, and tracking CLE. While they may be included in management decisions, Assistants play supporting rather than policy-making roles.

for a few large law firms. It arose in response to the growing need for associate training and gradually expanded to embrace other functions as well. The vagueness of the role is in part due to the haphazard way that organized professional development efforts arose in law firms. Historically, few professional development programs were fully conceived when they began. Instead, the process went something like this: A firm initiated a program, perhaps for recruiting and training summer associates. The program for summer associates was so well received that the firm thought it should do something for regular associates, too, so they started an orientation program for new associates. That grew into a training program for litigation associates, which subsequently led to training for corporate associates. At each step, a different person was usually in control. It became obvious that these various activities needed to be better coordinated, so the firm appointed someone to administer them.

Because of the gradual, opportunistic way the position evolved, the specialist's role tended to reflect the talents and interests of the particular individual in charge. For example, if the responsible person had a graduate degree in adult education, the job might concentrate almost exclusively on training. If he or she had a background in recruiting, the job might focus disproportionately on orientation of new associates. As a result, it was common for the position to be redefined every time a new person took over. When a transition occurred, some professional development activities might languish because professional development was defined by the motivation and particular interests of the person in charge, not as a delineated management function.

This lack of delineation also led each firm to shape the role differently, which resulted in remarkable variations across firms. Surveys conducted by the author in 1997 and 2001 of individuals responsible for professional development in law firms in the United States and Canada revealed an astonishing assortment of responsibilities. (See Table 2.) As this list suggests, the responsibilities are all over the map and many are unique to particular firms. No one would suggest, for instance, that audit inquiries or library management should be standard professional development functions. In spite of the huge variation in job responsibilities, however, a defined role for the professional development specialist has become apparent.

TABLE 2. Various Responsibilities of Professional Development Specialists

- Alumni relations
- Associate promotion/partnership decisions
- Associate relations
- Associate retention
- Associate work assignments/work allocation
- Audit inquiries
- Career guidance/counseling
- CLE administration/tracking
- Client relations
- Client training
- Compensation decisions for associates
- Compensation decisions for partners
- Coordination of professional development activities and procedures
- Development of performance benchmarks
- Diversity initiatives
- Diversity training
- Employment policies for lawyers
- Evaluations of associates
- Evaluations of partners by associates
- Evaluations of partners by peers
- Exit interviews
- Information Technology
- Integration of lateral lawyers
- Knowledge management
- Lawyers' benefits
- Leadership development
- Legal personnel
- Library management
- Marketing
- Mentoring
- Monitoring or assisting part-time lawyers
- Needs assessment
- Office space assignments
- Ombudsperson for associates
- Orientation for new and lateral associates
- Orientation for new and lateral partners
- Outplacement arrangements
- Practice specialization
- Pro bono work
- Public relations
- Quality of life issues
- Recruiting of lateral associates
- Recruiting of new associates
- Recruiting of partners
- Retreats
- Self-study learning resources
- Social event planning
- Strategic planning
- Summer associate program
- Teaching
- Technology support
- Training for associates
- Training for legal assistants
- Training for partners
- Training for staff
- Writing program

We can now identify twelve core areas of responsibility for the professional development specialist. These core areas embrace the four principal components of professional development (training, mentoring, work experience, and evaluation), along with other related development and management functions. Specialists should have expertise in all of these areas, although it is entirely appropriate for the firm to delegate certain responsibilities to others in the firm and to call in outside experts when necessary to supplement the specialist's capabilities. Even when professional development specialists do not have direct responsibility for each of these functions, they still need to coordinate and serve as a resource in all of these areas for the firm.

1. **Training.** The one almost universal activity run by professional development specialists is associate training. This is in large part because of how the role developed historically, as a response to law firm growth and the need to educate large numbers of associates about law practice. Today, professional development specialists are responsible for training program strategy, design, and implementation, not just for associates but for all lawyers in the firm. They understand and incorporate adult learning principles and work with lawyers in the firm to determine content and curriculum for each practice area. They conduct training needs assessments, design curricula, select appropriate training technologies and delivery systems, recruit and train in-house faculty, identify and negotiate with outside training vendors, and evaluate programs. They also supervise the CLE accreditation process for in-house programs. The ability to teach certain subjects is an added plus, but is not essential to the role.

TABLE 3. Twelve Core Areas of Responsibility for Professional Development Specialists

1. Training	7. Lawyer integration
2. Mentoring	8. Associate retention
3. Lawyers' work experience	9. Partner development
4. Evaluations	10. Planning and policy development
5. Career development	11. Coordination
6. Technology	12. Management

2. **Mentoring.** The professional development specialist promotes informal mentoring and helps to create an environment where mentoring relationships can flourish. When a more structured approach to mentoring is necessary, the specialist is responsible for designing, implementing, and monitoring a formal mentoring program.

3. **Lawyers' work experience.** Work experience includes both the nature of the work assigned and the evaluation of lawyers' performance. The specialist is responsible for developing systems to monitor associates' billable and pro bono work experiences, although practice groups or departments normally make their own specific work assignments.

4. **Evaluations.** Regular performance evaluations are necessary for lawyers to set and measure performance goals and assess their progress. The specialist oversees evaluation procedures and works with partners to establish performance criteria and standards for advancement.

5. **Career development.** In addition to day-to-day learning, professional development involves long-term career planning. The specialist is responsible for systems that promote career development, including work counseling, individual development planning, and policies regarding when and how lawyers choose areas of practice specialization.

6. **Technology.** Professional development specialists do not have to be experts in technology or information systems, but they must appreciate the many ways that technology promotes knowledge sharing and learning (as well as technology's limits). Working with the firm's technology experts, specialists select and utilize technology appropriately to support learning, expedite evaluation procedures, track CLE compliance, and enhance communication about professional development through the firm's intranet.

7. **Lawyer integration.** Integration begins with orientation, when new and lateral lawyers and the firm are introduced to each other. Orientation is a professional development responsibility (although it may be shared with the recruiting department). Integration of lawyers in the office includes how lawyers with different backgrounds and experiences deal with each other and how they relate to the firm. Diversity training is a professional development activity. Other programs and activities that support diversity may be shared with other groups in the firm.

8. **Associate retention.** Professional development is a fundamental part of any firm's efforts to retain associates. Specialists can lead the firm's

retention effort; at the very least, they are actively and closely involved in those efforts. They create programs and strategies to keep morale and motivation high and to foster associate engagement in work and in firm life. When associates leave despite these efforts, specialists conduct exit interviews to ascertain and reduce the causes of turnover.

9. **Partner development.** The professional development specialist ensures that partners have the training and resources they need to excel in practice. The specialist designs and oversees partner orientation, training courses, and leadership development. The specialist may also participate in partnership selection and succession planning, and work with the marketing department on matters related to practice development.

10. **Planning and policy development.** Professional development specialists participate in the firm's overall strategic planning process and are responsible for long-term planning for the firm's professional development program. They participate in the development of policies regarding training, development, and performance measurement for all lawyers, and policies regarding employment (e.g., part-time opportunities), advancement, compensation, and termination (e.g., outplacement services) of associates.

11. **Coordination.** The responsibility for coordinating all activities, policies, and procedures related to professional development rests with the professional development specialist. Specialists do not necessarily have responsibility for all related efforts (e.g., recruiting, summer programs, and hiring), but they do understand the processes and work with those in charge to ensure an integrated approach.

12. **Management.** Because specialists have the principal responsibility for professional development, they hire, manage, and supervise other professional development employees. They also prepare budgets, set priorities, allocate resources, and manage projects. In doing so, they organize retreats, meetings, and programs that require negotiating with personnel in the firm as well as outside facilities and vendors. Specialists manage information as well, ensuring that useful and pertinent learning resources are available and easily accessible to lawyers.

Many firms combine responsibilities for professional development with recruiting under a single director or department. Having one department responsible for both recruiting and development treats lawyers' learning and growth as a continuum that begins with their first contacts with the firm and lasts throughout their careers. Some firms take an even broader view, placing all professional and employment matters related to lawyers under one umbrella. Combining some or all of these functions makes sense for purposes of planning and coordination, but it expands the specialist's job beyond what one person can reasonably do. Because professional development can encompass so many diverse functions, it is important for the firm to define the professional development specialist's mandate and job description carefully. (See Appendix 3 for examples of job descriptions for professional development specialist positions.) Even though the job description may be fluid and likely to change over time, setting forth the specialist's position in detail will help the firm find the right specialist and help the specialist do the job right. It will also suggest the number of staff needed to support the specialist. The more distinct responsibilities that fall under professional development, the larger the staff should be. Having capable managers to perform the day-to-day work, and to assist in planning and implementation, enables the professional development specialist to concentrate on strategic issues and activities that make the best use of his or her knowledge and expertise.

Professional Development Specialists: Qualifications

Professional development specialists require certain skills and capabilities, but, at present, no established qualifications for this role exist. There is no specific training or certifying process to become a professional development specialist and no governing board or body to establish qualifications for certification. As the field continues to grow and specialists join forces to better define their responsibilities and establish standards, a certifying process will likely emerge. The Association of Legal Administrators (ALA) has shown that this can be done for the legal administrator — a role even more diverse than that of the professional development specialist. Legal administrators manage the law firm's business. They range from office managers in small practices who handle every detail of law firm management to the CEOs of the country's largest firms. Nonetheless, the ALA has identified 55 fundamental competencies that legal administrators need to master. Based on those competencies, it has developed coursework and a certification program for becoming a Certified Legal Manager (CLM). At some point, the core competencies for professional development specialists will also be identified and appropriate certification standards and procedures will be established.

In the meantime, notwithstanding the variation in roles and responsibilities of professional development specialists, certain qualifications for the job are manifest. Specialists must have expert management and leadership skills. To maximize the value of professional development to the firm and its lawyers, the specialist should also have sophisticated knowledge of how lawyers practice, learn, and develop. The success of a professional development program will depend more on an individual's capabilities in these areas than on any particular substantive knowledge or expertise.

■ **Expert management skills.** Professional development specialists manage people, projects, and resources. To do this effectively, they have to understand the business of the firm and how training and development impact business goals. They need to understand the financial implications of the programs they propose, and have the financial skills necessary to prepare, track, and control budgets. Specialists must be proficient in strategic planning, communication, and interpersonal relations. A hefty dose of common sense is mandatory; resourcefulness is vital; and a sense of humor is indispensable.

The specialist's multi-faceted role requires an ability to prioritize and juggle many different projects at once and to integrate many diverse systems into a coherent whole. Specialists have to develop, implement, and coordinate a variety of professional development activities, and address immediate issues concerning performance, programs, and personnel. At the same time, they have to concentrate on long-term planning and goal-setting. To accomplish this feat requires excellent organizational skills and an ability to work under constant pressure.

Effective communication is fundamental to any management role. Specialists must be able to articulate, verbally and in writing, the purpose and value of professional development in order to engage support and enlist participation. Specialists need to be attentive listeners as well. They have to listen carefully as they try to discover and respond to lawyers' needs and as they deal with the people they supervise. Managing people also requires good interpersonal skills, including the ability to collaborate with others, resolve conflicts, and build productive relationships.

A word should be said about resourcefulness. Professional development specialists must be able to roll with the punches. They have to have realistic expectations and a pragmatic attitude toward scarce resources, especially lawyers' time. When time, space, or budgets limit their options, specialists have to be innovative and imaginative in obtaining suitable, cost-effective trainers, materials, and technologies.

■ **Expert leadership skills.** The professional development specialist's position presents a unique challenge. The specialist runs a program without any power or control over the primary beneficiaries, i.e., the firm's lawyers. Lawyers struggle with constant time pressure and competing demands, and professional development is not their top priority. Consequently, leadership skills are unusually important, as the specialist must persuade lawyers to participate in professional development activities when their immediate priorities and attention lie elsewhere. Being in such a difficult role means that specialists must possess singular personal leadership qualities: credibility, decisiveness, and persuasiveness. In addition, they have to be advocates for themselves and for their programs, creative in generating and marketing new ideas, and politically savvy.

The specialist must be an advocate on many fronts. As internal consultants, they present the intellectual and practical justification for professional development. They exert influence on the firm's commitment to professional development and act as cheerleaders to build interest and enthusiasm. They push to establish a learning culture that supports and encourages professional development and fight for the resources they need to make it happen. When competing with others in the firm for limited resources, they are strong negotiators. They are bold not only in their willingness to try new things, but also in persuading others to agree to them.

Specialists design and act as catalysts for new initiatives. Generating new ideas, developing innovative strategies, finding solutions to difficult problems, and instituting new implementation techniques all require a creative mind. But specialists temper their creative vision with political astuteness. They have a keen awareness of the political dynamics of the firm and keep an eye on how firm politics may impact their work. They have to have clear access to — and support from — the true sources of power in the firm. While they recognize and respond to the key players in the firm, their motivation is to promote professional development, not individuals. They act as the ambassador for professional development throughout the firm, using diplomatic and collaborative skills. These skills also help them when their authority in a certain area is not well defined or the lines of authority are ambiguous.

■ **Knowledge of law practice.** Professional development specialists need not be lawyers, but they must understand how lawyers think, learn, and practice. This is the single most important requirement for a specialist in a law firm. Without this understanding, no professional development specialist can establish credibility or succeed in their work. In addition to being smart, competent, and professional, the specialist must have a thorough understanding of law practice in general and of their firm in particular. Before lawyers will accept the specialist's ideas and programs, they must be convinced that the specialist understands them and the intellectual and practice environment in which they work. This includes the pressures that lawyers operate under, the characteristic ways they approach problems, and the competing demands for their time and attention.

Specialists have to know enough about law practice to determine what lawyers need to learn and establish systems to facilitate their learning. This does not mean that specialists must have substantive knowledge of law; they can obtain guidance about content from the lawyers in the firm. But it does mean that they must be sufficiently familiar with legal concepts, terminology, and procedures to propose initiatives that are relevant and make sense to lawyers. They have to be aware of the unique features of law practice that impact the design of professional development programs (e.g., confidentiality constraints may restrict what can be discussed when outsiders are present).

Professional development specialists also have to understand how lawyers learn, not just in formal training programs, but also in the context of daily practice through work assignments, mentoring relationships, and self-study. And they have to understand what can and cannot realistically be expected of lawyers. As an example, corporate trainers may be accustomed to programs that are scheduled off-site for several days or a week at a time. Lawyers, however, will resist anything that requires more than a few hours away from their desks.

Finding Professional Development Specialists

Finding a fully qualified specialist in this still-evolving field may be difficult. There are relatively few individuals today who have sufficient experience and expertise to meet all of the qualifications and fulfill all of the responsibilities of a professional development specialist. But the pool of qualified people is growing. Many outstanding individuals are entering the field with credentials and experience in some but not all of the requisite areas. They are learning as they go, building on their knowledge base and growing into their leadership and managerial roles. These individuals are coming from four principal areas: (1) lawyers who leave or drastically reduce their practice but want to stay involved in the firm or the profession; (2) personnel who work in the firm in other capacities (especially recruiting) who are seeking new professional challenges or whose responsibilities are expanding; (3) human resources and training professionals from other industries, notably other professional services arenas; and (4) law school professors, deans, and administrators. Individuals from any of these backgrounds can be superb in the role. Still, there are practical considerations to keep in mind for firms contemplating promoting or hiring someone from one of these areas.

■ **Lawyers transitioning into professional development:** For lawyers practicing in the firm who make this transition, a full-time job dedicated to professional development is a natural extension of the historical, more limited role of the Training

Partner. This transitioning lawyer may be a practicing partner, but quite often is an associate with a few years of practice experience who is seeking a change in career direction. The position is also an attractive option for senior partners approaching retirement but not yet ready to leave the law firm.

Placing one of the firm's lawyers in this role has many benefits: familiarity, credibility, ease of entry, quick adjustment, understanding of the firm and its practice. On the other hand, there may be resistance from other lawyers who oppose the move or the particular individual. Some may be upset when a lawyer who has been billing clients remains on the payroll at a substantial salary but no longer generates revenue, and some belittle anyone who chooses to give up law practice for "non-legal" work.

For most "home-grown" lawyers who assume a professional development position, these criticisms readily subside as people grow accustomed to the change and begin to see positive results. Resistance is more difficult to overcome if the lawyer is new to the firm, especially if the position is also a new one. One example is the associate who told the firm's new professional development director, "We just figured you were a lawyer who couldn't cut it." While strong, vocal leadership support for a new professional development leader is essential under any circumstances, it is even more critical for a new person in a newly created role.

■ **Internal personnel transitioning into professional development:** The benefits to the firm when a firm administrator or manager moves into professional development are generally the same as for a transitioning lawyer. This kind of promotion also has an important collateral benefit: It signals to all employees that opportunities exist for career advancement within the firm. This can shore up the firm's efforts to retain good employees who might otherwise leave to pursue new challenges and growth opportunities.

The disadvantage is that because this person is not a lawyer, it will take more effort at the beginning to be effective in the role. This person will have to rely more on lawyers for input about practice needs and issues. Because many lawyers believe that only other lawyers can possibly understand and appreciate their work lives, the nature of their practice, and the pressures they face, some lawyers will also discount the expertise and authority of any "non-lawyer." However, even lawyers with many years of practice behind them do not understand practice areas other than their own and depend on other lawyers for guidance. Moreover, if the person is well known and respected in the firm and has the requisite experience, talents, and skills for the job, it may take a little longer but acceptance will ultimately come — even from the skeptics.

■ **Professionals from other fields and industries:** It is considerably more challenging when the professional development specialist is new to law practice. Experts in training, education, psychology, human resources, and many other fields have knowledge and expertise that provide enormous value to a professional development program. They may also have a business or management background that facilitates planning, coordination, and oversight of the program and its component parts. They may bring an abundance of creativity and energy to the job that can lead to innovation and rapid strides in lawyer development and retention. But without a firm footing in law practice, they will face serious obstacles along the way.

Transitioning from the business world to law practice can be tough. The law firm environment can be baffling and harsh to newcomers. One frustrated corporate trainer presented this litany of woe after his first few months as a specialist in a large law firm: "Law firms tend to be behind technically, processes are outdated and slow, demands on people are extremely high, [there is] lots of 'fire fighting,' human relations skills among lawyers are poor, and support for someone in [my] position tends to be low." The specialist's ability to carry out certain tasks may be undermined by a lack of understanding of how law firms operate and how lawyers work. It is important, therefore, to allow ample time for the new person to learn about the firm, its lawyers, and its practice. It is also important to provide resources (e.g., a mentor) to facilitate that learning and to encourage acceptance by the firm.

Professional development specialists who are new to the legal industry also have to prove themselves. In order to win the trust and cooperation of the lawyers in the firm, they must establish credibility quickly. Having an advanced degree in a relevant field helps; so does a substantial amount of related experience. But the most important thing is to demonstrate immediately an understanding of the lawyers, their firm, and their profession, and to undertake initiatives that are manifestly effective and successful. Over time, the resistance will wane as positive results are seen.

■ **Law school personnel:** People who come to law firms from law schools possess skills, knowledge, and understanding pertinent to professional development. These individuals frequently play a dual role in the firm, providing legal advice in their substantive legal specialties while administering the broader professional development program. They tend to be readily accepted by lawyers because their academic credentials pertain directly to their professional development role. They have an even greater advantage if they are returning lawyers who practiced law in the firm prior to embarking on an academic career. The challenge for them is to apply what they know about lawyers' learning and development to the "real world" of law practice. Law school experience does not always translate into skills needed in a law firm setting. These individuals may be handicapped if they lack management or law firm experience, or if their interest lies more in esoteric academic questions than in the practical issues involved in managing a law firm's professional development program.

Reporting Relationships of Professional Development Specialists

One important consideration is the place of the professional development specialist in the management chain of command. The line of authority is a very sensitive issue, especially in large firms. To function effectively and maximize their value to the firm, specialists need clear authority and direct access to top leadership. Professional development initiatives often require systemic changes, imposition of policies, and intrusions on lawyers' time. Because heads of professional development have no direct power over lawyers, they depend on access to and support from the firm leadership to verify their authority and enlist lawyers' participation. The level of leadership support, and the specialist's reporting position in the firm hierarchy, have significant influence on the way lawyers perceive the specialist's standing in the firm and the amount of respect and authority the specialist commands.

Perception of authority is important in any management job, but especially for those holding management positions in a law firm. Lawyers tend to have a "we/they" mindset; they categorize people as either lawyers or "non-lawyers" — and hold the latter group in less esteem. In areas affecting the way they practice and learn, lawyers are reluctant to depend on or defer to individuals who are not practicing lawyers. Even specialists who have previously practiced law have less stature once they move into a management role. Consequently, professional development specialists must establish their authority in the firm in order to be taken seriously.

As discussed earlier, much of this depends on the specialist's personal attributes and abilities. But it is also determined in large part by the organizational status and respect given to the professional development role. Firms that recognize the need for and value of expert leadership in professional development give the specialist a visible, pivotal role in designing strategy, establishing policies, and setting direction for the firm's professional development activities. They rely on the specialist for advice, information, and analysis when making decisions with implications for lawyer development, and make the specialist part of the firm's management team. This leaves no doubt as to the value placed on professional development by the firm, and invests the professional development specialist with the authority the job demands.

Not every firm is prepared to make the professional development specialist a full member of the top management team. Nonetheless, professional development specialists should be placed on a par with other key managers, e.g., directors of finance, marketing, information services, and human resources. The professional development specialist should be a high-level manager and report to top management in the firm or office, with as few intermediaries as possible. Specialists who head professional development firm-wide should report to the chair, managing partner, executive director, or executive committee. Specialists whose authority is office-based rather than firm-wide should report either to the firm-wide professional development specialist or to the managing partner or executive director of their office.

An executive management role for the professional development specialist is steadily gaining acceptance among law firms. Firms are beginning to recognize that professional development is critical to their success in the marketplace and that they need specialists to manage the professional development function. This is especially true as law firms increase in size, for they face a corresponding increase in organizational complexity. When they have hundreds or even thousands of lawyers at multiple sites, they must become more methodical about how they manage lawyers' development and performance. Fortunately, the number of professional development specialists qualified to perform that function is also growing. More law firms can be expected to institutionalize professional development as an executive-level management responsibility. Four firms that have already done so are highlighted in Table 4.

Professional Development and the Human Resources Department

There is some debate about whether lawyers' professional development belongs in the human resources department or whether it should remain separate and independent from human resources. This issue arises in firms with a corporate structure where human resources is an executive department.[1] Those proposing to fold professional development into human resources argue that it facilitates the integration and coordination of recruiting, training, and development activities for

---

[1] The issue does not usually come up if human resources is considered an administrative function or if the reporting line is reversed, i.e., the head of human resources reports to the professional development director.

TABLE 4. Examples of Firms with Executive Level Professional Development Directors

- **Dorsey & Whitney LLP (750 lawyers in 22 offices worldwide):** The Director of Professional Development is a partner who has full-time responsibility for professional development, although he also spends a limited amount of time practicing law. His responsibilities include new associate and new partner orientation, training, mentoring, and knowledge management, as well as paralegal and staff development. He supervises a staff of four to five people and coordinates the efforts of lawyers who serve as professional development coordinators in the firm's larger offices.

- **Fried, Frank, Harris, Shriver & Jacobson (550 lawyers in 5 U.S. and European offices):** The Executive Director for the Office of Associate Affairs is a former special counsel in the firm. He oversees all aspects of associate work life, including associate training, performance management, mentoring, employment policies and practices, compensation and benefits, career development, diversity, communications, and technology support. He supervises eight to ten people in the New York office, including directors and managers who run each function. The firm also has a Director and Office of Associate Development in its Washington, D.C. office with a separate but smaller staff.

- **Morrison & Foerster LLP (approximately 1,000 lawyers in 18 offices worldwide):** The Professional Development Director, a lawyer who is Of Counsel, leads the firm's Professional Development Group (PDG), which has responsibility for the firm's legal professionals, including lawyers, analysts, and legal assistants. She supervises four Regional Professional Development Managers as well as managers of pro bono work, knowledge management, and legal assistant training and development. The PDG is charged with providing strategic direction for the training, development, and retention of legal professionals. The PDG's responsibilities include evaluations, feedback, training, mentoring, supervision, orientation, and advising professionals regarding individual professional development matters. The Director is part of the firm's operations management team and reports to the firm's Managing Partners.

- **Wilmer, Cutler & Pickering (500 lawyers in 7 US and European offices):** The Director of Career Development is not a lawyer but has extensive experience in the field of lawyers' professional development. He co-chairs the firm's Career Development Committee, attends all partnership meetings, participates (but does not vote) in the partner selection process, and reports directly to the firm's Administrative Partner. His department includes about a dozen staff members and a Director of Legal Personnel and Recruiting, who is considered one of the firm's five top-level administrators. The department is responsible for recruiting, lawyer training and development, evaluations, career guidance, and all other aspects of lawyers' development.

lawyers and other professional employees. They point out that human resource functions include education and training, performance measurement, employee benefits, hiring and firing issues, diversity, and employment policies. Although human resource professionals are usually not lawyers, they are experts in retaining and developing human resources — including lawyers. They have a broad base of knowledge and often have experience in other industries and professions. They look at recruiting, development, and retention as a continuum of activities that flow into and interconnect with one another. Consequently, their approach to professional development is more holistic than that of a practicing lawyer or professional development specialist whose background and perspective are narrower.

The opposing view holds that professional development should be equal to the human resources department, not subordinate to it. Lawyers believe that human resources personnel do not understand the special complexities and intricacies of law practice, fail to appreciate what lawyers want and need, or have competing agendas that distract from lawyers' needs. Lawyers equate the human resources function with employee benefits and forms. As a practical matter, human resource directors do not have the same credibility or respect in lawyers' eyes as professionals who concentrate their efforts exclusively on lawyer training and development. Consequently, lawyers more readily accept professional development initiatives when they come from professional development rather than from human resources.

If the prevailing attitude in a firm is that human resources cannot address lawyers' professional development needs, placing professional development under human resources may deprive it of the respect and credibility necessary for professional development efforts to flourish. On the other hand, in firms that welcome the role of human resources in lawyer development, or whose culture is based on egalitarianism and teamwork, placing lawyer development in the human resources department would be appropriate. In fact, in such firms, separating lawyers from other employees for purposes of human resource issues would violate cultural norms. Regardless of where professional development stands in relation to human resources, what matters most is that professional development be accorded the full, visible, and enthusiastic support of — and access to — firm leadership.

Professional Development Committees and the Specialist

Another important issue concerns the accountability of the specialist in relation to firm committees involved with professional development. Most law firms have one or more committees that deal with training, evaluations, and other professional development concerns. These committees are accountable to the firm's managing partner or management committee but function autonomously. Professional development specialists have close working relationships with these committees, but, as firm managers, they should report to someone in the firm's management structure, not to a committee. They should advise and support the committees, participate actively as an equal member, and even chair them. But their responsibility is to the firm, not just to a committee, and their reporting relationship should reflect this fact.

Practical Suggestions for Professional Development Specialists

1. **Immediately establish yourself as a leader.** In order to be effective, you must establish your status as an executive or high-level manager as quickly as possible. One way to do this is to be sure that your title gives you parity with other managers and executives at the same level. Parity of title is not insignificant. If you are operating as an executive officer, you should be called a director, not an administrator. If you have been promoted to this position, you must change the firm's perception of you from a supporting player to a leader. To be seen as a leader, it is also important to have professional development responsibility for all lawyers in the firm, not just for associates.

2. **Define your authority up front.** It is important for you and the firm to have a clear agreement about the extent of your authority. The firm may tell you to "take the ball and run with it," but be sure you know exactly what that means. You need answers to some basic questions: For what am I accountable? To whom am I accountable? What kinds of decisions can I make independently and which require consultation with (and approval from) the professional development committee or some other individual or group? There will always be gray areas, but they will be easier to resolve if you have clarity at the outset about the anticipated scope of your authority.

3. **Know and be known.** When you take charge of professional development, especially if you are new to the firm, insist on being introduced to influential lawyers and managers in all the firm's offices, especially those who are active in professional development efforts. Ask the managing partner or other high-ranking partner to make the introductions and emphasize your role as a leader for professional development. Visit as many of the firm's offices as possible and meet as many people as you can. Learn how the firm's culture varies from office to office. Keep yourself visible so that people recognize you as the head of professional development and go to you with questions and ideas.

4. **Start with a quick success.** Even with the strong support of management, you have to demonstrate that you are both capable and dedicated to the best interests of the firm. Every new leader enjoys a grace period when people give you the benefit of the doubt. In most law firms, the grace period is very short. Lawyers are impatient; they want to see quick results. It is a good idea to begin with a small but prominent project that can be a clear-cut success and show how your efforts add value to the firm. As one success leads to others, it will confirm your merit and convert doubters into believers.

5. **Hold the firm to its commitments.** Perhaps the greatest single source of frustration for professional development leaders is their inability to hold the firm to its avowed commitment to professional development. As one professional development director commented, "This job requires 110 percent support from management in order to be successful." She was lucky enough to have that support, but many of her counterparts do not. A particular problem is partners who prevent associates from attending programs planned and publicized well in advance. This is true for all kinds of programs, but especially those that require a substantial amount of time away from the office, such as trial advocacy training. Partners who prevent associates from attending or pull them out after the program has begun, upset associates, frustrate program planners and participants, and thwart the professional development program's purpose.

    The best way to hold the firm to its commitments is to create a culture that places the highest value on professional development endeavors. You have no control over the firm's partners, but you can influence the firm's commitment and, in that way, impact its culture. This takes time, especially if the firm is new to organized professional development activities. Collaboration with and buy-in from influential firm leaders and partners are essential. So is smart planning. As discussed in Chapter 2, your plan should be realistic and comprehensive. Creating a professional development plan puts everyone on notice of the expectations for their participation and the participation of others — especially the associates they supervise. When the plan is accepted and put into play, you are in a stronger position to hold wayward lawyers to their commitment.

6. **Forge strong internal alliances.** A network of internal alliances can make your work easier and more successful. Start building alliances immediately. Determine the key players whose support you need, and devise a strategy to enlist both their support and firm-wide commitment. Build

and maintain bridges to all the individuals and departments with whom you work. Some of the groups that will be most important to you are:

a. *Office, department, and practice group leaders.* These individuals are your key sources of information about development needs and key sponsors of local training and development initiatives. You need to rely on them to carry out the policies and programs you create, and they need to have faith in your willingness and ability to help them.

b. *Firm managers and leaders.* Alliances with the top echelon of leadership and management are crucial, so marshal some powerful champions. You need management support for your professional development initiatives, budget, and daily operations, including space, facilities, equipment, and resources. You need leadership's vocal and enthusiastic advocacy to verify the importance and value of the undertaking, overcome resistance, and persuade others to support both the professional development program and your work.

c. *Marketing.* If professional development is tied to the firm's strategy and plan for the future, you must work hand in hand with the people in charge of marketing. Marketing and professional development interact in many ways. The firm's marketing strategy impacts the type of training, coaching, and work experiences you need to provide for lawyers. Many marketing directors and administrators can train or coach lawyers in business development and client relation skills. Marketing personnel with knowledge about industry trends can obtain industry and client information that enriches training efforts. The marketing department can help you market training and other professional development programs internally, to increase enthusiasm and participation, and create outreach efforts that include clients in professional development programs.

d. *Recruiting.* Much of what happens in professional development is interrelated with recruitment policies and activities. You should communicate and collaborate regularly with the head of recruiting on issues related to hiring, summer associates, and new associates. It is important for you to know what recruits want and think; it is important for recruiting that you help the firm stay attractive to potential hires.

e. *Associates and associates' committee.* You must have continuing input from associates, who are the recipients of most of the firm's professional development efforts. Many offices have an associates' committee that deals with associate affairs. This committee is your liaison with associates, and associates on the committee are your single most important source of information about associates' needs and desires. In addition to giving you information, associate members can distribute your ideas and plans to their peers; explain your intentions and promote your efforts; generate interest and participation; and translate for you when issues are unclear or mediate if they are controversial. If your office does not have an associates' committee (or if your committee is made up only of partners), seek out some cooperative and interested associates who can act as informal liaisons between your professional development team and other associates.

f. *Information technology.* Professional development relies heavily on technology in many ways, including knowledge retrieval, intranets, computer- and web-based training, evaluations, assignment tracking, and CLE. You need a strong collaborative working relationship with technology personnel to make effective use of existing technology, to fashion innovative new uses for what you have, and to stay apprised of new technologies that can be of benefit.

g. *Librarians.* Librarians can be of great assistance by conducting the research you need and training lawyers to use technology for their research. Librarians can also help gather and maintain resources for self-study. This is especially beneficial in states where self-study is an option for CLE compliance.

h. *Paralegals and staff.* In some firms, the professional development program embraces paralegals, secretaries, and other employees. Whether or not your program includes these employees, it is a good idea to build strong relationships with administrators and representatives from the rank and file. These groups can be rich mines of information about lawyers' training and development needs, especially in the area of management skills. Moreover, whatever lawyers do will affect the people they work with, so employees' understanding of what you are doing will make it easier to solicit their cooperation and support.

7. **Cultivate the professional development committee.** Much of your effectiveness depends on how well you support and facilitate this committee's work — and how much support the committee gives to you. Establish a strong and positive working relationship with committee members, especially the committee chair. Meet with the chair regularly, and spend time with each member as well. Get to know their special interests and pet peeves, learn what kinds of efforts they support and where you can expect opposition. Be a resource to them. Communicate regularly. Invite responsibility. Stay on top of lawyers' needs and activities. Generate and keep track of ideas and program proposals. Maintain budget data and timetables. When leading or participating in committee meetings, be well organized and prepared, and ensure that everyone has a chance to be heard. Being seen as an effective committee chair or facilitator can enhance your credibility and boost support for your work.

8. **Streamline decision-making.** Try to simplify planning and implementation procedures, and keep the number of people involved in decision-making to a minimum. Although some aspects of your work require thoughtful deliberation and a long time to study and reflect, most of the questions and issues you face require quick responses. A small decision-making group can be more agile, efficient, progressive, and innovative than a large and cumbersome committee. Decision-making is impeded when policy decisions must be made by partners who are too busy or distracted to pay attention, or by a large group that avoids making decision or gets wrapped up in competing agendas.

9. **Show how you add value.** It is important that lawyers appreciate the value of what you do. Do some internal marketing. Let lawyers see how much you can do for them. Respond to lawyers' requests and inquiries promptly; use their ideas and suggestions (and give them credit); present training programs for their clients; create brochures about the firm's professional development program so that lawyers can include them in written business proposals to prospective clients. Demonstrate to lawyers how the professional development program differentiates your firm and creates a competitive advantage.

10. **Find a champion.** If at all possible, find someone in the firm who will champion your efforts. The more prominent and influential the person is, the better.

APPENDIX 3

Two Sample Job Descriptions for the Position of Director of Professional Development

The following sample job descriptions from two different firms illustrate some of the varied ways the position of Professional Development Director can be structured. These are adapted from actual sample job descriptions and are not intended to represent ideal models for law firms.

For a 180-lawyer firm in six offices in the United States and Europe

The Director of Professional Development is a management position reporting to the Firm's Co-Managing Partners. The Director oversees the design and implementation of the Firm's associate training and development program. To that end, the person works with Firm and department leadership to design and implement systems (including work assignment and tracking systems; formal training programs; and review, evaluation, and compensation systems) which impact on associate training and development. In addition, the Director of Professional Development acts as an individual adviser to associates with regard to issues related to their professional development. The Director of Professional Development also oversees all aspects of the Firm's Summer Clerk Program.

The Director of Professional Development is a standing member of Firm committees that affect associates and, in those roles, coordinates the committees' work on various aspects of the associate training and development program and participates in Firm policy decisions to the extent that they affect associate training and development. The Director of Professional Development also oversees the Firm's Mentor and Alumni Relations programs.

The Director of Professional Development must have a J.D. degree and preferably will have large law firm experience, as well as experience practicing in other settings.

Leading the Professional Development Program

For a 650-lawyer firm in eight offices world-wide

Reporting Relationship:

The Director of Professional Development will report to the Executive Committee through the Firm Managing Partner. The Director will meet frequently with the Executive Committee, practice group leaders, and department heads and will also attend partners' meetings and retreats.

Overview of Position:

The Director is responsible for the creation and implementation of educational and developmental programs and policies required to improve the long-term professional development and satisfaction of our lawyers. The Director will help achieve the firm's goal to build a pre-eminent global law firm with excellent lawyers providing the highest quality client service. The Director will focus on the design and implementation of firm-wide professional development programs while each office will be primarily responsible for the day-to-day operation of the programs.

Primary Responsibilities:

- Develop a strategic direction for education and development to meet the Firm's objectives.

- Chair a National Associates' Committee that will include a partner charged with the responsibility of overseeing the professional development efforts in each office.

- Conduct an assessment of lawyers' needs for education and development.

- Develop an educational curriculum that meets professional, business, and client service goals.

- With practice group leaders, department heads, and office managing partners, develop and implement training in substantive law, practice skills, practice group-specific subjects, management training, and other development programs for lawyers.

- With practice group leaders, department heads and office managing partners, develop and implement firm-wide and practice-specific training retreats, orientations, and seminars.

- Develop and implement a strategic benchmarks/core competency program to uniformly assess associate progress.

- Develop a national evaluation system that will include annual reviews, upward evaluations, and completion of career development plans by lawyers. Provide summary reports to the Executive Committee and each office managing partner on the outcome of the upward evaluations.

- Work with the office managing partners and the Executive Committee to ensure that the upward evaluation reports are followed up with positive recognition and reward or remedial action.

- Revitalize the mentor program and work with the Associates Committee to ensure that each office supports and participates successfully in the mentoring program.

- Develop and oversee the budgets for continuing legal education in each office. Work with designated individuals in each office who will administer the approval of in-house and outside education programs.

- Develop hiring criteria for recruiting associates and implement an interview training program for all interviewers.

- Prepare information highlighting professional development activities for inclusion in recruiting materials.

- Keep up to date on professional development initiatives through literature, seminars, conferences, and membership in appropriate professional organizations.

- Deliver an annual report describing the Director's activities and accomplishments for the prior fiscal year.

The Director will be located in the Firm's home office and will travel to each of the Firm's offices approximately twice per year.

Secondary Responsibilities:

The Director of Professional Development coordinates activities with those responsible for other aspects of Firm administration, in the manner indicated —

- Prioritize professional development initiatives according to Firm business development objectives.

- Maintain current library of training materials, including client and CLE presentations, and coordinate with new knowledge management initiatives.

- Solicit feedback from attorneys regarding current risk management training and suggest improvements to Attorney Development Committee.

- Coordinate training efforts with Legal Assistant Department and encourage inclusion of non-lawyer personnel in team training efforts.

CHAPTER 4

How Law Firms Help Lawyers Learn and Develop

Law firms are only as good as their intellectual capital, which is the accumulated knowledge and experience of their lawyers. Like other forms of capital, intellectual capital can be invested, put to productive use, and made to yield benefits. The intellectual capital of the firm grows and increases in value as lawyers learn and develop. When the firm systematically invests in learning, the growth of intellectual capital accelerates. This investment gives a firm a considerable competitive advantage that yields high returns in professional and financial performance.

A professional development program is your firm's investment in intellectual capital. Its purpose is not to promote learning for its own sake, but to expand lawyers' expertise, improve their professional capabilities, and produce the talent required for the firm to achieve its business strategy. When an organization makes continuous learning a core component of its long-term strategy, it creates a win-win situation. Individual lawyers benefit by becoming more effective practitioners and enjoying more personal fulfillment. The firm is rewarded by superior professional services and higher financial returns.

To make a firm's investment worthwhile, lawyers have to put their learning to good use. Lawyers acquire new knowledge every day, but the value of that learning lies in how it is used. Learning should be productive; it should result in better performance. What ultimately matters is not just what lawyers know, but what they do with their knowledge, how they utilize their abilities and resources, and how they translate all of these elements into effective client service and career fulfillment. It is this process, over time, that transforms everyday learning into professional development.

An investment in intellectual capital also requires that new learning be continuous. Law firms reward lawyers primarily for exploiting their existing skills by billing high hours and bringing in new business so others can bill high hours. But smart firms also prize lawyers who strengthen the firm by enlarging their own and others' skills and capabilities. These are the lawyers who not only use what they know productively, but who continually assess their current levels of expertise and attempt to move beyond them. Rather than simply playing to their existing strengths or trying to correct their weaknesses, they constantly build *new* strengths and look for ways to compensate for weaknesses they cannot eliminate. These lawyers do not just try to do the same things more efficiently; they thrive on new challenges. Not satisfied with being experts, they strive to become virtuosos in the legal profession.

To inspire and sustain this enthusiasm for learning, professional development must be conscious and purposeful. It is true that much development happens by chance; left to their own devices, most lawyers learn through trial and error what they need to know in order to be effective practitioners. As they practice, they acquire a great deal of knowledge tacitly, i.e., "without intention to learn or awareness of having learned."[1] But a firm that places a high priority on learning and development can ensure that lawyers have plenty of learning opportunities that target, streamline, and accelerate the learning process. In order for your firm to make such opportunities available, you must first understand how lawyers learn, informally as well as through formal training programs. This is best understood against a backdrop of how adults learn in general; then we can see how the principles of adult learning can be used to design effective learning opportunities for lawyers. Armed with this knowledge, you can successfully design systems and produce an environment that promotes and supports constant learning and development. Let's look at these points and see how your firm can implement a program that keeps lawyers learning and developing — and producing high returns on investment — throughout their careers.

Adult Learning

For the last century, educators, psychologists, and social scientists have been studying how adults learn and how to make their learning effective. In his seminal research on adult learning, Malcolm Knowles posited principles that are widely accepted as the bases for effective learning in adults. Knowles' two most significant

---

[1] Robert J. Sternberg and Joseph A. Horvath, Eds., *Tacit Knowledge in Professional Practice*, Lawrence Erlbaum Associates, Mahwah, NJ, 1999, p. 21.

contributions to adult learning stressed the centrality of experience and shifted the focus from teacher to learner. He championed the idea that adults learn most effectively through experience and that educators should concentrate more on the process of learning than on content.

Education researcher David Kolb further elaborated the experiential basis of learning. He proposed that learning is an active, continual, and cyclical process of transforming experience into knowledge. (See Figure 1.) In Kolb's model, individuals begin the learning process with a concrete experience (Step 1). They reflect on that experience and consider it from different perspectives (Step 2). Learners integrate these reflections and observations into concepts and generalizations from which they form logical theories (Step 3). They use and test these theories in future situations and in solving future problems (Step 4). These actions then become the new experiences that continue the learning cycle. The learner's development spirals upward and advances with each cycle as new experiences — and new learning — become more complex and sophisticated.

The work of Knowles, Kolb, and others has yielded certain principles that form the basis for effective learning in adults. (See Table 1.) In designing professional development programs for lawyers, it is important to keep these principles in mind.

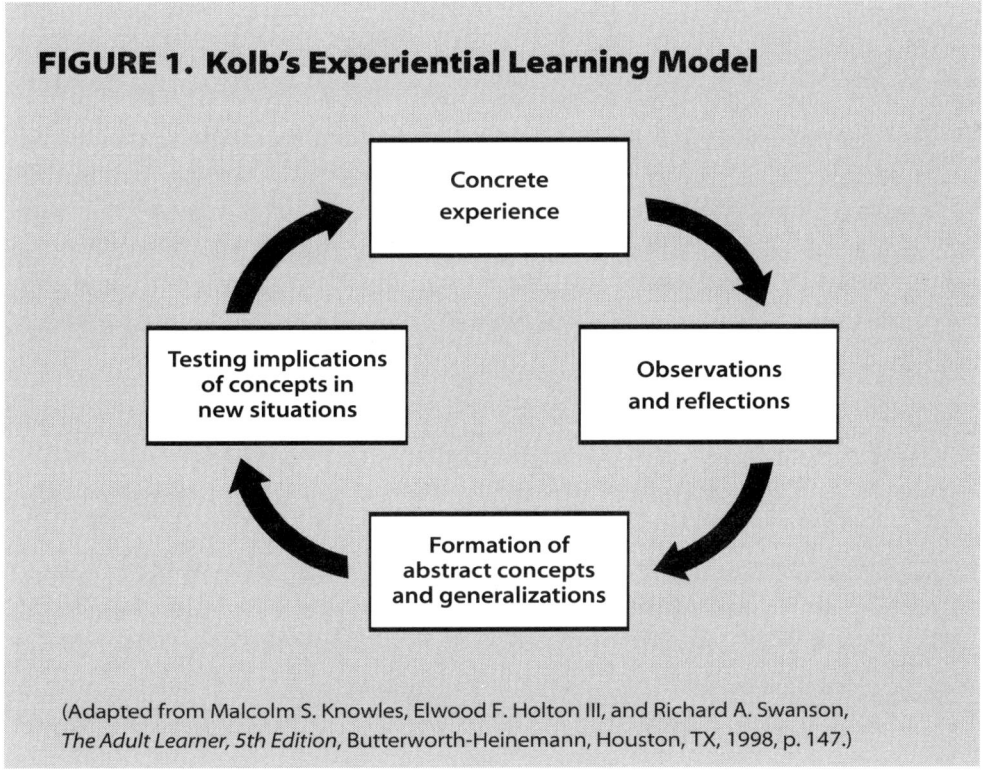

FIGURE 1. Kolb's Experiential Learning Model

(Adapted from Malcolm S. Knowles, Elwood F. Holton III, and Richard A. Swanson, *The Adult Learner, 5th Edition*, Butterworth-Heinemann, Houston, TX, 1998, p. 147.)

> **TABLE 1. Principles of Adult Learning**
>
> - Adult learning is focused on the learner, not the teacher.
> - Adults want to take responsibility for learning.
> - Adults want to know why they are being asked to learn something.
> - Adults are naturally motivated to learn.
> - Adult learning is experience-based.
> - Adults learn from each other.
> - Adults are self-directed learners.
> - Adults want to learn what will help them.
> - Adult learning is task-oriented.
> - Adults have individual learning styles.

1. **Adult learning is experience-based.** Adults bring all their life's experience with them to a learning situation. This makes each person unique in terms of needs, motivation, and learning preferences. It also means individuals can and do learn from each other, so they should be encouraged to share their knowledge and viewpoints. Learning techniques are most effective when they access lawyers' own experience, build on it, and connect new learning to what they already know. Orientation programs and mentoring relationships in which lawyers learn from other lawyers are experience-based methods to transfer knowledge and promote learning.[2]

2. **Adults are self-directed learners.** Adults are naturally motivated to learn and want to control their own learning. As self-directed learners, what

---

[2] It should be noted that the experiential basis of learning can also interfere with new learning. Organization and management experts Chris Argyris and Donald Schon have written extensively about the difficulties — and importance — of overcoming natural biases against new ideas that challenge what you know or believe. When new information fits into existing values or ways of thinking, people continue to perform efficiently. But when the new information does not fit, or existing values and ways of thinking are no longer appropriate to a situation, learners have to make fundamental changes — which they have a natural tendency to resist. An example is the adjustment that lawyers and firms have had to make to the entry of women and minorities into the legal profession. Prior assumptions, personal experience, and cultural norms created barriers to entry and advancement of these lawyers. Considerable new learning and adaptation have been — and continue to be — needed to overcome those barriers. In situations like this, *unlearning* existing knowledge and attitudes (or *re-learning,* as part of Kolb's continuous learning cycle) becomes as important as acquiring new learning.

lawyers want from their firm is an explanation of the firm's performance expectations; once they know what the firm expects, they will do and learn whatever they need to achieve those expectations. Firms can facilitate self-directed learning by providing an environment that encourages, promotes, and supports continuous learning. Firms can help lawyers become aware of themselves as independent learners and thinkers, capable of sustaining life-long learning.

3. **Adults want to learn what will help them.** Adults are more motivated and willing to learn when they believe that what they learn will be useful and relevant to them. They prefer to learn things that will help them do what they need or want to do and want evidence that their learning will have a practical, personal, and direct benefit for them. Because lawyers want to understand what they need to know and why they need to know it, informal feedback and annual performance evaluations are excellent opportunities to promote learning.

4. **Adult learning is task-oriented.** Adults are most ready to learn if they perceive that learning will help them solve real problems in their personal or professional lives. Adults learn best when new information is presented in a real-life context and they can see how to apply what they learn to accomplish a task or solve a problem. That is why techniques like case studies and interactive, hands-on exercises do more than impart new knowledge. These techniques help lawyers understand why they should — and how they can — apply new learning to the problems and issues they actually face. Lawyers are able to try out what they learn, test it, get feedback, and apply the insights they gain.

5. **Adults have individual learning styles.** Adults think and learn in different ways. Lawyers are most accustomed to learning by reading materials or listening to lectures, but many lawyers learn more effectively by solving concrete problems, watching demonstrations, or discussing issues with colleagues. When firms design training programs for lawyers, they have to pay as much attention to the training process as to the content. To reach lawyers with different learning styles, effective programs use multiple learning modalities.

How Lawyers Learn

While some lawyers learn for intellectual interest, pleasure, or stimulation, most lawyers are motivated to learn in order to accomplish organizational and personal goals. Organizationally, they learn what they need to know to do their work and serve their clients in the best way possible. Individually, their goals may be based on a sense of personal achievement (e.g., to do their work expertly) or a desire for recognition and acceptance (e.g., to be promoted to partnership). Your firm can help lawyers mobilize that positive energy by creating conditions where learning can flourish. Those conditions include both informal learning opportunities and formal programs that promote learning and development.

What Lawyers Need to Learn

The American legal profession is unusual in that it does not have a mandatory internship or post-graduate period of guided learning. Most professionals in the United States — doctors, accountants, psychologists, and teachers, among others — must spend some time after graduation practicing under the watchful eye and guidance of experienced professionals in the field. Entry to law practice in many countries, including Great Britain, Canada, Italy, France, and Japan, is conditioned on additional practical training following graduation from law school. But this is not the case in the United States. Unlike most other professionals, lawyers in the United States only need to pass an examination to obtain a license. Passing the bar exam requires only book learning; it does not measure competency to practice law. Consequently, even the most brilliant law school graduates have to learn a great deal before they are ready to represent a firm's clients. In the absence of some sort of post-graduate practice training system, law firms and other legal employers must provide the supervised learning that an apprenticeship or internship might otherwise provide. Employers must also provide learning opportunities for experienced lawyers to stay on top of new developments in the law, update their current skills, and acquire new abilities.

The intellectual learning required of all lawyers falls into three categories: cognitive knowledge, practical knowledge, and understanding. These three areas represent a progression of learning, increasing in importance and value as lawyers move toward understanding and wisdom:

1. **Cognitive knowledge** *(know-what)* — Lawyers must have a thorough understanding of the basic principles and rules of law, and mastery of the basic legal skills required to practice law. They begin acquiring this

knowledge in law school, but need to expand that knowledge throughout their careers as they encounter new subject areas and new kinds of clients. Cognitive knowledge is the most fundamental learning required for practice, but it is not by itself sufficient for success.

2. **Practical knowledge** *(know-how)* — Lawyers must be able to apply what they know and learn to increasingly complex, real legal problems. With repetition, guidance, and conscientious application, practical knowledge can be transformed into expertise.

3. **Understanding** *(know-why)* — Lawyers must acquire a rich understanding of how the legal system works, how to maneuver within it, and how to use it most effectively for a client's benefit. This understanding enables a lawyer to plan for the future; anticipate and deal with unintended consequences; and appreciate subtleties and dynamics of practice not otherwise apparent. Understanding comes with guidance, experience, and insight. It forms the foundation for professional judgment.

All three categories of learning are essential if the firm is to deliver consistently reliable legal services of the highest quality. The specific subject areas that lawyers have to learn include the following:

- Substantive legal knowledge,
- Technical legal skills,
- Critical thinking and problem solving,
- Client skills, including establishing and managing client relationships,
- How to manage their work,
- How to manage and develop the people with whom they work,
- Business principles that enable them to advise their clients,
- Business principles for managing the law firm,
- Leadership skills,
- Communication skills,
- Firm culture and politics, and
- Professionalism, including legal ethics, responsible behavior, and professional judgment.

In each of these subject areas, the *know-what* can be taught and, with practice and guidance, mastered. Lawyers can readily acquire basic information about each subject by reading books, listening to instructors, watching demonstrations, and memorizing principles, rules, and procedures. They can develop deeper insight by studying explanations and reasons for the information they acquire. But cognitive knowledge alone has little value. To *know* does not necessarily mean you can *do*. Knowing what goes into drafting a contract does not prepare you to negotiate terms or decide which provisions to include or exclude; knowing the elements of an effective client interview does not prepare you to deal with a client who is emotional, belligerent, or untruthful. In all of these subjects, learning content — the *know-what* — is the easy part; what's harder is making the content meaningful, putting it to effective use, and channeling it into *know-how* and *know-why*.

Practical knowledge can only be acquired through experience. All experts begin as novices. As reported in the book *How People Learn*,[3] researchers have found that novices rely on memorizing rules and information. Experts approach problems using more sophisticated thought processes that they learn and develop over time. Some of the characteristics that distinguish experts from novices include:

- Thinking at more abstract levels.
- Recognition of patterns in disparate situations.
- Intuitive abilities based on accumulated knowledge and experience.
- Deep knowledge of subject matter.
- Vast repertoire of knowledge, efficiently organized.

Expert lawyers approach a new problem differently than novices. They categorize information into related patterns and groupings, which makes them better able to see which information is meaningful and relevant. They notice features and recognize types of problems that novices do not see. Rather than searching through everything they know, experts can selectively retrieve the information relevant to a task with little conscious effort. Experts are more likely to recognize the strategic implications of what they do, and therefore to start problem solving earlier and at a higher level.

Experts have a storehouse of accumulated knowledge and experience. They do not jump to a solution right away; they start by digging deeper into what the

---

[3] John D. Bransford, Ann L. Brown, and Rodney R. Cocking, Editors, Committee on Developments in the Science of Learning, National Research Council, *How People Learn: Brain, Mind, Experience, and School*, National Academy Press, Washington, DC, 2000; http://www.nap.edu/catalog/6160.html.

problem really is. They do not necessarily accept what they are told at face value; they probe the problem from all angles. They look for patterns based on their own past experience, what they have learned from others, and what they intuit. They retrieve from memory the knowledge most relevant to the problem, even though it may come from an unrelated context. They know how to apply their knowledge specifically to this problem and this context. They then decide how to solve the problem by crafting a strategy and making choices that will achieve the right solution.

The difference between how experts and novices approach a problem is illustrated by the following case in point. A firm was asked to represent a family in a case arising from the death of their teenage son in a car accident. There were several potential defendants, including a utility company, a construction company, and a government entity, in addition to the driver of the car. Because of the way damages would be calculated under the applicable statute, the lawyers knew the potential value of the case with some degree of certainty. A junior associate was asked how he would approach the case. He immediately began to discuss which causes of action to include in the complaint, possible venues for filing suit, and the steps prerequisite to filing a claim against a public entity. All of these were correct and logical steps. However, they assumed that a suit would be filed right away — a reasonable assumption for an inexperienced lawyer who was accustomed to thinking in terms of rules and procedures. The more experienced partner suggested that instead of filing suit, they invite all the potential defendants to a meeting to discuss the case and propose a settlement (a move that did, in fact, lead to a prompt resolution). The associate was startled by the proposal and asked, "Do you mean we can talk with the defendants about the case *before* we file suit?" Nothing in this associate's education or experience to that point had prepared him for such a move.

The kind of thinking demonstrated by the partner exemplified not only her expertise but also a more sophisticated degree of understanding. The kind of learning that leads to understanding is the most difficult to acquire — but is also the first step on a lawyer's journey to a more advanced level of professional development. As lawyers learn more about the intricacies and nuances of the legal system and how to operate within that system, they realize a broader array of options and become more resourceful in representing their clients. It is this kind of learning that evolves into the defining characteristic of great lawyers: professional judgment. Professional judgment is the ability to perceive and evaluate the consequences of behavior (both your own and others') and to make wise decisions based on that assessment. Lawyers exercise professional judgment every time they evaluate the merits of a case, decide how to deal with opposing counsel, or advise clients on legal strategy. Judgment involves making choices and knowing when to make short-term sacrifices for the sake of long-term gains. It allows lawyers to be more creative in solving problems and in turning adversity to their advantage.

Having good judgment is not the same as being smart. It requires an ability to perceive and measure relative values and make good choices based on those values. It is the ability to distinguish between reasonable alternatives and wise ones. Knowledge enables lawyers to pursue desired ends, regardless of the value of those ends; judgment is what enables them to determine which ends to pursue. Professional judgment is the product of accrued experience shaped by ever-increasing wisdom. It is something that cannot really be taught. Although good judgment can be observed, analyzed, studied, and demonstrated, it can only be developed over time through self-awareness, practical experience, and continual learning.

Emotional Intelligence

Like intellectual learning, emotional intelligence (the competencies necessary for effective personal interactions) can be acquired or improved through training and practice. Lawyers excel at and place great importance on "cerebral" intelligence, i.e., the ability to understand, analyze, and apply information to solve complex problems. They are less adept at and place less value on the personal and interpersonal skills that make up emotional intelligence. Yet research has shown that people with high emotional intelligence experience more professional success and career satisfaction. IQ alone is a poor predictor of either one. Studies show that cognitive intelligence only accounts for about 25 percent of career success, while emotional intelligence accounts for 75 percent. In executive and leadership positions, emotional intelligence is even more significant, accounting for 90 percent of high-level success.[4] While intellectual ability is the threshold requirement for entry into the legal profession, emotional intelligence determines how quickly and how far a lawyer will advance.

There are four principal dimensions of emotional intelligence: awareness of one's own feelings and the feelings of others, and the ability to manage oneself and others. These four dimensions involve a broad range of competencies, including the ability to give, receive, and process feedback, deal with stress, collaborate with others, and manage client relationships. Having these personal and social competencies is essential for effective workplace relationships and superior workplace performance. Lawyers need these traits in order to be effective and trusted legal advisers, managers, and leaders.

---

[4] Daniel Goleman, *Working with Emotional Intelligence*, Bantam Books, New York, 1998.

Learning emotional intelligence competencies frequently involves changing one's attitudes, emotions, and behaviors, which presents special learning challenges. It is hard to learn new behaviors — and harder still to change established behaviors — whether you are a brand new lawyer or a veteran. A person's emotional patterns and behavioral habits develop over a lifetime; changing them does not happen overnight. Anyone can read a book or take a course that explains how to become more empathic or collaborative, but knowing what those behaviors look like is not enough. Lawyers first need to understand and accept why emotional intelligence is important and the critical impact it can have on their success. They have to be receptive to a heightened sense of self-awareness and carefully guided to achieve it. They need to be willing and motivated to learn new behaviors, and they must have access to models of positive behaviors, a place to practice those new behaviors, and patience, support, and positive reinforcement from co-workers during the learning process.

Informal and Formal Learning

Firms can help lawyers develop cognitive skills, practical knowledge, understanding, and emotional intelligence through both informal and formal learning processes. Let's look at the way these learning processes work.

Informal Learning

Most lawyers' learning is informal. This simply means that it takes place outside the classroom, without a structured curriculum or program, and the firm does not determine the specific content or learning process. Informal learning happens as you interact with others, research an idea, or try out a new technique. "Informal" does not mean "unplanned." Indeed, informal learning is enhanced when it is planned, either before the event or in retrospect to analyze or reflect on past experience.

The most common informal learning activity is daily work. Lawyers learn about law and become more accomplished practitioners as they research issues, draft agreements, appear at hearings, or prepare for negotiations. They learn by observing other lawyers, interacting with them, and asking them questions. This kind of learning is effective because it satisfies the principles of adult learning: It is relevant to the lawyer's particular needs, can be applied immediately, and allows a high degree of personal control.

Informal learning occurs through many different methods. Table 2 lists some common activities that are rich in potential informal learning opportunities. Infor-

TABLE 2. Activities That Provide Informal Learning Opportunities

- Client interaction
- Committees or task forces (especially leading them)
- Computer-based communications (e.g., intranet chat rooms, discussion boards, listservs, weblogs)
- Feedback (giving and receiving)
- Firm/department/practice group meetings
- Information exchanges (e.g., brown bag lunches, book clubs)
- Inquiries (asking questions of colleagues)
- Knowledge management systems
- Meetings (especially running them)
- Membership in professional associations
- Membership in civic associations
- Membership in trade groups
- Mentoring (both mentor and mentee)
- Observing more experienced lawyers in action
- Personal development plans
- Self-study resources (e.g., books, articles)
- Site visits
- Special interest groups
- Supervising people
- Work assignments

mal learning occurs when a supervisor gives an associate feedback on a project or when one lawyer asks another for ideas on how to approach a thorny problem. It can occur when a team meets to debrief a presentation made to a prospective client, or to analyze a recently concluded client engagement. At many firms, lawyers learn informally through affinity groups formed by lawyers who share an interest in a particular subject and want to explore it together. Such special interest groups might get together to study new developments in a field of law, learn a language to help them communicate better with foreign clients, or explore emerging industries for possible business development. Many firms endorse and sponsor these groups (e.g., by paying for lunch and study materials), but the groups create their own agendas and exist only as long as the interest is there.

As valuable and important as informal learning is, it also has some drawbacks. When lawyers learn informally, what they learn may be too narrow, superficial, or incomplete. If the firm relies on informal learning alone, lawyers may miss the lesson, learn the wrong lesson, or learn bad habits. Lawyers also may fail to see how their experience and the lessons derived from it fit into the firm's overall strategy, or how they relate to other systems and processes in the firm. That is why informal learning is not enough. The firm needs to direct certain areas of learning through formal training programs.

Formal Learning

When people think about learning, they usually think of formal classroom teaching. Although most learning takes place outside the classroom, formal training programs are the most visible vehicles for learning. Formal programs accelerate the learning process by providing structured opportunities to learn. They present study subjects in a larger professional context. And they provide a setting within which learning can take place: where lawyers can practice what they learn, receive feedback from experienced observers, exchange information, and learn from each other.

Training programs also ensure that important points about law and practice are uniformly disseminated to lawyers throughout the firm. They allow the same information or skills to be transmitted to a wide audience and minimize the variability of the content presented. For that reason, formal programs are especially useful for teaching standards, procedures, and principles. Through a well-planned, comprehensive curriculum, law firms can teach the skills and knowledge that lawyers need to know at different stages of their careers. And by emphasizing the importance of learning, formal programs reinforce a culture of learning.

Formal and informal learning are not at odds; they complement each other and work synergistically. Learning legal ethics is a clear example. Lawyers learn informally by dealing with ethical issues in the course of their work experience. They bring this experience to the classroom, where formal training programs present ethical rules and use case studies to help them understand how to apply the rules. When lawyers bring to the classroom the lessons they learned informally while handling real ethical dilemmas, they can think more critically about what is taught and participate more meaningfully in the course discussion. Chapter 8 explores formal training programs in greater depth.

Creating a Learning Environment

In a learning environment, teaching and learning are institutionally and culturally embedded in the firm and perceived to be beneficial to the firm and its individual lawyers.[5] (See Table 3.) Research has shown a clear correlation between a firm's culture (i.e., it's norms, values, beliefs, and practices) and the extent and variety of learning that takes place.[6] Firms that value learning provide resources and incentives — and remove institutional obstacles — so that people can take responsibility for their own learning. They create an environment where learning occurs naturally and easily. As one author has pointed out, creating a learning environment is much like Lewis Thomas' prescription for inspiring bees to make honey: "What it needs is for the air to be made right. If you want a bee to make honey, you do not issue protocols on solar navigation or carbohydrate chemistry, you put him together with other bees…and you do what you can to arrange the general environment around the hive. If the air is right, the science will come in its own season, like pure honey."[7]

The problem is that creating and sustaining this kind of culture takes time. Learning requires time to stop and reflect, while the workplace has a bias for action. The pressure is to bill, not to take time away from work. In most firms, lawyers take action based on current knowledge to get results. If the action works, they do more of it. If it doesn't, they try something else. This leaves little chance for real learning to occur. In a learning environment, people are asked to go further. After they get results, they ask, "Why did we get those results? How can we do it better next time?

---

[5] *The Teaching Firm,* Center for Workforce Development, Education Development Center Inc., Newton, MA, 1998, cited in Chris McMeekin, "Informal Learning in the Workplace," www.usd.edu/~knorum/learningpapers/informal.html.
[6] *Ibid.*
[7] Lewis Thomas, *The Lives of a Cell,* Viking Press, New York, 1974, p. 102. Quoted in Morgan W. McCall, Jr., *High Flyers,* Harvard Business School Press, Boston, 1998, p. 179.

TABLE 3. Indicators of a Strong Learning Environment

1. Partners teach associates as they work together.
2. Associates have ample opportunity to observe various role models.
3. Associates receive frequent, prompt, and constructive feedback.
4. Associates have mentors who guide their learning and development.
5. Associates have diverse, interesting, and challenging work assignments.
6. Associates receive close and careful work guidance from supervisors.
7. Someone monitors and assesses what associates learn.
8. Someone monitors and assesses how associates perform.
9. Associates develop strong relationships with clients through their work.
10. Associates have time for reflection and sufficient guidance for effective learning to take place.

TABLE 4. Action Steps for a Learning Environment

- Make learning strategic.
- Think long-term.
- Treat people individually.
- Promote life-long learning.
- Ensure diverse work experiences.
- Encourage goal setting.
- Teach people how to learn.
- Integrate work and learning.
- Promote collective learning.
- Encourage mentoring.
- Reward learning.
- Link learning systems.
- Supply learning resources.
- Give ample feedback.
- Protect risk-taking.
- Carve out time for reflection.
- Remind lawyers to learn and teach.
- Make the firm accountable for learning.

How can we use those results to expand what we know?" The firm's responsibility is to create conditions that encourage lawyers to ask these questions, and to provide resources and systems that enable them to learn. Can your firm foster a learning environment? To do it successfully, take these action steps. (See Table 4.)

1. **Make learning strategic.** Lawyers' innate drive to learn can be a major competitive advantage if lawyers use their learning to pursue firm goals. Make continuous learning one of your firm's highest priorities. Show lawyers how learning is connected to the future of the firm. Treat learning not as a luxury but as a business imperative.

2. **Think long-term.** Development occurs over the course of a lawyer's entire professional life. Learning is not limited to new lawyers; the need and desire to learn never end. Throughout their careers, lawyers need intellectual stimulation and challenge to remain engaged and motivated. Professional development efforts should address the many stages of a lawyer's career. The needs of a new associate who has to learn the basics are markedly different from those of a seasoned partner looking to expand his or her practice. Your professional development program should speak to them both.

3. **Treat people individually.** People learn in different ways, and lawyers are no exception. They have different learning curves, talents, and styles of learning. They have their own approaches to work and communication. Acknowledge these differences and accommodate them as much as possible by offering an array of learning opportunities and resources. Every lawyer learns at his or her own pace and direction, with different needs at different times. When setting career development milestones or benchmarks for lawyers, space them widely enough apart to accommodate variations in developmental rate and progress.

4. **Promote life-long learning.** Learning is promoted by social norms that value the search for continuous learning. Promote the ideal of the lawyer as a life-long student. This model lawyer is highly skilled and highly regarded but realizes there is always more to learn. When an environment respects intellectual curiosity, constant self-improvement, and a willingness to ask for help, lawyers are free to continue learning even after achieving prominence and expertise. Resist the model of the "omnipotent" lawyer. If the model of success in your firm is the expert who knows everything and has all the answers, lawyers will be reluctant to ask for help for fear of being perceived as incompetent.

5. **Ensure diverse work experiences.** Make work assignments as interesting, challenging, and exciting as possible. Give associates a broad spectrum of work experiences and expose them to different kinds of supervisors and clients. Try to find projects that address an associate's developmental needs, and "stretch" assignments that offer the greatest potential for learning.

6. **Encourage goal setting.** Explicit goals affect behavior; when people know what they need to learn and do, achieving stated goals becomes a significant motivator. Create development benchmarks or guidelines that tell lawyers what the firm expects in terms of their development and how their progress toward development goals will be assessed. Ensure that the benchmarks are used in evaluation and promotion discussions and during conferences between associates and mentors. Encourage lawyers to use them as a framework within which to set their own development goals. When individuals set their own goals, the goals are more meaningful and more likely to be attained.

7. **Teach people how to learn.** Lawyers encounter learning opportunities every day, and the most potent learning experiences often occur unexpectedly. Lawyers have to recognize and seize those occasions. They need to take the initiative to learn what they need to advance their own careers. For example, associates who do not get enough feedback should learn how to ask for it; those who want to learn about a particular subject should look for programs that teach it. Teach lawyers how to pursue their own learning and development. Show them how to identify their learning needs, ask for feedback, recognize personal blocks to learning, create a learning plan, find learning resources, reflect on what they have learned, and evaluate their progress.

8. **Integrate work and learning.** Use lawyers' work experience to facilitate the learning process. Most learning occurs when lawyers solve real problems for real clients. Emphasize the learning that occurs through everyday work encounters, and show lawyers how to use those daily interactions as teaching opportunities. When learning and work are thoroughly integrated, the process becomes transparent. A good example of how to do this is the "Shadowing Program" at Proskauer Rose LLP. First-year associates are permitted to log up to 200 hours, and all other associates up to 125 hours, each year to accompany ("shadow") senior lawyers to client meetings, depositions, and other events that are considered worthwhile

learning opportunities. Clients are not charged, and the time is credited toward associates' billable hours.

9. **Promote collective learning.** Learning happens in groups, not just individually. Participation in project teams, committees, and social groups is a fundamental form of learning, and lawyers should be encouraged to take an active part in various groups. These groups offer an excellent way to learn collaborative, management, and leadership skills. They foster respect for diversity, as people with different perspectives and background work together to achieve common goals. They promote open dialogue, inquiry, and challenges to existing ways of thinking. In doing so, they spread and expand the learning of individuals, and often lead to improvements in organizational operations and effectiveness.

10. **Encourage mentoring.** Mentors are among the foremost sources of learning and development in the firm. Mentoring focuses on the learning and development needs of the mentee. By taking an interest in furthering a mentee's career, mentors have enormous influence over their mentees' development. Be sure that lawyers in your firm know how to be effective mentors, how to work with mentors, and how to recognize and utilize mentoring opportunities.

11. **Reward learning.** Institute policies and incentives that reward learning. Even the most self-motivated learners and teachers need encouragement. Hire and promote people who demonstrate a capacity and eagerness to teach. Use compensation policies to give recognition and credit for training, mentoring, and other activities that promote learning. Advance associates based on learning and progress rather than class year alone. Offer career counseling, tuition reimbursement for outside training programs, and coaches to support individual learning efforts (e.g., improving leadership skills, assertiveness training).

12. **Link learning systems.** Because all the components of your professional development program are interrelated systems that promote lawyers' learning and development, they should be linked together in every way possible. Performance criteria, for example, should form a link connecting a firm's work assignment process, performance reviews, training curriculum, mentoring activities, and career development plans. Similarly, technology should help you exploit the interrelatedness of communication, knowledge distribution and management, performance management, and training.

13. **Supply learning resources.** Lawyers must have easy access to resources that expedite learning. The quality of these resources can exert a profound influence on the speed and extent of lawyers' development. The variety of learning resources is limitless. Perhaps the most important learning resource is the firm's partners. Transferring their accumulated knowledge, wisdom, and guidance to more junior lawyers is enormously important both to advance learning and inspire commitment. Another key learning resource is information. Increasingly, firms use systems to capture and disseminate information that can help lawyers learn. A simple system might be a form file containing samples of documents drafted by lawyers in the firm. At the other end of the spectrum are sophisticated computer-based knowledge management systems that also contain document samples but add an online tutorial program that teaches the proper use of each. Still other learning resources include in-house orientation and training programs; materials that facilitate self-study (e.g., audio- and videotaped training programs); and technologies that provide access to courses offered by online CLE providers.

14. **Give ample feedback.** Feedback is well known to be a critical component of learning. Giving and receiving feedback should be customary and routine, not limited to yearly evaluations. All lawyers should be skilled in giving — and expected to give — regular, informal, positive and constructive feedback. Informal feedback is best when provided in reference to clearly defined learning expectations, performance criteria, and career and development options.

15. **Protect risk-taking.** How much tolerance is there in your firm for mistakes? Learning is risky. A learning environment supports learning from experience and treats surprises, failures, and mistakes as learning opportunities; it permits second chances. Trial and error is a legitimate and effective way to learn. Indeed, it is probably the most common learning technique and is essential for the development of professional judgment. But risk-taking is squelched — and learning is compromised — when risk takers are penalized for their mistakes. Rather than punish errors, people in learning environments try to determine the causes of mistakes and take steps to prevent them from happening again. In this kind of environment, lawyers distinguish between foolish and reasonable risks and between system failures and human errors. They know — and trust — each other well enough to offer guidance and support for reasonable risk-taking.

16. **Carve out time for reflection.** Learning requires time for reflection. Lawyers need time to analyze and consolidate new knowledge and experience. Reflection should take place regularly. It does not have to be a solitary process. Mentors and supervisors can help associates reflect on the lessons learned from experience. Client teams and committees can analyze and assess what went well and what could have been gone better at the conclusion of cases, transactions, and major projects. This can lead to more effective team and firm performance. Most reflection can take place in the normal course of a lawyer's schedule. At different points in their careers, however, lawyers need a larger chunk of time for self-assessment and renewal. Many firms offer sabbaticals for this purpose.

17. **Remind lawyers to learn and teach.** Even in the most learning-centered firms, the press of business distracts lawyers from learning and teaching. Help them remember by issuing reminders, holding events, or awarding recognition for outstanding practices. At San Francisco's Farella Braun + Martel LLP, for example, professional development and mentoring are on the agenda at almost all partnership and department meetings.

18. **Make the firm accountable for learning.** The firm must accept as its responsibility the training and development of its lawyers. Individuals may be responsible for their own learning, but the firm controls the context in which its lawyers learn. Accordingly, the firm's actions must be consistent with its avowed developmental values. It should promise and provide high-quality learning opportunities for all lawyers. Partners should be role models for the learning and teaching behaviors they want to see in associates. They should be evaluated on how fully and capably they carry out their training and development responsibilities, and those who excel should be amply rewarded.

References Related to How Professionals Learn

Ida O. Abbott, "Getting Along to Get Ahead," *Developing Legal Talent*, NALP, Washington, DC, 2001.

Russell L. Ackoff, Ph.D., "Never Let Your Schooling Interfere with Your Education," *Ackoff's Best*, John Wiley & Sons, Inc., New York, 1999.

Chris Argyris, "Teaching Smart People to Learn," *Harvard Business Review*, May-June, 1991.

John D. Bransford, Ann L. Brown, and Rodney R. Cocking, Editors, Committee on Developments in the Science of Learning, National Research Council, *How People Learn: Brain, Mind, Experience, and School*, National Academy Press, Washington, DC, 2000; http://www.nap.edu/catalog/6160.html.

Daniel Goleman, *Working with Emotional Intelligence*, Bantam Books, New York, 1998.

Malcolm S. Knowles, Elwood F. Holton III, and Richard A. Swanson, *The Adult Learner, 5th Edition*, Butterworth-Heinemann, Houston, TX, 1998.

David Kolb, *Experiential Learning: Experience as the Source of Learning and Development*, Prentice Hall, Englewood Cliffs, NJ, 1984.

Morgan W. McCall, Jr., *High Flyers,* Harvard Business School Press, Boston, MA, 1998.

Morgan W. McCall, Jr., Michael M. Lombardo, Ann M. Morrison, *The Lessons of Experience: How Successful Executives Develop on the Job*, The Free Press, New York, 1988.

Robert J. Sternberg and Joseph A. Horvath, Eds., *Tacit Knowledge in Professional Practice*, Lawrence Erlbaum Associates, Mahwah, NJ, 1999.

Edward C. Stark, "Great Unknown: Young Attorneys Need Guidance, Training Before They Begin Their Career Tracks," *San Francisco Daily Journal*, October 19, 2001, p.4.

PART II

Four Essential Components of a Professional Development Program

CHAPTER 5

Work Assignments: The Core of Learning

Lawyers learn by working. Considering the centrality of work to learning, the quality of work assignments deserves far more attention than it receives. Associates repeatedly identify work assignments as "the most singularly important variable" affecting their job satisfaction and chances for advancement.[1] They know that the lack of exposure to a wide variety of experiences and partners "will doom even the most promising associate to a lack of stimulation and development."[2] In order to learn, advance, and stay motivated, associates need interesting, diverse, and progressively more challenging work. From a developmental standpoint, and for the long-term interests of the firm, it is critical to match associates with projects that will help them acquire new knowledge and skills, expose them to many partners, and give them a broad range of experiences and responsibilities. However, in the contest between associates' development needs and partners' staffing needs, development usually places second.

This is because most staffing decisions are made on the basis of current skills, availability, and urgency — who has the know-how and time to do what has to be done right now? Partners want to work with associates who are sufficiently experienced and independent to handle client matters. When they can select their own associates, partners tend to choose the same associates over and over again, because those associates have demonstrated proficiency in the task required for the assignment. This approach is certainly reasonable from a staffing standpoint. After all, it is more efficient to assign an associate who already knows how to do the job and needs little supervision or training. This is an easy way to staff current cases and transactions, but it does not build the superior and loyal workforce that your firm must have to meet the demands of the future.

---

[1] *Perceptions of Partnership: The Allure & Accessibility of the Brass Ring,* The NALP Foundation for Law Career Research and Education, Washington, DC, 1999, p. 81.
[2] *Id.,* p. 85.

Work assignments should not address just immediate or short-term staffing issues; they must be purposefully developmental. To ensure that associates acquire the learning and experience to meet future challenges, your firm must vigilantly promote associates' professional development through careful work assignments. To keep promising associates from leaving, the firm must keep their needs and interests in mind when new work is distributed. Finding the right balance between serving clients and developing associates can distinguish your firm as a place where both clients and associates receive added value. McKinsey & Company, the consulting giant renowned for its extraordinary professional development program, asserts that one of the reasons it is known as a great place to work is its belief that developing people in order to serve clients and serving clients in a way that maximizes the development of its people are both equally worthy goals.[3]

Ideally, every assignment would be analyzed for developmental implications and then matched with the associate most suited for it. Realistically, however, expedience rules the day. Firms are more concerned about getting cases staffed promptly and keeping associates busy. There are simply too many short-term assignments that must be made quickly, without time to go through a developmental analysis. But, if your firm takes professional development seriously, this analysis must be done for all major, long-term assignments and should be done whenever possible for routine or short-term assignments. If your systems regularly collect information about associates' development status and the true nature and scope of the assignments to be made, the analysis takes little time and results in better staffing decisions.

A systematic approach that consciously uses work assignments to advance associate development can make your firm a great place to work and a place where great work is done. The key is to develop legal talent by providing associates with a variety of exciting and engaging assignments in which they constantly face stimulating challenges and acquire new skills. To make this happen, it is necessary to understand how to recognize and exploit the developmental potential of work assignments, and then to establish systems to allocate and monitor associates' work experience.

The quality of work assignments is important for partners as well as for associates, but the assignment systems discussed in this chapter deal primarily with finding work for associates. With few exceptions, associates have little or no control over the work they receive. The firm as an employer has a responsibility to provide associates work that keeps them learning, not just busy. It owes

---

[3] "How McKinsey Does It," http://www.mckinsey.com/articles/how_mck_does_it.html.

no such responsibility to its partners, who, as owners of the organization, must bring in the work that they and their associates do.

Developmental Work Assignments

Professional development needs are created by a gap between a lawyer's current capabilities and those capabilities that the lawyer must acquire. A developmental assignment is one that enables an associate to narrow that gap. In order for a work allocation system to have a developmental focus, the people who assign work need to be able to identify the developmental potential of the assignments they make, i.e., they must know both the associate's development needs and whether and how the assignment can address those needs. This requires answering two questions:

- What are the development needs of the associates available to do the work?
- What is the learning potential of the work to be assigned?

To answer the first question, your firm must be familiar with each individual associate's development needs in order to match the associate with suitable, developmentally appropriate assignments as they become available. Information about associates' development status is most easily obtained when there is a coordinated system in place to track it. Such a system includes:

- Development benchmarks that identify the experiences, skills, and performance standards that the firm expects of associates at various points (e.g., by years of work, by promotion levels).
- A detailed record of each associate's work history, including projects, responsibilities, and client interactions.
- A comprehensive associate evaluation system that utilizes the firm's development benchmarks and associates' self-assessments.
- A process for setting and monitoring associates' development goals.
- Regular feedback from supervising lawyers on associates' abilities and skills.
- Mentors who help associates identify and deal with development needs.
- Training to help supervising lawyers recognize associates' development needs and help associates address them.

Using the information obtained through these processes, and from discussions with associates, their mentors, and supervising lawyers, the associate's particular development needs can be identified. Because associates' needs change over time, the information has to be reassessed at frequent intervals. In addition to associates' needs, you should also inquire about associates' interests — the kinds of work experience that associates would like to have. For example, an associate might want to work with a certain partner or on a particular matter outside their practice area. Firms often encourage associates to request particular kinds of work assignments, and many firms provide forms on which associates can make their desires known.

The assignment process seeks to match the right associate with the right work. A good match brings an associate work that provides appropriate opportunities for learning and development. Sometimes you begin with the development needs of a particular associate and try to find a work assignment that will address those needs. Sometimes you start with the assignment itself and look for an associate who will benefit developmentally from it. In either case, when you know the development needs of your firm's associates, you can examine the work available and try to make the right matches.

Keep in mind that not all assignments involve client matters. Working on committees and firm-related projects can also provide significant development opportunities. These assignments teach associates about firm management and governance. They give associates a chance to work with and get to know others in the firm in a more casual way, and they present a forum where associates can demonstrate talents and strengths that may not be recognized or called for in a client-focused work assignment. A junior associate who is just a minor contributor on a large transaction team can be a star on a small committee, taking on responsibilities and gaining recognition that might otherwise take years to get on client matters.

Work assignments are transformed into learning experiences when they strengthen and expand existing capabilities. Work-based learning can take many forms. Table 1 lists some learning outcomes that can occur during work assignments and how these outcomes can be learned.

An assignment's inherent learning potential may not be as easy to assess as it first appears and may require more in-depth analysis. Some assignments that sound limited can actually offer great learning opportunities. Others that sound exciting and cutting-edge may actually offer the associate only mundane or tedious duties. Analysis of the following elements, listed in Table 2, can help determine the development potential of an assignment.

TABLE 1. Work-Based Learning Outcomes and Examples of How They Are Learned

Learning Outcome	Examples
Business development	Managing client relations; business networking
Interpersonal skills	Working with partners; supervising others; relating to clients; examining others' perspectives
Leadership	Strategic thinking; exercising professional judgment; handling power; balancing toughness and compassion
Management	Setting work priorities; resolving conflicts; organizing work; motivating and developing others
Self-awareness	Setting personal priorities and career goals; realizing personal ambitions and limits; developing self-confidence
Self-control	Coping with stress and ambiguity; dealing with adversity; developing resiliency to setbacks
Substantive expertise	Expanding legal or procedural knowledge
Technical expertise	Enhancing trial advocacy, negotiation, computer, writing and presentation skills
Values	Behaving ethically; being sensitive to the human side of practice

TABLE 2. Development Potential of Assignments: Elements

1. Content
2. Supervising partner
3. Case team
4. Client
5. Scope of work
6. Challenges presented and opportunities to "stretch"

Content —
 Does the nature of the work fit the interests of the associate?

In a perfect world, every associate would work only on assignments that are exciting, challenging, and perfectly matched to their interests. This cannot always happen, but a firm should try to give its associates work that comes as close as possible to that ideal. Assignments that feed an associate's curiosity in a particular subject can take advantage of the associate's natural motivation to keep learning and developing. The more interest an associate has in the work, the more engaged he or she is likely to be. When an associate is excited about the subject matter of the case, working with a particular supervising partner, or getting to know a certain client, the level of productivity and commitment goes up. When success depends on learning and mastering new skills, or on proving oneself capable of handling new challenges, associates are inspired to do their best. When presented with difficult new challenges and dilemmas, more often than not, associates rise to the occasion. They learn and do whatever they need to get the job done and do it well.[4]

Sometimes there is little choice but to assign associates to a matter, team, or partner they dislike or that promises little opportunity for development. When this happens, acknowledge that the assignment is not desirable and explain the reason for the assignment along with the importance of the task. Try to help the associate find a way to benefit from the assignment and promise to look for better work next time. Be sure to follow through on this commitment. If you break promises to the associate, or keep making unpopular assignments, the associate will lose both motivation to work and faith in the firm.

A special kind of undesirable assignment is one that raises personal moral or religious objections. Associates should not be required to work on cases that they find morally repugnant. For example, an associate who has profound moral objections to tobacco companies should not be forced to defend one. However, if tobacco defense work is a major part of the firm's practice, encourage such associates to take a good look at whether they are in the right firm.

---

[4] Interesting work is also a key factor in associate retention. In the *American Lawyer 2001 Midlevel Associates Survey*, 70 percent of respondents said that the interest level of their work was one of the two top criteria in their decisions about whether to stay at their current firms (the second was treatment by partners). Laura Pearlman, "Whistle a Happy Tune," *The American Lawyer*, October 2, 2001. Additionally, research has repeatedly shown that "dollars don't drive retention. Exciting work and challenge continue to be the leading factors for engaging and retaining talent regardless of the industry, economic conditions, or business challenges." Beverly Kaye and Sharon Jordan-Evans, "Retention in Tough Times," *Training and Development*, January 2002, p. 32, 34.

Supervising Partner —

 Will the supervising partner support the associate's development?

The influence of supervising lawyers in developing associates cannot be overstated. Studies repeatedly show the enormous influence of supervisors on retention, job satisfaction, performance, and the firm's bottom line. On the basis of his research, David Maister argues emphatically about the "disproportionately" high impact of good supervisors on the financial success of a firm.[5] Associates learn a huge amount from their supervising lawyers, not just the subject matter of the assignment, but also about management, ethics, behavior, and other practical lessons. Good supervising lawyers share certain attributes (Table 3), the most salient of which are a concern for the people they supervise and the ability to inspire people to do their best. But associates take away lessons from all kinds of supervisors, good or bad. That's why it is important for them to work with a variety of supervisors in a variety of assignments during their years as associates. A positive experience with a supervisor — where the partner and associate get along well and both are satisfied with the work product and the work relationship — can lay a sound foundation for the associate's long-term career at the firm. A difficult experience with a supervisor, if managed properly, can make the associate stronger and more resilient. A bad experience with a poor supervisor can be devastating — but the impact may be mitigated by a positive relationship with another supervising partner.

Supervising lawyers play many different roles, any of which may be beneficial — or detrimental — depending upon the associate's situation. The same supervisor may be excellent for one associate and harmful for another. A lawyer who monitors associates closely may be perceived by some as a micromanager and by others as a conscientious teacher; one who leaves associates alone to handle assigned responsibilities may be seen as either encouraging associates to "stretch" or as "uncaring and inaccessible." Some partners nurture, counsel, and protect associates, while others play the role of "heavy" — criticizing, confronting, and pushing associates to perform better.

Although no firm should countenance bad supervision, assigning someone to a difficult supervisor is not always a bad thing. For a resilient, self-confident associate, the challenge of working with a partner who is hard to please can be a valuable learning experience. It is important, after all, for associates to be able to

---

[5] David H. Maister, *Practice What You Preach*, The Free Press, New York, 2001.

TABLE 3. Attributes of Good Supervisors

Good supervisors:
- Are concerned about the people they supervise.
- Take supervision seriously.
- Give associates work that is interesting and intellectually challenging.
- Delegate assignments clearly and completely:
    — Provide sufficient information and context.
    — Explain how their work fits into the overall strategy.
    — State what is expected in terms of scope of work, work product, format, budget, and deadlines.
    — Estimate the time commitment required and are clear about the urgency and priority of the project.
- Manage work efficiently and proactively.
- Communicate effectively.
- Keep associates and the team informed of major developments and reasoning behind strategic and tactical decisions.
- Notify associates and the team when priorities shift.
- Supervise carefully but appropriately, without micromanaging.
- Make themselves accessible.
- Respect associates' time:
    — Set deadlines that are reasonable.
    — Set deadlines that are real, not arbitrary or phony.
    — Explain when work has to be rushed.
- Promote constant learning.
- Observe, teach, and coach associates.
- Take professionalism and client service seriously.
- Act as excellent role models.
- Demand high performance.
- Place value on the quality of the work, not just the hours put into it.
- Give prompt, constructive feedback.
- Commend associates for outstanding performance.
- Include associates in meetings, phone calls, conferences, and hearings.
- Give associates meaningful and direct client contact.
- Give associates substantial responsibility and as much autonomy as they are ready to handle.
- Pay attention to the associate's progress, and spot danger signs that suggest an assignment is not going well.
- Are sensitive to associates' setbacks and help associates learn how to deal with them.
- Help associates take responsibility for their own development.

adapt to different types of partners. Moreover, surviving a partner known to be unreasonably demanding can increase the stature and reputation of the associate.

Partners should be taught how to be good supervisors (preferably early in their careers, when still associates) and rewarded for being good at it. Partners who are abusive toward associates should not be tolerated; they should be asked to leave the firm or, at the very least, prohibited from working with associates. But many partners fall somewhere in the middle. They may be difficult to work with generally or with certain types of associates (e.g., with those who are shy, who ask a lot of questions, or who work part-time). There are also partners who simply lack the skills, interest, time, or patience to be good supervisors. For vulnerable associates, an assignment to a poor supervisor can be demoralizing and harmful — and a reason to leave the firm. When there is no choice but to assign an associate to someone known to be a less-than-ideal supervisor, you should anticipate potential problems and help the associate guard against personality clashes, unreasonable partner demands, or other conditions that can lead to disappointing work experiences and regrettable departures.

The appropriateness and wisdom of assigning an associate to a particular supervisor for a particular assignment depends on the answers to the following questions. (Considering these questions will be helpful any time a work assignment is made, even without regard to developmental implications.) When staffing large cases or transactions where several partners and senior associates may be supervising junior associates, bear these questions in mind for all the likely supervisors, in addition to the partner in charge.

- What are the supervisor's strengths, and how do they match up to the associate's development needs?

- Will the assignment expose the associate to a supervisor with a different style, temperament, client base, or approach to practice?

- What is the supervisor's track record in working with other associates who have similar personalities, styles, or development needs?

- What is the supervisor's track record in working with other associates of the same race or gender as this associate?

- Does the supervisor delegate interesting work?

- Does the supervisor like to challenge associates?

- How much responsibility and autonomy does the supervisor give to associates?

- How closely does the supervisor monitor associates' work?
- Will the supervisor permit the associate to have direct client contact?
- How effective is the supervisor at managing work?
- How effective is the supervisor at managing people?
- How reasonable are the supervisor's expectations of associates?
- Does the supervisor regularly give feedback to associates?
- How patient is the supervisor?
- Is the supervisor a good role model?
- Does the supervisor enjoy teaching associates?
- Is the supervisor known to be a good mentor?
- Are the supervisor's and the associate's personalities compatible?

If the supervisor's strengths, temperament, and traits match up well with the associate's experience, personality, and needs, the associate stands a good chance of having a positive learning experience.

Sometimes the firm may want to match an associate with certain supervising lawyers for specific developmental reasons. This is often done for senior associates headed for partnership. To advance in the firm, associates need to work with and be known to many different partners. The firm may want to assign associates to partners who are superlative teachers or role models, experts about a particular legal field or industry, effective mentors and rainmakers, or wielders of power whose influence and support are necessary for becoming a partner.

Case Team —

 What will the associate's role be on the team?

The number of team members and the composition of the team impact the associate's development opportunities. A small team usually means the associate will have a lot of responsibility. On a large team, a senior associate might have front-line responsibilities and occasions to excel, while an inexperienced associate may get lost in the crowd. It is important to consider the experience levels of the various team members and where the associate will fit in. Who will be the associate's direct supervisors? How much direct contact will the associate have with partners?

How much direct contact will the associate have with clients? Will the associate be at the forefront of the case? Will the associate supervise other team members?

Another consideration in making an assignment is the history of the team and its dynamics. If the team is starting up, the associate can grow with the case. Getting in on the ground floor offers the best chances for getting good work, working closely with the partners, finding a comfortable niche, and getting to know the client. On the other hand, if the associate is being assigned to an existing team, consider how the associate will be integrated into the team. One important issue is how well the team gets along. There may be special concerns when an existing team has a troubled history because of inadequate communication, high turnover, poor client relationship, or weak management.

Client —

 Will the assignment create opportunities for the associate to work directly with the client?

Associates desire and expect early client contact. They know how important it is for their development. Direct exposure to clients is essential for associates to learn how to interact with, serve, and manage clients. Associates need assignments that present ample opportunities to work directly with a client and experience firsthand the dynamics of an attorney-client relationship. Associates need this kind of contact to stay engaged and interested in their work, and to feel as if they are truly representing a client — not just doing work. They also need client contact to learn how to become rainmakers. Lawyers cannot attract new clients unless they are adept at working with existing clients.

In making an assignment, some thought should be given to who the client is. Some clients are intolerant of inexperienced associates. You should know in advance if the client will be receptive to the associate you are considering, or whether you will have to make a case for the associate's participation on the matter. You also need to ensure that the associate's hourly billing rate is within the client's acceptable range.

Scope of Work —

 How broad a range of tasks, experiences, and responsibilities does the assignment entail?

A variety of work experience is critical in today's unstable, fluctuating legal environment, where adaptability is essential for long-term career success. Unless diversity of work is a conscious goal, a lawyer might spend years doing the same task expertly without learning anything new. One associate who left her firm after three years complained that she was trapped by her own success. The partners for whom she worked thought she had a brilliant understanding of privilege issues and continually asked her to supervise document productions and produce privilege logs. She often requested different work, but was told her special expertise made her too valuable where she was. The supervisors' admiration for her exceptional performance blinded them to her need for growth and led to an unfortunate departure.

In a rapidly changing world, lawyers must be versatile and multi-dimensional, which requires a broad base of experience on which to draw. Particularly in firms where early specialization is the rule, lawyers may become too narrowly focused. While they may become experts in a specific area, they run the risk of becoming one-dimensional. These lawyers are ill equipped to deal with issues outside their limited range of expertise.

Development potential increases when an assignment presents many different kinds of tasks and responsibilities. For development purposes, it is important that associates have a steady increase in both the scope of work and scale of responsibility. For well-rounded development, associates also need diverse assignments that provide a balanced overall experience. Over time, they should have both short-term, highly focused assignments and long-term assignments that involve broad roles and responsibilities; both stand-up work that requires quick, on-your-feet thinking and assignments that are analytical, methodical and take a long time; both the experience of working alone and of being part of a team. The use of benchmarks, experience checklists, or other guidelines that chart developmental progress can ensure that key development experiences are not overlooked. (See Chapter 7.)

Good supervisors recognize the importance of delegating interesting, challenging work to promote associate development. Some partners, however, hoard the most interesting assignments and give associates only mundane, tedious, or uninteresting tasks. This occurs most often in firms that value billable hours more than associate development. When work is scarce, partners do lower level work to keep up their own billable hours. This shortsightedness harms the associate, the partner, and the firm. The associate is denied meaningful developmental work. The partner wastes his or her time on work that should be done by associates, and fails to do the business development that could bring in needed new work. Here the firm loses out twice: Associates do not develop and the firm's business does not grow. Firms can reduce hoarding by basing partner compensation at least in part on factors that promote development. Some firms have done this by tying compensation to team performance: The better the entire team performs, the higher the partner's compensation. This encourages partners to give everyone on the team work that is developmentally appropriate.

The lack of good assignments for associates is not always due to hoarding. Some partners just do not recognize the importance of developmental assignments for associates, do not have good managerial skills, or do not trust others to do the work (e.g., "no one can do this as well as I can," "it will take less time if I do it myself"). To prevent under-delegation, firms must teach partners why and how to delegate good work and give them incentives for doing so.

Challenges Presented and Opportunities to "Stretch" —

Will the assignment challenge the associate and encourage professional growth?
What are the risks to the client, associate, and firm if the associate handles a stretch assignment?
What can be done to reduce those risks?

Lawyers gain professional know-how quickly through repeated exposure to real-life client problems. Many lawyers enjoy doing repetitive tasks because it allows them to work toward perfection. But perfection is not the same as development. A lawyer who handles only routine and familiar problems is more likely to respond to a new problem the same way as in the past. This may make that lawyer an expert at a particular task, but it affords no real opportunity for learning and growth. For most lawyers, repetition can actually stunt learning. Routine work leads to boredom, complacency, and a professional dead end.

As associates progress, they need assignments that present ever-increasing degrees of complexity, responsibility, and autonomy — work experiences that will help them learn and polish leadership, management, and client relations skills. As associates master certain competencies, they should be given assignments that require them to develop more advanced skills. This is important for associates' maturation and for the firm's benefit as well. As associates handle incrementally more complex challenges, their growing capabilities will generate commensurately higher profits.

Research has shown that job challenges, especially difficult work assignments, are the best teachers for up and coming executives.[6] Assignments that provide the most intense opportunities for learning are "stretch" assignments, where the associate has to reach beyond the comfort of familiar work and secure abilities into new

---

[6] Morgan W. McCall, Jr., Michael M. Lombardo, and Ann M. Morrison, *The Lessons of Experience*, The Free Press, New York, 1988.

arenas that may present elements of surprise or discomfort. Associates usually greet stretch assignments with a combination of attraction, because such assignments are exciting, and fear, because they are risky. Stretch assignments require not just substantive and technical knowledge but also leadership abilities: dealing with crises, managing work and people under pressure, and making decisions when faced with risk and uncertainty. These assignments force lawyers to apply past learning to new situations, to take risks, to think creatively as well as analytically, to experiment with new ways of thinking, behaving, and feeling, and to use capabilities they may be unsure they have. These assignments build confidence along with new learning, both of which are necessary for professional development.

Associates should be urged to take advantage of "stretch" opportunities that arise unexpectedly. Sometimes unplanned circumstances force associates to accept responsibilities earlier than they would in the normal course of events. These situations occur when, for instance, staffing shortages caused by departing lawyers foist higher-level work on associates than would typically be assigned, or when a client relies on an associate because the supervising partner cannot be reached. One partner's experience is illustrative. When he was a second-year litigation associate, he accompanied a partner to another state for two weeks of expert depositions. After three days, the partner was called back to the office because of a family emergency, leaving the associate to take the remainder of the depositions. The associate had to respond quickly, face up to his self-doubt and uncertainty, and deal with these unexpected demands. At first, he was "a nervous wreck, afraid of blowing the whole case." But when the depositions were concluded he felt, he says, "like I grew into a real lawyer almost overnight. Nothing scared me anymore." Situations like this can be powerful learning experiences, and associates should be encouraged to make the most of them.

Whether planned or not, stretch assignments also present risks for all involved. The greatest risk is a poor outcome for the client if the associate does not handle the work as competently as a more experienced lawyer would. The associate risks failure and its implications, including stigmatization, disgrace, and being fired. The firm risks excessive write-offs, loss of a client, and perhaps even malpractice liability. These risks are most pronounced in the same high-challenge, high-visibility stretch assignments that present the best learning opportunities. Even in the most development-oriented firms, avoiding such risks to the client or the firm will trump the associate's learning needs.

Occasionally, a partner deliberately makes an assignment to an associate who lacks the requisite skills, believing that the associate will somehow learn whatever is necessary in order to do the job. This extreme "sink or swim" approach can indeed lead to intense learning, especially when successfully executed, but, more often, it poses a serious risk of failure. Assigning work to an associate who is completely unprepared is foolish and jeopardizes the client and the firm. If someone is not ready to handle a situation, pushing them prematurely may also lead to a ruined reputation for the associate and a profound loss of self-esteem.

A more calibrated approach is less risky and more likely to have a satisfactory outcome. Although risks cannot be totally eliminated, they can be sufficiently reduced so that stretch assignments can be made without much fear. It is best — at least in the early stages of a lawyer's career — to begin with "moderate" stretch assignments where mistakes can be tolerated and the cost of failure to the client, the firm, and the associate are relatively low. While you would not place a client or the firm at risk by assigning work to someone totally unprepared, selecting an associate who is ready for the challenge and then providing appropriate guidance and support makes the risk reasonable and manageable. Specific steps that can help reduce the risks of stretch assignments include the following:

- **Assess the associate's abilities.** Pay careful attention to the associate's strengths, accomplishments, and deficiencies, in terms of both skills and experience. Find out what the associate has and has not yet learned and done.

- **Assess the associate's readiness.** Determine whether the associate has the motivation and state of mind to accept the challenges presented.

- **Match the right associate with the right learning opportunity.** Be sure that the opportunities of the assignment match the abilities and readiness of the associate.

- **Explain to the associate why the assignment is being made.** Associates need to understand why they are selected for an assignment and what learning outcomes are anticipated. Failure to make this clear may result in misunderstanding. The associate may perceive the assignment as undesirable or as a demotion. In one instance, a "star" associate was assigned to a matter because the team needed someone who could take a lead role in the case. The partners who made the assignment considered it to be a showcase for the associate's numerous talents — but did not tell the associate that. Unfortunately, the case and the team handling it had reputations within the firm as "losers." The associate believed that the assignment was a "dump" and took it as a message from the firm that he had no chance for partnership. So he left.

- **Warn the associate about potential problems.** When you make an assignment, let the associate know where problems might be anticipated. Discuss with the associate how those problems might be avoided or handled.

- **Be prepared to defend the assignment.** You may need to explain to the client (and perhaps to the firm) why this associate is the best person for the job. A thorough understanding of what the associate brings to the assignment will enable you to do so.

- **Supervise the associate carefully.** Stretch assignments require closer supervision than routine assignments. Supervisors should be willing to observe, teach, and support the associate. This requires that the supervisor be available and accessible. The associate and supervisor should set specific times to assess progress and address any significant issues that arise. But take care not to supervise so closely that it stifles the associate. Allow the associate the freedom to take risks, exert autonomy, and develop self-reliance. That is what a stretch assignment is all about.

- **Give the associate feedback.** Feedback is always important. It should be regular and frequent, not just a yearly performance review or "post-mortem" debriefing at a project's end. The supervisor should observe how the associate is handling the job and gather input from others working on the project as the work goes along. Using this data, the supervisor can reinforce good practices and make specific suggestions for improvement. Candor and honesty are critical but should be tempered with compassion.

- **Encourage the associate to ask for feedback.** If feedback is slow in coming, the associate should know how to ask for it without appearing insecure or needy.

- **Ensure the associate is processing the experience.** Ask associates from time to time what they have learned from their work so far and where they are heading. If they appear to be off track, use the opportunity to redirect them.

- **Keep mistakes and failures in perspective.** Associates will inevitably make mistakes. Try to transform these mistakes into learning events. Look at how the associate deals with the situation. Offer second chances that make recovery possible. Winston Churchill once said, "Success is the ability to go from failure to failure without losing your enthusiasm." His point was not to encourage failure but to stress the importance of resiliency. Similarly, your firm needs to help associates keep setbacks in perspective and get them back on their feet to try yet again.

Giving associates this level of support during their early stretch assignments makes successful completion of projects more likely. As associates' experience multiplies and their confidence grows, so does their ability to tackle independently later challenges that are unexpected or extreme. Firms invest far too much in their associates to stand by and let them fail. It is a much better policy, for the firm as well as its associates, to teach them how to succeed.

Allocating Work Assignments

Effective work allocation systems give associates assignments that will promote their professional development and distribute work effectively and fairly. Ultimately, the responsibility for using work assignments to develop associates' skills and talents lies with the firm's leaders. Only the firm's leadership can make work-related professional development an institutional priority, ensure that it happens, and shape the firm's culture to support it. In smaller law firms, professional development specialists may be involved in making work assignments and can exert leadership directly. In large firms, they rarely participate in the work assignment process, but they, along with the firm's professional development specialists and partners in charge of professional development, can also lead the way by emphasizing the importance of work assignments that are developmental, not just expedient. Professional development specialists in all firms can influence the work allocation process by educating assigning partners to recognize and consider the developmental potential of assignments; informing assignment brokers about associates' development needs; and persuading the firm to embrace a work assignment system with associate development as one of its goals.

The day-to-day responsibility for assignments lies with the partners who are closest to the associates. It is commonly accepted that associates have the responsibility for their own learning, but they cannot learn by themselves. It is the job of partners, especially department and practice group heads, supervisors, and mentors, to provide the work experience, teaching, and guidance that give associates the chance to learn. The best way to bring this about is to institute systems designed to promote work-based learning. These systems should hold partners accountable for carrying out their associate development responsibilities; assigning work fairly and with associate development in mind; and monitoring associates' experience to make sure they are getting good work.

Partners must take their work allocation duties seriously. This sometimes means subordinating their short-term staffing needs to long-term associate interests. But, as the owners of the firm and managers of the firm's associates, they have an obligation to the lawyers they hire, to the survival of the organization, and to their clients, to educate and develop associates into a superior talent pool. That requires exposing associates to learning and development opportunities through varied developmental work assignments. To meet these obligations, partners need to have a systematic method of allocating work to associates.

Work Allocation Systems vs. Laissez Faire

A work allocation system allows you to be methodical, fair, and judicious in selecting the right associate for a job. When making an assignment, many factors must be considered: staffing needs, client expectations, partner preferences, associate availability, associate development needs, and associate requests. But many firms have no system in place for allocating work. Instead, they take a laissez faire approach and let partners staff their cases and transactions by simply assigning work to the associates they choose. Assignments are random and without any consideration for the associate's development needs. They are made to suit the interests of partners, not associates.

When there is no organized system for making assignments, partners choose associates at will. This process can work satisfactorily in a small firm or practice group because lawyers are more apt to be familiar with group members' abilities, workload, availability, interests, and development needs. But in a large group, a laissez faire approach can be a free-for-all that results in frustration for associates and mismanagement of work. In one firm that uses what they call the "grab'em method" (partners walk down the hall and "grab" whomever they see), an unusual pattern resulted. Associates on the 14th floor worked almost exclusively with partners on 14, associates on the 15th floor worked with partners on 15, and so on.

In a laissez faire firm, associates find it hard to manage their work because they never know when and from whom the next assignment will come. They feel considerable pressure and find it almost impossible to decline work assignments made this way. All the control is with the partners, while the burden of "escaping" work rests on the associate. This approach is unfair to associates, counterproductive to development, and almost certain to lead to trouble.

In a laissez faire setting, it is particularly difficult to restrain domineering partners who intimidate or abuse other lawyers in the work assignment process. These are the powerful partners who view their work as more important than anyone else's and "pull rank" whenever they need assistance. With no centralized assignment system to curb their behavior, they bully partners and associates alike. They place excessive demands on associates, treat them rudely, or criticize them unjustly. In addition to upsetting associates, this impinges on the rights of other partners to find associates for their clients' work. Partners who always assert priority prevent partners with less power or influence from getting the staff they need for their cases and deals. When other partners cannot get adequate staffing for their matters, their ability to serve clients is compromised, and their progression within the partnership is stymied. A laissez faire approach can be unfair to clients, too, because no orderly effort is made to staff cases based on selection of the best associates to meet the demands of the work.

Matters can be more efficiently and appropriately staffed if the search for suitable associates is made in a systematic way. An organized system for distributing work remedies the failings of laissez faire and allows the assignment process to address development issues along with staffing needs. Firms use many kinds of work allocation systems, but the most common approach by far is to delegate responsibility for assignments to one or more individuals, sometimes called "assignment brokers." These individuals are usually partners, administrators, or a combination of both. In small firms, they may make assignments for all of the firm's associates, but in large firms they make assignments for associates within a particular practice group or department. A handful of firms use a "free market" system that allows associates to pick the work they will do. In this system, partners try to recruit associates to work on their cases or transactions, but the decision lies with the associate.

■ Assignment Broker Systems

When assignment brokers are used, the responsibility for matching associates and staffing needs is commonly delegated to one or more partners. Assignment partners are most often department or practice group chairs (or their designees) or assignment committees comprised of partners from a department or practice group. Some firms use department or practice group administrators, who may or may not be lawyers, to make work assignments.

Placing this responsibility in the hands of designated individuals means that they can become familiar with the associates they monitor and take associates' interests and development needs into consideration when making assignments. They are more likely to recognize the developmental potential of assignments. In addition, this system saves time and trouble for partners who need to have work staffed. When they need associates for new matters or to expand existing teams, they contact the assignment brokers, give them the job parameters, and let them do the legwork.

Having a system in place prevents associates from being pigeonholed in ways that can negatively impact their careers. Many associates receive less than optimal work if no one is watching out for their developmental interests. Assignment brokers can protect associates whose performance on one project was so-so by assigning them to another project that puts them back on track. Brokers can guard against discrimination based on stereotypes or incorrect assumptions, e.g., by seeing that minority or part-time lawyers are not unfairly blocked from significant work assignments. They can also ensure that associates who are placed on the fast track to partnership continue to get the kind of work and support they need to excel and advance rather than burn out.

A few large firms use a variation of the assignment broker system by breaking departments not only into practice groups but also into departmental subgroups (usually called "pools," "pods," or "families") that cut across practice areas. The purpose of subdividing the department this way is to expand lawyers' exposure to people and work throughout their department. This allows associates to become familiar with the variety of work in their department rather than limiting them to any particular practice area. One firm that uses this approach is McCutchen Doyle Brown & Enersen LLP.[7] The firm's litigation department has 305 lawyers from 17 practice groups who are divided into seven pools of 10 to 15 partners and 15 to 30 associates from different practice groups within the department. Junior associates are assigned to both a partner in a practice group and a pool. They receive half of their work assignments from their assigned partner and the other half from either the pool leader, who has primary responsibility for supervising the associate's overall performance and work experience, or the Associate Development Chair, who supervises the pool leaders and keeps track of workflow throughout the firm. (Assignments may also come from a Practice Group leader or from informal associate networking.)

In another variation of delegating work allocation responsibility to certain individuals, some firms assign new associates to one partner from whom they get all or most of their work. When the associate and the assigned partner are compatible, the work relationship can be great and partners frequently become informal mentors. This approach has the advantages of simplicity and accountability, but there can be serious pitfalls. Working exclusively with one partner limits an associate's professional experience and inhibits an associate's integration into the firm's professional and social networks. If the associate and partner are not compatible, if the partner's work is unexciting or not highly valued by the firm, or if the partner is a poor supervisor, the associate's development and satisfaction may suffer. In some cases, the wrong partner assignment can effectively stop a lawyer's career before it gets started.

---

[7] As of July 1, 2002, McCutchen merged with the law firm of Bingham Dana to form Bingham McCutchen LLP. The work assignment and professional development procedures of the merged firm had not been finalized at press time.

Assignment brokers apply several criteria to locate suitable associates to staff assignments. These criteria usually include a combination of various objective and subjective factors, such as current workload, available time, experience, expertise, billing rate, and the dynamics of a particular team. If assignment brokers are alert to developmental aspects of assignments, they will consider whether an associate has done too much of a particular thing or has too little experience in the area, and whether the assignment will help the associate learn new skills or handle new responsibilities.

If the firm is divided into specialized practice groups, assignment brokers usually look first within the practice group to see if anyone suitable is available for the assignment. If no one in the group is available, they may look outside the practice group to the wider associate pool, sometimes including associates in different offices. When they find a candidate, they discuss the options with practice group leaders and the partners in charge of the matter before an assignment is made. Perfect fits are rarely found, but using a systematic approach usually results in staffing decisions that are better for both the client and the associate.

■ Free Market Systems

A few firms allow associates to select their own assignments. These firms do not assign associates to particular cases, clients, or partners. Instead, associates in a general practice area (e.g., litigation or corporate) choose the kind of work they want to do and the partners with whom they want to work. Here, partners seek out associates who are available and interested in the assignment they have to offer, but the associate is free to accept or decline. The underlying philosophy in such firms is that lawyers — including associates — should do the work they want to do and enjoy the work they do. The free market system works best for associates who are ambitious, self-directed, entrepreneurial, and eager to be responsible for directing their own work experience and career development.

However, the free market system can be daunting. Even highly independent, self-assured associates struggle with decisions about what work to take, which partners to work with, and the impact such decisions will have on their careers. Some fear repercussions if they turn down work from certain partners or clients, and many have a hard time saying no to work that interests them. Either way, they accept too much work and have difficulty managing their time. They usually need counseling to guide the decisions they make, at least in the first few years. They may not realize, for example, that working exclusively with one partner, no matter how important the partner is, may be a detriment to advancement. Or the assignments they choose may cause them to become too specialized or too scattered.

Because it requires a unique culture to place so much control in associates' hands, very few firms have a real free market system. Many firms that claim to have free market systems in fact operate under a laissez faire arrangement. Those firms tell associates they are free to select their own work and to decline unwanted work without explanation, but, in reality, partners expect associates to accept proffered work and pressure them to do so, directly or indirectly. Associates who turn down work, especially from a powerful partner, are penalized by being labeled "slackers" or "uncommitted," or are not given another chance.

Free market systems work well so long as three conditions exist: (1) the firm recruits and hires associates with the traits necessary to flourish in such a system; (2) the firm culture supports it completely, so that associates truly are free to turn down work without fear; and (3) the firm provides tools and resources that help associates succeed within the system (e.g., written criteria for career development, detailed forms to direct and track their work experience, and mentors to provide advice and guidance).

Monitoring Associates' Work: Productivity, Progress, and Human Resource Management

Work allocation systems enable the firm to monitor and manage associates' workload more efficiently. Almost all firms track associates' billable hours. Some firms also track non- billable time, including time spent in pro bono, training, mentoring, business development, or administrative activities. Most firms use this information for compensation purposes and as an indicator of associate productivity. They can also use this information to keep an eye on the type of work associates are doing, the kind of experiences they are having, and the work assignments they need to progress further in their development. In addition, watching and comparing monthly reports of lawyers' hours enables the firm to assign associates where they are most needed, resulting in more efficient utilization patterns. For all of these purposes, individuals making assignments need information about associates' workload, availability, work experience, development needs, and interests. This information leads to more meaningful and equitable assignments.

■ Associate Productivity

Assigning work requires knowledge of associates' workload and availability. This is determined on the basis of associates' recorded hours and self-reports. Reports of associates' recorded hours provide a picture of their workload during the previous month; self-reports provide information about current and anticipated short- and long-term workload. Self-reports can be obtained from associates through face-to-face meetings, phone calls, standardized forms, or automated e-mail inquiries. A self-reporting system of shorthand signals is often used to indicate associates' ability or willingness to take on new assignments. For example, in a "traffic signal system," associates simply indicate "red," "yellow," or "green" to show whether they can take no more work, could take some new work, or need a new assignment. Some firms find such color codes too vague and prefer to have associates indicate whether they are "extremely busy," "busy but available to take on a simple project or emergency," "reasonably busy but could help out on some other matters," or "can take more work." (This system sometimes defaults to "can take more work" if an associate fails to respond to the inquiry.)

When comparing associates' recorded hours and self-reports, there is sometimes a "disconnect." When a discrepancy is noted, it is important to follow up and determine why. Some associates record their hours improperly; others are afraid to accept new work even though they can (or should) take it; some believe they cannot ever say no to new work; still others may be having performance or personal problems.

Recorded hours and self-reports do not provide the whole picture of an associate's productivity or the quality of their work experience. In terms of associate development, assumptions based on workload data alone are misleading. Associates who consistently seem to be working too little or too much may have productivity or performance problems, and both should be investigated, especially if there is a significant change from prior months. Some associates' hours are low because they do not get enough work. There may simply be a lull in the matters to which they are assigned, or the supervisor may not realize they have available time. Sometimes, however, the associate has a performance problem that is being ignored. When an associate is perceived as a poor performer, it is very common for partners to withhold work from them. This creates a dilemma for the associate: Partners do not want to work with a poor performer but they don't want to deal with the performance problem, either. So they just avoid giving that associate anything to do or they pass the associate along to other teams.

On the flip side, assignment personnel should also investigate associates who consistently record extremely high hours. Associates who are known to be high performers typically receive a great deal of work. Partners assume that associates who are busy must be getting good work and that those associates are pleased with their assignments. But because associates are very busy does not mean they are working appropriately, getting the right balance of work, or satisfied with the work being assigned. Some associates work inefficiently; they take too long to get work done, or have trouble managing priorities, allowing their assignments to back up. High hours may mean that an associate is the victim of an overly demanding partner or is assigned to long projects that are tedious and uninteresting. If no one intervenes, the hardest working associates can burn out.

■ Progress

Monitoring associates' work is essential to guiding their professional growth and development. Information about the kind of work associates have done and the kind they would like to do should be collected regularly through questionnaires, yearly evaluations (including self-evaluations), and associates' individual marketing and development plans. (See Chapter 7.) Data should be obtained from associates' mentors and from supervising lawyers familiar with the associates' performance, talents, and development status. Associates should also be encouraged to track their own experiences and identify their own perceived needs, and to make that information known to the people in charge of assignments.

Data collection should be the responsibility of associates' advisers or mentors, professional development specialists and staff, or other designated individuals. The information should be used to counsel associates about work assignments and other experiences they should seek to further their development. Pool leaders at McCutchen Doyle Brown & Enersen LLP, for example, conduct an Associate Development Assessment process. Associates are invited to complete and submit forms describing what kind of work they have been doing and what kinds of experience they would like to have more or less of.[8] Skills checklists are provided to help associates appreciate the types of skills and tasks they should be developing at their class level. The pool leader reviews the forms with the associate, offers guidance about work experience and career goals, forwards a summary of key goals for the upcoming year to the associate's assigned partner and mentor, and keeps the information in mind when new work comes in. If the new work suits an associate's development needs or interests, the pool leader considers that associate as a candidate for the job.

Another way of collecting data about associates' work experience is through electronic tracking systems. These systems designate billing codes for various tasks and projects. Data can be sorted to analyze an associate's work history by any number of categories, including task or project type, supervising partner, client, and percentage of time spent in each category. The data is weighted and ranked.

---

[8] As of July 1, 2002, McCutchen merged with the law firm of Bingham Dana to form Bingham McCutchen LLP. The work assignment and professional development procedures of the merged firm had not been finalized at press time.

Assignment personnel can use such reports to make developmentally focused work assignments. Some firms go a step further, tying their electronic work and time reports directly to the firm's associate evaluation system. This gives associates and their evaluating partners a more detailed picture of the associate's work experience during the evaluation period.

No matter how sophisticated the tracking system, reports that focus on hours, even if sorted by categories, do not sufficiently describe the quality of an associate's experience. They cannot tell you whether an assignment was challenging, or whether it piqued or dulled the associate's interest in the field. The only way to find this out is to ask associates directly, or to have them complete self-assessments that include information about what they have done and what they want to do. Many firms devise forms that can be used for this purpose. Fenwick & West LLP gives associates extensive, detailed forms to help them direct and track their work experience. One set of forms (called "Skills Assessment and Self Inventory Application") lists the work experiences required to become proficient in general corporate skills and in the specialized areas of the firm's corporate practice (i.e., start-ups, mergers and acquisitions, and public offerings and securities). For each experience listed, associates are urged to record their level of proficiency (ranging from "Novice" to "Master"), the number of projects completed in each skill area, and their level of interest in the work (low, medium, or high), and to discuss their goals with their mentor. (See Figure 1.)

FIGURE 1. Fenwick & West LLP Skills Assessment and Self-Inventory Application

General Skills	Level of Proficiency				Projects Completed				Interest Level		
	Novice	Require Much Direction	Require Some Direction	Master	0-2	3-6	7-9	10+	low	medium	high
Legal Research	○	○	●	○	○	●	○	○	●	○	○
Contract Review	●	○	○	○	●	○	○	○	○	●	○
Contract Drafting	●	○	○	○	●	○	○	○	○	●	○
Due Diligence Investigation	●	○	○	○	●	○	○	○	○	●	○
Closing Documentation	●	○	○	○	●	○	○	○	○	○	●
Negotiation	●	○	○	○	●	○	○	○	○	○	●
Delegation/Support Management	●	○	○	○	●	○	○	○	○	●	○
Training of Associates on New Projects	●	○	○	○	●	○	○	○	○	●	○
Client Relationship/Client Management	●	○	○	○	●	○	○	○	○	○	●
Manage Associates Working on Your Clients	●	○	○	○	●	○	○	○	○	●	○
Project Management and Leadership	●	○	○	○	●	○	○	○	○	○	●
Public Speaking	●	○	○	○	●	○	○	○	○	●	○
Spreadsheet Creation and Use	○	○	○	○	○	○	○	○	○	○	○
Prelitigation Counseling	○	○	○	○	○	○	○	○	○	○	○

Monitoring associates' work experience is also important to make sure no one inadvertently falls off the learning curve or is stigmatized by an early bad work experience. These situations occur when an associate does not receive enough challenging or exciting assignments; gets the same kind of work repeatedly; works for an extended period with a poor supervisor; or has a bad work outcome that brands him or her as a poor performer. In these situations, associates may pick up bad habits, fail to learn advanced skills, or no longer receive stretch assignments. Early identification through a work monitoring system can lead to early intervention, help the associate get up to speed, and correct misperceptions about ability.

■ Human Resource Management

Firms need to take a systematic approach to work assignments for effective human resource management. They need to distribute work efficiently among their lawyers. One of the most common sources of inefficiency is workloads that are severely lopsided, i.e. when some associates work hundreds of hours more than others. The repercussions of extreme workload disparity can be enormous: Dissatisfaction rises and morale plummets within associate ranks, associates' development suffers, and the firm's profitability declines.

Workload disparity commonly happens when there is too much work in one practice area and not enough in another. Associates in the busier group may be working around the clock while those in the slower group are going home early. It also occurs when no one is responsible for monitoring assignments (i.e., in a laissez faire firm). When no one is in charge, partners direct work to their favorite associates, while associates who are no one's favorite get little to do. The result is that one associate may be billing 3,000 hours while another in the same practice group bills 1,600 hours per year.

Firms that track associates' work hours can use the information to prevent or correct such imbalances. When one or more partners regularly monitor those hourly reports, they can identify patterns within and across practice groups that indicate less than optimum utilization of associates' time. In addition to greater efficiency, this can also save the firm from unnecessary hiring. When there is too much work in a practice group, the first response of partners in the group is to hire more lawyers. Someone who is familiar with the workload and capabilities of the firm's associates can tell these partners if there are underutilized associates in the firm who can do the needed work. Those associates might be in different practice groups in the same office, or in different offices of the firm. Supplying needed lawyers internally adds to the firm's revenues by putting underutilized associates to work rather than incurring the unnecessary effort and expense of hiring another lawyer. Cross-staffing helps to even out workloads among offices and practice groups, and promotes communication and relationship building among lawyers throughout the firm. In law firms contemplating associate layoffs, this process can also help the firm determine if associates can be redeployed to other practice areas rather than being let go.

Components of an Effective Work Allocation System

Monitoring associates' work and experience requires a sound, well-designed system. Like any formal management system, your firm's scheme will only succeed if it is thoughtfully planned and implemented. Six elements must be present:

1. Commitment from firm and practice group leaders;
2. Designated individuals with authority and support;
3. Written procedures and ground rules;
4. Fair and consistent application;
5. Links to other professional development systems; and
6. Administrative support.

---

1. **Commitment from firm and practice group leaders.** As explained earlier, firm leaders must guarantee the integrity of the system. Practice group and department leaders must guarantee its implementation. Unlike mentoring, evaluations, and training, which can be effectively managed at a firm-wide level, work assignments are best managed by the leaders who are closest to the work. Since most assignments are made "locally," i.e., by practice groups or departments, practice group and department leaders must be committed to the work allocation system.

2. **Designated individuals with authority and support.** Specified individuals must be accountable for the system's successful operation. Their authority must be clear and unequivocal. All lawyers must know who is authorized to make assignments and how to reach them. One or more partners should be designated to oversee work assignments in each department or practice group. This can be the department head, practice group leader, or others, including administrators, to whom authority is delegated. Two important issues must be addressed if the firm delegates this responsibility to an administrator, especially if the administrator is not a partner in the practice group.

To be effective in making assignments, the administrator must understand the skills needed, the people and practice groups involved, and the possible political repercussions of each assignment. Without a profound understanding of what the work entails, the administrator will not have enough insight or credibility to make assignments that partners will honor. This does not mean that the administrator must be a lawyer, but it does require that the individual have considerable knowledge of legal practice generally and familiarity with the group's practice in particular.

The firm must ensure that partners accept the administrator's authority. Administrators usually do not make significant assignments independently; they first confer with the requesting partners and possibly with the associates who are being considered. Nonetheless, partners may resist their authority. Partners own and manage the firm. They are responsible for serving their clients' legal needs, and they want to decide who will work on their clients' matters. Many partners find it hard enough to accept staffing decisions made by other partners, but they will ignore or vigorously resist decisions made by administrators unless the firm's leadership definitively supports the administrator. This means that if a partner challenges an administrator who is properly carrying out assignment responsibilities, the leaders of the firm — especially at the department or practice group level — must unequivocally back the administrator's actions.

3. **Written procedures and ground rules.** The assignment system procedures should be clearly documented. Written procedures define the mission, goals, and expectations of the system and promote a common understanding of how the system operates. They should include a process for emergency assignments that cannot wait for standard procedures to be followed. Emergency situations should be circumscribed and reflect unexpected urgency, not poor partner planning. Ground rules should also lay out when and for what reason associates may turn down proffered assignments (e.g., when the associate is working to capacity), and under what conditions the system can override short-term staffing needs in the interests of an associate's long-term development.

A work assignment system need not be uniform across the firm. In large firms, different practice groups may each have their own systems, depending on their size, on how their lawyers work together, on staffing needs and patterns, and on the composition of the associate pool. Large practice groups may require a staff of several people to process staffing requests. Smaller practice groups may be informal and need only one person in charge. So long as every practice group has a system that contains the necessary elements, the firm can permit practice groups considerable flexibility and creativity.

Procedures should provide guidelines to follow in case of disagreement over an assignment. One frequent cause of disagreement involves dueling partners. Associates often work with more than one supervising partner. Sometimes, two or more partners claim an urgent need for all the associate's time or entitlement to most of the associate's time. They put the associate in the middle of their quarrel over who has priority. This is not the associate's problem, it is the partners' problem. Unfortunately, however, the associate is the one who suffers. When an associate has no control over competing partners' claims, the partners should be the ones to work out the problem. The associate should present the dilemma to all the partners involved and request that they resolve it. In extreme situations, a firm's procedures could instruct the associate to consult with a mentor, practice group leader, ombudsperson, or assignment broker. The assignment committee, partner, or administrator should try to foresee and forestall such problems when making assignments, but, when competing claims arise, they can help to mediate the dispute with all parties.

4. **Fair and consistent application.** The firm must adhere to its written procedures and ground rules. Without such resolve, the system will break down. If the system is perceived as unfair, inconsistent, or arbitrary, it will lose credibility and become ineffective. Especially problematic are partners who refuse to abide by the rules and who "grab" or "cherry pick" associates. They try to do an end run around the assignment procedures. They insist on choosing their own associates, resist assignments by others, and coerce associates into accepting their work. The effect of their actions ripples throughout the firm. Because these lawyers give associates work outside the proper channels, associates may wind up neglecting other partners' projects. When this happens, the neglected partner gets angry with the associate, with the transgressing partner, and with the system; the associate gets caught in the middle; and the whole system is undermined.

To prevent obstreperous lawyers from defeating the system, it is imperative that firm leaders back up the assignment brokers and impose penalties on partners who try to circumvent the assignment process (e.g., releasing the associate from the coerced assignment, giving the offending partner last priority on future staffing requests). In addition, when they arrive at the firm, associates should be instructed not to accept assignments outside established channels, and they should be protected when partners try to pressure them to take on work without following established procedures.

The purpose of a work allocation system is not to prevent long-term work relationships between an associate and a partner but to ensure that associates who work with the same partner over and over again do so willingly. There are advantages to having associates work frequently with the same partners. Lawyers feel more comfortable with someone they already know and are accustomed to. Mentoring relationships intensify with time and frequent contact. Many partners who mentor associates are most effective when the two work together regularly. A deeper professional relationship develops and the mentor becomes the associate's champion and sponsor. This benefits the associate's development and advancement. The partner benefits as well when the associate becomes familiar with the partner's client. The associate's knowledge and expertise make the associate more efficient and valuable in subsequent work for the same client.

But the assignment system should also give those associates a chance to work with other partners, with other clients, and on other matters. This is critical to associates' overall development and advancement in the firm. An assignment system also protects associates from unfair assumptions or stereotypes that might lead partners to exclude or overlook them for certain assignments (e.g., assumptions that mothers of babies do not want to travel). It makes the assignment process more equitable to partners, too, ensuring that certain partners do not always have first choice of associates.

Similarly, associates should be encouraged to request assignments. The firm should inform associates about assignments that become available and encourage associates to apply for assignments they desire. Firms can post new assignment opportunities on their intranets, distribute them by e-mail (weekly or as they come in), or announce them at regular practice group meetings. By announcing work opportunities widely and to everyone at once, the process gives all associates a fair chance to go after the assignments they want and greater control over their work lives. The process keeps associates interested and engaged in their work, reassures them that the firm respects their ability to take responsibility for their development, and ensures that associates who are ready for and interested in certain kinds of work are considered for those assignments.

Although their work requests should be given strong consideration, partners and associates should understand that they are not entitled to any particular assignment (except in those instances where a certain assignment has been promised). The individuals in charge of making assignments may deny the requests but should give the parties an explanation for the decision and clear reasons for the refusal.

5. **Links to other professional development systems.** The assignment process is integral to the firm's entire professional development effort, and must therefore be linked to other professional development systems, including the summer program, orientation, evaluation, mentoring, and training. All of these systems can operate independently, but, to be effective in promoting lawyers' development, they must be connected to each other. Technology can be especially helpful in linking them.

    The links among different professional development systems also affect partners. Through an upward review of partners and senior associates, assignment brokers can learn about supervising lawyers' mentoring, management, and supervisory abilities. (See Chapter 7.) Assignment brokers need this information in order to analyze the development potential of assignments, prepare associates who are assigned to difficult partners, and match associates to specific partners for particular developmental purposes.

6. **Administrative support.** Assignment personnel require clerical, administrative, and technological support to implement the work allocation system. Collecting, processing, and keeping track of information pertinent to assignment decisions takes considerable time and effort. The burden of contacting associates weekly or more often to obtain information about workload, availability, interests, and needs varies with the size of the associate pool and the amount and frequency of work that customarily needs to be staffed. To fulfill these responsibilities, assignment personnel need assistance. For large departments or practice groups, this may mean contacting and following up with dozens of associates each week. The best way to obtain this information is for the same people to regularly gather and track it. Assignment partners often do this directly, but it may take too much of their time. Administrative clerks or assistants can do the data collection and organization as long as the assignment personnel receive the information and become familiar with the development profiles of the associates in the pool.

Specialization and Practice Group Assignments

A discussion of work assignments necessarily raises questions about how soon associates should be expected to select a practice area in which to specialize. The legal marketplace is driving lawyers to specialize earlier and earlier. A 2001 study of law office trends by The Affiliates, a legal staffing service, boldly declares, "The concept of a general practice attorney will soon be obsolete."[9] Because of this trend, many firms are no longer asking whether associates should specialize, but rather how quickly must they make a commitment. Answers to this question reflect different philosophies about law practice.

One view asserts that client expectations and high billing rates force law firms to assign only experts to client matters. In order to comply with these client demands, firms must push associates to specialize very quickly. Firms with this view require associates to select a practice group as soon as they join the firm, and make it hard for them to take assignments in other areas. Another view argues that associates should have a broad understanding of law in order to be competent legal advisers and advocates. Proponents of this view reason that, even when associates are sure they want to specialize in a particular practice area, without some exposure to other fields they cannot acquire the broad-based perspective, experience, knowledge, and appreciation of options and consequences that turn lawyers into outstanding professionals. These firms allow or encourage associates to accept assignments from various practice areas, or to rotate through different practice groups, before settling into a specific practice field.

Associates need to understand the implications of selecting a permanent practice group before they are expected to choose one. Assignment to a particular practice area has significant consequences for an associate's career, especially if the choice has to be made early. In most firms, practice groups have varying degrees of importance, leverage, and power. Associates in the firm's central, most lucrative practice groups often make more money and have a better chance to make partner.

Another implication of joining a practice group early is that associates limit their development of legal skills and may get stuck if work in their practice area dwindles. Legal activity is cyclical in many practices, with periods of intense activity alternating with periods of little work. Some practice areas dry up entirely as a result of new legislation or shifting economic priorities. When business is slow, or the firm decides to phase out a practice area altogether, associates in that area may find themselves in marginalized or dying practices. Unfortunately, associates rarely find out about

---

[9] "Future Law Office," The Affiliates, 2001, www.futurelawoffice.com.

these changes in time to protect themselves. When a firm makes decisions that impact the compensation or job security of associates in particular practice groups, the firm should allow or even encourage reassignment to other practice areas and give associates the training and support they need to make the transition. Associates who have had some exposure to other fields before specializing have an advantage when making such a change.

New Associate Practice Group Assignments

There is no standard policy among law firms regarding when or how new associates are assigned to specialized practice groups. Some firms require new associates to select a particular practice area immediately, especially if the associate has an interest in a field and the firm needs lawyers in that area. Other firms allow undecided associates to sample different practice areas before committing to a particular group. They permit new associates to choose two or more practice areas they would like to try out either within or outside their department.

New associates usually move into practice groups in one of three ways: They commit to one practice group right away, or, before making a commitment, they either rotate through two or more practice groups in one department or spend a period of time "floating" through different departments, unassigned to any practice group. Most firms use only one of these three approaches. This last, unassigned approach requires no initial practice group choices. Initial assignments under the first two arrangements are based on associate preferences, and most law firms try to honor associates' choices.

At firms that require immediate specialization, summer associates are asked to start thinking about practice groups during the summer and, if hired as associates, to choose a practice area when they accept the firm's offer. Typically, associates are asked to list practice group preferences, and firms usually try to ensure that associates will receive their first or second choice, provided that the groups can use the associate. Intellectual property, biotechnology, and other highly technical fields consider the associate's special education or training (or lack of it) as a factor in deciding whether the associate should be brought into the group.

In a rotation system, associates spend a set period of time assigned to particular practice groups from which they receive all or most of their work. Associates usually work in one group at a time, though some firms assign associates to two practice groups simultaneously. Associates move on to the next practice group when the rotation period ends, usually after three to nine months. After their last rotation, associates are asked to make a permanent practice choice. Rotation systems permit associates to spend concentrated time in at least two to three practice areas over a span of nine months to three years or even longer.

In firms that do not assign associates to practice groups, associates float throughout the firm, handling work assignments from many different practice groups. This allows them to sample a wide variety of the firm's transactions, cases, lawyers, and clients. After a set period of time, usually nine months to three years, associates are expected to find a practice group "home" in which to settle. This is the approach taken by Los Angeles-based Latham & Watkins. New associates at Latham & Watkins generally remain unassigned to any particular department or practice group until they become third-year associates, at which time they choose a department. During their unassigned period, they can select work assignments in different practice areas and participate in a core training curriculum that educates them about all aspects of the firm's practice. (See Appendix 8-A.) Once they join a department, they concentrate on a specific field.

For rotating or floating associates, firms face legitimate economic issues that require certain financial adjustments. Firms are willing to make these adjustments because of the value they place on giving associates broad work experience. But the costs are real. In a rotation system, there is a loss of continuity in the work team and an increased cost during the associate's move from one group to another. If they have to withdraw from a project before its natural conclusion, associates have to ramp up for their next assignments while other lawyers have to get up to speed to replace them. Not all of these costs can be passed along to the client. Moreover, compared to a specialist, rotating or floating associates bring no added value to an assignment because their knowledge of each new legal field is limited. As they become more senior, or when they finally choose a specialty, it may be hard at that time to defend their high billing rates. How can the firm justify the billing rate of a third-year associate when that third-year associate has only nine months of experience in the chosen field? Firms appreciate this problem, but because of the developmental value of the experiences, they are willing to absorb these modest costs by lowering associates' billing rates until they get up to speed. Most associates learn quickly what they need to know, so the adjustment is only temporary.

Interdisciplinary Practice Groups

Many firms are experimenting with interdisciplinary groups (sometimes called "special interest groups" or "SIGs") based on common legal themes, industries, or professional interests. These hybrid groups cut across many different practice areas and offices and are often firm wide. One of the most rapidly growing interdisciplinary practices deals with privacy. In privacy practices, lawyers with expertise in many different fields of law join together to advise clients on their right to collect, retain, and use information during the course of their business activities. In a firm that represents financial institutions, for example, a privacy practice group might comprise lawyers who specialize in banking, government regulation, technology, and intellectual property. Lawyers in interdisciplinary groups are usually not assigned or limited to any one SIG. They choose one or more groups because of a shared interest or the group's need for their expertise.

Changing from One Practice Group to Another

Associates sometimes change their minds. They join one practice group but decide after further reflection or experience that they prefer another field of law. This occurs even in firms with rotation or floating systems where associates are able to sample different practice areas. Associates' requests to change practice groups are handled on a case-by-case basis. The usual criteria are the associate's performance and standing in the firm, and whether the desired practice group has a business need for the associate. Additional considerations include whether the associate's current group will be negatively impacted if the associate leaves, and the level of the associate's genuine commitment to the new practice group. As a practical matter, if the associate is perceived as a star, the firm tries hard to accommodate the change in order to keep the associate happy and in the firm. However, if an associate is performing poorly in the present practice group, the proposed move may be perceived as "buying time" and firms are disinclined to grant such requests.

Some firms place conditions on an associate's practice group reassignment. Conditions might include a waiting period to complete their current projects; a waiting period until the target group has sufficient work for the associate; a reduction in the associate's compensation while the associate learns about the new practice area; or a delay in consideration for partnership. Such conditions are generally imposed when the change requires the associate to learn a new skill set, become educated in a highly technical field, or become acquainted with a new client base.

Creating Learning Opportunities

Certain important learning experiences are not always available in the normal course of the firm's practice. When these experiences do not appear naturally, the firm can create opportunities outside the firm or find substitutes for the experience within the firm.

Some types of important work experience are so rare that not all associates will have them. Going to trial is a prime example. While there is sufficient pre-trial discovery to give every young civil litigator a chance to propound interrogatories and take a deposition, the number of cases actually going to trial is minute. Consequently, many litigation associates suffer a significant "experience gap," i.e., they get little or no exposure to the courtroom. To overcome that gap, firms have found ways to create real or simulated trial experience for their associates. Three popular methods are (1) giving associates small revenue-generating and/or pro bono cases with a high likelihood of going to trial, (2) training associates in trial skills by sending them to the National Institute for Trial Advocacy (NITA) or holding NITA-style programs in-house, and (3) "loaning" associates (and occasionally junior partners) to District Attorneys' or Public Defenders' offices where they are promised one or more trials. In a "loaner" program, the associate remains on the firm's payroll but works in the local, state, or federal government office. The assignment typically lasts for three to six months, during which the lawyer gains trial experience that might take years to get in a general civil practice.

Another type of loaner program that creates outside learning opportunities for business lawyers is secondment. This practice, more common in Canada than in the United States, is usually in response to a client's request for on-site legal assistance, either to handle a specific project or to staff legal matters when in-house lawyers are unavailable. But some firms offer to loan associates to clients in order to give the associates hands-on business experience.

A seconded lawyer is placed in the offices of the client for a designated period of time. The lawyer works directly with the client, doing the client's business and developing an intimate knowledge of that business. Typically the firm continues to pay the associate's salary and agrees to bill the client at a certain (usually reduced) rate for the associate's work. Seconded associates have direct and regular access to both corporate lawyers and business people in the company. When they return to the firm, their familiarity with the issues, operations, and people in the company elevates the level of their subsequent service for the client.

Loaner programs, whether in a law enforcement agency or a client's legal department, have several potential drawbacks. They take an associate away from the firm for several weeks or months while the firm continues to pay the associate's salary. Some loaned associates find that their outside work does not give them the kind of experience they need to advance when they return to the firm, or they find they prefer criminal law or in-house legal work and decide to leave the firm to pursue those options. In addition, if they have been absent for a long time, these associates might lose a sense of social connection to their peers upon returning. For most firms that loan out associates, the value of the associates' development opportunities and the benefit to the firm of stronger client relationships and community good will outweigh these concerns. Most associates who participate in loaner and seconding programs find the experience to be highly desirable and beneficial to their careers.

Firms with international practices permit lawyers to expand their range of knowledge, practice, and business contacts by practicing for a period of time in other countries. Some firms send lawyers to work in the firm's own offices abroad. At Shearman & Sterling, many fifth- and sixth-year associates are offered a chance to spend up to three months working in any of the firm's offices worldwide. Firms that belong to international networks of law firms, like Lex Mundi and the Pacific Rim Advisory Council, send their lawyers to work in offices of member firms in other countries. By practicing in another country, lawyers learn firsthand how law and business are conducted there, and they develop personal and professional relationships with local lawyers, firms, and clients.

Pro Bono Assignments as Learning Opportunities

Pro bono work has a powerful influence on lawyers' professional development. Many lawyers and law firms do pro bono work to serve the community or to ensure equal access to justice. These are important and worthy reasons, but the developmental value of pro bono work should not be overlooked. When the firm consciously uses pro bono assignments for developmental purposes, the benefits for lawyers are impressive:

- **Pro bono representation accelerates learning**. Associates who work on pro bono matters are usually given more responsibility and autonomy than they receive on paid client work. They "exercise skills and judgments more independently and at an earlier state than comparable work for commercial clients."[10] As a result, they learn advanced skills more quickly than in the normal course of corporate or litigation practice.

---

[10] Esther F. Lardent, *Making the Business Case for Pro Bono*, The Pro Bono Institute, Washington, DC, 2000.

- **Pro bono work increases work satisfaction.** Lawyers who work on pro bono matters usually do so voluntarily. When they represent disadvantaged individuals or work to influence social policies, pro bono representation makes them feel they are doing something meaningful. It ignites their passions and gives their legal efforts greater purpose. When the firm supports their efforts, they feel validated and hold the firm in higher regard.

- **Pro bono work promotes associate advancement.** Pro bono cases frequently put associates in more prominent roles than they have on billable work assignments. This allows associates to demonstrate their legal skills, maturity, and judgment to supervising partners.

- **Pro bono work facilitates mentoring.** Because pro bono matters tend to be thinly staffed, associates have an increased opportunity to work closely and directly with supervising partners. Their shared interest in the matter and close work relationship make it easier for supervisors to give feedback and advice, and for mentoring relationships to develop.

- **Pro bono work increases associates' socialization.** Many pro bono efforts, such as staffing legal clinics or collaborating on lawsuits to impact public policy issues, bring together lawyers from different departments and legal teams. These lawyers have opportunities for social interaction that are often missing from their usual work routines, and they get to know colleagues they otherwise might not meet.

- **Pro bono work expands lawyers' appreciation of the world.** Many lawyers who represent pro bono clients deal with hard issues affecting real people. Lawyers in corporate practice find value in these less exalted but no less important aspects of life and society. Pro bono representation enriches lawyers' understanding of the world in which they live and practice. It keeps them aware of the needs of the underprivileged, makes them appreciate the impact they can have on society, and inspires them to use their legal expertise in worthwhile and creative ways.

Pro bono work also benefits the firm. From a business standpoint, pro bono work aids in recruitment and retention; elevates the image and reputation of the firm; improves client relations and business development; promotes good will and pride within the firm; and has a positive impact on the firm's economic performance.[11]

---

[11] *Ibid.*

Rather than leave pro bono undertakings up to individual lawyers, many firms create high-quality learning opportunities through organized pro bono programs.[12] Some firms sponsor fellowship programs or externships that allow lawyers to spend a set period of time working for a specified legal services firm or public interest organization (much like the loaner programs discussed above). Fellows receive training and hands-on experience, and the organization benefits from free, on-site legal assistance. Still other firms allow senior associates to take a paid leave of absence in order to undertake full-time pro bono work. All of these programs were begun not simply for the public good but also to develop and retain good lawyers.

Firms that recognize the relationship between pro bono practice and professional development frequently combine the two. Many firms appoint a partner or professional development specialist to run both the professional development and pro bono programs. This facilitates integration of the pro bono program with the work allocation process so that developmental considerations can be applied to pro bono assignments. There are a few issues to keep in mind, however, about pro bono assignments.

- **Most pro bono work is voluntary.** Few firms mandate pro bono work, but many expressly allocate a certain number of hours per lawyer to pro bono activities. If pro bono assignments are voluntary under the firm's pro bono policy, then they will not be assigned to associates without their agreement. Instead, associates are invited to volunteer for specific pro bono projects that afford good development opportunities for them.

- **Credit for pro bono hours.** How does your firm treat pro bono hours for purposes of determining productivity, promotions, and pay?[13] If the firm treats pro bono work as less important, or penalizes lawyers for doing it, associates may not take advantage of these assignments and the learning opportunities they provide. Firms approach pro bono credit in many different ways. Some firms are very direct — they do not give billable hour credit for pro bono activities. Any pro bono work is done on a lawyer's own time. Others track pro bono hours, but do so in a second "non-billable" category, along with client development, firm committee work, and administrative firm responsibilities. These firms generally claim that they give credit for

---

[12] Information on establishing pro bono programs is available from The Pro Bono Institute (www.probonoinst.org), The Corporate Pro Bono Project of the American Corporate Counsel Association (www.CorporateProBono.Org), the American Bar Association Pro Bono Project, and many state and local bar associations.

[13] For a discussion of this issue and suggested approaches, see ABA Commission on Billable Hours Report, August 2002.

pro bono time, but they tend to be vague about the weight they give it. This ambiguity frequently causes misunderstanding and friction. A great many law firms claim that lawyers receive equivalent credit for pro bono and billable hours, usually up to a certain number of hours per year. Firms that make such promises must abide by them. It undermines the firm's credibility to avow a policy of parity but decide compensation, bonuses, or promotions on the basis of billable work alone.

- **Supervision.** While pro bono assignments present wonderful opportunities for associates to work independently, associates still need to be supervised. A partner must have ultimate responsibility for every pro bono representation the firm accepts. You might put a specific partner in charge of supervising all pro bono matters or put one partner in charge of each matter, but someone must have oversight responsibility for every pro bono assignment.

- **Limits on pro bono.** The firm should be precise about what it considers a reasonable and acceptable pro bono time commitment. Associates who take on a substantial amount of pro bono work can get into trouble if their hourly billing targets are not met. Unfortunately, pro bono policies tend to be vague about three important points: if and how pro bono work is applied toward billable hour requirements (discussed above), how much pro bono is deemed "too much," and the repercussions of exceeding that limit. Mentors and assignment brokers should review associates' pro bono hours before a new pro bono engagement is undertaken and counsel those whose pro bono hours are greater than the firm deems prudent.

- **Non-litigation pro bono projects.** In most communities, there are plenty of pro bono opportunities for litigation lawyers, but it is often hard to find pro bono matters where transactional lawyers and lawyers in other fields of practice can put their expertise to use. State, local, and specialty bar associations, volunteer legal services clinics, and public interest groups can help you find pro bono work for these lawyers. Moreover, all lawyers can represent pro bono clients in matters requiring legal skills that are not practice-specific, like problem solving, negotiating, and counseling.

"You make a living by what you get and you make a life by what you give." — Sir Winston Churchill

CHAPTER 6

Mentoring: Promoting Development Through Relationships

"Our chief want is someone who will inspire us to be what we know we could be." — Ralph Waldo Emerson

Mentoring is a vital and highly desired professional development process. Its positive impact on lawyers is firmly established.[1] Mentors do not guarantee a lawyer's success, but they can save talented associates from failure and turn ordinary lawyers into stars. Mentoring is a developmental relationship in which one member helps the other to achieve personal goals and career success. In the context of a law firm, people usually think of mentors as partners. A partner who cares about an associate's development can guide that associate's experience, steer the associate to assignments that let the associate shine, get the associate appointed to key committees, introduce the associate to important business contacts, and boost the associate's reputation and prestige in ways that lead to rapid advancement. Lawyers can achieve great success without any help from mentors, but few would turn down such help if it were offered.

The benefits of mentoring for lawyers and for the firm are well known.[2] Mentoring:

- Accelerates learning and helps lawyers develop professional excellence in a cost-effective way.

- Increases lawyer productivity and law firm profitability.

---

[1] Ida O. Abbott, *The Lawyer's Guide to Mentoring*, NALP, Washington, DC, 2000; Jean E. Wallace, "The Benefits of Mentoring for Female Lawyers," *Journal of Vocational Behavior* 58, 366-391 (2001); David A. Thomas, "The Truth About Mentoring Minorities: Race Matters," *Harvard Business Review*, April, 2001; Catalyst, *Women in the Law: Making the Case*, New York, 2001.

[2] *The Lawyer's Guide to Mentoring*; *Keeping the Keepers: Strategies for Associate Retention in Times of Attrition*, The NALP Foundation for Law Career Research and Education, 1998, and *Perceptions of Partnership: The Allure and Accessibility of the Brass Ring*, The NALP Foundation, 1999.

- Helps recruitment by demonstrating the firm's commitment to professional development.

- Improves work satisfaction.

- Increases associate retention.

- Assists the career advancement of associates, especially women and minorities.

- Promotes the firm's continuity and stability by building loyalty, transmitting firm culture, and developing new leaders.

Many lawyers believe that mentoring takes place in a structured way, with assigned roles and scheduled encounters. But most mentoring happens naturally and informally every day as lawyers work together. It occurs during the frequent, one-on-one interactions in which one lawyer shares with another the skills and art of the profession. No one labels this mentoring at the time, but the elements and effects of the mentoring process are readily apparent. Informal mentoring is more likely to occur in small practice groups or teams, where partners and associates work side by side. Partners explain their thinking, model professional behaviors, and routinely offer feedback and suggestions. Associates learn by observing, listening, and being included in the partners' work. Relationships develop in which partners become associates' career advisers and sponsors. It is through such mentoring relationships that associates learn and develop. As they progress, their competence and satisfaction grow, as does their commitment to their work and to the firm.

Mentoring also has important benefits for mentors. Although the mentoring process focuses on the development of the mentee, mentoring relationships are reciprocal. Mentors acquire new perspectives, hone professional skills, and derive personal satisfaction from helping promising lawyers learn and grow. Mentoring also aids mentors in their daily work. Good mentors attract and keep good associates, which makes it easier for them to provide high-quality service for clients.

The conditions of today's law practice inhibit mentoring. In the haste and pressure of practice, partners are too busy to form mentoring relationships. These relationships are even harder to achieve in large practice groups and teams, where few associates have a chance to work closely with a partner. The economics of law practice, particularly the primacy of billable work and competitive pressures among partners, contribute to this failure.[3] In addition, many partners do not realize the substantial role mentoring plays in associate development, lack the skills

---

[3] See ABA Commission on Billable Hours Report, August 2002.

to be effective mentors, and are not urged by their firms to be mentors. This ultimately harms the firm, because the absence of widespread mentoring leads to dissatisfaction, morale problems, poor performance, low productivity, and high turnover among associates.

Mentoring is especially critical for women and minority associates. Studies of women and minority lawyers consistently find that the absence of mentors is a serious impediment to their career advancement.[4] But these lawyers have a harder time finding mentors. They face an inherent disadvantage because of the dearth of women and minority partners, and the reluctance of many majority male partners to serve as their mentors. Women and lawyers of color also tend to be excluded from informal social networks where many lawyers meet their future mentors. As a result, they do not find mentors as easily or frequently as their white male counterparts.

Because mentoring is an essential part of professional development, firms must promote its occurrence. As a general rule, research has found that neither the availability nor the quality of informal mentoring is consistent or equitable in law firms.[5] Consequently, while informal mentoring is preferred and should be encouraged, formal mentoring programs are also necessary. Formal programs ensure that all associates have access to mentors. Effective mentoring programs have limited and well-defined goals and a realistic design supported by sufficient resources. Through published guidelines, programs set specific standards for participants to honor. By training participants, firms make it more likely that they can meet those standards.

Formal mentoring programs are only one of several development systems that *together* foster the development of lawyers. Mentoring programs should not be expected to produce profound, long-term mentoring relationships, or serve as panaceas for associate attrition or morale problems. Instead, they should be seen as providing associates the chance to work with one person who acts as a mentor for a limited purpose focused on the associate's development. Accordingly, associates cannot rely entirely on assigned mentors for their professional development and career guidance. They should learn what they can from their assigned mentors and use that knowledge and experience to find other mentors who can help them throughout their careers.

---

[4] Thomas, *supra*; Catalyst, *supra*; *Perceptions of Partnership, supra*.
[5] *Perceptions of Partnership*, p. 52.

The Influence of Mentors

Mentors fulfill two sets of distinct but related functions: career and psychosocial.[6] Career functions promote career development and advancement and include such activities as work assignments, coaching, introductions to clients, networking opportunities, appointments to committees, and sponsorship for promotion and higher compensation. Mentors accelerate mentees' skill development through teaching, role modeling, and inclusion in client activities. They provide access to information about how the firm operates that is not always available through official channels. The career aspect of mentoring improves associates' performance and facilitates their advancement.

Psychosocial functions enhance the mentee's sense of confidence, competence, and effectiveness. These functions promote identity formation and socialization in the firm. Mentors bring mentees into informal social networks that make them feel included, and give mentees insights into firm dynamics that facilitate their adaptation to the work environment. The psychosocial function has a positive influence on work satisfaction, work commitment, work-related stress, and turnover. It also leads to more realistic career expectations.

Lawyers need mentors at every stage of their careers, especially when they assume new responsibilities or face changes, challenges, or transitions. Young lawyers often mistakenly assume that they need just one influential mentor in the firm. While having the "right" mentor can indeed provide a huge advantage, the length of a legal career, plus the uncertainty and fluidity of today's legal workplace, makes reliance on a single mentor unwise. Because turnover is high in both associate and partner ranks, associates cannot rely on a mentor remaining in the firm forever. Moreover, one mentor can provide valuable assistance in various ways but can rarely fulfill all of an associate's development needs. Consequently, associates are better advised to build a "personal board" of several mentors and advisers who can help them in different ways at different times in their careers. This process does not end when associates become partners. New partners continue to need mentors to help them face new responsibilities; senior partners need mentors when they assume advanced leadership roles or face retirement.

Many associates find mentors naturally and without special effort. They tend to be associates who exhibit qualities and traits that make them more attractive to potential mentors: excellent work product, good work habits, eagerness to learn,

---

[6] K. E. Kram, *Mentoring at Work: Developmental Relationships in Organizational Life,* Scott, Foresman, Glenview, IL, 1985.

positive attitude, ambition, and a drive to succeed. All associates should be encouraged to initiate mentoring relationships in order to promote their own development and enhance career success. In order to find partners or other individuals willing to act as mentors, associates should be encouraged to display the traits that potential mentors find appealing. They should be aware of their developmental needs and identify potential mentors who can help them address those needs. Sources of this information include their annual or semi-annual evaluations, informal feedback, and discussions with current mentors and supervisors. Because finding their own mentors may be unfamiliar and uncomfortable for many associates, firms can provide specific training to demystify the process.

Enhancing Informal Mentoring

Firms that want to concentrate their efforts on enhancing naturally occurring mentoring relationships should foster and reward informal mentoring practices. For mentoring to occur routinely and seamlessly, all partners must personally model good mentoring practices and teach them to others. On an institutional level, the firm needs to provide training in mentoring skills, reward good mentoring practices, and consider mentoring activities when evaluating lawyers and making promotion decisions.

- Mentoring becomes the norm when partners regularly act as mentors to associates and to each other. Such partners serve as excellent role models. They adopt high standards for mentoring and hold themselves accountable to those standards. They expect all lawyers who supervise associates to do some informal mentoring, and they welcome training programs that teach mentoring skills. Most importantly, they do not let the firm tolerate behavior that is contrary to the principles of good mentoring.

- Your firm can promote mentoring through training programs that teach lawyers the principles and skills necessary for effective mentoring. In addition to holding periodic training workshops or demonstrations, you can supplement formal training with other measures that educate lawyers about mentoring practices. Here are four simple steps to augment formal training:

  — Distribute written materials that contain useful ideas and suggestions about mentoring, e.g., articles from journals about mentoring, lists of "mentoring tips" and "best mentoring practices" (preferably generated by your own lawyers), profiles of outstanding mentors,

and announcements of special firm-sponsored activities that promote mentoring.[7]
— Hold conferences and informal get-togethers (e.g., brown bag lunches) to discuss mentoring issues. To give these sessions a mentoring focus, you might invite special guests, such as clients to talk about mentoring in their organizations, prominent individuals to describe significant mentoring experiences they have had, or mentoring consultants to answer questions about mentoring relationships.
— Build a library of books, videos, journals, and similar resources dedicated to mentoring. Encourage lawyers to use and contribute to the firm's collection of mentoring resources.
— Dedicate a page of your firm's intranet to mentoring. On that page, post the firm's mentoring resources, display a calendar of mentoring activities, and link to web sites that deal with mentoring. Create a chat room where lawyers can post questions and discuss mentoring issues.

■ All mentors should be publicly recognized and rewarded, and time devoted to mentoring should be given favorable consideration when determining partner compensation. When associates act as mentors, their efforts should also be acknowledged and considered when calculating bonuses. Rewarding good mentoring practices reinforces the importance of good mentoring, singles out mentors who are the best role models, and highlights practices to emulate.

■ Mentoring activities should be a consideration in evaluating and promoting lawyers. All partners should be evaluated on their performance as mentors. Firms should begin to evaluate lawyers' mentoring competencies while they are still associates. In this way, the firm sends a powerful message that mentoring is important and that all lawyers are expected to exercise good mentoring habits. Being an active and effective mentor should be a prerequisite for making partner. Through partner peer reviews or upward evaluations by associates, partners who are good mentors should be identified and their efforts supported, recognized, and reinforced. Partners who are found to be poor mentors should be given coaching or additional training and expected to make a stronger mentoring effort.

---

[7] Handy resources include two booklets, "Being an Effective Mentor: 101 Practical Strategies for Success," and "Working with a Mentor: 50 Practical Suggestions for Success," written by Ida O. Abbott, published by and available from NALP (www.nalp.org).

Firms can also enhance informal mentoring by making it easier for people to initiate and engage in mentoring relationships. You might maintain a list of individuals who are interested in being or having a mentor and make this information available to all lawyers in the firm. Additionally, you could appoint an individual to field questions about mentoring, help associates find a mentor, and assist lawyers who are having problems in a mentoring relationship.

Establishing a Mentoring Program

A mentoring program represents an effort to systematically promote the professional development of a targeted group of lawyers through assigned and focused mentoring relationships. Rather than leave mentoring to chance, a formal program facilitates mentoring by creating mentoring relationships between pairs or small groups of willing participants, and providing the training, resources, and support needed to fortify effective mentoring practices. Law firms often implement mentoring programs as part of new lawyer orientation and for many different reasons (e.g., retention, diversity, leadership development, learning in a particular field). While most mentoring programs feature partners and senior associates as mentors and associates as mentees, many innovative approaches are being used to suit various law firm needs. Some firms use group mentoring, matching one or two partners with a small group of associates. (See sidebar.) One variation of this approach employs a small team of partners to serve as mentors for all new associates. Another approach is "upward mentoring," where junior associates are paired with senior partners but with the usual roles reversed: the associates act as mentors to the partners. The purpose of upward mentoring is twofold: to promote interaction between partners and associates, and to have associates share their specialized knowledge with partners. Associate mentors might teach partners how to utilize technology more effectively or provide insight to partners on how young lawyers perceive the firm or the way it is managed.

To be successful, formal mentoring programs must be carefully planned, implemented, and monitored. Appendix 6-A at the end of this chapter is a checklist to help you carry out that process. The program should provide sufficient structure to facilitate and support mentoring relationships, and enough flexibility to accommodate participants' personal interests and needs. The program design should also be adaptable. Your firm might establish one mentoring program for the entire firm or permit different offices or practice groups to design their own programs as long as they are all consistent with the firm's vision for formal mentoring. Keep in mind, however, that oversight becomes more complicated and expensive when different groups structure their own programs.

> **Group Mentoring**
>
> Not all mentoring is one-on-one. A program model that is generating growing interest is group mentoring in which one or two mentors are matched with a group of three to six associates (or junior partners). When certain mentors are extremely popular, or when mentors are in short supply (e.g., women and minority mentors), this allows a single partner to maximize his or her exposure to associates without becoming overloaded. Mentors may lead a group singly or pair up with another mentor, and two or more mentoring groups might also meet together from time to time. Similarly, mentors can invite associates within the group to pair up as one-on-one peer mentors. These pairs mentor each other and may also work on special presentations for the group.
>
> One firm has a group mentoring program that divides associates into groups according to seniority. There are groups for first-year associates, mid-level associates (second- to fourth-year), and senior associates (fifth-year and up). The purpose of the program is to promote associates' professional development, collegiality, and retention, and its design exposes associates to at least two partners who are expected to provide career guidance. The groups also cross practice boundaries, so lawyers from different practice areas get to know each other. Breaking the associates into seniority-based groups allows mentors to address development issues of greatest concern to associates at different stages of development. Each group of two mentors and four to six associates meets at least once a month for a year and works on issues that the group agrees upon.

Some people think mentoring programs are just for large firms. To the contrary, small and mid-size firms also benefit from mentoring programs designed to ensure developmental experience and guidance for associates. One 31-lawyer firm that has successfully implemented a mentoring program is Morgan, Miller & Blair in Walnut Creek, California. The firm's mentoring program is designed to help build and retain successful lawyers by addressing associates' professional development needs. A mentoring committee of five partners and associates runs the program. Associates are asked to identify development needs and matched with mentors who can help them address those needs. Where two lawyers already have an informal mentoring relationship, the firm tries to keep them together. All but the most junior associates may be mentors in the program, and some of the firm's experienced associates are both mentors and mentees.

Most people would prefer to have a "natural" mentor rather than one who is assigned through an institutional program. When mentor and mentee gravitate to each other naturally, their self-selection reflects a level of interest and motivation that increases the likelihood of a successful relationship. Formal mentoring programs are not intended to replace informal mentoring but to supplement it. Programs that provide formal mentoring experiences are limited in scope, time, and purpose. However, working with an assigned mentor makes it easier for associates to acquire informal mentors in the future. Occasionally, assigned mentoring relationships do move beyond the parameters of the formal program to become more intense and long-term. But at the very least, associates benefit from the careful attention of at least one assigned mentor.

Mentors should be distinguished from "buddies." Firms customarily assign an associate to every new and lateral lawyer to make them feel welcome, introduce them to others, and answer questions about the firm. Many firms call these assigned associates mentors, but in fact, they really act as buddies. They perform important socializing functions and have the potential to become a peer mentor. But associates need mentoring relationships that go directly to the heart of professional development: work experience.

For maximum developmental impact, assigned mentors must be involved in the work the associate does. They do not have to supervise the associate's assignments or critique work product, but they have to know what the associate is working on and who the associate is working with. Without that knowledge, mentors cannot give associates the advice they need to make decisions, plans, and necessary moves to aid their professional growth and development. How mentors get involved in associate's work experience varies with each program. In some firms, mentors demonstrate, model, and teach, while in others they are simply available as needed to discuss progress on work assignments. In some programs mentors act as coaches. In that role, they help associates set development goals, develop a plan to achieve those goals, and support them while they carry out the plan. In other programs, mentors take part in the evaluation process or the work assignment process, monitoring the amount and quality of the associate's work and helping the associate find appropriate developmental assignments.

Formal mentoring programs usually begin enthusiastically with high hopes and expectations of success. Unfortunately, many programs fail after the initial surge of eagerness. The reasons for failure are numerous, but most can be prevented by carefully designing the program to fit the specific culture and needs of the firm.

Mentoring Program Elements

Effective mentoring programs share certain essential elements:

- Leadership commitment.
- Clear and specific program objectives.
- Program guidelines.
- A program coordinator.
- A process for selecting and matching mentors and mentees.
- Incentives for participants.
- Training in mentoring skills.

Leadership Commitment

No mentoring program can succeed without the vigorous support of the firm's leaders. It is the leaders' job to make the strategic case for a mentoring program. They must work to achieve consensus within the firm about the value of mentoring and the strategic importance of the program. The firm must fully appreciate, accept, and support mentoring as a means to achieving its business goals. Tying mentoring to business strategy is not hard. Mentoring produces the talented, highly proficient lawyers that the firm needs in order to survive. Mentoring is directly and positively related to associate recruitment, performance, loyalty, and retention.[8] It increases the firm's financial performance by increasing productivity of both mentor and mentee.[9] These facts clearly establish mentoring as a business imperative.

Leaders must champion the mentoring program as a firm priority and create an environment where mentoring will thrive. They must promote the firm's commitment to mentoring as a means of professional development; persuade the firm to underwrite mentoring activities; reward mentoring efforts; and actively participate in the program as mentors and role models. Leaders must not only build support for the concept of mentoring as a firm priority, but also hold partners accountable for making the program work.

---

[8] Abbott, *The Lawyer's Guide to Mentoring*.
[9] *Ibid.*

Clear and Specific Program Objectives

Mentoring programs require realistic expectations. The key to managing these expectations is to clarify program objectives. Clearly articulated program objectives tell participants what they can expect and what is expected of them in the mentoring program. Many mentoring programs fail because participants are confused about what the program is supposed to accomplish and what they are supposed to do. When objectives are not defined, expectations for mentoring programs tend to be unrealistically lofty. Participants may believe that mentors and mentees are bound together for a lifetime and that mentors will turn mentees into expert practitioners, protect them against failure, and ease their way into the partnership. It is essential that these expectations be brought down to earth.

One way to begin is by articulating the purpose of your firm's mentoring program and how it supports the firm's strategic goals. Explain why the program is needed and how it can address development needs. When your purpose is clearly understood, you can write program objectives and identify the group or groups to be mentored (e.g., all new associates, lateral associates, junior partners). By going through this process, you may find that your program has several objectives that affect different target groups. In that case, state program objectives for each target group.

Program objectives should be narrowly defined, realistic, and measurable. Specificity ensures that everyone will know exactly what the program hopes to accomplish. Realism ensures that the program can succeed in your firm's work environment and culture. Measurability is necessary in order to determine whether the mentoring program accomplishes your objectives.

One type of mentoring program that demonstrates the value of clear and narrow objectives is performance-based mentoring. As its name suggests, a performance-based mentoring program primarily addresses the mentee's performance. This type of mentoring program emphasizes the mentor's role as coach. (See sidebar.) Mentors and associates focus on a few specific performance goals to be achieved within a prescribed period of time. The mentoring relationship concentrates on the identification and achievement of those goals, which usually involve learning new skills, improving existing skills, or having a particular kind of work experience (e.g., handling a negotiation, more contact with clients, public speaking). The performance-based mentor's role is to help the associate find resources, assignments, or opportunities; coach and support the associate along the way; and get to know the associate better in the process. Because the program objectives and responsibilities are so clearly, specifically, and narrowly defined, participants can readily accomplish them.

Coaching and Mentoring

Many people refer to coaching and mentoring interchangeably. Both processes have much in common: They promote learning, require special interpersonal skills, and have an impact on a lawyer's career. But there are some important distinctions.

A coach helps you identify and set goals and develop a strategy to achieve those goals, then gives you support while you implement your strategy. Coaching deals primarily with improving performance or productivity; it is result-oriented and works toward specific goals. Coaches frequently work with lawyers one-on-one in particular areas of performance, such as presentation skills, time management, leadership style, or writing. Mentors and supervising partners frequently act as coaches, but if the issue involves changing a lawyer's problematic behavior, law firms and individual lawyers often hire professional coaches instead.

Mentoring is broader in scope and purpose than coaching, and mentoring is based on a deeper, more meaningful relationship than coaching. The quality of the mentoring relationship, and the factors that determine quality — trust, mutual respect, and mutual learning — are critical to the mentoring process. Mentoring potentially covers more wide-ranging career issues than coaching because it deals with mentees' overall professional development, not simply certain performance goals. Coaching is just one of the techniques mentors use, along with confidence building, role modeling, counseling, and advocacy. Mentors are more likely than coaches to use their own experiences, insights, and advice to help the mentee learn.

When your mentoring program's objectives are fixed and the mentees targeted, you can define the role of the mentor. The responsibilities of assigned mentors should be consistent with the objectives of the program. If you have different objectives for different target groups, the mentors' responsibilities will likely vary for each group. It is not uncommon to have two or three separate roles for mentors within the same mentoring program, and many firms appoint two mentors for every associate, each mentor serving a different purpose. At Wiley Rein & Fielding LLP, every lateral associate is matched with five different mentors. Three of them — a junior associate, senior associate, and partner in their practice area — serve as "primary mentors" who provide assistance with work assignments. Two lawyers outside the associate's practice area act as "support mentors" and take responsibility for the lateral associate's social integration in the firm.

> **TABLE 1. Responsibilities of Two Types of Assigned Mentors**
>
> **I. Mentors responsible for integrating new associates into the firm and the practice**
>
> — Introduce associate to other practice group members.
>
> — Provide or arrange for at least two initial, diverse, and significant work assignments.
>
> — Foster professional relationships with other lawyers by inviting the associate to social events and small group lunches.
>
> — Provide information regarding the firm's policies, lawyers, and practice groups.
>
> **II. Mentors responsible for associates' career development and preparation for partnership**
>
> — Provide career counseling, using the firm's career benchmarks as guidelines.
>
> — Help associate align work assignments with long-term career goals.
>
> — Identify and arrange introductions to partners whom the associate needs to meet in other practice groups and offices.
>
> — Provide guidance and opportunities for business development.
>
> — Advise the associate on how to establish and maintain strong client relationships.
>
> — Provide information and guidance on partnership opportunities.

Table 1 illustrates responsibilities that might be expected of two different types of assigned mentors, one who assists with associate integration and one who focuses more on career development. When a program targets more senior associates, mentors might focus specifically on skills and practices required for partnership, such as leadership and business development. In mentoring programs for new partners, mentors might function as sponsors and champions, enabling mentees to maneuver and rise within the new and unfamiliar world of partnership politics.

Mentoring programs, work assignment, and evaluation processes all interrelate, and, in a comprehensive professional development program, they should be integrated. Mentors can participate in assignments and evaluations directly, by supervising mentees on work assignments, steering them to new assignments, monitoring existing assignments, overseeing evaluations, or being involved in associates' performance reviews. If the firm uses career benchmarks in the evaluation process, mentors can use them in counseling associates about career development.

Occasionally, mentoring programs use "Learning Contracts" or "Mentoring Agreements" to provide even greater clarity and accountability to the mentoring relationship. Mentoring agreements memorialize what the mentor and mentee agree to do during their time together. These agreements remind the mentoring pair of what each is supposed to be doing and make it easier for them to accomplish their purpose. By referring to the mentoring agreement when they get together, they can follow their progress and see what they have accomplished — or neglected. Although mentoring agreements can resemble formal legal documents, it is better to keep them simple and straightforward. Mentoring agreements need simply be statements of what the associate and mentor have agreed to do. They usually set down such items as when the two will meet, how they will stay in touch between meetings, what issues they will explore, what goals the associate has set, what actions they will take in furtherance of those issues or goals, and how they will handle confidential information. See Appendix 6-B.

Program Guidelines

Program objectives outline the purpose and scope of the mentoring program. Guidelines go into greater detail. They clarify what is expected of participants, provide direction, and minimize the chances for confusion. Guidelines need not be exhaustive, but they should be sufficiently detailed to provide direction to program participants. Items to be included in mentoring program guidelines are listed in Table 2. Guidelines should be written and distributed to all lawyers.

The topics listed in Table 2 are discussed throughout this chapter. Following are a few additional points:

- **How participation is determined.** Because it involves a personal relationship based on trust, mentoring must be voluntary. A program can facilitate mentoring, but it cannot mandate that mentoring shall occur. Lawyers who are unwilling to participate should be permitted to decline without penalty.

- **Duration of the assigned mentoring relationship.** For development purposes, assignments should be at least six months to one year. A shorter period is insufficient for mentors to monitor associates' specific development goals. Assigned relationships can conclude at the end of the agreed upon term, although mentoring pairs who wish to continue informally beyond the time period set by the program should be encouraged to do so.

TABLE 2. Contents of Mentoring Program Guidelines

- Program purpose and objectives
- How the program objectives should be met
- How program objectives will be monitored
- How the program will be evaluated
- Responsibilities of mentor
- Responsibilities of associate
- How the mentoring relationship works
- Role of program coordinator
- How mentors and associates will be matched
- Duration of the mentoring relationship
- Time commitment
- How mentoring activities should be recorded (i.e., billable or non-billable)
- Confidentiality
- What to do if problems arise in the mentoring relationship
- Budget

■ **Time commitment expected from participants.** The amount of time participants should devote to mentoring has to be limited, realistic, and spelled out clearly. One of the most serious handicaps in mentoring programs is an unrealistic expectation of the time lawyers are able and willing to commit to assigned mentoring relationships. Mentoring does take time, but not as much time as most lawyers believe. When the objectives and scope of the mentoring relationship are sharply focused, and participants understand how to utilize their time to achieve specified objectives, mentoring can be done in a time-efficient manner. To dispel any misunderstanding or anxiety about the time commitment expected from participants, the guidelines should give lawyers an estimate of the time they should devote to mentoring on a weekly or monthly basis. While some firms prescribe a set amount of time, most prefer just to make recommendations.

■ **Scope of the relationship.** Explaining what is and is not within the scope of the mentoring relationship makes it easier for participants to concentrate on achieving program goals. Although they may decide on their own what kinds of issues they want to address, it is important for participants to understand at the outset what kinds of development issues they should cover, and what if anything is expressly outside the scope of the mentoring relationship.

■ **Confidentiality.** Mentoring involves risk. Mentors and mentees often discuss issues that are sensitive or embarrassing. It is important for the integrity of the mentoring relationship that the question of confidentiality be decided at the outset. Your firm can issue a confidentiality policy, or it can leave the decision up to the lawyers in each mentoring pair. A policy about confidentiality might provide that all communications are confidential or that all communications are not confidential. If the policy favors confidentiality, mentors and associates are expected to keep communications between them in strict confidence. Even when policies promise confidentiality, however, there are exceptions to the rule. Two common exceptions are: (1) the mentoring pair can override the policy by mutual agreement, or (2) when disclosure is required by law, rules of professional responsibility, or another firm policy.

- **Financial support from the firm.** Many firms provide financial support for mentors. Mentors use the funds to take their assigned mentees out for a meal or an event. Financial support is especially important for associates who are acting as mentors in your program. The guidelines should state the amount of the mentor's budget, how it should be used, and how to access the money.

Because the nature and quality of each mentoring relationship is unique, guidelines should allow for flexibility in mentoring relationships or activities and not try to regulate them. The success of any relationship depends on many variables, including the motivation, commitment, and mentoring skills of each party; how well the mentor's abilities match the associate's needs; and each party's work demands and personal distractions. The firm cannot guarantee that associates will derive any particular level of satisfaction or meaning from their assigned mentoring relationships. The best it can do is to recommend objectives, provide guidelines, sponsor activities for the participants' benefit, and hold people accountable for their commitments to the program and to each other.

A Program Coordinator

In every mentoring program, there should be one person who is accountable for implementation and oversight. If you are responsible for directing professional development in your firm (whether in a full-time role or as part of a broader job description), you are in an ideal position to coordinate the mentoring program. The role of program coordinator is also often assumed by a professional development partner. Firms with several offices should have local coordinators in each location where the program is in effect. Whoever coordinates the program must be allotted sufficient time and administrative support to do the job.

Program oversight is indispensable for a mentoring program's success. An informal national survey of law firm mentoring programs conducted by Morrison

& Foerster in 2001, found that the most effective mentoring programs had ongoing oversight. Conversely, lack of adequate monitoring is one the main reasons that programs fail. Mentoring programs are not self-executing. If mentoring were prevalent in a firm, there would be no need for a program to make it happen. By their very nature, programs impose specific responsibilities on very busy lawyers with other priorities and demands on their time. To ensure that responsibilities are carried out, someone must constantly enlist participants, issue reminders, monitor performance, make sure the program works as intended, and adjust it when necessary to keep things going smoothly.

Program coordinators see that mentees' needs are being met and that the program's purpose is being achieved. They perform a variety of specific functions, including the following:

- Manage program logistics.
- Direct the process for matching mentors and mentees.
- Monitor mentoring participants to ensure that they are engaged and pursuing program objectives.
- Watch for and respond to any problems in mentoring relationships.
- Evaluate the program to determine whether it is achieving its stated objectives.
- Facilitate continuous improvement of the program.
- Integrate the mentoring program with the firm's other professional development systems.
- Manage the budget.

Because of the delicate political and interpersonal issues that can arise, program coordinators must have the trust and respect of all participants. Because of the monitoring responsibilities involved in the job, coordinators should be tactful yet firm.

A Process for Selecting and Matching Mentors and Mentees

Matching associates with mentors is not as daunting as it seems. You are not arranging lifetime relationships. You are not deciding an associate's fate. You have a simple, narrow purpose: to pair people up to achieve specific, well-defined goals during a set period of time. By gathering information about the participants' strengths, needs, and interests, and by being sensitive to differences in personality and style, the matching process can work smoothly and with good results.

■ **Matching criteria.** Matching criteria should be delineated. The most important factor in a successful match is finding a mentor who is able to address the associate's development needs. Other criteria include compatible personalities and common interests, experiences, or backgrounds (e.g., colleges, law schools, hobbies). The more information you have before making matches, the better your matches will be. If the people doing the matching are familiar with the lawyers in the mentoring program, they may have sufficient knowledge of associates and partners to make effective matches. If more information is needed, it can be acquired from résumés, surveys, recruiting personnel, and interviews with participants. Consider using an online questionnaire to solicit pertinent information from potential program participants. An online questionnaire can make data collection easy and allow you to sort the data according to your matching criteria. This can facilitate the matching process, especially if you have large numbers of lawyers in your program who are unknown to the people making the matches.

■ **Matching process.** The program coordinator should supervise the matching process, in collaboration with others who are familiar with the associates and mentors in the program. Practice group leaders or department heads, and lawyers, administrators, recruiters, or staff who work with an associate might also be involved. Information about associates' development needs can be obtained from the evaluation process, work supervisors, and the associates directly. For new associates, sources of this information would most likely include the recruitment director, members of the hiring committee, the people who run the summer program, or a questionnaire.

■ **Choice.** Although the firm makes the final matching decisions, formal mentoring relationships have a better chance of success when the firm allows participants to select their mentoring partners. Your program should permit as much lawyer choice as possible in the matching process. You might allow associates to choose mentors, mentors to choose associates, or both. Relationships feel more natural and comfortable, and participants work better together, when they start with a positive regard for each other. New associates who have participated in your summer program or lateral associates who have friends in the firm may have enough information to request certain mentors. However, some new and lateral associates may not know enough about potential mentors to make requests. You can allow them extra time to make a choice or suggest mentors for them.

As with requests for work assignments, associates' requests for mentors should be honored whenever possible so that associates can be assigned mentors whom they like and respect. Ask associates to identify two or three people with whom they would like to be matched. The program coordinator should discuss the choices with the associate and make every effort to match the associate with one of the listed choices. Be sure to ask prospective mentors to approve a match before it is announced.

There may be situations when an associate's request for a particular mentor cannot or should not be honored. A requested partner may be unavailable during the time period or unwilling to mentor a particular associate. The partner may have personal problems unknown to the associate that would prevent effective mentoring or be harmful to the associate. The partner may not have the skills needed to help the associate with certain critical development needs, or a different partner might have special skills that could better address the associate's known needs. When an associate's request is not honored, the reasons should be explained as fully as possible, along with the reasons for the match that is made. The associate who is denied a particular partner should be assured that just because that partner is not formally assigned to them does not mean that a mentoring relationship with that partner is not possible. Indeed, associates should be encouraged and shown how to initiate mentoring relationships with lawyers they would like to have as mentors in the future.

■ **Recruiting mentors.** All partners should be encouraged to participate in the mentoring program. Every firm has a few lawyers who are naturally good mentors and associates love to work with them. But cast your net widely; with motivation and training, all lawyers who want to be mentors can do a good job for some associates. In recruiting mentors for the program, take into account the behaviors, attitudes, and work styles the firm would like to perpetuate, and look for mentors who will be effective role models, teachers, and counselors. Ask prospective mentors to assess their strengths and motivations as mentors, and be sure they can realistically devote sufficient time to mentoring activities. By identifying mentors' special talents, interests, and abilities, you can match prospective mentors with the associates who can benefit most from their attention. An associate who needs to focus on improving writing skills should be paired with a mentor who writes well, is patient, and likes to teach. An associate who needs a mentor to provide introductions to business contacts should be matched with a rainmaker who is well connected. If your mentoring program permits mentors to select mentees, circulate a list of prospective mentees to all lawyers who have agreed to be mentors.

You may need to recruit mentors for associates in small regional offices or practice groups where there are not enough on-site mentors. This means that mentees may not always work in the same office as their mentors. In "long-distance" mentoring, mentors and associates regularly communicate by telephone or e-mail and meet in person whenever possible (e.g., at firm-wide events).

■ **Mentors as supervisors.** One issue for the firm to decide is whether mentors will supervise mentees' work. Some law firms encourage a supervisory relationship between mentor and mentee, while others caution against it. In some programs, for example, mentors are expected to supervise their assigned associates on at least some work projects so that assigned mentoring relationships coincide as closely as possible with the natural mentoring relationships that arise as lawyers work together. Mentoring relationships in law firm programs tend to be more successful when mentors and associates spend some work time together. Contact and interaction occur more frequently and casually. The relationship seems less artificial and more spontaneous, and the pair have business interests in common, which leads to easier, less forced conversations. The associate finds it easier to approach the mentor to talk or seek advice, and has more opportunities to observe the mentor as a role model. Mentors are more inclined to pay attention to lawyers doing work for them; in this setting, they do not consider mentoring to be an extra time burden. Mentors who also supervise some of the associate's work tend to follow through more reliably on their mentoring responsibilities. They can also observe the associate's professional development firsthand and identify areas where growth is needed.

However, difficulties often arise when supervisors act as mentors. When mentors are also associates' work supervisors, associates may be inhibited from voicing insecurities or concerns for fear of damaging the mentor's opinion of them and thereby damaging their chances for advancement. Associates who do not get along with their assigned mentor/supervisor face a similar predicament. When the mentor is the problem, to whom does the associate go for help? Or what if the mentor treats the associate as a "personal associate," monopolizing the associate's time? The associate may feel vulnerable and stuck. In corporate mentoring programs, supervisors do not act as mentors; they are generally two or more levels apart in the organizational structure. The reason is to ensure that the mentor has no direct control over the mentee's evaluations or promotions, and to foster confidentiality and openness. The same reasoning holds true in a law firm, but the way most firms are organized makes this type of program structure hard to achieve.

Whether or not mentors should be permitted to supervise their mentees depends in large part on a program's objectives and the trade-offs necessary to realize them. If your firm's program will allow mentors to supervise associates, be sure to include mechanisms to address these foreseeable problems. Having someone available to help the associate deal with mentor/supervisor issues alleviates dilemmas that arise from the mentor and associate's work relationship. A program coordinator who regularly checks on the associate's mentoring experience can intervene in situations involving mentor-mentee incompatibility or conflict. When mentoring pairs are asked to assess the progress of their relationship, they can be given the option of requesting a new or additional mentor or mentee. An ombudsperson can also be a source of assistance if the associate needs relief. (See Chapter 17.) Whatever your firm's procedures are, they should be spelled out in the program guidelines.

■ **Associate evaluations.** Mentors should be a source of support to their assigned associates during the performance evaluation process. Mentors should receive copies of the associate's written evaluations, either in their entirety or in summary form. They may act as advocates for the associate during partner discussions that precede the review, and may even take responsibility for collecting and processing the written evaluations. Mentors should prepare the associate for the review and debrief with the associate immediately afterward. Many mentors also participate in the review session. Because evaluations are an important source of information about the associate's performance strengths and deficiencies, the mentor and associate should refer to them when setting future development goals.

Incentives for Participants

A growing number of law firms give lawyers incentives for time spent in mentoring activities. They usually take the form of billable hour credit, compensation enhancement, or positive consideration in promotion decisions. These measures show that mentoring is valued and reduce the chance that lawyers will defer mentoring in favor of billable work. Firms that determine compensation only on billable hours and business origination send a signal that developing talent for the long term is not as valuable an activity as producing revenue today. Although a great deal of mentoring occurs during the production of billable work, mentoring and informal training also take place during non-billable activities. If firms do not reward these activities, most lawyers will not engage in them. Even lawyers who enjoy being mentors will be discouraged if they are criticized or financially penalized for spending "too much" time mentoring associates. This myopic attitude robs associates of important developmental guidance and hinders the development of superior associates for the long-term benefit of the firm.

A few law firms reduce the compensation of partners who are assessed as bad mentors. But most firms that value mentoring and are committed to development emphasize the positive; they find ways to recognize and reward lawyers who do it well. In some firms, compensation incentives are tied directly to mentoring, and partners who are outstanding mentors receive bonuses. In firms where mentoring is part of a retention program, mentors who reduce attrition among their associates may also receive a bonus.

Many firms give other kinds of tangible rewards to good mentors. Dorsey & Whitney, for example, has established a Partner of the Year Award to honor its best mentors. The award is more than just a token; in addition to a plaque and firm-wide recognition, the winner receives two round-trip, first-class airplane tickets to any city in the United States or coach-class tickets to any city in the world. The benefits of this award extend beyond the winning mentor to the firm at large. The names of all nominees and the reasons for their nomination are posted on the firm's intranet so that others can see and learn from them. In this way, the award recognizes good mentors, publicizes best mentoring practices, gives all lawyers incentives and specific suggestions to improve their own mentoring practices, and improves the quality of mentoring throughout the firm.

Training in Mentoring Skills

All lawyers need to be prepared to assume their roles in a mentoring relationship. Training gives lawyers a chance to learn and practice the skills necessary to make mentoring relationships successful. Mentors require certain specific competencies: management skills such as supervising, coaching, and giving feedback; interpersonal skills such as listening, counseling, and confidence building; and a capacity for empathy, self-awareness, and trust. Lawyers are not always proficient in these mentoring competencies. In fact, many superb lawyers are inept mentors. Training can give lawyers who are awkward or deficient in mentoring skills the concrete practices and techniques to increase their comfort and effectiveness in mentoring relationships. Training also benefits lawyers who are good mentors by reinforcing and improving their positive mentoring practices, and by teaching them new mentoring skills and techniques.

Associates also need training to prepare for their roles in the mentoring relationship. Younger lawyers must realize that mentoring is not something that "happens" to them. Associates must be proactive and inquisitive. They cannot sit back and wait for someone to mentor them. They have to take the initiative, seek mentors out, and engage them in conversation. They have to think about their career plans, identify development goals, seek feedback, and accept a mentor's advice and support. These activities are intuitive for some associates, but they are alien to many others. A training program should show associates how to do what it takes to build and get the most out of mentoring relationships.

Every formal mentoring program should include an introductory orientation that presents mentoring concepts and principles, and explains the expectations and guidelines for participation. A training curriculum should also be developed to address the skills, behaviors, and competencies that participants need to carry out the objectives of the program. (See Appendix 6-C.) The topics selected should cover the interpersonal dynamics of the mentoring process, teach specific mentoring skills, and raise awareness of the attitudes and behaviors necessary for effective mentoring relationships. Some of the core topics are listening and communication; supervision; giving and receiving feedback; identifying development needs; goal setting and coaching; and trust-building.

APPENDIX 6-A

Establishing a Mentoring Program: Checklist

A. Leadership commitment
   — How committed are your firm leaders to a structured mentoring program?

B. Program objectives
   — What do you want your mentoring program to achieve?
   — How will a mentoring program further the firm's business strategy?
   — What are your program objectives?
   — Are your objectives practical, realistic, and measurable?
   — Which attorneys will the program serve?
   — What professional development needs will it address?

C. Program parameters
   — How long will the mentoring relationship last?
   — What types of issues and concerns are within the scope of the mentoring relationship?
   — How much time should the mentor and associate spend in mentoring activities?
   — What should mentoring activities include?
   — How much money should mentors spend on mentoring activities?
   — Who will pay for these activities?

D. Procedure and criteria for matching mentors and associates
   — How will associates and mentors be matched?
   — What criteria will be used?
   — Will participants select their own mentors and/or protégés?
   — Who will make the matching decision?

E. Program management
   — Who will be your program coordinator?
   — What will the program coordinator do?

Source: *The Lawyer's Guide to Mentoring* by Ida O. Abbott, Esq. (NALP, 2000).

F. Training
- What will be included in your mentoring training curriculum?
- Who will provide the training?
- When will training be given?

G. Ongoing support and monitoring
- What kind of support will the program coordinator give to participants?
- How will the program be monitored?

H. Evaluation
- How and when will the program be evaluated?
- Who will do the evaluation?
- How will individual mentoring experiences be evaluated?
- How will success be measured?

I. Written guidelines
- Do your written guidelines cover all essential elements of the program?

J. Mentoring incentives
- How will you encourage and reward people who engage in mentoring activities?

K. Mentors
- Who are the potential mentors in your program?
- What attributes will you look for in potential mentors?
- Who can be mentors: partners? associates? retired partners? counsel? non-lawyer personnel?
- How will mentors be recruited?

L. Associates
- Which lawyers will be mentored in your program?
- Will you include all lawyers in a certain group?
- Will you limit participation to certain individuals?
- If the program will be limited, what will the selection criteria be?
- Will your program include part-time attorneys?

M. Mentor-associate relationships
- What will mentors' responsibilities be?
- What will associates' responsibilities be?
- Are mentor-associate communications confidential?
- Are there any limits on confidentiality?
- How will you deal with problems that arise in mentoring relationships?
- Will the mentor supervise the associate's work?
- If mentor and associate work together, how will that impact confidentiality?
- What will be the mentor's role in associate evaluations?

(M. Mentor-associate relationships, continued)

- How will the mentor be expected to handle sensitive information about the associate?
- What role, if any, will the mentor play in deciding the associate's work assignments?
- How will the mentor relate to the associate's supervising attorneys?
- How many mentors will be assigned to an associate?
- How many associates will be assigned to a mentor?

N. Pilot project

- Which individuals, groups, and offices, will be included?
- How long will the pilot project last?
- What procedure is in place to monitor and make adjustments?
- How will it be evaluated?

O. Marketing the program

- What will you use to market the program inside the firm?
- Do your materials inform and promote the program?
- Are your marketing materials designed to recruit participants for the program?
- Are your marketing materials designed to attract lawyers and clients to the firm?
- How will you launch your program?
- How will you educate your lawyers and staff about the program?
- What publicity materials will you use?

P. Integrating professional development activities

- Is your mentoring program coordinated with other professional development activities?
- Will the mentoring program coordinator coordinate any other aspects of associates' professional development?
- Will mentors play a role in coordinating any other professional development activities?

APPENDIX 6-B

Sample Mentoring Agreement

Mentee's Goals:
 1.
 2.
 3.

What mentee will do to achieve goals:　　　　　　　　　　**Time frame:**
 1.
 2.
 3.

What mentor will do to assist or support mentee:　　　　**Time frame:**
 1.
 2.
 3.

Duration of relationship: _____

Next meetings:
 How often: _____　　When? _____
 Where? _____　　　　How long? _____

Confidentiality:

Additional points:

Mentor: _____　　Mentee: _____　　Date: _____

APPENDIX 6-C

Mentoring: Core Training Curriculum

1. **Mentoring dynamics:**[1]
   - Why mentoring is important
   - How the mentoring process works
   - Commencing the relationship
   - Building trust
   - Building confidence
   - Support for risk-taking
   - Dealing with conflict
   - Transitions within the mentoring relationship
   - Ending the mentoring relationship

2. **Mentoring skills:**
   - Attentive listening
   - Communication styles and differences
   - Learning styles and differences
   - Modeling
   - Counseling
   - Coaching
   - Setting development goals
   - Negotiating development plans
   - Delegation
   - Supervision
   - Feedback
   - Objective performance evaluations
   - Advocacy

3. **Mentoring attitudes and behaviors:**
   - Self-awareness
   - Empathy
   - Dealing with differences[2]
   - Setting reasonable expectations
   - Taking initiative
   - Persistence
   - Demonstrating commitment
   - Being a worthy participant
   - Reflection
   - Showing appreciation

Source: *The Lawyer's Guide to Mentoring* by Ida O. Abbott, Esq. (NALP, 2000).
[1] For group mentoring, mentors need to also understand group dynamics and facilitation skills.
[2] Generational, gender, racial, ethnic, sexual orientation, disabilities.

CHAPTER 7

Using Evaluations to Promote Lawyers' Development

> *O wad some Power the giftie gie us*
> *To see ourselves as others see us!*
> — Robert Burns

In any profession, what counts is performance. The lawyers who join your firm have plenty of ability and potential, but they will not succeed unless they can perform at the level and in the way that the firm expects of them. You know that and so do they. What they don't always know is what kind of performance the firm expects from them. Remarkably few law firms give lawyers meaningful guidance on this crucial point. Instead of defining expectations and standards, firms assess associate performance by relying on the number of hours billed as an objective measure, and the "we know it when we see it" test as a subjective measure. This ill-defined approach does a disservice to both associates and the firm.

Associates need clearly defined performance standards that tell them not just how much work to do but also at what level of performance. They need guidance about what it takes to advance in the firm and what criteria the firm will apply in judging their readiness for promotion. And they need feedback that tells them to what extent their performance meets those criteria and expectations.

Partners fare no better. Partners are responsible for the firm's financial success by bringing in profitable business; for superb client service by managing work effectively; and for developing the lawyers they supervise through coaching, mentoring, and training. But they generally receive little or no guidance on how to carry out these responsibilities. Partners' achievement in the first category, profitability, is roughly reflected by the amount of money distributed to them at the end of the year, but they usually receive little or no feedback about the effectiveness of their performance in the last two categories.

Every firm has a critical interest in optimizing the performance and potential of all its lawyers. The best way to do this is through feedback based on clear, predetermined standards and an evaluation system to deliver feedback regularly and systematically. The most obvious purpose of giving lawyers feedback is to ensure that they work effectively and productively to serve clients and achieve the firm's business goals. An equal but less obvious purpose is to ensure that lawyers make the most of their talents. It is this developmental aspect of performance evaluations that is radically changing the way law firms approach and use evaluations. Firms that want to take advantage of the new developmental approaches to evaluations need to have a culture conducive to feedback, ongoing informal feedback, explicit performance standards, and a structured system for conducting regular evaluations. When these elements are in place, the firm can design and institute an evaluation system that maximizes lawyers' ongoing learning and achievements.

Informal Feedback and Formal Evaluations

Feedback conveys information about what others have observed and concluded about a lawyer's knowledge, skills, and behaviors at work. This information is central to determining whether a lawyer is performing up to accepted standards. It is well established that feedback has a profound and positive influence that improves performance and promotes development. (See Table 1.) When feedback is given regularly in the normal course of work, its immediacy and relevance help lawyers learn and understand what works well, what needs to be changed, and why. Daily, on-the-job, informal feedback is the quickest, most effective, and least expensive way to accelerate lawyers' learning, spur productivity, and upgrade overall performance. This is the feedback that associates most want and need.[1] It is the stimulus that provokes lawyers to continue what they do well, prevents them from forming bad habits, and corrects poor performance or bad behavior. Law firms also periodically need to give lawyers a more formal, comprehensive, and rigorous assessment of their performance. They customarily do this for associates through annual or biannual performance appraisals, which they call "evaluations" or "reviews."[2] Evaluations that cover six- to twelve-month intervals provide a summary

---

[1] *Keeping the Keepers: Strategies for Associate Retention in Times of Attrition,* The NALP Foundation for Law Career Research and Education, Washington, DC, 1998.

[2] Although "evaluation" technically refers to written assessments, and "review" means the in-person interview to discuss the assessments, the two terms are used interchangeably.

> **TABLE 1. How Feedback Influences Performance and Development**
>
> **Effective feedback:**
> - Guides lawyers to the level and quality of work that the firm expects.
> - Explains how the firm views lawyers' performance.
> - Informs associates whether they are progressing appropriately.
> - Inspires high performers and acts as an impetus for superior performance.
> - Motivates average performers to reach higher.
> - Reinforces and encourages positive behaviors.
> - Corrects undesirable behaviors.
> - Lets poor performers know what they must do to meet standards.
> - Requires partners to pay more serious attention to the associates they work with.
> - Shows lawyers the firm values them and takes an interest in their development.
> - Recognizes lawyers' good work.
> - Acts as a reality check. Reassures high performers and enlightens poor performers.

assessment of lawyers' performance and progress. When done well, these evaluations weave together the separate strands of informal feedback received from multiple sources over the intervening months. They allow us to see the larger patterns of performance and measure them against the firm's expectations. Evaluations let associates know whether they are reaching the levels of performance required for their jobs. If they are meeting expectations, they are rewarded by money and promotion; if not, they are usually given a chance to improve or they are asked to leave.

The need for feedback is not limited to associates, and firms are beginning to give serious attention to feedback for partners on their performance. Although few law firms currently conduct systematic evaluations of partners, the numbers are growing rapidly. As in associate evaluations, many reviews of partners are done for appraisal purposes, i.e., to assess adequacy of performance and determine compensation. But firms can also use partner evaluations to promote partners' development as law firm leaders and managers. One form of partner evaluation is the peer review, in which partners assess each other's contributions to the firm for purposes of compensation decisions. Some firms are also starting to conduct "upward" reviews, in which associates review the partners who supervise them. A small number of large firms are using more comprehensive "360° reviews," in which partners are evaluated by peers, subordinates, staff, managers, and clients.

A Culture Conducive to Feedback

Evaluation systems thrive in a trusting culture. The correlation and interdependence among performance evaluations, work environment, and firm culture are well established.[3] Most lawyers want a culture that holds people to high standards of performance in an open, trusting environment.[4] In this kind of environment, lawyers are willing to give feedback, able to deliver it effectively and constructively to others, and receptive to hearing feedback about themselves. They understand that evaluations serve a strategic function by strengthening lawyers' performance in pursuit of the law firm's goals.

Because evaluation systems are built on trust, lawyers must believe that the motivation behind the evaluation system is beneficent: to aid in learning and development. Punitive or authoritarian cultures act as a brake on candor. People will not be open and forthcoming about others' performance if they fear that honesty will bring punishment or retaliation. Conversely, well-designed and implemented evaluation systems can actually help build trust. Trust building is cumulative. If the purpose of evaluations is clearly understood, and if the process and its outcomes match the promised intentions and goals, trust in the firm and in the evaluation system mounts up with each successive review cycle. As people come to recognize the value of others' input, lawyers' receptivity to evaluation grows.

Another cultural precondition for an evaluation system is that reviewed lawyers must be given the opportunity and resources to learn needed skills and make necessary corrections. The firm must support development by leveraging the review into an occasion for learning by providing pertinent experience, training, mentoring, or coaching. Evaluations that point out deficiencies, even when done constructively, are not sufficient. Lawyers need guidance on *how* to improve and opportunities and support to let them learn and practice improvements.

There are many steps a firm can take to foster a culture where feedback will flourish. One important step is to adopt a set of performance standards that elucidate the firm's performance expectations through the criteria used in evaluations. When lawyers know and agree on the standards, they can more easily ask for, give, appreciate, and make use of feedback.

---

[3] *Fair Measure: Toward Effective Attorney Evaluations*, American Bar Association Commission on Women in the Profession, 1997, p. 6.

[4] *The War for Talent*, Ed Michaels, Helen Handfield-Jones, Beth Axelrod, Harvard Business School Press, 2001; David H. Maister, *Practice What You Preach*, The Free Press, NY, 2001; Ida O. Abbott, "'Happy Lawyer' Is Not an Oxymoron," *Developing Legal Talent*, NALP, Washington, DC, 2001, p. 237.

Basing Evaluations on Explicit Performance Standards

Law firms have long used evaluations for administrative reasons, to form the basis for decisions about promotion and compensation, and to create a record documenting the reasons for ultimate removal of a poor performer from the firm. They are now expanding the use of evaluations to influence lawyers' performance, aid their development, and track their progress. The use of specific, enumerated performance standards adds substantial value to the evaluation process by describing the skills, accomplishments, behaviors, and other factors to be evaluated. (See Table 2.) Such standards enhance fairness, produce clearer messages, result in better assessments, facilitate future planning, and prove the firm's commitment to the development of its lawyers.

■ Fairness

Enumerated performance standards promote fairness in evaluations. When the firm reaches consensus on the specifics of good lawyering, reviews are more relevant to the firm's business goals and the standards are more fairly applied. Using objective and observable performance standards lessens the potential for bias that exists when reviewers use their own subjective assumptions and value judgments. It also means that lawyers know in advance the bases upon which their performance will be evaluated; reviewers know what to look for in observing a lawyer's performance; and the chance that a lawyer will be unfairly surprised or blindsided by a reviewer's comments is significantly reduced.

No firm should tolerate bias or discrimination in evaluations. While firms are generally alert to overt signs of bias, it often shows up in subtle, less obvious ways. The most serious concern is that reviewers may hold stereotypes, assumptions, or prejudices that interfere with objective performance assessments of women and minority lawyers. Bias also creeps into evaluations when the reviewer dislikes or holds a grudge against the person being reviewed. Criticism of poor work quality is warranted; criticism that results from a personality clash or personal animosity is not. Explicit performance standards act a safeguard against such biases.

Careful drafting of performance standards also promotes fairness by requiring evaluations to be based upon objective and observable facts, behaviors, skills, and events, not mere conclusions. This is especially important to protect women and minorities against unfair assumptions.[5] When someone says that a lawyer is "not

---

[5] *Fair Measure, supra.*

committed" or "not a team player," those are often code words that camouflage stereotypes or biases about certain groups and signal that individual lawyers are not being evaluated on their merits.

Lawyers may also be evaluated unfairly when they work on a team or in an environment that is dysfunctional or politically charged. A lawyer's performance — and, consequently, his or her evaluation — is affected by many factors that the

---

TABLE 2. How Performance Standards Enhance Evaluations, Performance, and Development

Performance standards:

- Communicate the kinds of behaviors, skills, expertise, and attitudes the firm values and expects.
- Give all lawyers a common language for discussing performance.
- Produce greater consistency in evaluations.
- Explain to associates how they are expected to help the firm achieve its professional and business objectives.
- Avoid surprises in evaluations; reduce defensiveness.
- Make it easier to receive and process feedback.
- Ensure that attorney development and performance are aligned with firm expectations and values.
- Enable individuals to integrate personal aspirations and abilities with the firm's professional values and business objectives.
- Accentuate the need for ongoing performance improvement and career development.
- Encourage associates to think long-term about their careers. Promote goal setting and career development planning.
- Enable partners to coach and mentor associates more meaningfully.
- Facilitate career counseling.
- Emphasize skills and performance levels instead of class year.
- Promote merit-based advancement and pay.
- Improve hiring and staffing decisions.
- Allow lawyers to track their development and progress over time.
- Identify individual development needs at the earliest stage.
- Help the firm decide where to devote training and development resources.
- Ensure that associates perform all required professional activities.
- Reduce friction with clients over billing rates for associates.
- Assure quality of client service.
- Enhance managerial skills of all lawyers.
- Facilitate change. Introduce new skill-sets needed to implement a change in strategy or direction.
- Speed up adoption of new technologies.

lawyer cannot control (e.g., lack of resources, poor group communication, mismanagement by team leaders, competition within the team). The firm should watch out in evaluations for signs of institutional and systemic problems that adversely impact performance. Some of these signs are complaints by partners that some or all associates on a team or in a practice group make the same mistakes, have similar bad habits, or have "attitude problems."

■ Clearer Messages

Another benefit of using explicit standards is that the message of the evaluation becomes easier for the recipient to understand and digest. Referring to the standards forces lawyers to focus on concrete skills, behaviors, activities, and events. Directing the parties' attention to written standards reduces the chances of misunderstanding and facilitates a more focused, less emotion-laden discussion.

Very often, reviewers present more information than an individual can easily process during a brief review. There is not enough time to go over most matters in depth, so reviewers tend to simplify the message and work from overall impressions rather than specific details. Because people use their own unique mental frameworks to process and remember feedback, recipients attach more weight to what fits their self-image and less weight to what is inconsistent with it. This often results in misunderstanding or a lack of agreement on the real message of the evaluation. The anxiety that accompanies most reviews compounds the problem. Most lawyers are uncomfortable in performance reviews; they dislike "sitting in judgment" on another lawyer or listening to judgment being passed on them. In particular, reviewers are reluctant to give negative feedback, and recipients become defensive listening to whatever the reviewer says, good or bad. Even though the review is supposed to be professional, it feels personal. In contrast, reviews based on standards can organize the feedback in a way that makes the message more coherent and easier to understand. Important items can be addressed in depth, while extraneous or trivial items can be omitted or put into the proper perspective. Focusing on standards makes the review less emotional. The standards provide some distance; they emphasize objective criteria and downplay the personal elements.

■ Better Assessments

When feedback is based on specific standards, evaluations more accurately assess performance. The standards enumerate the specific knowledge, tasks, skills, behaviors, and activities that the firm values and expects lawyers to achieve. The things that need to be evaluated get the attention they deserve; lawyers spend their time on important issues, not on things that don't matter.

■ Future Planning

Most feedback is retrospective. It looks at an individual's past performance to determine whether it warrants a bonus, promotion, or continued employment. When feedback is based on specific performance standards, the review can become prospective as well. In addition to determining how an individual measures up to prescribed performance levels, the review can concentrate on developing new skills and improving existing ones.

■ Proof of the Firm's Commitment

Using carefully enumerated standards proves to associates that the firm is committed to their development and willing to give them the information and feedback they need to move ahead. It demonstrates that the firm has thought about and agreed on what it takes to succeed as a lawyer. Associates take performance reviews very seriously. A thorough, systematic evaluation process based on specified standards shows that the firm is serious about it, too.

Two Types of Performance Standards: Benchmarks and Competencies

Many law firms are starting to express performance standards and expectations in terms of career benchmarks and core competencies. Benchmarks and competencies identify precisely what lawyers need to learn and do to advance and succeed in the firm. "Career benchmarks" set forth the progression of skills, experiences, aptitudes, behaviors, and personal characteristics an associate must develop on the path toward partnership. "Core competencies" describe the knowledge, skills, behaviors, and attitudes that lawyers must have to excel in their work. Together, benchmarks and competencies provide a roadmap for successful professional development.

Benchmarks and competencies are especially common in law firms that use a merit-based system of associate promotion and compensation rather than the traditional lockstep approach. In a lockstep system, all associates receive the same base compensation and are promoted to the next seniority level regardless of variations in performance. Associate pay and promotions are based on the year of graduation, so all associates in the same class move ahead at the same pace. The system makes some accommodation for individuals through merit-based bonuses, but even those do not produce striking differences. Unless an associate stands out as a poor performer and is held back (a rare occurrence), compensation and advancement are virtually equal and automatic for the entire class. In a lockstep system, the highest performers receive little extra reward and poor performers get more than they deserve. Many firms find that lockstep is out of step in the competitive business environment in which law firms operate today. Instead, they are adopting merit-based systems in which associates are evaluated, promoted, and compensated on the basis of explicit performance standards.[6] Under these merit-based systems, each associate's performance is measured against enumerated benchmarks and competencies, and decisions about advancement and compensation are made on an individual basis.

Whether using lockstep or merit-based systems, law firms that place a high priority on professional development are making benchmarks and competencies the centerpiece of a comprehensive professional development program. The terms "benchmarks" and "competencies" are often used interchangeably. In large part this is because benchmarks and competencies contain common elements and are used for similar purposes. To avoid confusion in this chapter, benchmarks will refer to career path guidelines for associates, and competencies will denote performance standards for excellence among all lawyers. The procedures for selecting and articulating benchmarks and competencies are discussed in a later section of this chapter.

■ Career Benchmarks

Benchmarks point out the path for associates' progression from entry level to partnership. They provide guidance about what lawyers should know and accomplish for normal progression, i.e., what is necessary to move up from one level to another toward partnership. In most cases, benchmarks are nothing more than guidelines; they are neither prerequisites for nor promises of promotion. When used in the evaluation process, they reveal developmental and experiential needs and provide focal points for discussions regarding an associate's progress. By stating expectations about the skills, experiences, and behaviors required for advancement, benchmarks increase the fairness and worth of associate evaluations.

Benchmarks delineate the legal skills and experiences that associates should achieve by the time they reach certain career milestones. They serve as reference

---

[6] For a description of how one firm replaced lockstep with a tiered "level system," see Peter B. Sloan, "From Classes to Competencies, Lockstep to Levels," (Blackwell Sanders Peper Martin LLP, 2002).

Blackwell Sanders' Level System

On January 1, 2001, Blackwell Sanders Peper Martin LLP, a 320-lawyer international firm based in Kansas City, Missouri, replaced its lockstep system with an Associate Career Development Process, which they commonly call the "Level System." The Level System uses specific performance guidelines to determine associate advancement and compensation, and is completely integrated with the firm's career development, evaluation, and training systems.

A committee of associates and partners worked intensively over a period of six months to design the Level System. Under the system, instead of grouping associates by class, the firm now places each associate in one of four "levels," depending upon their experience and performance. Partnership progression is governed by acquisition of competencies and skills, not by any specific time frame. The firm uses general performance criteria and department- and practice group-specific lists of expected skills and abilities to decide the right level for each associate. Together, these performance criteria and skills lists determine when associates can advance from one level to the next until they reach partnership.

The performance guidelines are also used in associate evaluations, which are done twice a year. A spring evaluation focuses on the associate's development; the fall evaluation addresses performance. In the spring, department or practice group chairs deliver the associate's review and work with each associate to create a one-page, twelve-month Career Development Plan using a form provided by the firm. Associates use the plan to track their progress and to measure their developmental accomplishments in subsequent reviews. The fall review includes an associate self-evaluation and an assessment of the associate's performance in relation to peers. Both reviews include a discussion of the associate's readiness for promotion, which can occur in either the spring or the fall. If the associate is not ready for promotion, the department or practice group chair and associate jointly discuss what the associate must do to become ready.

A comprehensive training curriculum is tied to both associate evaluations and the Level System. One of the firm's equity partners administers the Level System and coordinates lawyer recruiting, training, and development on a full-time basis. As this partner explains, when training, evaluations, and career advancement are integrated, "… it all snaps into place. Associates know they need to develop certain skills to be promoted, they are evaluated on those skills, and we provide training on those skills. In running the evaluation and review process, I can see exactly who needs additional help in what skill areas, so I can target the training and development resources where they are needed most."

points against which to measure career advancement, ultimately setting forth the basic experiential and technical requirements for partnership. The simplest type of benchmark is a checklist of skills and work experiences that lawyers should have at certain career points. Some benchmarks apply to all associates (e.g., ability to write clearly and persuasively), but benchmarks may also relate specifically to different practice areas and levels of seniority. For example, the following benchmarks may apply to a third-year litigation associate:

> At the end of three years, a litigation associate should have
>
> 1. completed all benchmarks for first- and second-year associates,
> 2. taken and defended at least ten depositions,
> 3. arbitrated at least three cases,
> 4. had primary responsibility for preparing and arguing one summary judgment motion,
> 5. regular contact with clients, and
> 6. sufficient legal knowledge, expertise, and initiative to manage cases with minimum supervision.

For purposes of applying benchmarks, firms divide associates according to either seniority levels (i.e., number of years out of law school) or competency levels (i.e., performance quality and achievements). Most firms use class years as dividing points for determining seniority levels. They have different benchmarks for each class year (e.g., first-year associates, second-year associates), or they group two or more class years together (e.g., first- and second-year associates, third- and fourth-year associates). Other firms use competency-based "tiers," with progression to higher tiers based on achieving certain performance levels, regardless of class year. At one such firm, associates move upward through four tiers before becoming a partner. The firm defines specific qualifying performance standards for each tier, and bases those standards on competencies, not on particular years of experience. Associates may spend several years in one tier, skip over a tier entirely, or even go down a tier, depending on their performance and level of commitment. This system recognizes that individuals' progression is not always linear and that at times in their careers (e.g., because of outside personal interests or part-time work), lawyers' development rates and directions vary.

For all their value, benchmarks pose risks to the firm. The risks can be avoided by making the intent and implications of the benchmarks crystal clear. There are two principal areas where benchmarks are easily misconstrued:

1. What are the ramifications of the benchmarks — are they "desired" or "required"?

2. How will associates get the training and experience called for by the benchmarks?

Regarding the first issue, associates will want answers to the following questions:

- Are the skills and experiences listed in the benchmarks the minimum that an associate must achieve in order to move ahead? Are they the "norm" or the "average" for associates? Or are they the "ideal"?

- Will failure to achieve a benchmark result in an associate being held back or dismissed?

- What happens to an exceptional associate who is highly capable but who does not meet the benchmarks?

- What about an average associate who achieves all of the stated skills and tasks but does not excel at any of them?

Unless the firm makes clear exactly what the benchmarks represent, the purpose of the benchmarks can be blown way out of proportion. Associates will make assumptions that may or may not be true, namely that: (1) associates must have all benchmark experiences in the order listed, (2) if associates comply with the benchmarks, they will become partners, (3) the firm promises to give every associate every one of the listed experiences, (4) benchmarks will be used unfairly to hold associates back, or (5) if associates do not comply with the benchmarks in every detail they cannot advance or become partners. To prevent or disabuse associates of false assumptions, firms must clearly communicate the real intent of the benchmarks. Of equal importance, they must implement the benchmarks the way they say they will. Failure to do this breeds distrust and undermines the firm's interest in having benchmarks in the first place.

Another risk of benchmarks is that associates may perceive them as obligating the firm to provide more opportunities for experience and training than is possible. While benchmarks do not create a promise for specific opportunities, it *is* the firm's responsibility to provide the work experience and training that will enable associates to achieve the benchmarks and progress along a "normal" career path. Associates in most law firms have little control over the work they are assigned, which determines to a great extent the experience and training they receive. Associates should be encouraged and expected to seek out the kind of work they need, using the benchmarks for guidance, but it is the firm's responsibility to ensure that associates have the designated experiences and related training in the time prescribed by the benchmarks. When the firm fails to provide the work and training that associates need to prove their capabilities relative to the benchmarks, associates should not be unfairly penalized.

As a roadmap, benchmarks can assist in pointing out where an associate stands in terms of the "normal" path of progression and areas where more experience is needed. But for evaluations, benchmarks alone are insufficient. Benchmarks describe what lawyers can do but not how well they do it. Achieving a specified benchmark does not by itself disclose the level or quality of the lawyers' performance. To conduct a worthwhile evaluation, and to promote development, the firm has to assess both achievement and proficiency. Core competencies provide a mechanism for doing that.

■ Core Competencies

Unlike benchmarks, which list the skills and experiences all lawyers must have to do the firm's legal work, competencies set the model for superior, successful performance. Competencies are a bundle of attributes (i.e., the knowledge, skills, aptitudes, attitudes, and behaviors) that distinguish the most capable performers from those who are merely adequate. Competencies are used to assess the level and quality of performance beyond technical mastery of the law. They cover such areas as interpersonal skills, team skills, client development, client relationship management, work and people management, and leadership ability. They define the capabilities that underlie high performance and reflect the values and strategic goals of the firm. The Colgate-Palmolive Company explains each competency with a description of behaviors that indicate strong performance and those that suggest improvement is needed. Table 3 contains one of the core competencies expected of Colgate-Palmolive lawyers.

Unlike benchmarks, which are directed at associates, competencies are used to evaluate all lawyers. They look at how capably lawyers are fulfilling their professional responsibilities and contributing to the overall well-being of the firm. By identifying the competencies of successful lawyers, the firm sets the threshold that lawyers must meet to become and remain partners.

Competency-based evaluations are the foundation for managing the performance and continued professional development of partners. They form the basis for upward and 360° reviews — setting performance expectations, but without any particular time frame or differences based on seniority. They can be linked to compensation decisions, but, more importantly for development purposes, they can be used to manage and improve partners' management and practice performance.

TABLE 3. Example: One of the Colgate-Palmolive Company's Competencies for Lawyers

DEVELOPING BUSINESS PARTNERSHIPS:
Building a close partnership with business partners; Helping partners achieve business results.

BEHAVIORS INDICATING STRENGTH:

- Understands the strategies and key initiatives of the business.
- Finds ways to participate as a member of business team(s).
- Helps business partners achieve aggressive business objectives while managing legal risks and complying with ethical obligations.
- Inspires trust and confidence through responsiveness and sound advice.

BEHAVIORS INDICATING DEVELOPMENT NEED:

- Focuses on potential problems without providing solutions.
- Acts only as an outside adviser rather than business partner.
- Fails to devote adequate time to learn the business.
- Accepts being contacted only after a problem arises.

Adopting and Implementing an Evaluation System

An evaluation system should reflect the unique values, structure, and culture of a firm and be designed to meet the firm's business goals and needs. The underlying principles should apply to all of the firm's lawyers, but procedures and approaches should be crafted separately for associates and partners. Four steps are required to establish or revamp a firm's evaluation system:

1. Making the case for the evaluation system.
2. Identifying and codifying performance standards.
3. Establishing evaluation procedures.
4. Allocating sufficient personnel and resources to the process.

Making the Case: Why Conduct Performance Evaluations?

As with other components of a professional development program, there must be agreement on the purpose and value of the evaluation process, and an understanding of its role in furthering the firm's strategic goals. Lawyers are likely to resist any new system or a major overhaul of the existing system. Associates will fear it is a ploy to hold them back, limit the number of new partners, or save the firm money at their expense. Partners will fear that it will cost them more money, impose unreasonable burdens on them, and create new associate demands and entitlements. The best way to deal with this resistance is to prevent it by getting everyone involved in the planning process and keeping them thoroughly informed through frequent and unambiguous communication.

■ The Purpose of Evaluations

Evaluations have two principal purposes. They are (1) an appraisal of accomplishments and results (what you did) and (2) an assessment of development (how you did it). In most law firm evaluations, the results element (e.g., hours worked, revenues generated, leadership contributions) forms the heart of the review because results are easier to measure and of most immediate concern to the firm. The development dimension concentrates on a lawyer's personal and professional growth (e.g., acquisition of new skills, ability to manage people). Development is harder and more subjective to measure and takes more time and attention.

Nonetheless, the continuing development and success of individual lawyers is vital to the overall development and success of the firm.

Most firms combine results and development in their evaluations without considering the implications of the differences between the two, which are significant (see Table 4):

- The purpose of a results-oriented evaluation is to look at a person's accomplishments over the intervening period to determine the kinds of rewards (or discipline) their performance warrants. The purpose of an evaluation for development is to assess current capabilities and set goals for expanding or improving them.

- In a results-oriented evaluation, the written assessment belongs to the firm and goes into the lawyer's personnel file. When an evaluation is done for development, the data belongs to the person being reviewed and the individual decides who will see it and how it will be used.

- Results-oriented evaluations assess the lawyer's ability to do past and current work at the performance levels the firm expects. Development-oriented evaluations focus on future expectations. They examine lawyers' overall experience, their performance relative to both their previous reviews and to their peers, how well they perform beyond mere technical abilities, and their progress toward partnership. An associate's results may be adequate to carry out current assignments but insufficient from a development standpoint for the responsibilities expected of a partner.

TABLE 4. Comparison of Features in Evaluation Systems Used for Results and Development

Feature	Results-Oriented	Development-Oriented
Purpose	Decide rewards/discipline	Assess capabilities
Who controls data	Firm	Individual
Focus	Past and current results	Future targets
Who sets goals	Firm	Individual, with firm input
Consequences	Firm rewards/disciplines	Personal
Context	Threatening	Supportive

- Results-oriented evaluations focus on accomplishments relative to goals determined by the firm. Failure to meet those performance goals leads to financial and professional detriment. In a development-centered evaluation, the focus is on setting personal targets for improvement. The firm supports the process, but there are no organizational repercussions if the lawyer's personal goals are not met (so long as the lawyer meets the firm's performance standards).

- Results-oriented evaluations are directly tied to pay and promotion. The review represents the firm's judgment, and raises feelings of fear and anxiety. People feel threatened and respond defensively. When feedback is given for the purpose of development only, the emphasis is strictly on becoming a better lawyer. This increases the recipient's comfort, willingness to listen, and ability to learn.

It is preferable to keep developmental evaluations separate from the annual performance review for compensation. Unless compensation is decided solely on objective criteria (e.g., hours billed or revenues collected), the developmental message too often gets lost in the concern about money, advancement, or continuing in the job. Moreover, to the extent evaluations are intended to motivate people to change behaviors, tying improvement to financial rewards has limited value and often heightens resistance to change. If the message contradicts a lawyer's self-image, defense mechanisms kick in. The lawyer may deny the problem or blame others for it.

The best way to proceed is to schedule two separate review sessions, one an appraisal for purposes of discussing compensation and its relation to past or current performance, and a second session that is exclusively to examine development issues. This is the approach being taken by many firms that have instituted benchmarks or competency-based evaluations. If two separate sessions are not feasible for your firm and compensation will be discussed along with development, then steps should be taken to defuse anxieties and keep the discussion focused.

- Explain the purpose of the review and what will happen during your time together. Encourage mutual candor.

- Create a positive environment, emphasizing the constructive nature of the feedback you will be presenting. Stress that the main purpose of the feedback is to address and foster the lawyer's professional growth and development.

- Refer to specific performance standards. Concentrate the discussion on what it takes to perform at designated levels.

- Give lawyers their written evaluations or a summary in advance of the in-person review session. A lawyer who can read the evaluation and discuss it with a mentor or adviser can think more clearly and be better prepared to discuss development concerns and goals during the review.

- Encourage dialogue during the review. Engage the recipient by asking questions or soliciting reactions to the review, and make the review interactive.

- Look ahead. Move from feedback to goal setting. Use the review as an opportunity to set targets for the next evaluation period.

Why Evaluate Associates?

The case for associate evaluations is clear, straightforward, and well established. The major reasons for conducting in-depth associate evaluations (many of which have been discussed in preceding paragraphs) include:

- Serving as a vehicle to communicate the key values, skills, behaviors, and attitudes that the firm seeks in lawyers.

- Setting performance standards and expectations for lawyers.

- Assessing associates' performance against the firm's expected standards.

- Promoting quality assurance and risk management.

- Improving performance and accelerating development by pointing out specific areas for growth and improvement.

- Giving associates feedback on performance and prospects for advancement.

- Reinforcing positive behaviors.

- Helping associates understand how they are expected to contribute to achieving the firm's strategic business goals.

- Stimulating and guiding development within the context of the firm's values, performance expectations, and strategic goals.

- Identifying top performers, those who can improve, and those who should be asked to leave.

■ Why Evaluate Partners?

While associate reviews are accepted and expected, reviews of partners are relatively new and rare. But as many law firms are beginning to realize, partner reviews are no less important.[7] Partner evaluations assess partners' interpersonal, management, and leadership skills, practice development, development of others, team building skills, self-improvement, client satisfaction, and firm citizenship. Evaluations can give partners the feedback they need to reinforce or improve performance in these key management and leadership areas. In medicine, education, and most other professions, reviews by peers, supervisors, and subordinates continue throughout a professional's career. The reason for the widespread popularity of development-oriented performance evaluations lies in their showing us how others see us, how our behaviors impact those around us, where our behaviors are beneficial, and where we need to be better. This knowledge makes us more emotionally intelligent and professionally effective.

Partner evaluations benefit partners and the firm in numerous ways:

- ■ **Self-improvement.** Assessing partners' strengths and pinpointing areas where improvement is needed enables partners to make positive changes.

- ■ **Improves client relations.** Feedback from clients allows partners to better appreciate and respond to client needs and expectations.

- ■ **Management skills.** Assessing partners' effectiveness and contributions in managing people and work calls attention to the importance of management and encourages partners to manage better.

- ■ **Communication.** Assessing partners' abilities to communicate, build consensus, and advance understanding within the firm emphasizes the importance of these activities and induces partners to communicate more effectively.

- ■ **Improves associates.** When evaluating partners, associates think more critically about what it means to be a partner.

- ■ **Improves evaluations.** By receiving feedback, partners become more empathetic and effective at giving feedback.

---

[7] A 2002 survey of professional development directors found that 21 of 37 responding law firms (57 percent) did upward evaluations and noted a significant growing interest in partner evaluations. "Upward Evaluations: Results of Our January Survey," *Professional Development Quarterly*, February 2002, p. 1, 2.

- **Recruiting.** A reputation for promoting excellent associate-partner work relations attracts good associates to the firm.

- **Retention.** Giving associates input into firm management and promoting all lawyers' professional development furthers the retention of capable and motivated associates.

Overcoming Resistance to Partner Reviews

Initiating reviews of partners is no easy task. The process is costly, takes considerable time, and can be highly threatening to partners who are unaccustomed to being formally evaluated by their peers, much less by subordinates. To make matters more difficult, the subjects of partner evaluations tend to be in areas where partners are least comfortable or self-assured.

Firms that want to implement partner reviews should be prepared for resistance. First there is the matter of time and expense. A competency-based partner review is both time-consuming and expensive. It requires a dedicated project manager, often working with an outside consultant, to identify and draft competencies, design and implement the program, collect and analyze the data, and provide feedback and follow-up coaching to partners. It is not unusual for a project manager in a large, multi-office firm to spend several weeks working on the upward evaluation process full-time. Bringing clients and staff into the feedback loop for a true 360° review adds to the expense.

The other major reason for resistance is partners' natural reluctance to be judged by others. Partners rarely receive any feedback on their performance. The only feedback most partners do get from their firms comes in the form of a check at the end of the year. That payment reflects what the compensation committee thinks of their value to the firm, but it does not come with an explanation. The check presents no performance standards to guide partners' future performance, and it does not give them a clue about what to do or how to change so that their performance may justify a larger check next year. Although some firms use objective mathematical formulas to allocate profits, even those firms usually include some vaguely defined subjective elements in the calculation as well.

However vague the criteria for compensation might be, at least they deal with tangible, measurable numbers that lawyers understand. The areas evaluated in upward or 360° reviews deal with management, leadership, mentoring, and other non-financial abilities that lawyers are not taught and may not understand. Consequently, feedback in these areas can be extremely threatening, especially when submitted by subordinates. Partners do not know what performance standards apply in these areas because these activities and skills have traditionally not been defined or evaluated. Many partners are surprised to learn that they have a responsibility to train, mentor, and develop associates. One tax lawyer who joined a law firm after twelve years working for the government explained that he made the move because, "In order to advance any further in the government, I would have to become a manager of people, so I went to the law firm instead where I could just be a partner." Imagine his shock when he learned upon arriving at his new firm that he would be evaluated on his competence in associate development.

On the bright side, evaluations can make partners feel terrific. Partners are frequently surprised to learn that associates recognize and appreciate their management, teaching, and mentoring efforts. When this happens, partner evaluations can be powerful tools for spurring partners to stretch to ever-higher levels of performance.

■ Establishing Trust in Partner Reviews

Some lawyers may recognize the value of partner reviews right away, but most participants do not appreciate their value until after the first year or two. There may be skepticism when partner evaluations are initiated. People begin to trust the system when they see that the evaluation instrument is valid, that anonymity is in fact guaranteed, and that the motives behind the system are truly to benefit the partners' development. Trust accumulates when the process is well run and the outcomes for participants are positive. Associates become confident that their feedback will be used constructively and will improve how partners manage them. Partners find that receiving feedback is relevant and useful, and they are given support and a chance to make improvements before being castigated for any deficiencies.

Selecting and Articulating Performance Standards

Evaluations based on performance standards collect and incorporate three types of information:

1. Quantifiable data (e.g., billings, business origination, realization rates) that measure accomplishments in terms of time, work, and money generated.

2. Evaluators' assessments of lawyers' performance based on the firm's performance standards.

3. Lawyers' individual development plans to measure what they have achieved and what still needs to be done.

Most firms can readily determine the information and baselines required for category one. Developing a set of relevant performance standards for items two and three is a more complicated process requiring a serious investment of time and effort. Once the effort is completed, however, the benefits will accrue for many years. The firm's performance standards, especially when expressed as benchmarks and competencies, will create a model of excellence for its lawyers. Because these standards are both current and prospective, it is important that you develop standards strategically, i.e., deciding what kinds of skills lawyers will need in the future to achieve the firm's business objectives. The type of skills, learning, and behaviors that allowed the firm and its lawyers to succeed in the past may not be sufficient to tackle the problems of the future. To develop performance standards, create assumptions about the near future — use trend information, forecasts, market research, as well as the firm's strategic goals. Infer from those assumptions what competencies will be needed, and combine them with current best practices.

Evaluations should deal with behaviors that can be learned and modified. No one should be expected to alter inherent personality traits. Innate characteristics (e.g., initiative, creativity, the ability to learn quickly) may be improved somewhat but are generally not amenable to significant alteration. Nonetheless, performance standards can establish baseline levels of acceptable or unacceptable behaviors when these characteristics are important to the lawyer's job. While evaluations will not lead to personality changes, they may inspire people to alter certain behaviors that are manifestations of innate personality (e.g., curbing angry outbursts through stress management techniques).

Some firms determine performance standards by themselves, but many find that working with an outside consultant familiar with law practice performance standards makes the process easier, faster, and more objective. This is especially true when the standards are to be integrated into an upward review system for partners. Whether working with an internal group or an outside consultant, developing specific benchmarks and competencies requires a methodical approach. Once the firm identifies the standards, they must be clearly and succinctly articulated and made known to the firm. They should be explained to associates when they arrive at the firm, contained in any orientation handbook provided to new lawyers, and posted on the firm's intranet so that lawyers can access them at any time.

Developing Career Benchmarks for Associates

The process of creating benchmarks involves analyzing what lawyers do in their practice and how they do it. These steps can assist in that process:

- Conduct an internal audit to determine the knowledge, experiences, and skills that associates should be expected to have at specific seniority points. It may be helpful to start at the end, i.e., to determine the knowledge, experiences, and skills that partners should have and then work backward, indicating the time frame in which associates should accomplish them.

- Ask partners to break down the lawyering process in their practice area into principal constituent parts and identify the primary tasks associated with each constituent part.

- Ascertain partners' expectations by inquiry and observation. Interview or survey partners to determine what they expect of associates at different levels of seniority. Ask partners to be specific and to give examples. Consider how reasonable their expectations are. Compare what partners tell you to what they say during associate review discussions. Where are partners' comments consistent and how do they differ?

- Delineate the lessons that associates must learn and the experiences they must have to meet partners' expectations.

- Search the literature for published benchmarks and resource materials that describe what lawyers need to know in different fields of law practice.[8]

- Review the firm's strategic plan to ascertain its expectations and potential impact on the performance, skills, and knowledge attorneys will need.

- Review the firm's employment manuals and policies, and orientation materials given to associates, to see what they say that may impact performance criteria. (Depending on the standards you adopt, those materials may require later revisions.)

---

[8] Examples of such resources are Stephen R. Chitwood, Anita F. Gottlieb, Evelyn Gaye Mara, *A Business Skills Curriculum for Law Firm Associates*, Association of Legal Administrators, 2001; Austin G. Anderson and Arthur G. Greene, *The Effective Associate Training Program*, The American Bar Association, 1999; and *Legal Education and Professional Development — An Educational Continuum, Report of The Task Force on Law Schools and The Profession: Narrowing the Gap*, ABA Section of Legal Education and Admissions to the Bar, 1992 (the "MacCrate Report").

Using Evaluations to Promote Lawyers' Development   205

- Decide whether the benchmarks will be mandatory for advancement or simply guidelines for development.

- Consider the impact of benchmarks on lawyers who work part-time, on the firm's diversity goals, and on lateral associates.

These steps should generate the information you need to start drafting your benchmarks. Benchmarks should represent baseline performance expectations of all associates, not the ideal or superstar performers. Be as specific as possible about skills, knowledge, behaviors, observable attitudes, and attributes. Specificity should include the seniority levels you will use (e.g., by class years, by tiers) and the tasks, experiences, responsibilities, and personal attributes appropriate for each seniority level. Some attributes are difficult to assess, such as whether an associate is trusted by clients. One way to deal with this is to consider what kinds of observable behaviors indicate that clients trust an associate (e.g., that clients call an associate directly for advice or send business to the associate).

Once you have drafted a prototype of your benchmarks, distribute them to partners and associates for comment and make adjustments based on feedback. When you have adopted the final benchmarks, it is a good idea to try them out in a pilot project before implementing them firm wide. When they are implemented, integrate the benchmarks with other professional development systems, including training, mentoring, and work assignments.

■ Developing Core Competencies

Benchmarks state levels of accomplishment; they list tasks and skills that a lawyer must be able to do in the course of developing proficiency. Competencies express qualitative elements; they describe the degree of excellence required for successful performance. The process for identifying and articulating competencies is similar to that for benchmarks, but there are some important distinctions.

- Identify four to six discrete areas of competency (e.g., superior client service, demonstrated leadership, associate development) that reflect and promote the firm's key values and strategic goals. The competencies you select to evaluate must be directly and distinctly relevant to successful performance. The firm's leaders can identify the areas of competency to be evaluated, but it is essential that the all lawyers accept them as valid. Don't bother evaluating people on teamwork and mentoring if the only thing that ultimately matters is the number of hours billed.

- Identify five to ten specific components to be evaluated for each key competency. If a competency is "superior client service," that competency must be dissected into specific, observable tasks, skills, attitudes, behaviors, and attributes that characterize what a lawyer must do to deliver superior client service.

- Use different techniques to analyze and determine the competencies to be evaluated:

    — Survey or interview lawyers individually and in groups to solicit what they believe are examples of superior performance.
    — Observe how high performers work and what they do to achieve superior results.
    — Ask partners how they achieved winning results. Inquire about challenges they faced; what they thought, did, and felt at the time; and what abilities helped them deal with the situation successfully.
    — Observe and compare average and high performers to identify the factors that differentiate them.

- Locate examples of competencies being used by clients, other law firms, other professional service firms, businesses, and associations that deal with performance issues.

Competencies are standards for excellence. In applying competencies, ask yourself the following questions:

- How will competencies be scored? Will an "average" score be acceptable or is superior performance required?

- Will lawyers be expected to excel in each set of competencies? Must they be at or near the top of the scale in one or two?

- Does every set of competencies have the same value or will some competencies carry more weight than others?

- How will results be interpreted in deciding compensation or advancement?

In adopting competencies, remember that the intent is not to create a single model of success. Although you are creating a model of excellence for lawyers to follow, you do not want a law firm filled with identical clones. To the contrary, performance standards must acknowledge diverse models of successful lawyer performance. Law firms need variations, not sameness. An assortment of personalities, skills, interests, styles, practice strengths, and even eccentricities is very important for a vibrant, energetic law firm. Every firm needs quiet, precise, analytical thinkers as much as it needs extroverted rainmakers. The reason for using competencies in evaluations is not to create a template to which all lawyers must conform but to assess lawyers' proficiency and effectiveness in their work, and to further their professional growth and development. The firm should plan for and accept differences in styles and approaches when evaluating lawyers' contributions, calculating compensation, and providing developmental guidance.

■ Articulating Performance Standards

Whether presented as benchmarks, competencies, or basic evaluation criteria, all performance standards should be reduced to writing. They should explain what evaluators should assess about behaviors, attributes, actions, and interactions. Evaluators should be able to assess these attributes through direct observation or be capable of making an inference based on surrounding events and evidence.

Each item to be evaluated should be briefly stated, followed by a detailed description that tells the evaluator what is being measured. Table 5 lists examples of performance standards. Performance standards should be as precise and observable as possible. They may include skills, knowledge, and behaviors that range from being easily seen and measured (e.g., preparing a document on time and without errors) to being quite difficult to perceive and assess (e.g., building and managing

---

TABLE 5. Examples of Performance Standards

- **Competitiveness.** Desires to succeed in negotiations, win for the client, and/or exceed stated expectations.

- **Delegation.** Assigns work to others at appropriate levels; explains assignments clearly and fully; provides prompt and useful feedback on work and behavior.

- **Attention to detail.** Is thorough and tenacious in completing complex and multi-faceted tasks; work product is neat and free of errors.

- **Client understanding.** Understands the client and the client's business; is able to relate legal concepts and theories to client problems and goals.

- **Team management.** Respects the work obligations of team members when assigning work and setting deadlines; helps people feel a sense of common purpose in working toward a quality work product.

teams). Assessing hard-to-evaluate behaviors can be made easier by referring to observable behaviors that raise inferences about performance (e.g., we can infer that a partner whose teams are highly productive with little turnover and consistently high performance is proficient at building teams).

Establish Procedures for Evaluations

Along with specific standards, you need procedures for conducting evaluations. To promote professional development through evaluations requires a comprehensive evaluation system with the following procedures and features:

- Collection and analysis of written performance assessments from evaluators.
- Collection of pertinent information from the lawyer being reviewed.
- Personal review sessions to deliver the collected feedback to those evaluated.
- Composing development plans for the person being evaluated.
- Decisions on specific procedural features:
    - Who will evaluate partners.
    - Who will evaluate associates.
    - Who will evaluate Special Counsel.
    - How evaluators will be selected.
    - How and by whom the reviews will be delivered.
    - How the program will be rolled out.
    - How often evaluations will be conducted.
    - What support and follow up will be provided.
    - How to maximize participation in the evaluation process.
    - Whether to permit appeals.

Using Evaluations to Promote Lawyers' Development 209

■ Collection and Analysis of Written Performance Assessments from Evaluators

Evaluation questionnaire forms

Performance assessment data is collected through evaluation questionnaires. The validity of the evaluation is determined in large part by the quality of the questionnaire. In drafting evaluation questionnaire forms, keep in mind the following points:

- ■ The questionnaire should be divided into categories, with specific aspects of performance listed for each category.

- ■ All terms should be defined and explained; glossaries, examples, and illustrations are useful. In defining terms, care should be taken to be objective, factual, and free from characterizations that may reflect bias.

- ■ Instructions for completing the form should be very simple and clearly spelled out. Attaching the firm's mission statement or statement of values, relevant portions of the strategic plan, or other materials that remind reviewers of the general standards expected of lawyers can be most helpful.

- ■ It is a good idea to phrase performance standards and criteria in a positive way, e.g., "Takes initiative" vs. ""Does not take initiative." Receiving feedback from forms that are filled with negative statements makes people feel defensive and less receptive to the data. Moreover, positive statements inform lawyers or evaluators what they should be doing; negative statements do not.

- ■ Forms should include numerical scales that ask evaluators to rate performance along the scale. The most simple is a three-point scale that asks whether performance "Exceeds expectations," "Meets expectations, or "Fails to meet expectations." Some firms use scales with as many as ten points, but more than five points calls for distinctions that are hard to define and measure. Smaller three, four, or five-point scales force people to rate lawyers' performance more definitively, without a lot of wiggle room.

- ■ Forms should ask for an overall rating (using the same rating scale) of the lawyer's performance in each general area of competency.

- ■ Evaluation forms should ask questions calling for narrative answers because numerical rating scales alone are insufficient. Questions should ask for insightful observations and in-depth comments about what the lawyer does well, where improvement is needed, and recommendations. These questions may follow the numerical assessment of each competency area and/or be placed at the end of the questionnaire. People often want to elaborate their ratings and observations or present pertinent information that is not specifically requested on the form. You may also leave space for these comments. For example, an associate may rate very high on technical skills, but an evaluator might believe that the associate's assignments have not been demanding enough to really test the associate's technical abilities.

- Evaluators should be required to provide a rationale (including specific facts, actions, and events) for their ratings and conclusions. This is necessary to reveal potential biases and to make reviewers think more carefully about their ratings. Not every numerical rating needs to be justified. One useful approach is to require an explanation for any rating that is higher or lower than a mid-range score, and to require comments about any conduct that raises issues about the lawyer's honesty, trustworthiness, or failure to adhere to ethical standards.

- Encourage evaluators to give specific recommendations for any skills or behaviors they believe need improvement.

- Make it easy for lawyers to complete the evaluations. Try to keep the evaluation form brief and the instructions simple. There should be no more than about 30 to 45 questions, and the questionnaire should take no longer than about 20 minutes to complete (except that evaluations of associates for partnership consideration may take more time). Most people will have to evaluate several lawyers, and brief, easy to complete evaluation forms will increase the likelihood of response, facilitate data processing, and enhance credibility and confidence in the system.

- Include technology personnel in designing the form so that it can be completed and processed online. Be sure that the system and the form are both user-friendly.

Interim evaluation forms

Because performance reviews happen six months to a year apart, lawyers should document special events and important evaluative data as they happen. Firms can provide written or electronic forms for documenting such interim data at the end of a major project or the conclusion of an assignment. Forms can be kept in the associate's file and retrieved by the author at the time of the full-scale evaluation. Recording this information close in time to the occurrence will give evaluators more accurate and reliable data. Otherwise, evaluators tend to rely on impressions or vague memories of things that happened long ago. Completing such forms when the knowledge is fresh in your memory also saves evaluators time. It eliminates the need to go back and review earlier files or work product to remember what and how the lawyer did on a project. The completed forms may also be shown to the associate or used as the basis for giving the associate informal feedback soon after the project's completion.

Analyzing the evaluation data collected

No matter how large or small the firm, collection and analysis of evaluation data is extremely labor-intensive. Using numerical rating scales makes the analysis and reporting easier, but it can still be daunting. Although this process can be done manually in small firms, firms with hundreds of lawyers require computerized data collection and processing systems. The Nixon Peabody LLP law firm found that when they implemented an electronic evaluation system, the return rate for completed evaluation forms increased from 60 percent to 90 percent, and staff time decreased because the system makes the process much easier for both evaluators and administrators. In firms of any size, questionnaires can be distributed, completed, and retrieved online, and technology can be used to collect, process, and present evaluation data. After the first year, the electronic evaluation system can be used to compare current and previous reviews to track lawyers' progress.

Many firms use their internal technology departments to create the software for evaluation systems, but there are numerous vendors who sell programs or services designed specifically for evaluation purposes.

Ensure that the system that you buy or design will allow you to sort information and produce reports, including tables and charts, which describe the numerical ranges, means, and averages of performance ratings for the firm as a whole, for each department or practice group, and for each office. Looking at aggregated results and cross-comparisons among these groups will help the firm locate well-managed teams, pinpoint problem areas, and determine where management training, coaching, or other support should be directed. For example, if evaluation results show that many lawyers are not sufficiently skilled at legal writing or client management, then the firm knows it must shore up its efforts in those areas. Correlating evaluation data with productivity figures for these groups also helps the firm determine the validity of the performance criteria being used. If working with a consultant or vendor, it may be possible to compare the firm's results with those of lawyers in other firms.

To save time and maximize participation in the evaluation process, the system should allow you to track compliance. If the system is to be taken seriously, the firm should require that everyone participate. Two indispensable aspects of the evaluation process revolve around the identification of evaluators and the timely submission of their completed evaluations. Evaluators should be individuals who have worked with the lawyer being reviewed for a substantial time or on a significant project. In addition, lawyers to be evaluated should be asked to name people who should evaluate them. Once the evaluators are known and the forms distributed, the firm must ensure that evaluators complete and return their evaluations promptly. Because of inertia, resistance, or competing demands, many lawyers fail to name evaluators or return their completed forms. The firm must constantly remind lawyers to comply, which is a time-consuming undertaking that no one likes to do because it requires nagging. A program that tracks compliance and sends automatic reminders reduces the need for someone to make nagging calls. Even with auto-reminders, however, project managers, practice group leaders, or managing partners may need to send personal reminders, emphasizing the importance of the evaluations and the consequences of non-compliance.

Once you have collected completed evaluation forms, the analysis can begin. The analysis looks at both the numerical grading and the narrative comments. In addition to compiling reports about individual lawyers, the program should have the ability to search for and eliminate irrational, biased, unfair, or untrustworthy reviews. Ensure that no one individual can drastically influence the evaluation (e.g., an "easy grader" partner who gives every associate the highest scores, or a disgruntled associate who gives all partners low scores.) Watch for severe criticism based on one isolated episode. Be alert for "outliers," i.e., extremely favorable or critical comments that clash with other data collected for an individual. Outliers should be investigated and put into proper perspective or excluded from consideration.

Narrative comments from the evaluation forms should be integrated into a consensus or composite summary. This summary will be the major focus for discussion at each lawyer's review. Narrative comments can be collected and organized electronically, but someone must personally analyze and summarize the data. Summaries should be constructive and highlight areas where there is substantial agreement on the lawyer's performance. Individuals writing the summaries should know which issues are important and which should be discounted or ignored. They should not shy away from tackling poor performance issues, sugar coat tough messages, or exaggerate positive remarks. Firms usually appoint one or two attorneys in each practice group to prepare summaries. Other options are appointing a project manager from inside the firm (e.g., someone in the professional development or human resources department) or delegating the task to an outside consultant.

Even those law firms that show associates all of their evaluators' narrative comments are well-advised to prepare evaluation summaries. Associates reading individual reviewers' comments may exaggerate, underplay, or obsess about particular remarks, and they may not understand how the firm views their overall performance and career prospects. An evaluation summary puts the various comments into perspective, directs an associate's attention to the points that the firm deems most important, and delivers the message that the firm wants the associate to hear. Moreover, it is a good idea to have someone review evaluators' comments rather than give them to associates "as is" in order to screen out statements that raise legal concerns, reflect bias, or are otherwise inappropriate.

Who will see the summaries

Each lawyer being reviewed should be shown his or her evaluations or at least an evaluation summary. This should be done before the review so that the lawyer can reflect on the assessment and prepare to discuss it more thoughtfully at the review session. If you give lawyers the summary for the first time during the review, they may need extra time to think about its implications and an opportunity to respond at a later time.

Associates' performance summaries are available to all partners, who are their employers. Partners typically get together by practice group, department, or in their entirety, to discuss associates' performance before the evaluations are finalized. Mentors and advisers who work with the associate on professional development issues should also receive copies.

Partner evaluations have more restricted distribution, as discussed later in this chapter. In addition to the partner being evaluated, summaries are customarily shown to the partner's practice group leader and the outside coach or consultant if there is one. Some practice group leaders may prefer to see only the evaluations of partners who are rated exceptionally high or exceptionally low. Reviews that reveal extraordinary abilities or serious problems should also be shared with the chair or office managing partner.

Anonymity

The question of maintaining confidentiality of evaluators' comments is different for associate and partner evaluations. Upward reviews of partners require absolute anonymity, as associates' fear of retribution is the single greatest obstacle to partner evaluations.[9] Associates and other employees will not give honest answers about their employers if they fear the employers will find out what they say. But partners

---

[9] "Upward Evaluations: Results of Our January Survey," p. 9.

do not need anonymity when evaluating associates. To the contrary, as managers and employers, partners have an obligation to give associates direct feedback about their performance and prospects.

Partners often try to avoid this responsibility, and reviews rarely attribute comments about associates to the partners who make them. The rationale is that attributing negative comments to the partner might damage that partner's work relationship with the associate. Some argue that partners will be less candid about an associate's shortcomings in order to keep the associate working on the partner's assignments. While this approach may be expedient, it helps no one. Associates who do not know partners' real opinions of them are at an unfair disadvantage; partners can hold back associates' long-term advancement for their own short-term needs. This ultimately leads to the associate's disappointment, loss of trust in the partner (and the firm), and even humiliation. In the meantime, the benefit of anonymity to the partner is not that great. Partners who do not fully believe in an associate's abilities have to spend time worrying about the associate's inadequate work and monitoring them more closely. This can result in excessive write-offs or the client being overcharged for the partner's extra supervision.

On the other hand, letting associates know which partners made which comments allows better, more straightforward dialogue during the review and makes the evaluation process more honest and fair. One firm whose experience confirms this reasoning is Alston & Bird LLP, which consistently appears on the list of *Fortune Magazine*'s "100 Best Companies to Work For" (ranking number 9 on that list in 2002). At Alston & Bird LLP, associates receive written evaluations that identify evaluating lawyers and their comments. The firm finds that because partners know that their comments will be shown to associates they give careful thought to what they say. But rather than inhibit candor, this transparency produces more honest, open, and meaningful evaluations. Associates learn the particular expectations of the partners with whom they work and can determine what they must do differently to satisfy those individuals. Associates who desire more clarity or who disagree with a partner's comments can discuss them with the partner. As a result, associates are able to put comments into perspective and defend themselves against evaluations they believe to be unfair.

■ Collection of Pertinent Information from the Lawyer Being Reviewed

Self-assessments should be a part of the evaluation process because they increase self-awareness, a critical component of professional development. They have particular value in making lawyers more aware of their strengths and development needs. Self-evaluations also foster lawyers' sense of responsibility for their own professional development and help them identify goals that will boost their careers.

The self-evaluation system can have lawyers use the same criteria (and evaluation forms) as those on which others will assess them. This allows lawyers to compare their own evaluations with the ratings that others give them. Comparing the lawyer's self-image with the observations and conclusions of those with whom the lawyer works acts as a reality check. It gives both reviewers and the reviewed lawyers insight into whether they have a pretty good idea of themselves and how others see them. A vast disparity between a lawyer's self-assessment and others' evaluations can be a red flag that the lawyer lacks confidence, is overly confident, or does not appreciate the impact of their performance and behavior on others.

Self-assessments are useful when working with a mentor, adviser, or coach on development goals or career directions. Using a self-assessment in combination with informal feedback, feedback from evaluations, advice from a mentor, and the lawyer's own professional interests and desires, lawyers can establish a baseline of their current capabilities and begin to formulate career plans that set long-term development goals and more limited objectives for the next review period.

Self-assessments have value for partners as well as associates. The memos that partners send to the compensation committee at the end of the year (often called "brag memos," "begging memos," or "I love me memos") are not developmental self-assessments. Those memos explain what lawyers have accomplished in the past year, how they have contributed to the firm, and why they deserve a large share of the firm's profits. In some firms, the memo is based on a form that requires partners to answer specific questions; other firms leave it up to individual lawyers to say whatever they want in whatever format they wish. Regardless of what the memos look like, their main subjects are the partners' billings, collections, business origination, and client development successes. Some firms also want to know about the partners' activities in developing associates, pro bono work, and internal committee work, but the real issue is money. These memos emphasize a partner's lucrative accomplishments during the previous year and do not address the lawyer's personal development.

Because these memos are so self-serving, they are not reliable for development purposes. What should be used are self-assessments that ask the same questions asked on an upward or 360° evaluation form. Those questions reflect skills, behaviors, and activities that the firm has deemed important for partners to have and constitute a more valid basis for partners' professional development plans.

■ Personal Review Sessions to Deliver the Evaluation

Delivering associate reviews

Associate reviews serve many purposes: to tell associates how they are performing, individually and in comparison to their peers; to discuss the past year's achievements and how they measured up to the firm's expectations; to elucidate associates' strengths and weaknesses; and to explain the firm's expectations for the associate in the year ahead. Unfortunately, too often these reviews end up centering on productivity (the quantity of billable work performed) and money (the amount of this year's bonus and next year's salary). The reason is that when discussions of money are combined with discussions of performance, money talks louder. Ideally, reviews for development should be separated from reviews about compensation. It is unrealistic, however, to keep the two issues completely separate because compensation is largely based on the level and quality of demonstrated performance. As noted earlier, the best approach is to conduct an annual evaluation that deals with performance for purposes of compensation and promotion, and a second evaluation during the year to assess performance in terms of development and progress.

Reviews should present feedback gleaned from the evaluations and engage the associate in a dialogue about his or her performance. The review should give a global assessment of the associate's performance during the review period, using particular facts and events to substantiate the conclusions presented. Reviews should focus on observed skills, behaviors, and activities. Feedback should be candid and constructive. Associates should leave a review with a clear grasp of their standing relative to firm expectations, career benchmarks, and promotion criteria. The discussion of development issues can go into greater depth if the associate has received regular, informal feedback on performance throughout the review period. The associate and reviewers can concentrate on the associate's current and needed capabilities, and short- and long-term development plans, instead of covering minor issues or incidents that occurred months before.

The associate review should not be a monologue. It is an important time for associates to voice their views on their experience in the firm and to provide information that the firm may need to know about their interests, concerns, and plans. It is also important to elicit the associate's comprehension of and reaction to the current review. The associate should be encouraged to offer information that clarifies or explains comments of evaluators that appear on the evaluation summary or are voiced during the review.

Delivering partner reviews

Partners also need to discuss and assimilate their reviews. All partners should receive a written report of their evaluation, including how they were rated compared to the way they evaluated themselves. Upward reviews tend to generate a lot of other comparative data including comparisons of their own performance with other partners' on each competency and overall, and how lawyers in the firm's different departments, practice groups, and offices compare to each other. These findings need to be interpreted so that partners understand what they mean and what the implications are. Presentation of results can be done one-on-one and in groups. The best approach is to have someone meet with each partner to discuss individual evaluations and with all the partners together to present and explain the firm-wide and group data. Individual review discussions are especially important if the partner, their practice group leader, or the managing partner requests it.

Individual partner reviews should be conducted sensitively because they can be very threatening. While some partners welcome the feedback that such reviews offer, others are unaccustomed, uncaring, and unwilling to hear what others think of their performance. Some managers believe that each partner's evaluation should be available for all partners to see, but, from a developmental standpoint, it is better to limit the distribution of evaluations to a few key people, e.g., the partner's department or practice group chair, the managing partner, a member of the evaluation committee, or the person in charge of evaluations. Any of these people can deliver individual reviews, but review discussions may be more fruitful and less anxiety provoking when handled by someone outside the firm. Professional development consultants and executive coaches are good resources for this function.

Training to deliver and receive reviews

Lawyers need training in how to give and receive feedback. Even when the message is positive, reviews make most people uncomfortable. Lawyers do not like to sit in judgment of others or to hurt colleagues' feelings. Constructive criticism is still criticism, which is value-laden and judgmental. Feedback recipients are even more apprehensive. Appraisals can undermine both a positive self-image and the basic need for security, so people avoid listening to the message. Because of the discomfort, unease, and awkwardness of the situation, reviewers often sugarcoat difficult messages and listeners hear what they want to hear. Lawyers should be sensitive to these emotional factors and trained to focus on observable facts, accurately presented. Lawyers should also be trained to receive and process feedback in a useful, non-defensive, and constructive manner.

■ Composing Development Plans

Most performance reviews live up to their names: They look backward at past performance. While this is suitable to justify bonus or promotion decisions, evaluations for professional development purposes must also face forward. Events of the past should be analyzed for their developmental implications and used as the foundation for future planning. Reviews should culminate with the creation of a personal development plan.

Reviews are the time for associates to draft or update plans to further their professional learning and growth. The development plan should incorporate the associate's goals, the firm's goals for the associate, and the specific work assignments, experience, and training needed to reach the stated goals. Goals may focus on new learning and experience or on addressing areas that need improvement over the ensuing few months. They may be of a technical and legal nature, or they be related to management, marketing, client, business, or interpersonal skills, depending on the particular associate's interests, needs, and performance level. Resources and actions needed to implement the plan should be identified and a timetable included for achieving interim steps and final goals.

The plan can be written before, during, or after the review session:

- ■ Associates can come to the review with a draft plan that is discussed and fine-tuned with the reviewer.

- ■ Associates and reviewers can draft the plan together during the review.

- ■ Based on discussions during the review, the associate can draft the plan after the review and discuss it with the reviewer, a mentor, or an adviser at a later time.

Many firms provide templates for lawyers to use in creating these plans. Appendix 7 is one such template. After the plan is finalized, associates should meet periodically (at least quarterly) with a mentor or adviser to monitor progress and make any necessary adjustments. At the associate's next review, the plan forms one of the starting points for evaluation and discussion.

Development plans are valuable for partners, too. Partner reviews should be a time to align partners' management and leadership responsibilities with the strategic goals of the firm. While many compensation committees now ask partners to submit plans that set out business goals and expectations for the coming year, few firms ever ask partners to draft plans that address management or leadership development. The partners' performance review is the perfect opportunity to do this. In drafting a plan, partners can consult the reviewer or other lawyers about how to deal with issues raised in evaluations. Alternatively, they can work with professional development specialists, consultants, and executive coaches who have expertise in the field and are more objective. Development plans are for the partner's use and do not have to be shown to anyone. However, if a partner has a serious performance problem, the managing partner or practice group leader should see the partner's plan in writing. Partners should refer to their plans in their self-assessments in subsequent evaluations as a way to measure progress, accomplishments, and unattained goals.

■ Decisions on Specific Procedural Features

Who will evaluate partners

Associates are typically evaluated by partners and more senior associates. When partners are evaluated, the type of evaluation determines who the evaluators will be. Depending on the evaluation process, partners may be evaluated by other partners, associates, firm employees, clients, and community members.

- **Peer reviews of partners.** Partners sometimes review their peers as part of the firm's compensation process, but peer reviews are also useful for development purposes. All partners implicitly or explicitly agree to carry out certain management, leadership, and business responsibilities. Peer reviews give partners feedback on how their peers perceive their performance in these areas. The process lets partners know when they are appreciated and admired by their peers (which seldom gets communicated otherwise) and areas where professional growth is needed. As with any type of performance review, it can be a springboard to planning future development efforts. However, because feedback from peers can have serious political and financial implications, peer reviews must be run and delivered by firm leaders who are trusted and respected and can do the job with great sensitivity and tact. Peer reviews are more effective for development purposes when they are combined with reviews from associates and 360° reviews.

- **Upward reviews administered by associates.** In many firms, associates control the upward evaluations of partners. Associates choose the categories of skills and behaviors on which to rate partners, such as:

    — Delegates responsibility effectively.
    — Sets fair and reasonable deadlines.
    — Gives frequent feedback.
    — Allows direct client contact.

— Is accessible.

— Explains budgeting and billing practices.

In this kind of evaluation, the categories that associates choose let partners know what associates want, value, and deem to be of greatest importance. Associates complete written evaluations and sometimes hold meetings to discuss their evaluations of partners. At those sessions, they listen to other associates' comments and share advice about how to work more effectively with different partners. A group of associates collects and processes the data from the evaluations and discussions, and prepares written summaries about each partner. Each partner receives his or her summary. These summaries may also be sent to the department or practice group chair or to the managing partner. The feedback from the evaluation summaries informs partners about how associates perceive their effectiveness in managing and developing them, and reminds partners of their responsibilities as mentors and trainers. Partners who receive especially favorable ratings may be singled out for commendation or reward. Partners whose evaluations signal serious problems may be counseled, offered coaching assistance, or disciplined.

■ **Upward and 360° reviews administered by the firm.** Evaluations of partner performance that are run by the firm are more complex and far-reaching than associate-administered upward reviews. These upward and 360° reviews are based on core competencies, which represent the firm's standards in areas of strategic importance (e.g., management, leadership, business, clients, and associate development). Associates may have input into what the competencies should be, but the competencies on which partners are evaluated go beyond the issues of associate management and development. In upward and 360° reviews administered by the firm, a professional development director, human resources director, or project manager oversees the collection and analysis of the data. Associates complete written evaluations in both upward and 360° reviews. In 360° reviews, peers, firm employees, clients, and community members also complete evaluations of the partners' competencies — hence the term "360°" because this type of review attempts to collect information from the full spectrum or circle of professional contacts.

The extraordinary impact of the 360° review is in large part due to the broad base of feedback presented. There is considerable power in numbers. One firm cites the example of a partner who was a terrible manager of people. Twenty people in the firm evaluated him as part of a 360° review, and the consensus of the evaluations pointed out serious behavioral problems. While he might have been able to shrug off one or two such comments, the weight of these numbers, and the consensus of opinion, was simply too great for him (or the firm) to ignore.

Client evaluations can be the most powerful and immediate instrument of learning and development for partners. They teach partners what clients care about the most in their legal relationship, and how partners can serve clients better. Although many partners recoil from the notion of seeking evaluations from clients, others recognize how precious that data can be. Evaluations of law firm partners are already occurring in many client companies, although companies use the evaluations for internal purposes and do not share the results with those partners. Corporations that retain large numbers of outside counsel routinely rate outside lawyers and distribute the information among the corporation's in-house legal staff. Corporate counsel use these evaluations to make or withhold recommendations about outside lawyers for future engagements. While corporations might not reveal their internal assessments, they are usually willing to participate in 360° reviews that are intended to promote lawyers' development and improve the quality of legal services. Firms that seek client feedback typically send clients written evaluation forms and sometimes follow up with personal interviews. Some firms elect to have a third party conduct those interviews. If someone inside the firm interviews the client, it is usually the managing partner, department chair, practice group chair, or a designated client relationship partner. Asking the client for feedback gives partners especially valuable insight into what must be done to keep — or win back — corporate clients.

One consideration in partner evaluations is the need for a sufficient number of evaluators. For this reason, upward and 360° reviews may not be feasible in small firms or practice groups. An alternative approach in these smaller venues is to have a partner, director, or outside consultant interview associates individually or in groups to obtain feedback on the partners' performance. The person conducting the interviews can then present overall findings and specific feedback to the evaluated partners while maintaining the evaluators' anonymity.

Who will evaluate associates

All firms ask partners to evaluate associates, and many ask senior associates to evaluate the junior associates whom they supervise. Some firms also invite upward reviews of associates, in which junior associates evaluate the more senior associates who act as their supervisors. This usually occurs when lawyers work on large teams and senior associates on the teams customarily assume supervisory responsibilities.

Firms may find it useful to broaden the scope and content of associate reviews as associates approach partnership eligibility. When partnership is at issue, a more rigorous and intensive review is warranted. If the firm has systematically and thoroughly reviewed associates all along, there should be sufficient evaluation data from the firm's lawyers to determine associates' basic readiness for partnership. If progress is documented and tracked over years, the firm will be able to discern associates' achievements and growth over time, their leadership potential, and the extent to which they are motivated and striving to reach partnership.

An intensive pre-partnership review should include input from a variety of additional sources, not just partners and other associates. Evaluations from clients, administrators, staff, and community contacts can be highly informative and contribute significantly to the decision about whether an associate should be made a partner. In addition, the type of information collected should be more far-reaching for this review. Instead of applying just the standards that measure senior associates' proficiency, you need to assess the associates' potential for and expression of management and leadership abilities. You might use the same competency-based upward evaluation criteria used for partners, or create a separate set of performance criteria that set out the standards for admission to partnership.

Intensive pre-partnership reviews should not be done at the last minute, i.e., the year of eligibility for partnership. They should be initiated at least one or two years before the associate is up for partnership, to identify factors that propel the associate forward as well as deficiencies that may hold the associate back. This allows the associate to receive feedback about prospects for advancement, identify development needs, and work out a plan to deal with those needs. Subsequent re-evaluations can help the firm and the associate monitor whether the associate remains on track for partnership, make adjustments where necessary, and make alternative plans if partnership looks unlikely. This process makes the ultimate partnership decision much easier and more equitable.

Who will evaluate Special Counsel

Many firms permit associates to attain a special intermediate status often called "Counsel" or "Special Counsel" after a few years at the firm. These lawyers are neither partners nor associates. When they are elevated to this special status, they often receive (in addition to financial benefits) management training to help them transition into managerial roles. Special Counsel also receive business development training and assistance to prepare them for partnership. These lawyers should be evaluated both by the partners with whom they work and the associates who report to them. The evaluation instrument can either be a combination of the forms used to evaluate associates and those for upward reviews of partners, or a special form adapted for lawyers who hold this status.

How evaluators will be selected

The larger the number of evaluators, the more comprehensive an assessment can be. When lawyers work with many other people during a reporting period, multiple reviewers can evaluate them. There are four principal sources for identifying potential evaluators:

- ■ Time records.
- ■ Suggestions from billing partners.
- ■ Lawyers' choice of their reviewers.
- ■ Unsolicited evaluations.

Using time and billing reports, the firm's accounting office can generate lists of the matters to which lawyers have billed time and the billing partners on those matters. Those lists should identify the lawyers with whom associates or partners have worked most extensively during the evaluation period. If the accounting department does not have this information, then further inquiry is necessary to identify appropriate evaluators. The billing partner and supervising partner (who are not necessarily the same person) should know all team members and their work assignments, and are therefore important sources of this information.

It is important to invite the lawyers being reviewed to choose their own evaluators. These would be people with whom the lawyer has worked and who have observed the lawyer during the review period. Time records may not reflect their names, and billing or supervising partners may not know about them if the work involved activities that are not recorded on time sheets (e.g., business development efforts or community projects).

Some firms open the evaluation process to anyone who wants to comment on the performance of lawyers with whom they have worked. People who for one reason or another want to evaluate a lawyer will do so, but this open-ended request may not be sufficient to generate enough feedback for a meaningful evaluation. This invitation should therefore supplement the other three methods. The best option is to use all four sources of input about potential evaluators.

Everyone who fills out an evaluation form should state how much direct contact they have had with the person they are reviewing. They should indicate how closely and for how long they had a chance to observe that person's work and behavior. The depth and breadth of a reviewer's experience with the person being evaluated should be given appropriate weight.

How and by whom the reviews will be delivered

Conducting effective and constructive reviews is a management skill that requires tact, training, practice, and careful preparation. The people who deliver reviews should be positive, supportive, and sympathetic. Reviewers should feel and demonstrate genuine interest in the reviewed lawyer's development and welfare, and seek to understand any problems the lawyer is having. When the message is a tough one, they should deliver it constructively, sensitively, directly, and clearly.

Delivery of partner reviews was discussed earlier in this chapter. For associates, a supervising partner, mentor, project group leader, or someone on the evaluation committee should deliver the review. Although one person can do this task, most firms have two people do it together. Having two people deliver reviews takes more lawyer time and may be intimidating to the associate. But if there is controversy over the content of the review, having two reviewers can make sure that the message is accurately communicated and understood. It also adds more than one viewpoint to the discussion.

How the program will be rolled out

Before the evaluation system is implemented, everyone must understand the purpose of the program, how the performance standards were derived, and how the system will work. Consider at least one pilot program before rolling out a new evaluation system firm wide so that you can troubleshoot any problems and fine-tune the process. Large firms may want two or even more simultaneous pilot programs in various offices and for different practice groups before attempting full-scale implementation.

When the program is new, it is best to concentrate on its developmental purpose. Although you might want to reward people whose evaluations reflect outstanding performance, do not use the first set of evaluations to decide promotion or compensation. Wait to use evaluations for deciding those issues until after you have established the baseline for a lawyer's performance in the first evaluation and ascertained whether the lawyer has tried to meet expectations by the second review.

One interesting phenomenon that often occurs is that the ratings given to lawyers in the first pilot evaluations tend to be higher than in subsequent firm-wide evaluations. This may be because the first group subjected to evaluations are often volunteers who tend to be the lawyers who are the least threatened by the new system and the most effective in the competencies being measured. It could be because evaluators tend to be more generous the first time around because they are unsure of the effect of the ratings on the lawyers being reviewed, so they err on the side of caution. In later evaluations, they don't feel the need to play it safe. Or it could be something else entirely. But it is something to watch and prepare for, especially if the next groups to go through the process expect to receive similarly high ratings. Their disappointment can lead to anger and resistance to the program.

How often will evaluations be conducted

All associates should be formally reviewed at least once a year. In associates' first two or three years of practice, two reviews per year are preferable. Conducting reviews at the same time each year can make implementation easier because people learn to expect and plan for the process. In very large firms, to make the process more manageable, lawyers can be divided into groups that are evaluated at different times, perhaps on a rolling basis. Most firms conduct annual reviews in the fall, just before compensation decisions are made. This emphasizes that the review is for compensation purposes. Firms that also want to emphasize development hold a second, separate review for that purpose.

It is a good idea to give associates some formal feedback after their first three months in the firm. Rather than an evaluation that goes into their personnel file, this review should be "off the record," intended merely to give associates some input on their early progress. This also gives the firm a chance to find out from associates about their work, experience, integration, and general happiness at the firm, and to uncover any problems that associates may be having. The first formal associate evaluation should take place after six months.

The frequency of partner reviews depends on their purpose and the level of complexity. Upward reviews and peer reviews should be done every year; a more extensive 360° review may be too burdensome to conduct that often. The Law Department at ChevronTexaco alternates 360° reviews for managers with more frequent, less comprehensive evaluations. The Law Department conducts annual evaluations of all lawyers based on fifteen "performance dimensions," including job knowledge, client interaction, advocacy skills, timeliness, and teamwork. Every lawyer in the company is evaluated, including the General Counsel, who is evaluated by the CEO. Those lawyers who act as managers also go through a comprehensive 360° review every two years.

What support and follow up will be provided

Evaluations must be integrated with training, mentoring, and work assignment systems. Telling lawyers that their behavior is inadequate may be informative, but it is not especially helpful in promoting their development. After drawing attention to lawyers' problem areas, the firm must direct them to trainers, mentors, or coaches who can help them make improvements. These resources may be within the firm or outside. For associates, outside assistance recommended by the firm is usually provided at the firm's expense. Partners should also be offered at least a few hours of firm-paid executive coaching or training at the firm's expense.

It is difficult to change established behaviors. Change takes time and is often frustrating. Lawyers need to be shown how to make necessary changes, given opportunities to practice what they learn, and offered ongoing support and encouragement. Partners are more likely than associates to deny problems and resist change. Even partners who are highly determined get distracted or neglect their resolution to change. Experienced coaches and consultants can help busy lawyers set goals, develop a plan, and stay focused and motivated.

Lawyers whose performance is below firm standards should at first be given guidance, training, support, and reasonable opportunities to improve. If they do not or cannot raise their level of performance, they should be asked to leave. When the poor performer is a partner, the problem is thornier but the firm must confront it directly. These partners are not good role models, mentors, or managers, and high-performing lawyers dread working with them. The firm should place poor performers in different roles or move them out. Failure to act decisively on low-performing partners blocks advancement opportunities for more productive lawyers, denies associates and more junior partners effective training and development, and depresses productivity and morale.

How to maximize participation in evaluations

For evaluations to have validity and impact, adequate feedback must be obtained. Associates should be evaluated by at least each of their supervisors on significant projects. In general, evaluations are more worthwhile if there are multiple sources of feedback.

For upward reviews of partners, it is essential to collect evaluations from at least three or four associates in order to protect evaluators' anonymity and to have sufficient data for a meaningful review. Any partner who is not evaluated by at least this minimum number of associates should not be reviewed. Alternatively, if only one or two associates submit evaluations of a partner, you can give those associates the option of showing or withdrawing their evaluations. Some associates will not mind showing their comments to the partner; others may fear disclosure of their identities.

In order to get maximum participation in the evaluation process, the firm's leadership must institute concrete measures. People need to be constantly reminded to submit names of those who should evaluate them and to return the evaluations they complete about others. Overcoming lawyers' inertia and resistance often requires dogged persistence, especially if lawyers believe there will be no adverse consequences for non-compliance. Firms apply pressure to comply in various ways.

In one firm, the evaluation project chair sends periodic statements to practice group leaders about the participation rates in each group, including comparative participation rates, while the evaluation process is underway. In a true spirit of competition, leaders of practice groups with low participation rates push their members to comply. In addition, the managing partner personally contacts individual lawyers who do not respond and lets them know that their lack of cooperation will be looked upon with disfavor in compensation decisions.

Whether to allow appeals

Reviews sometimes deliver unexpected negative feedback. Associates who believe an evaluation to be unfair or inaccurate should be permitted to set the record straight by requesting additional data or clarification, or introducing information in their defense before the evaluation is entered into their personnel record. In some firms, associates are permitted to appeal or challenge criticism about their performance, compensation, or promotion decisions, or the way a review was conducted. Some law firms also permit partners to challenge or question evaluations, but many do not.

Allocating Sufficient Personnel and Resources

The evaluation process is highly labor intensive, not just for the lawyers who have to complete evaluation forms and deliver reviews but for the administrators who oversee the process. A simple upward review run by associates takes a great deal of time but little outlay of money. A competency-based review, however, is both time-consuming and costly. Someone has to do the following things: obtain time records from accounting to identify potential evaluators, elicit information from every lawyer about their potential evaluators, encourage unsolicited evaluations, distribute evaluation forms, remind people to complete and submit them, collect completed evaluation forms, tabulate the numerical data, analyze the narrative comments, synthesize all of the data into evaluation summaries, match reviewers with lawyers to be evaluated, arrange for lawyers to meet together (sometimes flying in from other offices) to discuss the evaluations, schedule meetings to deliver reviews, follow up with individuals to monitor development plans, and coordinate evaluations with mentoring, training, assignments, and other professional development systems. This requires a huge amount of time and considerable expense.

The entire evaluation process requires a dedicated leader and substantial support staff. Many firms have evaluation committees of lawyers who carry out most aspects of the evaluation process with help from clerical and administrative staff. In some firms, professional development directors manage the evaluation process, working with an evaluation committee or running the entire project themselves. Some professional development directors are intimately involved in the associate evaluation process, sitting in on or delivering all associate reviews and doing the follow up monitoring of associates' development plans. In partner reviews, the role of the professional development director depends in large part on their level of authority in the firm. They often manage the partner evaluation process and occasionally take part in delivering and interpreting the data from the evaluations.

■ Aids to Get the Firm Started

As this chapter shows, initiating a comprehensive evaluation system is a complicated undertaking.[10] Table 6 presents some key questions that you should answer and key points to keep in mind as you design and implement your evaluation system.

---

[10] Other helpful resources are *Fair Measure: Toward Effective Attorney Evaluations*, American Bar Association Commission on Women in the Profession, 1997, and *Beyond the Nuts and Bolts of Associate Evaluations: System Development and Process*, NALP, 1995.

TABLE 6. Key Questions to Answer in Setting Up an Evaluation System

1. Why are evaluations being done?
2. What will be evaluated?
3. What standards will be applied?
4. Who will be evaluated?
5. How will reviewers be selected?
6. How will evaluation data be collected and processed?
7. How will the data be used?
8. Who will see the data?
9. How often will reviews be done?
10. How and by whom will reviews be delivered?
11. What support and follow up will be provided?
12. How will the evaluation system be introduced?

APPENDIX 7

Associate Practice and Development Goals for 20___ *[Calendar Year]*

Associate's Name: _____

Practice Group: _____ **Mentor:** _____

I will focus attention on the following practice and development goals (fill in any or all categories below):

Category *[handwritten: GOAL]*	Resources/ Assistance Needed *[handwritten: Activity]*	Timetable *[handwritten: How to Accomplish it]*	Changes/ Comments (Mentor or Practice Group Chair)

1. Skills to learn or improve
   a.
   b.
   c.			

2. Type of work experience
   a.
   b.
   c.			

3. Partners to work with
   a.
   b.
   c.			

(Associate Practice and Development Goals, continued)

Category	Resources/ Assistance Needed	Timetable	Changes/ Comments (Mentor or Practice Group Chair)
4. Clients to work with 　a. 　b. 　c.			
5. Business development activities 　a. 　b. 　c.			
6. Other goals 　a. 　b. 　c.			

CHAPTER 8

Training

To train or not to train? Unlike Hamlet, your firm has little to mull over — it has no choice. For most law firms, training is an imperative. Firms must teach new associates the basics of practicing law, but they cannot stop there. All lawyers need training in areas like management, technology, and business development that are essential for contemporary law practice. Of the four principal professional development activities (along with work assignments, mentoring, and evaluations), training is the most labor-intensive, time-consuming, and expensive — but it cannot be avoided. It is simply a cost of doing business today. Consequently, the firm must make sure that its training efforts are cost-effective, respond to real needs, and support strategic business goals.

Training customarily refers to organized educational events that follow a pre-set agenda to deliver specific content. The ultimate goal is to transfer knowledge, teach skills, and promote behaviors that lawyers must have to be successful in their profession. Within a professional development framework, the emphasis is not simply on formal instruction, but on providing structured opportunities for learning. Training can occur in the classroom, in front of a computer, or in the car, listening to an audiotape during a long commute. Whatever the format, training must be carefully planned and executed.

The need for law firms to sponsor training derives from the new economics of law practice. Law schools prepare graduates to think like lawyers, not to practice law. This has always been true, even though many law schools now offer clinical experiences that give students a taste of real-life practice. The difference is that in the past, law school graduates would spend their first year or two as an apprentice — learning to become a lawyer through mentoring, close supervision, firsthand work experience, and frequent client contact. They could be given small cases and first-chair responsibility, and clients would be charged for their learning time. This model required leisure time and clients who paid bills willingly. Today, sky-high salaries, grueling work demands, clients' cost-controls, and limited interaction with partners or clients make the apprenticeship model a relic. Although associates in small firms and practice groups still enjoy this kind of experience, for most associates, mentoring is ad hoc and informal training is haphazard. More commonly, associates are thrown into a very deep pool and expected to swim laps like an Olympic champion.

Partners often grumble that the "sink or swim" approach was good enough for them, and, to mix metaphors, "the cream will rise to the top." There is some merit to this view, as lawyers often learn best when they are tested under pressure by new challenges. But this approach is hard on associates and also creates problems for the firm. Without guidance and supervision, learning outcomes may be dysfunctional or even endanger the firm's interests. Associates will learn bad habits or acquire only limited knowledge; they will not discern the learning value of a challenging experience; they will feel abandoned; and their inferior work will put clients and the firm in jeopardy. Few firms can afford the risk of totally random trial-and-error learning by associates. Law firms must provide direction to make the learning process more predictable and orderly, to channel and enhance the learning that occurs naturally, and to ensure that the quality of associates' learning meets the firm's performance standards and advances its strategic goals. Considering the talent and investment that are lost if associates "sink," isn't it better to teach them to swim?

Some firms believe that they can avoid training by hiring lateral associates who already have practice experience. But firms cannot rely on "buying talent," especially in a time when law firms are all competing for the best associates. Aside from sacrificing cultural cohesion and institutional memory, that strategy is too expensive and risky. If law firms do not support training, they will not be able to grow talent from within, and it is not a sure bet that the right laterals will be available when the firm needs them. Nor will firms that avoid training be able to attract the laterals they want. New and lateral associates want to be in firms with supportive, learning-oriented cultures in which they can develop and grow professionally. Without such an environment, firms will not be able to recruit and retain the talented lawyers they need.[1]

The need for training is not limited to inexperienced associates. To a large degree, law firms have become institutions of continuing legal education for all their lawyers. They have to make sure that lawyers keep their knowledge and skills up to date, and that lawyers learn the new things they need to compete. Law practice is not static and lawyers must be able to adapt to changes in the law, the firm, and the marketplace. As firms become more businesslike and competitive, these changes require new skills and responsibilities in areas like management,

---

[1] "How Executives Grow," *The McKinsey Quarterly,* Number 1, 2000, pp. 116-125.

leadership, business, technology, and marketing. But lawyers do not learn these skills in law school or on the job. Law firms must provide this education for their lawyers — and the firm — to survive.

As important as training is, it must be kept in the proper perspective. Training is not a panacea, a quick fix, or a solution to systemic problems. Many firms offer training programs as a way to address institutional problems they are not able or willing to tackle head-on. When lawyers are frustrated or feel that something is not working as well as it should, they look to training as the intervention of choice. They mistakenly view training as a cure for interpersonal conflicts, poor performance, low productivity, high turnover, or similar institutional ailments. Examples abound, but here are three common areas where training alone is not the solution:

- **Time management training for overworked associates.** A time management program may teach associates worthwhile skills, but it won't necessarily solve the underlying problem. Associates may be overworked because partners do not organize, delegate, or manage work effectively, or because the firm's technology or administrative support is inadequate.

- **Diversity training as the way to increase the number of minority lawyers in the firm.** Training is an important piece of an overall strategy to increase ethnic diversity, but by itself it will do little to increase the number of minority lawyers in the firm. Instead, the firm must look at the underlying reasons for its lack of diversity and address those reasons through a comprehensive initiative. If the culture of the firm does not make minority lawyers feel welcome and does not give them the support and opportunities they need to excel and advance, diversity training will have little impact on the institutional problem.

- **Writing classes.** Many firms employ writing instructors, conduct in-house writing workshops, and send associates to outside writing programs when the real problem is not associates' writing but rather partners' failure to explain the purpose and context of the assignment, the issues to be covered, or their expectations for the final product.

Training can improve performance, but it cannot solve every performance problem. If the problem is one of poor attitude or inappropriate behavior rather than a lack of knowledge or skills, training can raise awareness, expand knowledge, and demonstrate better techniques, but training alone cannot change the person's behavior. Change will happen only if the person is motivated and the workplace environment reinforces and supports the desired behavior. In fact, some work environments negate the benefits of training, as when lawyers are taught not to engage in sexual harassment but the firm continues to tolerate offensive behavior by prominent rainmakers. Also, many performance problems are better addressed through methods other than structured training, such as individual coaching, closely supervised stretch assignments, and mentoring. These methods are more personalized and often more efficient and cost-effective than training.

It is important that formal training not be used as an excuse for partners to shirk their responsibilities for associates' professional development. Partners may assume that an extensive, high-quality training program relieves them of the obligation to educate and mentor associates. Partners reason that since associates are going to classes to learn practice skills, they can rely on those classes to teach associates whatever they need to know. Sometimes these partners become upset when associates cannot immediately perform up to their expectations. It is a mistake for partners to think that law firm training courses will instantaneously make associates proficient. Professional development still takes time and requires partners to take part in active, informal teaching.

Lastly, the purpose of your firm's training effort is not to put on programs but to provide education that meets lawyers' needs, promotes the firm's business interests, and maximizes the value of learning. If your firm is going to pay for training, then it should be wise and prudent about how it spends its money. Training is expensive and should be designed with the same strategic purpose as your overall professional development program. If poorly executed, training can be a black hole that sucks up money with little to show for it. But when carefully thought out and efficiently implemented, training can add substantial value to the firm's services and its bottom line. Stephen Mayson, Professor of Legal Practice and Director of the Centre for Law Firm Management at England's Nottingham Law School, emphasizes this point:

> "It is often said that training is an investment and not a cost. It is both. It cannot (and should not) be denied that training costs time and money. It becomes an investment when it is properly conceived, properly managed, and properly used. This raises issues of the firm's culture and structure (as well as the way in which it accounts for training time and training costs). Only when the firm's approaches to all of these things are consistent will the true value of training be realised *(sic)*.[2]

---

[2] Stephen Mayson, *Making Sense of Law Firms: Strategy, Structure & Ownership*, Blackstone Press Limited, London, 1997, p. 380.

Training has a central place in the professional development scheme, but it must be appropriately used and adequately supported. Training provides instruction, direction, and a chance to try out new skills in a safe environment. But learning, which is the ultimate purpose of training, requires that lawyers be able to apply what they learn in class to their daily work. That means that training must be viewed not as a separate function, but as an integral and interrelated part of a comprehensive, dynamic professional development program that includes supervised work assignments, mentoring, and feedback. Training should be tied to these professional development systems, to your lawyers' specific learning needs, and to your firm's specific business goals. The first step is to conduct a training needs analysis.

Needs Analysis

Training refers to organized group instruction designed to meet particular learning objectives. Training efforts begin by identifying what needs to be learned. The purpose of a needs assessment is to determine what training programs your firm should present in-house or make available through outside providers in order to address those learning needs. A full-scale training needs analysis is a major, time-consuming project and should be undertaken if your firm is (1) initiating a training program, (2) considering major changes in its training program, or (3) responding to significant internal or external events that require a new in-depth look at training in the firm (e.g., merger, new technology, severe economic downturn, large number of lawyers with serious performance gaps). Firms with an existing training program should also conduct an in-depth analysis of training needs every four or five years. In other years, it is sufficient to reassess and update training efforts as part of the evaluation and budgeting processes. (See the section on Evaluating Training Programs later in this chapter and also Chapter 10 on Budgeting.)

In addition to helping you determine the content of training, a needs assessment can produce extra dividends. It increases the visibility of professional development efforts, allows you to collect critical incidents and case study materials, permits the professional development specialist to meet and get to know lawyers throughout the firm, and gives lawyers a stake in the firm's training program. If lawyers feel invested in the outcome of the training survey, it will be easier to get their buy-in for the ensuing program.

Many firms conduct needs analyses through their own training and professional development personnel, but some find it advantageous to use outside consultants for this purpose. The principal advantages of having the firm's own professional development personnel conduct the needs analysis are that it (1) funnels the information directly to them, (2) allows them to develop personal relationships with lawyers, and (3) builds up goodwill, credibility, and support for them throughout the firm. These individuals are also familiar with the firm's culture and pragmatic about what training proposals are and are not feasible. The advantages of using outside consultants are: (1) their experience, expertise, and independent perspectives; (2) their objectivity in evaluating the results of the training inventory and interpreting lawyers' perceptions of what training they need; (3) their ability to elicit more candid information from lawyers; and (4) the ability to free up professional development personnel for other work. On the other hand, outside consultants have to be educated about the firm and its culture, and their fees add to the expense of the undertaking.

The steps in a training needs assessment are similar to the steps outlined in Chapter 2 for setting up a professional development program, but they focus more narrowly on formal training efforts:

1. **Clarify the firm's business goals and strategy.**
2. **Determine the capabilities lawyers will need to achieve the firm's goals.**
3. **Inventory current training activities.**
4. **Identify perceived training needs.**
5. **Set realistic and achievable priorities.**
6. **Design a training plan.**

■ Clarify the Firm's Business Goals and Strategy and Determine the Capabilities Lawyers Will Need to Achieve the Firm's Goals

These initial steps should have been carried out as part of your professional development program planning (Chapter 2), and determination of lawyers' needed capabilities as expressed in benchmarks and core competencies (Chapter 7). If this has not been done, see those chapters for guidance. These steps are critical to show how training will be integrated into the professional development program and enable the firm to move successfully toward its strategic goals.

A full-scale needs assessment should cover all of the firm's offices and practice areas, and your findings and recommendations should be reported to all departments and practice groups. Each constituent group can take charge of the decisions, design, and implementation of its own specialized training, although firm-wide professional development personnel should work with these smaller groups to assist and coordinate training programs.

■ Inventory Current Training Activities

Taking an inventory of current training activities sounds straightforward but can be quite complicated, especially in multi-office firms. Formal training may occur in many places within the firm, so entries for your training inventory will come from many sources, including:

- All courses conducted by the firm-wide training group.

- Training that goes on in individual offices, departments, and practice groups, including both stand-alone courses and training that is incorporated into business activities (e.g., business development training conducted by the marketing director, legal development updates during practice group meetings).

- Orientation programs.

- Summer associate programs.

- Programs that lawyers attend which are conducted by outside CLE vendors, including those that firm lawyers have attended outside the firm, outside programs that lawyers have attended in the firm via computer or satellite, and programs that CLE providers have presented inside the firm.

If your firm tracks CLE, searching the firm's CLE database can facilitate the inventory process.

In taking an inventory of current training, you should also locate training resources used by the firm. These would include individuals, educational materials, and references that are part of the firm's training efforts, including:

- Lawyers and managers in the firm who have expertise, experience, and interest in teaching;

- Clients, judges, business people, and professional contacts who have served as in-house faculty;

- Teaching guides and instructional materials from past courses;

- Videotapes and other self-study materials;

- Previous and existing contracts with online and community-based CLE providers;

- The administrative staff in each firm office and their capabilities; and

- The technology available to support training (including video and telephone conferencing capabilities, net-meeting and webcasting ability, and a tracking system for CLE compliance).

One vital resource that should be ascertained is the level of the firm's commitment to training, beginning with top leaders and the professional development/training committee. It is important for the professional development director to know their level of commitment and support. It is also important to find out if the firm has any plans, or would be receptive to proposals, to increase or change its technology support for training.

■ Identify Training Needs

The heart of a needs analysis is to find out what lawyers need so that the firm can design a training program that responds to those needs. The three principal areas that most needs fall into are: (1) the basic practice skills and knowledge that new lawyers must have to become effective practitioners; (2) the competencies that all lawyers need to achieve business goals; and (3) the CLE requirements in all the jurisdictions in which your lawyers are licensed. CLE requirements can be obtained from each state licensing entity or at www.cleusa.org, the web site of the Organization of Regulatory Administrators of CLE (ORACLE). While you investigate the areas where training may be needed, keep in mind what you have learned about the firm's current training activities and resources during the inventory process. Consider how you can use, improve, recycle, or build on those existing efforts.

Begin by surveying lawyers to determine what training they need. One of the challenges in a training needs analysis is to distinguish between what lawyers want and what they actually need. Sometimes the two coincide, but often lawyers want training that is irrelevant to the firm's business or training goals, too trivial or limited to warrant a formal program, or unfeasible for the firm to present. To be fair, lawyers may not understand what is or is not a suitable subject for training or they may not really know what training they need, especially if they are new to practice or to the firm. Often they request training to address issues that reflect systemic problems in the firm that cannot be remedied by training. They tend to base training requests on their present needs, not their long-term needs, which limits their responses. They also find it easier to identify deficiencies in others than in themselves. One way to deal with this last issue is to ask lawyers first "What training do you think *other* lawyers need?" and then, "What training do *you* need?"

In addition to general questions about their perceived needs, your survey should ask about specific areas where training might be useful. Along with technical and substantive subjects, this inquiry should cover areas that are not legal in nature but may be vital to lawyers' practice, such as management skills, foreign language proficiency, or business etiquette. For example, training in cultural diversity may be especially important if you have international offices or your lawyers are working across international borders. Lawyers do not always think of those subjects as being under the aegis of law firm training and may not mention them spontaneously.

A written survey is the easiest way to collect all of this information, but personal interviews and focus groups are more effective and generate more detailed data. Prepare questions carefully. When you conduct the survey in person, listen attentively and ask appropriate follow-up questions to clarify and expand answers. For greater consistency and validity, it is advisable to prepare a list of open-ended questions, and to have one person or a small group of people conduct all the interviews using the same questions. Using common questions will also make data analysis easier.

Be sure to obtain input from a cross-section of the firm, from new associates to senior partners, across all practice groups and offices. It is also useful to survey paralegals, managers, and staff to ascertain the kind of training they believe lawyers need. Practice group leaders are especially important to survey because they may be privy to information about anticipated events that may require special training (e.g., a shift of emphasis in a group's business plan from public offerings to corporate finance). New and lateral associates should be asked what promises, if any, were made to them about training during the recruiting process.

In conjunction with your survey, a review of various firm documents and records can also shed light on lawyers' training needs. Some of the records to review include:

- **Benchmarks and competencies.** Benchmarks list the basic knowledge and skills required for practice at different career points, and competencies identify additional knowledge, skills, and behaviors needed for successful practice. When you know what capabilities lawyers need to succeed in your firm, you can then assess whether they are performing up to expectations. If they are not, determine whether the gap between expectations and performance can be remedied by training.

- **Performance evaluations.** Summaries of lawyers' performance reviews indicate areas where individual improvement is needed. While you would not necessarily conduct a program for one or two lawyers, look for broader patterns, especially within practice groups or by classes. If, for example, many second-year associates appear to have poor research skills, then a legal research workshop for that group may be worthwhile.

- **Client surveys.** If your firm (often through the marketing department) conducts client surveys, the results may suggest areas where training could be beneficial.

- **Evaluations of previous programs.** A review of the evaluations for past training programs will show which courses have been well received, where there has been ample training and where there has been little, and what suggestions have been made to repeat, improve, or drop specific courses.

- **Recruiting and marketing materials.** These materials may raise expectations about training in the firm. Compare what they say to what the firm does.

- **Exit interviews.** Specific comments as well as patterns that emerge in these records may suggest areas where training is needed.

■ Set Realistic and Achievable Priorities

Most needs analyses generate far more training ideas than the firm can realistically implement. It is necessary to set priorities that reflect the firm's and its lawyers' most pressing needs. Priorities are very hard to set in the face of numerous competing needs and demands, but the process is easier when the firm's strategic business goals and learning goals are clear. Then you know what the firm deems most important, what it is trying to accomplish, and what specific training will help achieve those goals. Buy-in and support will also be more forthcoming from the firm's leaders.

Keeping in mind the firm's strategic plan, benchmarks and competencies, and the other data you have collected, outline the goals for the training program and decide your priorities accordingly. These decisions will determine where the firm will direct its training money and resources. The training or professional development committee should be actively involved in deciding these priorities. One of the first issues in setting priorities is to decide the scope of the firm's training endeavors. Does the firm want a comprehensive curriculum or one that is targeted to particular topics (e.g., client relation skills) or constituencies (e.g., new associates)? Similarly, does the firm want to provide training primarily for entry-level lawyers or offer more advanced programs as well? Is there something happening in the firm that dictates where training should be concentrated? For instance, if the firm is introducing a new computer system, technology training for all lawyers might be the primary focus of training efforts for the whole firm. If the firm wants to provide training in all mandatory CLE subjects, then those topics will drive your training plan.

Once your overall goals and program scope are set, you can prioritize specific courses. Analyze the data you have collected and determine the various training courses that will respond to lawyers' identified needs. After you have listed all the potential courses, divide them into three different priority levels: *Essential*, *Desirable*, and *Wishful Thinking*. *Essential* courses include those that are of vital importance and must be taught in some way, shape, or form. The *Desirable* group consists of courses that the firm would like to have if sufficient resources and time permit. The *Wishful Thinking* courses are those that appeal only to a small group of lawyers or have little impact on business goals, but which nonetheless have educational value. These categories will help you shape your plan but do not necessarily dictate what will go into it. Most courses will come from the *Essential* group, but you may also decide to include lower priority courses, especially is there is a groundswell of interest or a special purpose that may not be based on training needs alone.

■ Design a Training Plan

Once you know your priorities, you can devise a training plan that names the courses you will present during the year. The initial outline of your plan should include all the courses you have selected and a timeline for presenting them. Do not omit or limit programs at this stage because of anticipated costs or available resources. Once you determine the overall curriculum, you can pare down the list and adjust the training program to meet budgetary and logistical constraints.

In prioritizing topics for curriculum planning, people sometimes forget that their goal is to provide appropriate training to meet lawyers' needs, not to put on a lot of courses. The final program design should carefully select courses that are relevant, practical, and worthwhile. The process of setting priorities and developing a training plan is dynamic and fluid. Priorities change, as do budgets, so keep your priority list updated and handy. Although its immediate use is for the current year, the training plan should also act as a blueprint for future planning. Priorities will shift from year to year, but your findings and plan should facilitate later planning efforts.

Curriculum Considerations

A curriculum delineates all the courses your firm's training program will offer. Preparing a curriculum:

- Demonstrates the coherence, structure, and educational value of the firm's training efforts.

- Expresses what the firm wants its lawyers to learn and how the firm will provide formal opportunities for learning.

- Helps lawyers achieve firm-generated benchmarks and competencies.

- Facilitates coordination of training with evaluations and other professional development systems.

- Ensures that important areas of training are not overlooked.

Subject areas that are customarily included in law firm training curricula appear in Table 1. Appendix 8-A at the conclusion of this chapter contains descriptions of the curricula at four law firms.[3] In selecting courses for your curriculum, do not restrict your vision to substantive law training. Be creative. Conduct courses that address the many different learning needs of your firm's lawyers. Below are some common categories in which law firms present courses:

- **Orientation.** Orientation programs provide new associates and lateral lawyers with information about how the firm operates, what the firm expects of them, and how they can get their work done.

- **Substantive law and procedure.** These courses impart knowledge needed for effective practice. They include basic courses for new associates, specialized programs for experienced lawyers, and updates on new developments for all lawyers. This training is usually department or practice group specific.

- **Practice skills.** All lawyers need to learn and improve practice skills. For junior associates, training may focus on basic skills such as interviewing and

---

[3] Three additional resources for designing law firm curricula are Stephen R. Chitwood, Anita F. Gottlieb, Evelyn Gaye Mara, *A Business Skills Curriculum for Law Firm Associates*, Association of Legal Administrators, 2001; Austin G. Anderson and Arthur G. Greene, *The Effective Associate Training Program*, The American Bar Association, 1999; and *Legal Education and Professional Development — An Educational Continuum*, Report of The Task Force on Law Schools and The Profession: Narrowing the Gap, ABA Section of Legal Education and Admissions to the Bar, 1992 (the "MacCrate Report").

TABLE 1. Subject Areas Customarily Included in Law Firm Training Curricula

- Litigation skills and procedures
- Business/transactional skills and procedures
- Practice specialties
- Business development
- Technology
- Management skills
  — Self-management (time, stress, organization)
  — Managing people
  — Managing work
- Mentoring
- Negotiation
- Dispute resolution
- Legal writing
- Ethics and professionalism
- Law firm economics
- Principles of business
- Communication/presentation skills
- Diversity and elimination of bias

legal drafting. For experienced associates, it may include work management, oral advocacy, or editing the writing of others. For partners, it may concentrate on leadership. Some skills courses apply to all lawyers (e.g., delegation) while others are department or practice group specific (e.g., taking depositions).

■ **Interdisciplinary courses.** Lawyers need to understand how other disciplines impact their legal work. Specialized courses can teach lawyers about other professional fields. Some interdisciplinary courses cross legal specialties (e.g., bankruptcy law for litigators, methods of dispute resolution for business lawyers), while others address the interrelation between law and other disciplines (e.g., understanding financial statements, medical complications of toxic products).

■ **Management.** Courses that teach lawyers how to manage themselves, their work, and other people have become increasingly important as lawyers assume greater management responsibilities. Courses that fall into this category include supervision, stress management, and dealing with conflict.

■ **Business.** Lawyers need to know about the business of their clients and the business of the firm. Knowledge about business — including how to run a business — is becoming more important for lawyers who serve as counselors to their clients. Knowledge about the firm's business is necessary to make sure the firm runs efficiently and profitably.

- **Professionalism.** Professionalism courses today go beyond teaching legal ethics or the rules of professional responsibility. They include such topics as civility and appropriate behavior in dealing with clients, courts, and opposing counsel. They also include firm practices and procedures in managing risk, avoiding conflicts of interest, and preventing malpractice.

- **Client relations/business development.** To be effective lawyers and rainmakers, lawyers must know how to serve existing clients and attract new ones. Lawyers need to learn the knowledge, skills, and behaviors necessary to attract, manage, and retain good clients.

- **Communications.** Many firms provide communication training to help lawyers communicate better. These courses are often adjuncts to larger training programs in management, business development, or client relations.

- **Technology.** The use of technology is now fundamental to law practice. Most lawyers cannot practice without computers and high-tech communication tools, including handheld devices and laptops that allow them to work from home or on the road. Firms need to teach lawyers to use technology appropriately and effectively in practice.

A curriculum should identify the core programs that are deemed fundamental for practice. This primary core curriculum includes courses for all lawyers in the firm, but each department or practice area may also have a separate core curriculum to cover subjects essential to its own unique practice. Core curricula are predominantly directed at first-year lawyers (see Table 2), but they should also offer courses for lawyers at different experience levels. These can be new subjects introduced after the first year or advanced courses that build on the basic ones. In addition to the core subjects, a curriculum should include courses that are deemed important but not vital. These courses can cover any subject within the scope of your firm's training goals. They should appeal to lawyers at various seniority levels and with different practice interests. The main limitation on these programs is the amount of time and resources the firm is willing to commit to them.

Small firms with few resources may be more limited in what they can present, but their curricula can still provide an array of courses. For example, any size firm can schedule weekly "case reviews," i.e., discussions of recent court decisions, case developments, legislative enactments, or business transactions. Aside from being immediately applicable to the firm's practice, having different lawyers present the case and lead the discussion gets everyone into the habit of teaching and allows them to practice presentation skills. Table 3 describes other

TABLE 2. Potential Topics for Inclusion in Core Curricula for First-Year Associates

- **All first-year associates**
    - Legal research (including computer-assisted research)
    - Use of technology in practice
    - Legal writing
    - Introduction to business development
    - Diversity
    - Interpersonal office relations
    - Ethics and professionalism
    - Managing time and work
- **First-year litigation associates**
    - Early case assessment
    - Drafting and responding to pleadings
    - Drafting and responding to written discovery
    - Taking and defending depositions
    - Motion practice
    - Document productions
    - Settlements
    - Dispute resolution procedures
    - Strategies, negotiations, and documentation
    - Preparing for trial
    - Trial skills
- **First-year corporate associates**
    - Due diligence
    - Corporate mergers and acquisitions
    - Organization of businesses and how businesses make money
    - Letters of intent
    - Structuring a deal
    - Negotiating and drafting agreements
    - Representations, indemnities, and warranties
    - Closings
    - Legal opinions
    - Accounting principles

approaches and techniques that allow small firms (as well as large firms) to offer high-quality training. Using ingenuity and creativity to control costs and maximize benefits, firms of any size can offer excellent in-house training for their lawyers.

One of the factors to consider in designing a curriculum is the career point when training in a particular subject makes the most sense. If litigation associates will not go to trial before their third or fourth year, scheduling a week-long intensive trial skills course for first-year associates may not be prudent. The impact of the training is lessened by the long gap between the training and the time associates can actually utilize the skills they learned. Nonetheless, a firm may choose to schedule it this way for other reasons, e.g., to inspire associates or build morale.

TABLE 3. Cost-Efficient Training Approaches and Techniques for Small Firms

1. Have lawyers present and lead discussions of recent court decisions, case developments, or deals.

2. At the conclusion of a client matter, have the lead partner facilitate a discussion of what went well, what went badly, and what should have been done differently.

3. Ask lawyers who make presentations at conferences or to clients to repeat their presentations in the firm.

4. Ask lawyers who write articles to discuss the points made in the articles.

5. Use a videotape to jumpstart a discussion.

6. Have lawyers who attend outside CLE programs present what they learned.

7. Have a partner and associate prepare a course based on client work they have done together.

8. Invite partners to discuss their practices, clients, and practice areas, highlighting key learning points for associates.

9. Base programs on "best practices" in various subject areas (e.g., business development, arguing motions, handling difficult clients, lawyers, and judges).

10. Invite clients and community leaders to lead or participate in programs.

11. Solicit anonymous questions from associates about a particular topic and design a program in which partners answer those questions.

12. Join with other small firms to share the costs of hiring an outside instructor.

■ Curriculum Time Frame

Once you have the content of a core curriculum mapped out, determine the time period for it. While you may want to cover all topics in one year, an 18-month or longer cycle may be more realistic for a comprehensive program. Then, when you have this big picture time frame, determine at what point in the cycle you will schedule each program and how long each program will take. If you plan to repeat a program, decide when, how often, and in which offices it will be presented. For example, let's say that one of the curriculum topics you want to address this year is legal ethics for new associates. You may decide that the initial seminar will be held in October and again in March in your largest office, and that it will be presented once a year in your other offices every November. Organizing this information this way makes it easier for you to plot the programs, assess how the curriculum fits together across the firm, and prepare an accurate budget.

In-House Training or Outside CLE?

Law firms can provide training for their lawyers by doing it in-house or by sending lawyers to outside CLE providers. It is best to offer a combination of both, using outside CLE to complement and expand what the firm can present in-house. For particular courses, the firm can decide individually whether to use in-house or outside CLE resources. There are many reasons for law firms to conduct their own training courses. (See Table 4.) One important reason is that associates want to learn from the firm's own lawyers, and the firm can use the opportunity to transfer its collective intelligence and know-how to all associates. A second principal reason is control. In-house courses allow the firm to control the content, quality, and cost of training. Training courses convey both information and values. By designing the programs yourself, you determine the course content, including the information, skills, behaviors, and values that will be taught to your lawyers. In-house training ensures that all lawyers are taught the same lessons, and that those lessons are in accord with the firm's vision and principles. Certain programs, such as a course in the firm's risk management procedures, ought to be conducted by the firm because the content must be uniform and cannot be as effectively taught by an outside provider.

In-house training allows the firm to maintain a high quality of instruction. Mentoring, supervision, and other methods of informal teaching are directed at single lawyers. When lawyers teach other lawyers one-on-one, the teaching will vary and some may be amiss. Training programs present lessons to many lawyers at once and ensure that the message is consistent and delivered according to pre-set quality standards.

Conducting training in-house makes it easier for the firm to control its training costs. An in-house program makes training costs predictable and manageable. While it might be more cost-efficient to send a few lawyers to an outside CLE course, for a large number of lawyers, the per capita cost is usually less in an in-house program. By closely overseeing the budget and evaluation processes, the firm can assure that its in-house training is cost-effective.

TABLE 4. Reasons to Conduct Training In-House

- Teach a subject, procedure, or skill consistently to all lawyers.
    - Examples: Professionalism, risk management procedures, practice-specific ethical issues.
- Maintain quality control of courses.
- Control training costs.
- Promote camaraderie and acculturation.
- Real-life experience is not widely available or is too risky for a novice.
    - Example: Trial skills.
- Need a low faculty-to-student ratio.
    - Examples: Writing and presentation skills.
- Lawyers need essential skills training quickly.
    - Example: First-year classes in substantive practice and procedure.
- Training can be tailored to lawyers' exact needs.
    - Example: Language training for international lawyers.
- Lawyers will not attend outside programs.
- Outside programs do not adequately cover the subject.
- Teach firm-specific procedures and strategies.
    - Example: Settlement negotiation and philosophy.
- Showcase own lawyers' expertise.
- Promote client relationships and business development.
    - Examples: Use clients as faculty, invite clients to attend the firm's courses.
- Support the firm's recruiting and retention efforts.
- Support lawyers' business development efforts.
    - Example: Convert instructional materials from in-house courses into published articles and conference presentations.
- Make it convenient for lawyers to comply with CLE requirements.

Another important reason for doing training in-house is that its social and cultural value for the firm cannot be duplicated in an outside CLE course. In-house training sessions bring the firm's lawyers together to share their own experiences, ideas, and lessons. This enriches the firm's knowledge base, creates a sense of community among the lawyers, and provides a comfortable environment that promotes camaraderie. When lawyers join the firm as new associates, laterals, or through mergers, in-house training also provides an effective vehicle for acculturation and social integration.

On the other hand, law firms may prefer outside CLE courses when they cannot present those courses in-house or when it would not be cost-effective to do so. Using outside CLE providers saves program development time and lightens the teaching load of the firm's lawyers. There are many situations that make outside courses more appealing or affordable:

1. A course may be too costly for the firm to develop or implement.

2. There may be too small an audience for a course on a specialized topic.

3. The firm may not have anyone qualified or willing to teach a course.

4. The firm may have insufficient administrative resources to put on the course.

5. An existing outside course may be better than anything the firm could present.

Table 5 lists some of the factors to consider in deciding whether to send lawyers to outside training courses or present the training in-house. These factors are interrelated and no single one is determinative. They should all be weighed together in making your decision.

Even law firms that conduct extensive in-house training usually pay for their lawyers to attend some outside courses, although payment for out-of-town programs involving travel or extraordinary expenses may require justification. Firms take many different approaches to deciding how much they will pay for outside CLE. Three common approaches are to handle each request on a case-by-case basis; to budget a set amount for outside CLE every year, calculated as either a percentage of the training budget or on a "per lawyer" basis; or to allocate a maximum amount for each lawyer to spend for outside CLE.

Many CLE programs are offered at legal conferences, by bar associations, and by private CLE providers. Lawyers attend those training events for important reasons in addition to advancing their knowledge. Coming together with other professionals is necessary for a lawyer's professional growth. The universe in which

> **TABLE 5. Factors to Consider in Deciding Between In-House and Outside CLE Courses**
>
> - **Availability.** Are good programs available from outside providers?
> - **Number of lawyers.** How many lawyers need this program? Do the numbers justify the time and expense of in-house course development?
> - **Faculty and resources.** Does the firm have access to faculty and resources (e.g., facilities, equipment) needed for the program?
> - **Quality.** How good are outside CLE programs compared to what can be offered in-house?
> - **Specialized needs.** How specialized must the content be? Can outside programs provide the level of specialization and depth required?
> - **Cost efficiency.** On a per capita basis, is it less expensive to send lawyers to outside programs or bring the program in-house?
> - **Convenience.** How easy is it for lawyers to attend the outside program? How hard is it for the firm to put on the program?
> - **Travel.** Will lawyers have to travel out of town to attend the program? Is the added time and expense justified by the excellence, pertinence, or uniqueness of the outside program?
> - **Timing.** When is the training needed? Can the firm put it on when needed? Are outside programs available when lawyers need them?

lawyers practice is not confined to the firm; lawyers need to take part in the legal profession as a whole. At outside learning events, lawyers meet and learn from colleagues in other firms, locations, and employment venues. They hear about new and emerging legal issues and acquire new perspectives on familiar issues. They network with other lawyers and industry leaders, both to expand their business development prospects and for personal edification. And they return to the office inspired and reinvigorated.

Outside CLE programs are available in most legal communities throughout the country. Local and state bar associations, the American Bar Association, specialty bar associations, law schools, and private CLE providers, among others, sponsor these programs. Many of these providers make legal training courses available by telephone, on CDs, or online. Information about providers and courses can be obtained from many sources, including the Association for Continuing Legal

Education (ACLEA — www.ACLEA.org), a nonprofit association with more than 500 members representing over 200 CLE providers.

Technology in Training

Technology is fast becoming a familiar and convenient way to deliver training to lawyers. We now commonly speak of "technology-based training" and "e-learning," which refer to the transfer of instructional content or learning experiences via the Internet/World Wide Web, intranets, extranets, audio- and videotape, satellite broadcast, interactive TV, and multi-media CD-ROM. Among other advantages, the use of technology enables firms to provide "distance training," or educational experiences in which the instructor and students are separated by time, location, or both.

In 2001, the American Society for Training and Development (ASTD) issued a comprehensive report on e-learning which concluded that:

> "E-learning has the potential to revolutionize the basic tenets of learning by making it individual rather than institution-based, eliminating the clock-hour measures in favor of performance and outcome measures, and emphasizing customized learning solutions over generic, one-size-fits-all instruction."[4]

The ASTD study also projected that corporate e-learning in the United States would be a $7 billion market by 2003, and that web-based training in particular would surge by 900 percent between 1999 and 2003.[5] Another ASTD study of the training industry found that 11 percent of corporate training is now delivered by computer.[6] In this area, the business world is way ahead of the legal profession. It is estimated that only about one to three percent of CLE is now delivered online.[7] However, a recent survey of law firm professional development directors showed that technology use for lawyer training and development is growing: "In-house faculty are using more technology in the classroom. Firms are using more technology to get in-house programs out to all their offices and to store learning resources for access on demand."[8]

---

[4] "A Vision of E-Learning for America's Workforce: Report of the Commission on Technology and Adult Learning," ASTD, 2001 (http://www.astd.org/virtual_community/public_policy/jh_ver.pdf).
[5] Ibid.
[6] Tammy Galvin, "Industry 2001 Report," *Training*, October 2001, pp. 40, 42.
[7] Data presented by panel of CLE providers in San Francisco, October 2001.
[8] "In-House Uses of Technology for Professional Development," *Professional Development Quarterly*, August 2001, p. 3.

In spite of the interest in technology-based training, the use of technology — considered a "non-traditional" training format — is not recognized as a valid training modality by many state CLE accrediting agencies. Those states do not give CLE accreditation to courses that employ satellite broadcasts, webcasts, interactive software programs, or even videotapes in some cases. It is anticipated that this will change as non-traditional instructional formats become more widely used and accepted. As training technologies continue to become more refined and less expensive, as production qualities improve, and as their benefits become more widely appreciated, technology could indeed revolutionize the way training is delivered in the legal workplace.

■ Satellite Broadcasts, Web-Based Training, and Videoconferencing

Firms have used some forms of technology in training for many years; videotapes, CD-ROMs, and teleconferences have become CLE staples. Today, more sophisticated technologies deliver outside training to the office through satellite broadcasting and to the desktop through the World Wide Web.[9] Using videoconferencing, firms can easily connect all their offices for live, interactive in-house courses.

Satellite broadcasts are transmissions of live programs to locations equipped with a satellite dish. Some firms are equipped only to receive transmissions, but others also have the capability to broadcast from one office to another. This permits direct communication among all the offices that are linked together for the program. Web-based programs combine, and deliver online, live and taped presentations, text, video, audio, and graphics. In addition to course content, they may include real-time chat rooms or asynchronous discussions in which individuals post questions and faculty respond when they log on, which may be at completely different times. Web-based resources can include archived programs, libraries of course materials, and hyperlinks to references that lawyers can utilize whenever they please. A webcast presented by Practising Law Institute (PLI) following the events of September 11 attests to the power of technology to deliver training to a broad audience. That two-day program, "The Aftermath of Terrorism: Confronting the Legal Issues," presented on November 15-16, 2001, dealt with numerous issues involving crisis management, airlines, insurance, corporate/securities issues, bankruptcy, immigration, privacy, civil liberties, real estate, business, and estate administration. 1,256 lawyers in more than nine states around the country received the live

---

[9] For definitions of technology-based training terms and methodologies, see www.learningcircuits.org/glossary.html.

webcast by computer, and an additional 750 lawyers have since registered to view the archived program online.

Even more common than satellite and web-based training is the use of videoconferencing to deliver live in-house programs to distant offices. Real-time videoconferences have the benefit of being live and permitting interactivity among lawyers in multiple offices. Lawyers throughout the firm receive the same content at the same time. Multi-office firms, especially those that try to maintain a "one-firm" culture, find that distributing training by videoconference allows them to get a consistent message out to all offices and reduces feelings of isolation among lawyers in remote offices. The savings in time and travel costs are also important factors in the popularity of videoconferencing.

Notwithstanding these benefits, videoconferencing has limitations. Videoconferencing is best for presentations and for conferences for a small number of participants who can see and talk with one another in real time. Unfortunately, most firms are too ambitious in their aims for training by videoconference. They assume that any course can simply be presented before a camera without affecting the quality of instruction, so they do not adapt the program for a televised medium. They also try to include too many people in too many offices in the training. If the presentation is a straight lecture, this may work, but where interactivity and audience participation are desired, the medium presents too many obstacles:

- The instructor is either forced to remain in one place, which reduces spontaneity and interactivity, or to move out of camera range, which may leave lawyers in distant offices viewing a blank wall or the back of a talking head.

- The technology makes it very difficult for the instructor to engage or connect with audiences in distant offices. Audience members remain detached and rarely ask or answer questions.

- The technology is still imperfect. Many things can go wrong with the telephone and video connections, and image and production quality are often inferior.

Although the training director can take steps to improve quality and reduce these drawbacks,[10] videoconferencing has a far way to go to provide high-quality training experience for lawyers in distant offices.

---

[10] Christine White, "Videoconferencing: How to Set Up for Effective Presentation," *Professional Development Quarterly*, August 2001, p.1.

■ Comparing E-Training and Classroom Training

Technology-based training has several advantages over classroom training. Unlike classroom training, which is a one-time event, technology allows programs to be archived and accessed over and over again. Lawyers can "attend" programs at their own convenience. Technology allows them to create their own learning schedules and experiences by choosing the courses that interest them the most at the time when they most need to learn the subject matter. Lawyers can refresh their knowledge by going back to old programs and course materials on their computer screens. They can view entire programs at one sitting, watch portions of a program in sequence over a period of time, or select only certain portions of a program that are relevant to their learning needs. Lawyers can learn precisely what they want, quickly, easily, and just in time to put that learning to use. They can also test their learning by taking online quizzes that cover what they just viewed and get immediate feedback about the results.

Online training is also more efficient. It can reach many more lawyers than a classroom can — and reach them at any time of day or night. Lawyers do not have to go anywhere; they can attend training at their desks. Instead of trying to cover too much material, instructors can focus on a few key points, then list resources for lawyers who want to go farther or dig deeper — and lawyers can access those resources instantaneously through hyperlinks. Online discussions can follow as well, with participants "talking" to each other and with the instructors over many days.

Notwithstanding the benefits and potential impact of online training, technology will not replace the classroom. Many lawyers are not comfortable or receptive to taking a class alone through a computer terminal; they learn best by being engaged and challenged in a real classroom. Much of learning is social. Live, classroom-based training provides a social learning environment that enriches the learning experience. It is true that groups of people can interact online, but the social context is not as fulfilling as in-person encounters. Dr. Edward Hallowell of Harvard Medical School speaks of this need for face-to-face interaction as the "human moment."[11] Hallowell states that this need is both physiological and emotional. He explains that the human moment occurs when people are together in the same place, at the same time, and engaged in dialogue with one another. Using this definition, attending a class online does not present a human moment. Even if it is live and interactive, participants are not sharing the same physical space during the class, and the level of personal engagement is diminished.

---

[11] Edward M. Hallowell, "The Human Moment at Work," *Harvard Business Review*, January 1999.

A clear example of the need for the human moment in training is in courses that teach trial skills. Learning trial skills is more than just learning the rules of evidence or practicing closing arguments. Trial lawyers cannot become great in the courtroom unless they experience the emotional drama of a cross-examination and develop "gut feelings" that only come from practicing in a realistic courtroom environment. In that way, lawyers learn to respond to the emotional messages, body language, and chemistry of witnesses in stressful situations. Technology-based programs can teach cross-examination principles and take a lawyer through a cross-examination with a pre-taped witness, but the quality of learning cannot compare with the experience of a simulated mock trial in a courtroom, facing a live witness, in front of a judge and jury.

Classroom and online learning are best used to complement and leverage each other's strengths. Together, they combine the social learning of classroom training with the individualized learning available through technology to maximize the impact of training. Every person has a distinct learning style and preference. Some lawyers are visual learners, while others learn better by listening or by "doing." Some lawyers thrive in small, interactive learning groups, while others learn better through solitary study. A blended approach (i.e., offering both classroom and online training) can satisfy different learning styles and preferences. When both types of learning environments are available, the learning possibilities are richer.

■ Bringing Outside Training Inside: Contracting with Online CLE Providers

In addition to delivering your own in-house training courses online, your firm can contract with CLE providers to give your lawyers online access to their programs. Some CLE providers produce and distribute their own specially designed online programs, while other providers act as aggregators, i.e., they give lawyers access to programs that are produced by other CLE providers. The advantage of using providers that distribute their own courses is that they stand behind the quality of their offerings. The benefit of using aggregators is that they provide access to a larger variety of program sources. In addition, some vendors will convert recordings of a firm's in-house programs to a digital format, making those courses accessible to lawyers (and their clients) through their computers.

Online CLE providers use different pricing arrangements (e.g., flat fees, per lawyer or per program fees, payment based on time usage) and include different product and support features in their prices (e.g., CLE credit tracking, technical support, help desks). The online CLE industry is still very new and fluid, with vendors appearing, merging, and disappearing all the time. These uncertainties make contracting with vendors confusing and difficult. If your firm is thinking about contracting with an outside provider for online CLE, see Appendix 8-B, which offers a list of questions that you should ask before you make any deals.

■ Administrative Benefits of Online CLE Providers

An added — and very appealing — feature of contracting with online CLE providers is that it makes life much easier for CLE administrators. Online CLE vendors usually offer more than CLE programming. They also provide a host of services that include:

- Tracking lawyers' CLE credits;
- Keeping records of programs;
- Filing for CLE accreditation;
- Handling program registration;
- Printing out and storing certificates of attendance;
- Monitoring renewal periods for firm CLE re-accreditation;
- Monitoring lawyers' CLE compliance periods;
- Advising law firm administrators of changes in CLE regulations;
- Tracking training costs;
- Reporting on usage patterns, costs, and other data useful to the firm;
- Sending e-mail alerts to lawyers when programs become available; and
- Sending e-mail reminders of programs for which lawyers have registered.

Many online CLE providers offer these services across multiple states. Since all states have unique CLE requirements, this means that multi-office firms can have a central source of CLE information and recordkeeping that covers all lawyers, regardless of where they are licensed.

Course Design for In-House Programs

When designing a training course, it is necessary to address both content (what will be taught) and process (how it will be taught). The principles of adult learning discussed in Chapter 4 emphasize the need to make law firm training experiential, practical, useful, and interactive. The variability in lawyers' learning styles means that employing diverse formats and training techniques will engage a wider audience. With these points as a backdrop, you can design a training course by identifying the learning needs of the audience; setting learning objectives; selecting appropriate teaching methods; developing an agenda; and securing the resources necessary to implement the course.

■ 1. Identifying Audience Needs

The first step in designing a course is to determine who the audience will be and what their learning needs are. Determining those needs requires assessing the current level of lawyer performance, finding the gaps that can be closed by training, and determining what training to provide. Courses for lawyers should meet one or more of three basic training needs: what lawyers need to know (knowledge), what they need to do (skills), and how they need to do it (behavior). Courses are most effective when four conditions are met: (1) the lawyers in the audience are at a similar level of competence, (2) they need to learn the same material, (3) the material they need to learn is designed into the course, and (4) audience members will be able to put the training to use soon and frequently after the course.[12] Although program designers cannot control all four of these elements, every course should be designed with a particular audience in mind. For example, a legal writing course for new associates might emphasize research and style, while a writing course for partners might focus on editing. Trying to combine both groups in the same one-hour course would result in an unfocused, ineffective, and diluted program.

■ 2. Setting Learning Objectives

The next step in course design is to articulate what the audience will learn during the course. The question to answer is, "What should participants be able to know or do as an outcome of this course?" Learning objectives refer to the outcome of training. The emphasis is not on what the teacher presents but on what the

---

[12] Gaye Mara, "Making Training Count," *The Capital CLE Calendar*, June-July 1998, pp. 1,2.

audience will learn. Learning objectives guide program planners in putting the course together and let course participants know what they can expect to learn.

To be useful, learning objectives should state *specific, observable,* and *achievable* behaviors. To state behaviors that are specific and observable, use verbs that are not open to wide interpretation and that allow the learner to visualize the anticipated objectives. Examples of verbs that are specific and observable include: *write, identify, describe, conduct, draft, demonstrate, negotiate,* and *present.* Verbs that are open to wider interpretation and harder to visualize include: *understand, know, appreciate,* and *recognize.* A learning objective that states, "Participants will be good managers" is too vague. Make it specific and observable by stating, "Participants will be able to delegate work effectively."

Learning objectives should be *achievable* given the time and conditions of the training. They should focus on what can be realistically accomplished during the training period. Stating that participants in a one-hour seminar on leadership "will demonstrate leadership qualities" is too vague and unrealistic, but stating that participants "will be able to define the ten principles of effective leadership" reflects the simple, achievable purpose of the seminar. In setting learning objectives, keep in mind that while training can expand knowledge and skills, behavioral change is more difficult to achieve. Programs that deal with time management, leadership, or diversity, for example, can influence behavior and inspire a desire to change, but achieving real change requires more than a course. For new behaviors to take root, people need opportunities to practice what they learn, plus regular coaching, ongoing support, and perhaps follow-up training.

Learning objectives are further clarified by adding the *degree* of anticipated learning and the *context* in which performance should occur. Setting standards to measure the degree of learning makes it easier to evaluate whether learning objectives have been achieved. Examples of phrases that include a degree of performance include: "develop *logical* strategies," "deliver a *persuasive* closing argument," "draft an agreement that lists *all material* conditions," and "open a new client file *correctly.*" Adding the context further specifies how, when, or where the learning is to be applied. Some examples:

- "Develop logical strategies *for settling a lawsuit.*"
- "Deliver a persuasive closing argument *at the conclusion of a trial.*"
- "Draft an agreement that lists all material conditions agreed to by the parties *in the sale of a manufacturing plant.*"
- "Open a new client file correctly *using the risk management manual as a guide.*"

■ 3. Selecting Appropriate Teaching Methods

There are many ways to teach. Lawyers are most familiar and comfortable with lectures and panel discussions, but other teaching methods may be more suitable for teaching a particular course. Program planners need to consider alternative teaching methods, including case studies, role plays, hypothetical situations, debates, brainstorming, video clips, and games. (See Table 6.) Using more than one method in a program keeps the program lively and the audience engaged.

Interactive, learning-by-doing courses are especially effective ways to teach lawyers practice skills. This type of training has been available for litigators for decades. The format, popularized by NITA, combines practice exercises, videotaped performance, critique, and simulations. Many firms send lawyers to a NITA facility for training, while others conduct the training in-house, using NITA's course materials. There are now comparable training resources for business lawyers. Interactive business training materials include two modules available from AILTO, *Conducting a Due Diligence Review* and *Negotiating and Drafting the Acquisition Agreement*. Both modules use a hypothetical case (including pertinent documentation and supporting materials) as the basis for hands-on workshops. Firms can also create their own hypothetical case studies for business skills training. One type of program follows the life of a hypothetical company over several classroom sessions from incorporation to initial public offering, merger, or dissolution. At each stage, lawyers participate in discussions, role plays, and exercises.

A little imagination can make training in any area of law practice effective, engaging, and interesting.[13] The key is to select the instructional methods that are most appropriate for achieving the stated learning objectives. An excellent reference on teaching methods is *Teaching for Better Learning: Adult Education in CLE*,[14] a publication of the American Law Institute-American Bar Association Committee on Continuing Professional Education. This book describes many teaching formats, explains how each format can be used to achieve training objectives, and details how good lawyer training is designed and delivered.

■ 4. Developing an Agenda

A course agenda should list the specific topics to be covered and the time allotted to each. Having the program laid out this way provides structure and

---

[13] Abbott, *Developing Legal Talent: Best Practices in Professional Development for Law Firms* (NALP, Washington, DC) 2001.

[14] *Teaching for Better Learning: Adult Education in CLE*, American Law Institute-American Bar Association Committee on Continuing Professional Education, Philadelphia, 1999.

TABLE 6. Teaching Methods

Training format	Utility	Usual Teaching Purpose*			Interactive for audience	
		K	S	B	Yes	No
Brainstorming	Group discussion and joint problem solving	X			X	
Breakout or "buzz" groups	Small groups permit more people to take part in a discussion	X			X	
Case study	Address real examples of issues that arise in practice	X		X	X	
Debate	Present different sides of an issue	X				X
Demonstration	Model skill or behavior to be taught	X	X	X		X
Discussion of audience-generated questions	Answers from peers and experts to real problems	X			X	
Game	Engaging way to transfer information	X			X	
Discussion of hypotheticals	Address simulated issues that arise in practice	X			X	
Lecture	Delivers factual information	X				X
Panel presentation	Efficient sharing of information	X				X
Residential programs	Immersion in learning, few distractions	X	X	X	X	
Role playing/ simulation	Practice skills being taught; playing different roles gives different perspectives	X	X	X	X	
Seminar	Group learning based on discussion	X			X	
Skills workshop	Learn by doing; learn and practice new skills in a safe environment; polish existing skills	X	X	X	X	
Video vignette	Discussion of subject prompted by the vignette; vignette can model skill or behavior being taught	X	X	X	X	

* **K** = knowledge, **S** = skills, **B** = behavior.

discipline. It requires that the program presenter think through the course in its entirety and assign appropriate amounts of time for each part. Because time is precious, it is imperative that the stated learning objectives be accomplished within the time allotted. The time given to law firm programs always seems too short for what the instructor hopes to cover, and presenters are commonly criticized for trying to teach too much in the time they have. An agenda helps the instructor focus on what is most important.

Good training programs leave some time for questions or for reflection on how lawyers will apply what they have just learned when they return to work. Ideally, participants should be able to apply their new learning to their work immediately. Programs that intend to teach skills need to build in sufficient time to allow participants to practice what they learn. Follow-up sessions, in groups or one-on-one, can provide additional practice opportunities.

Straight lectures and panel presentations are best kept to about an hour. It is difficult for an audience to pay attention for a longer time unless they are actively participating. Interactive programs can be longer, e.g., a brief presentation followed by role playing and discussion. Courses that teach complex practice skills require larger blocks of time, sometimes several days, and should use multiple teaching methods. Any program can be expanded beyond the time in class by assigning work in advance (e.g., a case study to read before the course) or homework after a program (e.g., check in with someone a week later to discuss how you implemented something you learned). Although these activities do not show up on the timed agenda, they should be factored into the overall program plan.

■ 5. Securing Resources

To put on any training course, you need to obtain and coordinate many types of resources: faculty, instructional materials, a training site, administrative staff, appropriate technology, and financial support. All of these resources are discussed separately in this chapter.

The more complicated the program design, the more resources you will need. For example, trial advocacy programs require a complex array of resources, including personnel to handle logistics, audiovisual and technological support staff, and numerous people to serve as judges, jurors, court reporters, and witnesses. Rounding up these resources begins when the program is first planned but continues up to the last minute, when those in charge are scurrying around trying to locate mock jurors to replace those who cancelled.

Faculty

The most important resource in any program is your faculty. The best programs are taught by faculty who have both the substantive knowledge and the ability to teach it effectively. The quality of the instructors can make or break a program. Gifted teachers can bring even the most mundane subject to life; poor faculty can turn exciting, cutting-edge material into naptime. Finding the right faculty is essential to the success of each course offered. To the extent possible, most instructors should come from within the firm; outside trainers can supplement and expand in-house capabilities. The wisest approach is to use a judicious combination of in-house and outside faculty. Both in-house and outside instructors need to be located, carefully screened, and fully prepared. However, working with in-house faculty is different than hiring outside trainers, and understanding the differences will help you prepare your faculty better.

Inside Faculty

Most law firms possess a rich base of talented lawyers, many of whom are exceptional teachers. Whenever possible, it is best to use the firm's own lawyers to teach in-house programs. Teachers who are part of the firm understand the firm and have a personal interest in the learning and development of the colleagues they teach. In particular, in-house lawyers should teach substantive law courses. The firm may also have in-house experts in non-substantive areas like marketing and technology who can teach programs in those subjects. As firm representatives, in-house instructors embody the firm's commitment to the development of its lawyers, and their comments and advice carry great weight. Having in-house personnel teach courses allows these talented individuals to showcase their expertise and know-how and share it with the firm. It impresses junior associates, instills pride in firm lawyers, and preserves continuity and culture. The teaching of in-house faculty can have a greater impact because the audience perceives their comments as more realistic, practical, and believable.

Senior partners, especially those who are semi-retired or phasing out of active practice, are excellent teaching resources to tap. Aside from sharing their extensive knowledge and experience, having them teach younger lawyers provides continuity and protects much of their "institutional memory" from being lost when they leave the firm. In addition to leading structured programs, very senior partners can teach in a more conversational mode, speaking about their own experience. Associates can benefit a lot from hearing their war stories. However, their experience should be interesting and relevant to associates, and, like all faculty, they must be able to stay on message, communicate effectively, and point out practical lessons. Lack of focus, talking over associates' heads, and telling too many shapeless war stories can become a tedious bore.

Finding capable, committed in-house faculty can be a challenge. The difficulty lies in finding instructors who have both the knowledge and the teaching skills to be effective teachers. Many lawyers love to teach and are good at it. However, some lawyers who may seem obvious choices because of their expertise and renown are lackluster teachers. Similarly, lawyers who are subject matter experts may be superb presenters for experienced lawyers, but the depth and breadth of their knowledge sometimes makes it difficult for them to teach less experienced lawyers. You can help lawyers with a strong knowledge base to become better teachers, but realistically, even with extra effort, not all of them will excel in the classroom. Moreover, you may have to compromise in special cases, when, for example, the leading expert in an area is a prominent partner in your firm but a marginal teacher. The quality of that partner's presentation may be less important than the access of lawyers to his or her wisdom.

You can identify potential in-house faculty through individual inquiries, surveys, and evaluations of past programs. Ask lawyers, especially practice group leaders and members of the intended audience, for recommendations. Watch for new talent, i.e., lawyers who have an interest in teaching and may be looking for teaching opportunities. Send lawyers a survey that solicits faculty recommendations and invites lawyers to express any interest they may have in becoming faculty. (See Appendix 8-C at the conclusion of this chapter.) Review past program evaluations to see which faculty received high marks and which did not. Occasionally, someone who received poor marks asks to teach again. This can place you in an awkward and politically difficult position, especially if the lawyer is a powerful partner. If this occurs, there are steps you can take to mitigate against future substandard presentations. You can review the poor evaluation with the lawyer and discuss what he or she can do to improve; you can suggest that the person attend a "train the trainers" course (disussed in the next section); or you can design the program so that other, more effective trainers share the teaching responsibility with the poor instructor.

When you have identified the in-house faculty you want, invite them to participate. Some lawyers will accept your teaching invitation enthusiastically, but others will have to be persuaded. Many of those who are wary of saying yes are concerned about the time commitment involved. This concern may be due to work pressures or scheduling conflicts that are unavoidable. If talented lawyers cannot teach in the particular program you propose, you can find teaching opportunities for them at more convenient times. If, however, lawyers are worried that the non-billable time spent in preparing and teaching will have a negative impact on their compensation, the firm must find ways to reward capable in-house instructors or at least to protect them from financial penalties. Otherwise, it will lose out on many of its best teachers.

When you ask people to act as faculty, inform them of the program's learning objectives, what their responsibilities will be, and exactly what you want them to cover. Make sure they understand what you expect of them. Go over program dates, deadlines for materials, and other faculty who will participate. Describe the intended audience for the course. Let them know if the audience will be only lawyers from the firm or if it will include people who are not lawyers (e.g., clients, paralegals) or who are lawyers from outside the firm (e.g., clients' in-house counsel, lawyers invited from public interest organizations). Knowing who is in the audience will help instructors prepare remarks appropriately and make them careful not to disclose confidential or privileged information. Answer their questions and find out what kind of assistance and support they need. Many faculty will want to have an associate do research on the topic and help create instructional materials and handouts. Be prepared to tell them the kind and level of support you can offer.

Suggest a suitable program format for their presentation. Discuss how they can make effective use of written materials and visual aids. Encourage them to be enthusiastic and animated, and to move around during the course instead of remaining frozen behind a lectern. Urge them to use appropriate humor and show passion for the subject under discussion. Review the principles of effective presentations and suggest that they take a faculty-training course if they have not yet done so.

Table 7 lists topics that you should cover with faculty. Much of this information can be contained in written guidelines that can be made available in both hard copy and through the firm's intranet. A copy of the detailed guidelines that Cooley Godward LLP sends to in-house instructors for its "Cooley College" program is found in Appendix 8-D at the conclusion of this chapter.

■ Training In-House Faculty

Many in-house instructors can benefit from a course that teaches them how to teach more effectively. A faculty training program should cover the principles of adult learning, communication, feedback/critiquing, and presentation skills. Providing guidance and support to make lawyers better teachers will enrich their performance and the value of your firm's training programs. A faculty training program can teach skills and provide practice opportunities for lawyers who have limited teaching experience or ability. Such programs can also help lawyers who are naturally good teachers acquire a better understanding of learning principles and

TABLE 7. Topics to Discuss with Instructors

- **Program objectives**
  - Desired outcomes of training
  - Issues to be addressed
  - Reasons the program is being presented
  - Standard or customized program

- **Context**
  - Standalone program? Part of a series?
  - Relationship of program to core curriculum
  - If at a retreat or conference, the other subjects that will be covered and other presenters who will be there

- **Desired format (e.g., presentation, interactive)**

- **Location of each presentation**
  - Travel arrangements and accommodations

- **Schedule**
  - Program dates for each presentation
  - Time allotted for program
  - How often the program will be taught on each date
  - Deadlines for submitting course materials

- **Audience**
  - Number
  - Composition
  - Practice areas
  - Experience level

- **Instructional materials**
  - Handouts
  - Teacher's manual

- **Audiovisual and technology requirements**

- **Request to audio- or videotape the program**

- **CLE compliance in jurisdictions where program will be presented**
  - Whether the program meets CLE accreditation requirements
  - Whether the outside instructor is a qualified CLE provider
  - CLE recordkeeping

- **Price of outside instructors**
  - Fees
  - Expenses, including travel

- **Processes preliminary to presentation**
  - Meetings in firm?
  - Needs assessment?
  - Interviews or focus groups with firm lawyers?
  - Communications during planning process

- **Confidentiality**
  - Of materials and information provided to instructor
  - Of instructor's handouts

teaching techniques. Consider making this training "strongly recommended" for in-house faculty. This will make it easier for you to ask lawyers who are in need of such training to go through the class.

Some professional development directors and some lawyers who have gone through "train the trainer" courses may have the background and expertise to teach a faculty training course, but most of the time you will need outside faculty to teach this course. Suitable faculty can be found in consulting firms, universities, law and business schools, CLE providers, and theater companies. You can seek faculty referrals from other law firm professional development directors or from your corporate clients' training or human resources departments. Look for instructors who specialize in CLE, adult education, communication, and presentation skills.

Alternatively, you can send your lawyers to outside "train the trainers" programs. Organizations like NITA (www.nita.org) and the Harvard Program on Negotiation (www.pon.harvard.edu) conduct these programs. They also provide case materials that law firms can use to teach trainers in-house.

Outside Faculty

Law firms are filled with smart, talented people, many of whom are exceptional teachers, but it is unlikely that a firm can rely exclusively on in-house faculty to meet all of its training needs. Knowledge alone does not translate into teaching ability. In spite of their substantive expertise, the most gifted lawyers may be ineffective teachers. Outside trainers are teaching professionals who also have subject-matter expertise. Firms should retain outside trainers when in-house lawyers are not able to do the job. Your firm's lawyers may lack suitable subject matter expertise or teaching skills, have no time to prepare adequately for training, or be unavailable when you need them. In particular, you likely need outside trainers to teach non-legal topics like business, management, and leadership. In addition, outside consultants can address certain sensitive issues that may be difficult or awkward for firm lawyers to teach (e.g., sexual harassment, work-life conflict, diversity).

Once you have identified the specific training needs and decided to use an outside instructor, you must find and select the right person for the job. But your work does not end there. You must be sure that the instructor understands your expectations and is ready to meet them.

■ Finding Outside Faculty

Finding outside faculty can be easy or daunting, depending on the subject matter. If the firm has hired outside consultants to teach a course in the past, or if there are many well-known potential trainers in your community, the process may be a snap. But if you are starting from scratch, or looking for someone to teach a relatively obscure subject, you may need to invest some time in a search. The best way to find faculty is through personal recommendations from individuals whose opinions you trust. If you cannot find a personal referral, your next step is to search other sources of potential referrals. There are many places to look for recommendations, including:

- Professional development directors in other law firms.
- CLE vendors.
- Clients' legal, training, and human resources departments.
- ABA, state, local, and specialty bar associations.
- ABA Center for Continuing Legal Education.
- Law schools.
- Business schools.
- Consulting firms with expertise in the area you need.
- Legal associations that deal with professional development.
- NALP (www.nalp.org).
- Professional Development Consortium (PDC).
- American Institute for Legal Training in the Office (AILTO — www. ali-aba.org).
- Association for Continuing Legal Education (ACLEA — www.aclea.org).
- Association of Legal Administrators (ALA — www.ala.org).
- Specialty and industry groups (e.g., medical associations, accident reconstruction firms, economists).
- American Society for Training and Development (ASTD — www.astd.org).
- Legal journals and periodicals.

- Directories of experts published by bar associations.

- Mailings and advertisements that come across your desk.

Contact the recommended trainers who appear to suit your needs and explain what you are looking for. Be sure that candidates have the experience and the expertise to teach the program you are planning. Ask them to send you their marketing materials and/or refer you to their web sites. Inquire about their credentials, their experience teaching the particular course you are interested in, and references whom you can contact. Call these references and ask them about their experience with the trainer. In addition to considering expertise in the subject area, contemplate whether the trainer's personality, style, and approach fit the culture of your firm. Some individuals who are big hits at one firm (or even in one of your offices) may be duds at another.

If the trainer appears to meet your needs, arrange an interview by telephone or, preferably, in person. For a major project, it is worthwhile to have potential trainers come to your office to meet with professional development committee members, firm leaders, and the people who are planning the program.

During the interview, give the prospective trainer a clear and complete explanation of the project and the firm's expectations. (See Table 7.) Explain the program objectives, including the issues to be addressed and whether you want a standard "off-the-shelf" program or one that is customized for your firm. Describe the intended audience. Take advantage of the trainer's expertise and ask for feedback about your proposal. Be receptive to the trainer's ideas and input.

One of the key subjects to discuss is the program format that best achieves your learning objectives. Ask outside trainers to describe the content and format of their "standard" programs and their style of teaching. Some trainers will be able to send you videotapes, audiotapes, or CDs of their course or permit you to observe them in an upcoming program. If you have a preferred format, ask whether the trainer can present the program that way. Even trainers who can follow your preferred format may suggest alternative approaches in light of your objectives, audience, time frame, or budget. For example, interactive skills training programs require substantial time and a small teacher-to-student ratio. If you have only one hour and expect a large number of participants, this type of program may not be feasible. Trainers should be able to suggest other options.

Let trainers know if you expect them to create handouts and/or a teacher's manual and if any special CLE requirements must be met. Discuss any special technologies that will be used. State where and when each program will be held and the number of times the training will take place at each site. Go over logistics, such as travel arrangements, deadlines, and audiovisual needs.

The fees charged by outside faculty vary enormously, depending on many market factors. Be sure to ask prospective trainers what is and is not covered by their fee (e.g., training materials). You may be able to negotiate fee reductions on the basis of volume, perks (e.g., extra days at the resort where a retreat is being held), or promises of additional work in the future. If the firm will cover the trainer's expenses, set any ground rules that you deem necessary (e.g., air travel only at economy fare, fax and photocopies charged at cost). There are other ways to control expenses of outside trainers. For example, most large firms hire one trainer to teach the same course in their offices around the country. But another option that may be more economical and still meet the firm's training objectives is to hire local trainers to teach the same content in different offices. To do this requires you to spend more time finding faculty and ensuring consistency in program content and quality of delivery, but the savings in travel expenses and fees can be substantial.

■ Selecting Outside Faculty

Lawyers can be very tough on trainers, so selecting the right trainer is extremely important. You are investing more than money in these programs; you are investing lawyers' valuable time. Be especially cautious with trainers who are not lawyers or who have little or no experience working with lawyers. Lawyers are very smart, impatient, and exacting, and they often resist training by people who are "outside" the legal profession. Even when they are recognized experts in their fields, these trainers may find themselves confronted by a rude and hostile audience. When hiring outside trainers, you must therefore be sure that they understand how lawyers think and work, and that they are familiar with law firm culture, structure, and operations. Programs that may be highly successful in academia or the corporate world may not work in a law firm. Corporations, for example, allow more time for training programs than lawyers will tolerate. A course that would take several days in a corporation may be given only a few hours in a law firm.[15] If the trainers you hire are not savvy about lawyers and how they work, you will have to educate them. Otherwise, it is likely that the trainer will be frustrated and your lawyers will be displeased.

---

[15] Among corporate trainers, one- to three-hour training sessions are sometimes referred to as "quick hits," and anything under an hour as "hit and run" training. Sandra Torres, "Quick Hits," *Training and Development,* December 2001, p. 17.

■ Working with Outside Faculty

When you hire an outside trainer, make sure the trainer welcomes you as an active partner in designing and delivering the program. Establish a good work relationship with the trainer and keep lines of communication open. Share any relevant background information or concerns that will help the trainer prepare for the program (e.g., significant current internal firm issues that may distract the audience). Some trainers may ask you to solicit suggestions and topics that anticipated audience members would like to have the trainer cover in the course.

Stay in touch with the trainer, especially if there is a long time lag between your engaging the trainer and the date of presentation. If the firm makes any changes in plans, timing, or conditions, let the trainer know as soon as possible. It is a good idea to contact the trainer shortly before the program date to go over last-minute items, share information about expected attendance, and make sure everything is on track.

Be available during the trainer's presentation and debrief the trainer afterward. Each office where the trainer will present should have an administrator to set up the training room, welcome the trainer, take care of CLE registration, and generally oversee the implementation of the program. This administrator must be on site to address immediately any problems that come up. If videoconferencing or other complicated technology will be used, have technical support available. After the program, you should speak personally with the trainer. Discuss the program evaluations and any problems that were identified. Ask trainers for any insights they may have garnered that will be valuable for your ongoing professional development efforts.

Instructional Materials

After your faculty, the most appreciated part of a training program is the instructional material you provide. Instructional materials include handouts for program participants and teaching manuals for program presenters. Every training program should have written handouts for distribution to the audience. Handouts can be voluminous or merely an outline of key points presented in the program. They are important because people do not understand or absorb everything that is presented during a training program, and lawyers can refer to them later to continue learning after the program ends. Handouts can contain summaries of main points, lecture transcripts, articles, cases, sample documents, checklists, timelines, case citations, statutes, web sites, bibliographies, graphs, photos, copies of PowerPoint slides, questions to think about, and any number of other educational resources.

These materials are usually given to participants at the program, but they can be distributed before or afterward as well. It is helpful to send out program materials before the session when they provide background information that will make the teaching more meaningful and easier to understand or when the instructor wants participants to prepare something to bring to class, such as a writing sample for a class on persuasive writing. Sending additional instructional materials after the program can highlight and reinforce key learning points and present new avenues for exploration on the topic.

Just as handouts are helpful tools for learners, teaching manuals are helpful tools for instructors. Teaching manuals lay out in detail what the teacher should do to present the program and are especially useful for programs that will be repeated. They use narratives or detailed outlines to explain teaching goals and techniques, describe classroom exercises, supply questions to facilitate discussion, and present step-by-step instructions to guide everyone who will teach the same program. If the course uses a case study, the manual highlights issues and points for discussion as well as applicable legal standards, principles, and citations. Handouts, audio and video clips, slides, and all materials presented by instructors during the program should be placed in the manual. The idea is to create a self-contained package that will enable any instructor to teach the same class (perhaps with updated references) at a later time.

Your firm does not have to produce all of its instructional materials. Many types of legal education courses are available for purchase or license, and come with handouts and teaching manuals. These "off-the-shelf" instructional materials are designed specifically for law firms and include teachers' guides that facilitate in-house use. Some of these materials may need to be customized to particular practices or jurisdictions. Examples of ready-made training materials include trial and deposition case studies from the National Institute for Trial Advocacy (NITA — www.nita.org); transactional training materials on due diligence and corporate acquisitions available from AILTO (www.ali-aba.org); and videotape-based case study programs on legal ethics from the University of Pennsylvania Center on Professionalism, Loyola University School of Law, and New York University School of Law.[16]

A word of caution is in order about the use of copyrighted materials in training programs. Many people like to show slides of cartoons or distribute copies of pertinent articles that are copyright protected. Both in-house and outside instructors

---

[16] The University of Pennsylvania Center on Professionalism and Loyola University School of Law materials are available from the ABA Center for Professional Responsibility (www.abanet.org/cpr/); the New York University materials are available from NYU Law School (grays@juris.nyu.edu).

should be familiar with copyright laws that apply to the materials they use, and the firm should have guidelines and procedures in place for obtaining permission to use such materials. In addition, the firm needs to protect its own privileged information from disclosure and safeguard firm documents, forms, and other intellectual property from unauthorized distribution or misuse. Information about copyright issues can be found on the Library of Congress web site at www.loc.gov/copyright/, and lawyers in your firm may be able to give you guidance in this area.

Time and Place

Choosing the Time

Courses should be scheduled to maximize attendance and learning. When scheduling courses, you need to consider the time of day, day of the week, and time of the year. All of these timing issues can have a significant impact on program attendance. Even with the best planning, you may not be able to get all the lawyers in a target group together for an important program. If that happens, it may be necessary to offer repeat sessions on different days and at different times of the day. The professional development director should keep a master calendar of training programs and confer with all departments and practice groups when scheduling major courses. Conversely, no department or practice groups should schedule a major program without first checking the master calendar.

Generally speaking, holding a training session at a mealtime — and serving food — is one key to bringing lawyers to class. Lunchtime is the favorite time slot for training and works well when the program format is interactive. Programs at lunchtime must be designed to keep people awake and engaged. Presenting a substantive lecture immediately after lunch may cause people to nod off. As one professional development director points out, "The efficacy of substantive law seminars is lessened in direct proportion to the number of calories consumed by the listener."[17] She recommends holding lectures at breakfast, when people are fresher, the meal is lighter, coffee is abundant, and participants still have the day ahead to get their work done.

The day of the week should also be considered carefully, taking into account firm culture and tradition. Study what works best in your firm. For example, many lawyers and firms prefer not to schedule training on weekends, evenings, Mondays,

---

[17] Valerie L. Fitch, "Believe It or Not, A Substantive Law Program Can Be Less Dull Than Dishwater," *The AILTO Insider,* Volume 15, No. 1, Winter/Spring 2001.

or Fridays. Yet this can vary from firm to firm. Some firms prefer these times because they work best for their lawyers. Sometimes the length of time needed for a program dictates the schedule. If a course will take a full day, or if lawyers are traveling from different cities to one location to attend the course, it may be best to hold the program on the weekend. In scheduling this type of program, be sure to factor in travel time.

The time of year can also be a determining issue in scheduling training programs. For example, scheduling major corporate or tax law programs in December may limit attendance because of the end of the year rush to close client deals, while scheduling programs on mentoring in the summer can increase participation when tied in to a firm's summer associate program.

Choosing the Place

The easiest and least expensive site for a training program is the firm's own office. Many firms have large conference rooms, multi-purpose rooms, dedicated training facilities, courtrooms, and even conference centers that can be used for training. However, sometimes programs demand more space than is available in the office. Moving your program off-site also enhances the learning experience. It is less likely that lawyers will be interrupted, called away, or otherwise disturbed during the course. In fact, some states mandate that CLE programs be held in locations that promote learning and minimize the chance of interruptions.

If you decide to go off-site, there are many different kinds of facilities to choose from. The place you select depends in large part on the program design. Some courses need multiple breakout rooms, a courtroom, or an outdoor setting. Other factors to consider are whether the course is a stand-alone program or part of a multi-day symposium; the number of participants; where participants are coming from; the length of the program; hotel room accommodations; desired amenities; need for logistical support and technology resources; and, of course, budget. Good sites for training programs include training facilities, hotels, resorts, conference centers, universities, law schools, and courts. If a large number of people are flying in for a program, it may be important to be near an airport; if the training is part of a retreat, it may be desirable to be at a resort where people have time and amenities to relax and socialize.

Administrative Support

Training requires a great deal of administrative and clerical support. Every program requires personnel to handle planning and logistics and to carry out the myriad tasks required to run a training course. It is especially important for firms to designate a person to be responsible for CLE compliance, as discussed later in this chapter. Someone in the firm should be familiar with CLE rules to assist lawyers and act as the contact person with state regulators, even if the firm does not track individual lawyers' compliance. Aside from CLE administration, multi-office firms should have individuals in each office in charge of training activities, and those people should be coordinated by a firm-wide professional development director.

The firm's overall training program is the responsibility of the professional development director, either directly or through a manager of training. In addition to being responsible for overseeing and managing the entire training program, the professional development/training director handles numerous specific training-related responsibilities. (See Table 8.) Some firms hire full-time in-house trainers specifically to handle these tasks and, if the trainers have particular expertise, to teach certain programs.

TABLE 8. Representative Training Responsibilities of Professional Development/Training Directors

- Conduct needs assessments.
- Develop curricula.
- Design courses.
- Select faculty.
- Prepare, collect, and maintain instructional materials.
- Manage the interaction between training and other professional development systems.
- Handle negotiations with outside and online CLE providers.
- Approve lawyers' requests to attend outside CLE programs.
- Market in-house and outside CLE programs internally.
- Keep training information and resources current on the firm's intranet.
- Secure appropriate technology for learning.
- Teach courses (optional).

Technology

Most training programs use some form of technology, even if it is simply a microphone or an overhead projector. Part of your program planning is to ensure that the technology you need will be available at the facility you use and suitable for the program presentation. The use of technology in training is discussed at page 251.

Program Costs

Producing training courses can be expensive, so shop around and negotiate to obtain a price that is fair and reasonable. The largest professional development expenditures in most firms are training-related travel and food. These are areas where small adjustments can lead to large savings. Encouraging lawyers to attend local rather than distant programs, presenting more programs in-house, and using technology to deliver programs are just three ways that a firm can reduce travel costs. Changing caterers or reducing the food at training sessions may help you find money for additional programs. However, do not eliminate all food at training programs; lawyers expect something to eat during training courses and are less apt to come if you do not offer refreshments.

Two other major expenses are the cost of outside faculty and the use of outside training facilities. There is considerable variation in what and how outside trainers charge. They may charge by the project, hour, day, attendee, or a combination of methods. Some trainers charge separately for program materials, while others include them in the fee. Most consultants charge for travel expenses, and some charge for travel time. Using an off-site training facility is invariably more expensive than using your office. In addition to room rental fees, most hotels or conference facilities charge for food and technology support. Explore ways to negotiate price reductions with faculty and facilities. One example might be to find another firm to co-sponsor the program, including the faculty and facility costs.

You can control training expenses better by budgeting and tracking your costs carefully. Chapter 10 discusses how to do this.

Evaluating Training Programs

Every training program should be evaluated. If you follow the steps of assessing needs and formulating learning objectives, then your evaluation can measure how well the program has met those needs and objectives. Evaluations are also important for planning and improving the firm's future training efforts. Feedback from these evaluations should be used to modify and improve upcoming programs and to plan new programs. At least once a year, evaluate your overall training program by asking lawyers to assess the curriculum, including whether certain programs should be continued, changed, or dropped. This information can help you set priorities in the next year's training curriculum.

The most common method of evaluation is the written questionnaire, but other techniques can be used, such as observation, tests, reports, and interviews. Some state CLE regulations mandate that CLE programs be evaluated and even prescribe the questionnaires that should be used. It is important to match the right evaluation method to the program. For example, to evaluate a presentation skills program, it is better to view pre- and post-program videotapes of participants' presentations rather than use a written survey.

There are many ways to evaluate training programs, and each method is designed to obtain different information. These methods seek evaluative data at different evaluation "levels" and range from very simple questionnaires to highly complex analyses. The four most common levels of evaluation are:

1. **Reaction — Participants' opinions of the training.** Using evaluation forms, ask individuals what they thought of the program, its format, content, and instructors, and whether their expectations for the training were met. Level 1 measures satisfaction.

2. **Learning — The ability of participants to apply what they have learned.** This level measures whether participants learned what the program intended. A common technique for measuring learning is pre- and post-testing.

3. **Performance — Participants can demonstrate a learned skill and apply it appropriately to their work.** Level 3 measures whether performance has improved as a result of the training. It requires ongoing observation and appraisal of changes in performance. One approach is to ask supervisors to compare associates' performance before and after receiving training.

4. **Results — How the firm's performance has improved as an outcome of the training.** Level 4 evaluation shows how a particular course has led to higher revenues, reduced costs, or greater client satisfaction. A reduction in write-offs or improved responses from client surveys may indicate positive performance results. However, these results may be related to many other factors as well, so direct causal relationships between performance results and training are very hard to prove. Because this level of

evaluation is the most difficult to measure, most firms use only reaction, learning, and performance evaluation levels.

Whatever method you use to evaluate programs, be sure you make the most of them. If you use questionnaires, urge participants to complete and return them. When evaluating a training symposium that includes several discrete programs, have participants evaluate each program as well as the overall event. Make the evaluation forms easy to complete and submit, and provide time at the end of the program for people to complete them. Immediately after the program, send the questionnaire by e-mail to program participants and ask those who have not yet completed them to do so. Make sure that program planners carefully review every evaluation and provide copies, or at least summaries, of course evaluations to faculty. Most presenters and instructors welcome the feedback and will use it to make improvements in their future programs.

Measuring Investment in Training

Firms want to know if they are getting value for their training dollars. Evaluating the return on the firm's investment in the training and development of lawyers presents a tough challenge because the traditional "return on investment" (ROI) analysis is notoriously difficult when applied to training. ROI seeks to quantify dollar savings or revenue increases that are directly attributed to training. Although training expenses can be calculated without difficulty, there are too many variables that impact lawyers' development, performance, and retention to isolate the impact of any particular training course. Consequently, financial return as a measurement of training success is no longer the primary focus of training evaluation. Equal emphasis in now given to other strategic initiatives including the development and retention of talented personnel.[18] Firms recognize that their survival and success depend on their ability to recruit and retain the best talent, which they can only achieve through continuous training and development.[19]

Two other approaches to measure the effectiveness of the firm's training investment are "return on expectations" (ROE) and "return on knowledge" (ROK).[20] Both approaches focus on the outcomes of training. To measure ROE, you would ask lawyers and supervisors how effective a course was in relation to what they

---

[18] Stewart Whittingham, "Getting Beyond the Numbers: Budgeting for Professional Development," *NALP Bulletin*, October 2001.
[19] Michael A. Cusumano and Constantinos C. Markides, Eds., *Strategic Thinking for the Next Economy*, Jossey-Bass, San Francisco, 2001.
[20] Liz Simpson, "Great Expectations," *Training*, February 2002, p. 40.

expected its impact to be on performance or productivity. If those expectations are met, the program is considered successful. ROK asks whether training has increased the lawyers' knowledge and skills so as to increase the value of their work product to clients and the firm. It also asks whether the increase in knowledge and skills translates into higher performance and productivity. Training is successful to the extent that it builds up lawyers' competencies and expands the firm's intellectual capital.

The Law Firm as an Accredited CLE Provider

Every state has unique CLE rules and regulations, although there are efforts afoot to make the system more uniform.[21] The rules in some states are far more complex and confusing than others, but all states require a considerable amount of paperwork to accredit programs and ensure compliance. Just a few of the state-to-state differences in CLE requirements include:

- The number of CLE hours required.

- Compliance period variability (annual or multi-year).

- Mandatory CLE vs. voluntary CLE (penalties for non-compliance vs. incentives for compliance).

- Required subjects.

- Subjects that do not qualify for CLE credit.

- How lawyers are organized for compliance (e.g., by birth date, alphabetically)

- Special requirements for certain subgroups of lawyers (e.g., newly admitted lawyers).

- Requirement that in-house programs must be open to lawyers from outside the firm.

- Definition of a "CLE hour" as 50 or 60 minutes.

- "Partial hour" credit availability.

---

[21] See, e.g., *MCLE: A Coordinated Approach, Report and Recommendations,* The American Law Institute, Philadelphia, 2001.

- Availability of "comity," i.e., whether lawyers licensed in more than one jurisdiction can comply with the CLE requirements of another state by fulfilling the CLE requirements of the state in which they practice.

- CLE credit for self-study or technology-based training.

If lawyers in your firm are licensed in states with mandatory CLE, it is advantageous for your firm to become an accredited CLE provider if your state permits it. Having CLE provider status can save you and your lawyers a significant amount of time and effort. As an accredited provider, you do not have to seek accreditation for each course that the firm sponsors. If you have "blanket" accreditation, your courses will automatically qualify for CLE credit (so long as they otherwise comply with CLE regulations).

Monitoring CLE compliance has two aspects: compliance of courses and compliance by lawyers. Both aspects of compliance are especially complicated for large firms whose lawyers practice in multiple jurisdictions. If you want in-house courses to qualify for CLE credit in more than one state, the courses must comply with the CLE requirements in each of these states. Reconciling the various state-to-state differences is a time- and labor-intensive job. Ensuring that your programs comply with the rules for accreditation requires that the programs be tailored and implemented to meet all applicable state requirements.

As for lawyers' CLE compliance, the firm must decide whether it will track and monitor its lawyers' compliance or leave this up to the individual lawyers. Compliance is, of course, the personal responsibility of every lawyer, but many firms assist lawyers by tracking their credits and monitoring their compliance status. These firms notify lawyers of their progress and help them to obtain the necessary CLE credits within the compliance period. Firms that have sufficient resources do this as a convenience to their lawyers and also as a means of reducing the chance of lawyers dropping out of compliance. Non-compliance can lead to suspension from practice, which would have firm-wide, not just personal, repercussions. This service is useful for lawyers and the firm, but it is extremely laborious and time consuming.

■ CLE Tracking: Systems and Staff

Firms that decide to take on responsibility to monitor and assist with CLE compliance need systems and staff specifically for this purpose. Many firms have created their own software systems to track CLE, though this is a fairly expensive undertaking. Fortunately, today there are several software programs and vendors on the market that provide compliance tracking systems and services. Some of these providers customize human resources software for the legal market. Others are online CLE vendors who provide tracking services as an extra feature of their course offerings. Your firm's technology director should be able to help you with the technical aspects and requirements of any system or service you are considering.[22]

Whether your firm will build a CLE tracking system or work with an outside supplier, the following issues should be addressed before you begin:

- The number of lawyers in the firm and all of the states in which they are admitted.

- The states for which the firm will track data.

- The capabilities you want the system to have, e.g.:
    - Preparing periodic status reports for each lawyer.
    - Creating certificates of attendance.
    - Creating hyperlinks to course and CLE web sites.
    - Automatically notifying lawyers when their compliance periods are about to expire.

- What information you will capture and maintain.

- Whether and how lawyers will be able to access the system to enter data, make changes, print reports, and view their compliance status.

- How to track attendance data from in-house programs.

- The number and types of CLE programs that your firm puts on each year.

- Whether your CLE programming is likely to change significantly in the future.

- How to obtain and input data from lawyers who attend outside CLE programs.

- Whether and how the firm will maintain attendance records and issue attendance certificates to outside lawyers who attend in-house programs.

- How quickly the firm is growing.

- Whether the firm is contemplating a merger with another firm.

The size of the staff needed to track, monitor, and facilitate CLE compliance depends on the number of lawyers in the firm and the extent of the firm's commit-

---

[22] Also see the series of articles by Dottie Palazzo in *Professional Development Quarterly*, starting with "Building or Buying a Tracking System: Where to Begin," in the August 2000 issue.

ment to oversight. The professional development/training director manages the CLE system, interacts with state regulators, and makes decisions about technology and systems necessary for tracking. CLE staff, who report to the training director, carry out a wide array of tasks, many of which are clerical. Some of the activities that the CLE personnel handle include the following:

- Implementing the CLE rules for programs and lawyers in every applicable state.
- Understanding CLE rules and staying abreast of changes and proposed changes.
- Selecting, designing, and/or implementing the CLE software system.
- Tracking individual lawyer credits.
- Inputting data from lawyers and courses about course attendance.
- Preparing and storing certificates of attendance.
- Disseminating information about courses to lawyers.
- Communicating with the governing CLE boards in every state.
- Ensuring that program materials comply with CLE requirements.
- Maintaining the firm's CLE system and keeping it up to date.

To find out how to become an accredited provider, contact the CLE regulatory agency in each state in which you want to qualify. A complete listing of state CLE regulatory agencies and requirements can be found at www.cleusa.org, the web site of the Organization of Regulatory Administrators of CLE (ORACLE).

Multi-Office Firms: Special Training Considerations

Law firms with offices in many locations have complex training issues, especially if some of those locations are in other countries. One major challenge for multi-office firms is to ensure that certain subjects are understood and treated consistently across the firm. Issues related to professional responsibility and ethics, cross-border transactions, and the interplay between local custom and firm standards need to be addressed at both policy and training levels. Training can serve as a vehicle to distribute and explain firm policies and procedures, and to ensure consistency in the quality, format, and style of work product.

Another challenge is to deliver training to lawyers spread throughout the country or across the globe. In addition to the obvious problem of coordinating and scheduling multi-office training sessions, each office may have special training needs. Some offices may have hundreds of lawyers while others have only two or three. Firms have to find ways to provide the same level of high-quality training for all lawyers in all locations and to make associates feel that they are part of one firm, regardless of where they are located.

Associates in small, remote offices often feel isolated and apart, culturally as well as physically. Realistically, these associates may not get the same amount or quality of formal training as those in the larger main offices. However, a good training program can broaden their perspective and make them feel more connected to the firm. It can also give them a great deal of formal training, teach them how to take advantage of the informal learning opportunities in their offices, and show them how to access the training resources available throughout the firm. By tying lawyers in multiple offices into the training program, firms can promote the notion of "one firm" and help these associates identify more closely with the firm.

No matter where lawyers are located or how large or small your offices are, your firm can bring training to associates — and associates to training — in many ways. Some suggestions to help deliver training to lawyers in multiple offices include the following:

- Hold firm-wide training conferences for all associates from all offices to attend.

- Combine training conferences with retreats.

- Hold regional training sessions. Bring associates from several small offices together in one office.

- Fly faculty to various office locations to present programs.

- Deliver training sessions electronically through videoconference or webcasts. Alternate scheduled training times to favor offices in different time zones.

- Have some programs originate in smaller offices.

- Have lawyers in more than one office co-present a program.

When a firm grows by acquiring or merging with other firms, training can be an effective means of promoting cultural integration. Getting lawyers from the merging firms to develop, run, and teach a program together is a good way for them to get to know and learn from each other. As they present a program to the firm at large, they start to see themselves as part of a new law firm entity.

Law firms with overseas offices face additional challenges. A number of global firms have internal education requirements for all of their lawyers and must deliver the requisite training worldwide. All international firms have to prepare U.S. lawyers to practice in other countries and educate local lawyers in their overseas offices about American legal practice. American lawyers in foreign offices need to learn local laws and procedures and also be kept informed of legal developments in their home jurisdictions. Because states do not exempt lawyers from CLE requirements while they work outside the U.S., law firms must find ways to help American lawyers working abroad to comply with CLE requirements in states where they are licensed. Lawyers who rotate through international offices require orientation to practice abroad and re-orientation when they come home. Lawyers from other countries need to be educated in American laws and procedures and in how the firm expects them to conduct their legal business.

Lawyers in international offices need standard CLE programs but also require specialized training in areas such as legal ethics in international practice and cultural differences in negotiations. Much of this specialized programming may have to be developed in-house, either by the professional development/training department or by the lawyers in each overseas office. In some cities, such as London, where there are substantial numbers of American lawyers, local law schools and international CLE providers frequently present CLE programs on pertinent topics.

A few large firms send instructors to their international offices to deliver training, and many firms bring lawyers to the United States for orientation or training. Both of these options are very expensive, so most training of lawyers in overseas offices is done through technology. Despite the time differences, many firms provide simultaneous live programming to offices located overseas using various distance learning technologies, such as webcasts and videoconferencing. Other technologies make training available to lawyers at their convenience through video- and audio-taped presentations, delayed satellite transmissions, and online training.

A number of U.S. firms provide special training for lawyers who are graduates of foreign law schools and who work in the firm's international offices. This training may range from hiring a tutor to help lawyers improve English language skills to sponsoring foreign lawyers to attend one-year LL.M. degree programs in United States law schools. Many of these firms bring those lawyers to one of their U.S. offices for an extended period, usually six months to one year. The lawyers work closely with their American colleagues and attend the firm's regular in-house training programs. These firms sometimes develop unique in-house courses for those lawyers to explain the American legal system and how it works. At the end of the designated period, the lawyers return to their overseas offices with a better understanding of American law practice, with personal relationships with firm lawyers and clients, and with a better ability to integrate their local practice into the practice of the firm as a whole.

Common Training Questions

■ **1. Should attendance at in-house training be mandatory?**

In most cases, no. The purpose of the firm's training program is to encourage learning, not to punish lawyers who miss programs. Lawyers are high-achieving professionals and self-directed learners, and they should decide whether or not to attend the training events the firm offers them. If the training meets their needs and is well designed and presented, lawyers will go to them willingly.

Nonetheless, there are times when training has such importance that the firm might make attendance "expected," "highly encouraged," or "strongly suggested." Training that falls into this category includes new associate orientation, first-year associate training in the basics of practice, prevention of sexual harassment, and programs in risk management procedures that may be required by the firm's liability carrier. Firm leaders should impress on lawyers the value and importance of these programs, and reproach lawyers who fail to attend. If a lawyer's failure to attend important training programs is persistent, then the firm may take it as a sign of poor firm citizenship.

Some lawyers may have such a compelling need for education that the firm might make training mandatory. One example is an associate who lacks certain critical skills. The firm may require that the associate attend training courses to learn those skills. Another example is a lawyer whose behavior is so inappropriate that the firm requires the lawyer to attend classes on preventing sexual harassment, anger management, or interpersonal relations. Firms may also require attendance at some programs as prerequisites for promotion (e.g., a course in client relations before becoming a partner) or for taking more advanced courses (e.g., reading financial statements before a course on corporate valuation).

2. How can attendance at in-house training programs be increased?

Insufficient attendance at in-house training sessions is a ubiquitous problem. When busy lawyers bill by the hour, every work hour is precious and they give top priority to getting clients' work done. So the first rule for increasing attendance is to make the programs practical, interesting, and directly related to the audience's needs. As one training director put it, "Education for a billable-hour-conscious person must be direct, concise, and immediately useful."[23] Below are a number of suggestions to help you attract more people to your programs.

- Serve food. The better the food, the bigger the draw.

- Give billable hour credit for time spent in training. Many firms give associates a "bank" of training hours that count toward their billable time requirements, and some firms also give partners credit for teaching time.

- Give lawyers "firm" credit for time spent in training. Some firms require both billable hours and "administrative" or "firm" hours, both of which are taken into account for purposes of compensation and advancement. At Pillsbury Winthrop LLP, associates have a "total commitment" of 2,200 hours, 1,950 of which are billable. One hundred of the remaining 250 hours are to be spent in business development, including business development training.

- Respect people's time. Start and end programs on schedule.

- Involve target audiences in planning their own programs. This reinforces the message that you are designing programs to address their needs and interests and gets their buy-in, which increases the likelihood of their attendance.

- Market your programs. Make sure that programs are widely advertised and appear on the firm calendar and intranet. Ask your firm's marketing director to help you create a marketing campaign for your training program and for each individual training course. Create a "brand" for your training department, e.g., Cooley Godward LLP's "Cooley College" for first-year associates.

---

[23] Sharon M. Abrahams, "Training Lawyers to be Better Trainers," *CLE Journal*, January 1996, 22.

- Use catchy titles to draw attention and elicit interest in your program. For example, "Law Practice in the Palm of Your Hand" is a more alluring title than "Using Handheld Technology Devices."

- Give prizes. For example, one firm gives Palm Pilots to all lawyers who complete a technology course.

- In states where CLE is required, use CLE as leverage to draw people to training sessions. Present programs that cover state-mandated CLE subjects.

- Have practice group leaders, department heads, or the managing partner send reminders to the target audience, urging them to attend.

- Enlist supervising partners' assistance in getting associates to attend training programs. If associates repeatedly fail to show up for training, ask the partners to speak with them.

- Encourage partners, especially those in leadership positions, to attend. This sends a clear message that training is important and valued. Others will follow their lead, and some lawyers will not want to be absent when these leaders are present.

- Invite clients to programs, either as presenters or as guests. Lawyers are eager for opportunities to interact with and learn from clients. Partners will encourage lawyers to go to these programs so they can impress clients with good attendance — and avoid the embarrassment of poor attendance.

- Don't overwhelm lawyers with too much training. Be reasonable and realistic about how much time lawyers can spend in training.

- Break training down into small segments. For instance, design some 15- to 30-minute programs that can be tacked on to regular practice group meetings.

- Hold long training sessions. If it is difficult for you to get lawyers together for several training sessions, try holding one long session that encompasses everything you want to cover.

- Coordinate training across departments, e.g., tax implications of corporate mergers or bankruptcy law for litigators.

- Collaborate with another firm. To teach negotiation, for example, jointly create or license a negotiation case study and have the lawyers in your firm negotiate against the lawyers in the other firm. Use partners from both firms as faculty/observers.

- If lawyers resist technology training, integrate it with practical skills training. For instance, teach PowerPoint in a program on presentation skills, or Internet research in a course on incorporation procedures.

- Use "celebrity" faculty such as judges, politicians, community leaders, or well-known professors.

- Generate excitement about training. Produce a string of targeted, highly successful programs that build a reputation for high quality and usefulness.

■ 3. How can partners be persuaded to release associates to attend training programs?

The most important thing is to have unequivocal partner commitment to training. Make partners responsible for urging associates to attend programs. To accomplish this, you need partners to accept the importance of training. They need to appreciate how training associates will make their lives easier because associates will be more competent and productive, thereby decreasing write-offs and increasing the firm's bottom line.

Associates frequently miss training programs because partners pressure them to continue working instead. This is especially common for long programs that are held off-site, where the associate may be out of the office for a day or more. Sometimes there is a true emergency and the associate's absence cannot be helped, but more often, it is because of poor planning or organization by the partner. Firms that place a high priority on training do not condone these occurrences. In many firms, partners must get approval from the managing partner or the professional development partner in order to prevent an associate from attending firm-sponsored training programs. Sometimes the managing partner intervenes with a partner who is a "repeat offender" in keeping associates from training.

■ 4. Should the firm include clients in in-house training programs?

Including clients in in-house training — as guests and as faculty — is a great idea. Some partners worry that firm lawyers may say the wrong thing, make a poor impression, cause embarrassment, or steal their clients. Nonetheless, firms that include clients reap benefits that far outweigh any potential problems. Clients usually enjoy participating, as faculty, and welcome a chance to educate the firm's lawyers about their company, business, or industry. It offers a chance for more dialogue between lawyers and clients, with each developing a better understanding of how the other thinks. Inviting corporate counsel as guests gives you a chance to showcase the legal talent in your firm while also providing your guests with CLE credits.

One firm that uses clients as faculty in a unique way is Thelen, Reid & Priest LLP. This firm holds an intensive three-day "Client Satisfaction Workshop" for senior associates. Senior associates, partners, and invited clients from all over the country are brought to a single location. The workshop features clients in a variety of teaching activities: panel discussions, legal games ("Jurisprudence Jeopardy!"), case studies, and role playing. In the role plays, associates act out scenarios on client-related issues in front of clients, who then give the associates immediate feedback. Although associates may be nervous about doing this in front of clients, the feedback they receive, the insights they gain, and the relationships they establish with clients are invaluable. As an added bonus, the clients get to know the lawyers better and to appreciate the talented senior associates who represent them.

APPENDIX 8-A

Four Sample Law Firm Curricula

Severson & Werson

Severson & Werson demonstrates that smaller firms can provide ample training for their lawyers. This litigation firm, with 72 lawyers in two California offices, conducts a series of seminars and workshops for new associates on core practice topics and offers additional educational programs for all lawyers.

Core Curriculum for First-Year Associate Training

- Law Firm Economics
- Time Keeping
- Filing a Complaint (Part I)
- Filing a Complaint (Part II)
- Responding to a Complaint
- Attorney-Client Privilege
- California Discovery Procedures
- Document Production
- Legal Writing
- Federal Practice
- State Practice
- Expert Witnesses
- Settlement Negotiations
- Arbitration/Mediation
- Conflicts/Legal Ethics
- Evaluation Reports

Other Training Topics

- Consumer Finance
- Fair Debt Collection Issues
- Mortgage Banking
- Class Action Litigation
- Employment Law
- Real Estate/Title Insurance
- Business & Professions Code 17200
- Commercial Finance
- Insurance Coverage Issues
- Sexual Harassment
- Bankruptcy

Howard Rice Nemerovski Canady Falk & Rabkin

Howard Rice, with 133 lawyers all in one office, has core curricula for associates in the firm's Litigation and Business Departments. In addition to seminars and workshops on core curricula topics, the firm conducts a formal orientation program for new associates; holds educational programs on issues of broader interest, such as electronic discovery, interpretation of financial statements, and marketing and client development for women; and sponsors discussions and presentations at monthly or quarterly practice group meetings to which all lawyers are invited.

Litigation Department Associate Training Program

- Elements of Motion Practice in the California District and Superior Courts
- Using the Howard, Rice Style Manual and Cite Checking Guidelines
- Writing the Complaint
- Pre-Judgment Remedies: Attachments, TROs, and Preliminary Injunctions
- Attacking the Pleadings
- Planning Discovery—Interrogatories and Requests for Admission
- Document Requests, Document Management and Document Production
- Preparing For and Taking Depositions
- Primer on Electronic Discovery
- Writing the Summary Judgment Motion
- Settlement Negotiation and Mediation
- Preparing for and Taking Expert Depositions
- Trial Preparation and Jury Instruction
- Appearing in Court
- Writing the BIG (Appellate) Brief

Business Department Associate Training Program

- Equity/Venture Financing
- Securities Laws Basics
- Mergers & Acquisitions
- Choice of Equity
- Intellectual Property Overview
- Software Licensing and Distribution
- Stock Option Plans
- Due Diligence and Closings in Corporate Transactions
- Writing Legal Opinions

Hale and Dorr LLP

Hale and Dorr (with approximately 500 lawyers, 6 offices, and an independent joint venture law firm with offices in London, Oxford, and Munich) provides educational seminars and hands-on workshops for all partners and associates in a wide range of subjects including management, feedback, and supervision skills, communication skills, legal writing, negotiations, and time management. The firm offers intensive skills workshops, including a trial skills program for first- and second-year litigation associates that culminates in a mock trial. Departments and practice groups also conduct their own comprehensive educational programs. Below are the core curricula for Hale and Dorr's first-year associates and the programs presented by the Corporate, Litigation, Commercial, and Real Estate Departments.

CORE CURRICULUM: FIRST-YEAR ASSOCIATES

1. New Associate Orientation Program — Practicing Law at Hale and Dorr

- Legal Writing for Litigators
- Legal Writing for Transactional Attorneys
- Practice Management
- New Associate Retreat (Off-site)
- Conflicts and Ethics
- Management of Hale and Dorr
- Mentoring
- Public Service
- The Associates Committee

2. Hale and Dorr University: Corporate Department

- Drafting Transactional Documents
- Introduction to the Practice of Corporate Law
- Life of a Company
- Review of Federal Securities Laws – I
- Practical Guide to Conducting a Due Diligence Review
- Organizing a Transaction
- What Paralegals Do
- Start Up Businesses
- Introduction to Due Diligence – I
- Review of Federal Securities Laws – II

- Stock Option Plans
- Introduction to Venture Capital Financings
- Introduction to Mergers and Acquisitions – Overview
- Introduction to Mergers and Acquisitions – The Merger Agreement, Stock Purchase Agreement and Asset Purchase Agreement (*including related documents and disclosure schedules*)
- Introduction to IPOs
- Introduction to Due Diligence – II
- How to Conduct an IPO Closing
- Understanding Section 16
- How to Perform a "Tech Check" — Overview and Practical Applications
- Legal Opinions: Frequently Made Errors
- Edgarization and What an Associate Does at the Printer
- Reading and Understanding Financial Statements
- Corporate Tax/Choice of Entity
- Licensing Agreements
- Intellectual Property Law

3. Litigation Department Orientation Program

- Litigation Basics
- The Role of Litigation Paralegals and Litigation Support Services
- Initiation of Litigation
- The Defense
- Case Management and Discovery
- Drafting Discovery Requests
- Responding to Discovery Requests
- Depositions
- Deposition Examinations (three sessions; skills workshop)
- Motion Practice
- Motion Arguments (two sessions; skills workshop)
- Trial Preparation
- Settlement

4. Commercial Law Department Training

- Introduction to Commercial Law: An Orientation
- Chapter 11 (Parts I and II)
- Preferences, Fraudulent Conveyances, Strong Arm Powers
- Pre-Chapter 11 Planning
- Chapter 11 Financing: DIP Facilities and Cash Collateral
- Loan Documentation

- Legal Opinions
- Workouts & Restructurings
- Other Debt Transactions – Trust Indentures and Asset Securitization

5. Real Estate Department Training

- Purchase & Sale and Acquisition Due Diligence
- Leases I: Introduction to Leases
- Entities
- Introduction to Title & Survey
- Field Trip to Suffolk Registry and Advanced Title
- Environmental
- Zoning and Other Development Issues
- Leases II: Servicing of Corporate Dept. Leases
- Guarantees & Notes and Construction Loans
- Mortgages & Foreclosures, Assignment of Leases and Rents, Environmental Indemnities
- Construction Contracts and Architect Agreements
- Retail Leasing
- Authority & Enforceability Opinions

Latham & Watkins

Latham & Watkins, with more than 1,400 lawyers in 21 offices worldwide, offers a comprehensive array of educational opportunities for lawyers in all of its offices. The firm's course offerings include a core curriculum for new associates, advanced courses, skills workshops, and special "academies" for summer associates and first-, third-, and fifth-year associates. An overview of these programs is published as a brochure, which is reproduced on the following pages.

The L&W Formal Training Program

The Academies

- **LWU—SUMMER ACADEMY**
  A multi-day, off-site retreat designed to provide summer associates with substantive training in the firm's various practice areas. This program has been carefully crafted to expand upon the knowledge that summer associates are obtaining in law school and to provide them with the opportunity to meet summer associates from other offices in the firm.

- **FIRST YEAR ACADEMY**
  An intensive, multi-day, off-site training program offered each fall to incoming associates firm-wide. First Year Academy combines practical training programs with social activities that allow new associates to meet colleagues from other firm offices. The courses offered include a selection from the Core Curriculum designed to provide information about Latham & Watkins as a firm, general lawyering and practice skills, and substantive legal concepts in areas most relevant to our new associates.

- **THIRD YEAR ACADEMY**
  A two-day, off-site training program for associates in their third year of practice. This program concentrates on supervision training, tips for transition from junior to mid-level associates, and professional growth at this important juncture in an associate's career. Substantive tips for success in various practice areas are also included.

- **FIFTH YEAR ACADEMY**
  A two-day, off-site training program designed to provide the firm's fifth year associates with information relevant to the transition to roles assumed by senior associate in our demanding practice areas. Topics covered include partnership standards, business development, firm finances, mentoring, public speaking, as well as professional growth and development opportunities in general.

The L&W Formal Training Program

Core

The Core Curriculum is introduced to all first year associates at First Year Academy and continues via videoconference on the first Wednesday of each month throughout the year. The Core Curriculum is designed to provide all of Latham & Watkins' newest lawyers with an overview of the basic practical skills necessary to thrive in a law firm environment. The course list includes:

- Transition from Law School to the Practice of Law
- The Law Firm as a Business
- Good Client Service and Client Relations
- Law Practice Management & Office Procedures
- Anatomy of a Lawsuit
- Basics of Discovery
- Equal Employment Opportunities
- Corporate Law Fundamentals
- Transactional Due Diligence
- Legal Opinions and Audit Letters
- Basic Negotiation Skills
- Anatomy of a Deal
- Ethics
- Attorney-Client Privilege & Confidentiality
- Legal Research
- Environmental Law Fundamentals
- Legal Writing
- How to Read Financial Statements
- Commercial Lending Transactions
- Real Estate Law Fundamentals
- Insolvency/Work-out and Bankruptcy Fundamentals
- Corporate Finance 101
- Mergers & Acquisitions

Interdisciplinary

The Interdisciplinary Curriculum, offered to all associates, consists of practical courses that are designed to be of interest to all lawyers practicing in many substantive areas. The course list includes:

- The Art of Negotiation
- The Art of Supervision
- Employment Law for Dummies
- ERISA: What Every Transactional Lawyer Should Know About Compensation Plans
- Dealing with the Press
- The Federal Legislative Process and How to Influence It
- Legal & Contractual Pitfalls in International Commercial Transactions
- Securities Enforcement Litigation
- Antitrust: The Basic Principles and Practical Applications
- Tax for Non-Tax Lawyers
- What We Should All Know about Criminal Law
- Environmental Law for Transactional Lawyers
- Insurance: The Basic Policies and Coverage Issues
- Lawsuits 101 for Deal Lawyers
- Audit Letter Responses
- Winning the Business
- Frequently Asked Questions About Bankruptcy & Insolvency

Transactional

The L&W Formal Training Program

The Advanced Transactional Curriculum consists of a series of practical courses designed to give the firm's transactional lawyers an in-depth knowledge of "cutting edge" legal issues. These courses are delivered by partners in the firm's Corporate and Finance Departments, as well as outside experts, and are tailored to provide real-world skills as well as a knowledge of important substantive areas of law. The course list includes:

- EBITDA—What is it and Why You Should Care
- Public Offerings
- Venture Capital
- Regulation D and Private Placements
- Regulation M
- Regulation S and Offshore Offerings
- Debt Tender Offers
- The Investment Company Act
- The Margin Regulations
- High Yield Covenants
- Bridge Loans and Bought Deals
- Basic Securitizations
- Subordination
- The Anatomy of a Secured Loan
- The Basics of Acquisition Structuring
- The Architecture of a Public Acquisition Agreement
- The Architecture of a Private Acquisition Agreement
- Defensive Planning
- Fiduciary Duties of Directors in M&A Transactions
- Role of the Investment Banker in M&A Transactions
- Accounting Gamesmanship
- Accounting for Lawyers: Using Financial Data in Legal Practice
- Management Discussion & Analysis
- The Lawyers' Corporate Finance Program
- Understanding Corporate Financial Statements & Accounting for Corporate Transactions
- The Williams Act and Equity Tender Offers

The L&W Formal Training Program

Controversy

Highlights of the Advanced Controversy Curriculum include a three-day intensive deposition skills training program and a four-day, off-site national trial skills college. In each program, Latham associates practice their "stand-up" advocacy skills under the tutelage of an experienced faculty. In the deposition program, open to all associates interested in litigation, lawyers take and defend the depositions of fact and expert witnesses in a case that will then be used in mock trial exercises at the trial skills college. The national trial skills college, attended by the third and fourth year associates in the litigation department, also employs the "learn by doing" model. Associates conduct direct- and cross-examinations of expert and fact witnesses, argue evidentiary issues before a judge, and present open and closing arguments. They are given individual instruction by outside faculty and experienced Latham trial lawyers. Learning is reinforced by reviewing videotapes of each of their performances. In addition to these intensive programs, advanced courses are offered monthly throughout the year on such topics as:

- Experts: What They Can Do for You, and How You Find and Prepare Them
- Basic Pleadings
- Large Document Productions
- TRO's: What You Need to Know to Get One
- ADR, Arbitration & Settlement: Available Proceedings, Their Rules and Related Considerations
- Appellate Practice and Effective Written Advocacy
- Class Action Litigation Strategies and Issues
- Jury Selection Techniques and Issues
- Five Things Every IP Litigator Should Know

Latham & Watkins

APPENDIX 8-B

Questions to Ask When Choosing Online CLE Providers*

Content:

1. How many courses do you offer?
2. What subjects do you cover?
3. What materials are provided in conjunction with your programs? In what format? How are they accessed?
4. What is the source of your content?
5. How often is your content updated? Who updates the programs?
6. Which programs do you produce? Who produces the others?
7. For which jurisdictions do you offer credit? How many hours of content do you offer per jurisdiction? Is the content of your programs jurisdiction-specific?
8. Are your programs simply captured and digitalized or are they produced and edited specifically for online use? If they are produced, by whom?
9. How long are your programs?
10. Describe how the content is presented. What appears on the screen when a user is taking your program?
11. Please describe the audio/video/text quality of your online programs.
12. Do you ask for program evaluations? If so, how do you implement feedback?

CLE:

1. Do you offer participatory or self study credit, or both?
2. If you offer participatory credit, how is participation ascertained?
3. Do you offer CLE tracking services? What information do you track?
4. Do you have CLE and/or legal experts on staff?

---

* Adapted from a questionnaire created by Sandra Magliozzi of Heller Ehrman White & McAuliffe; Krista Juli of Morrison & Foerster; and Katya Miller of Thelen Reid & Priest.

5. How are CLE certificates issued? Do they include both 50-minute and 60-minute calculations? Do they include partial credit calculations?

6. Do you provide additional staffing toward the end of each compliance period?

Customer Support:

1. During what hours is customer support available?

2. What kinds of reports do you provide?

3. Do you provide usage reports? If so, how often? Are reports per lawyer? Per office? Firm wide?

4. Do you offer on-site training to teach attorneys how to use your services and programs?

5. Do your customer service representatives and other staff members have legal experience?

6. Are you doing research on online usage?

7. Are you considering becoming an aggregator?

8. What assurances do we have that you will be in the market in the next two to three years?

9. How do you promote your programs?

Cost:

1. How do you charge customers?

2. What types of billing options do you offer?
    — One firm bill?
    — Prepay for courses?
    — Flat rate?
    — Volume discount? If so, what types?

3. What packages do you offer for a firm the size of ours?

4. Do you require any guarantees? Or any minimum or maximum hours of usage?

5. Please delineate any penalties each particular package would cause for our firm.

6. What kind of flexibility, if any, would customers be able to exercise over the life of their subscription?

Ease of Technology:

1. Do firms need in-house tech support in order to use your programs?
2. Does a user need to download anything in order to take an online course?
3. What do the programs look like over 56K modems?
4. How many users can access through one T-1 line?
5. What is the ease of login: after logging in the first time, what happens after that?
6. Are users able to interrupt the program? If so, can they pick up where they left off? Please address "interruptibility" in general.
7. Please describe mobility within the program: can a user move back and forth, from screen to screen? Can a user study discrete sections of a program?
8. What type of security/firewalls do you provide?
9. Are there any additional or special technologies required for lawyers in international offices?
10. Are there any special issues if lawyers log on through their laptops outside the office?

APPENDIX 8-C

Annual In-House Survey to Identify Future Training Topics and Faculty: Sample Form

This form identifies five proposed in-house training programs and leaves space for you to suggest others. After each suggested program, there are columns in which you can indicate the proposed audience and practice groups (e.g., second-year corporate associates), the names of possible faculty from inside and/or outside the firm, and whether you would be interested in serving as faculty. There is also a column for comments, where you can provide any additional information, including specific points you would like to have addressed in a program and suggested formats.

Program topic	Proposed audience/ Practice groups	Recommended faculty	Would you teach?	Comments
Structuring acquisitions	First- and second-year business associates			
Accounting for lawyers	All associates			
Negotiating with government agencies	Second-year Regulatory Group associates			
Stress management	All lawyers			
Public speaking	All lawyers			

Your name (optional) _____

APPENDIX 8-D

2001-2002 Cooley College Faculty Guidelines

Many thanks to each of you for teaching associates in Cooley College for the 2001-2002 academic year. The enclosed schedule highlights the course(s) you are scheduled to teach. The positive feedback received for last year's Cooley College was a direct result of the effort placed by the instructors into the materials and the presentations.

The following guidelines provide answers to many questions posed by instructors over the past five years. Please feel free to comment or to raise additional issues. Even if you are providing a repeat performance, please review carefully as there are critical changes in this year's Cooley College, such as:

- This year, almost all of the Cooley College classes will be taught starting at [DATE] and ending [DATE]. The first years from other offices will fly out to the Bay Area on [DATE], go through firm orientation on [DATE], and stay at the [HOTEL] through [DATE]. To the extent possible, please try to use PowerPoint presentations or other visual aids such as easels with carts or diagrams. These really help punch up a presentation.

- Due to the schedule, the binders for all of the classes taking place from [DATE] to [DATE] must be ready to copy in the Copy Center by [Date] to avoid overtime charges.

Location

1. Almost all sessions this year will be held in all-day, off-site sessions at the [HOTEL] in [CITY].
2. Since we will have several programs scheduled throughout the day, it is imperative that you arrive on time at the hotel. The day will be very full and we need to keep to the times scheduled.

Materials

1. Written materials are mandatory. The completed materials (in the format described below) must be submitted to [NAME] by the deadlines set forth below.
2. The presenters from each session should meet well before the session to determine who will be responsible for modifying or adding the different materials in the

binder(s) for the session and who will cover which parts of the presentation. One person should then compile the final materials. We cannot be responsible for putting the binders together for you. We will try to review the materials in a cursory manner as a quality check but will not be able to compile the binders. The materials are the responsibility of each panel of presenters. We know that each of you is very busy, but we have hopefully given you enough notice to get the materials done.

3. The materials must include:
   a. Detailed Table of Contents.
   b. Discussion Outline — in the past some of the presenters spoke from great outlines, but they were not included in the materials. Many participants requested that the actual outline be included so that they can better follow the discussion.
   c. Copies of any slides or PowerPoint presentations. All PowerPoint presentations must be printed in black and white, on 3-hole punched paper, using the "3 slides to a page" print option. Please make sure that the background selected will allow for proper viewing in black and white (you may use whatever background you like for the presentation, but please make appropriate changes for printing). (Note: for those classes requiring submission of the binders on [DATE] you can as an alternative provide copies of the PowerPoint presentations at the session. Please make arrangements (with your secretaries or the Copy Center), to make 100 stapled copies on 3-hole punched paper, using the "3 slides to a page" option for printing. We plan to be at the [HOTEL] from start to finish and not able to come back to the office to pick up last-minute copies.
   d. Sample documents, forms, statutes, articles, and memos, as necessary and appropriate for the presentation. Please doublecheck the Forms List to see if there is an existing form to use rather than providing a sample.
      i. All form documents included must be current and updated. Please check the Forms List and print out the most current version before including the documents in the materials. Please read the forms you will use to see if they need to be updated. If so, please mark up the document and send it to [NAME] for processing. Please also use sample documents that are current (i.e., samples of Edgar documents and cover letters, filing letters that reflect the correct filing fees, periodic reports that reflect new rule changes, new Nasdaq materials, etc.). We would suggest that all samples used be no older than one year if possible.
      ii. Remember to copy the most current rule, regulation, or statute from the appropriate authority; many changes occur over a one-year period.
      iii. When reviewing prior materials, look for materials that should be deleted or added. The prior materials are just a starting point — do not just recycle them. Please feel free to add to the materials; in most instances new materials are expected to be added.
      iv. Please make sure a document number appears at the bottom of each document included.
      v. Please remove client references from the materials. For example, if an actual agreement that you wish to use is on the system, please try to change the

Training

          names from the actual parties to "Acme" or "Ajax" or your favorite politically correct alternatives.

e. All of the above materials should be compiled and tabbed and one copy sent to [NAME] for reproduction and delivery to the hotel. All presenters will receive a binder of the materials and directions to the hotel prior to the presentation (if you give the materials to [NAME] on time!).

f. Please have a copy of the PowerPoint presentation sent to [NAME] by [DATE]. We will have the presentation loaded on a laptop at the hotel. We will not be able to run the presentations at the hotel from the network. Note that many presentations far exceed the capacity of floppy disks. You may bring your own laptop with the presentation loaded on the "C" hard drive as a backup, but we need to have them loaded and ready to go.

g. A copy of last year's binder for your topic is included only for those presenters who did NOT teach the same session last year. If you taught the same class last year, please use your old binder as a starting point. If you don't have your binder, please let us know and we will get a replacement to you as soon as possible.

Deadlines for Submitting Materials

Please adhere to the following deadlines for submitting the materials listed above.

Cooley College Date	Deadline for Materials
[DATE]	[DATE]
[DATE]	[DATE]
[DATE]	[DATE]
[DATE]	[DATE]

Presentation Tips

1. Please let [NAME] know in advance if you need any special equipment for the presentation. We will have a laptop with an LCD projector for all of the presentations (unless you indicate otherwise), but need to know if you require an overhead projector, TV, special microphones, easels, or other materials. This should be as soon as possible, but please by [DATE].

2. Please try to use visual aids, such as a PowerPoint presentation or easels. Evaluations consistently show that visual or interactive presentations have the greatest impact.

3. All sessions will be videotaped — remember to repeat any questions asked by the audience for the benefit of those later viewing the tape.

4. Remember your audience at Cooley College is meant for very junior associates. Teaching the basics is the point. Focus on the tasks and documents a junior associate will be doing in any given project. Also, remember to "give the big picture" at the beginning to set the topic in context.

5. Encourage questions as time permits. Encourage those with "personal" questions to contact you after the program.

6. Stick to the time allotted for the presentation. Those programs with several presenters especially need to adhere to time allotted to make sure you get through the entire program. One comment from prior years was a tendency to rush through the last part of the materials. We know this happens, but it helps to have one person responsible for keeping time during the presentation.
7. Use real life examples when appropriate. Some war stories are interesting; too many detract from the presentation. Use humor.
8. IF YOU HAVE AN EMERGENCY AND ARE UNABLE TO PRESENT, YOU ARE RESPONSIBLE FOR FINDING A REPLACEMENT PRESENTER.

MCLE Faculty Credit

Now for the good part — how much MCLE credit will you receive for your presentation? Under the California MCLE rules, credit hours for panelists are computed by multiplying the length of time the panelist is assigned to speak by four. If specific speaking times are not assigned to the panelists, "the length of time the panelist is assigned to speak" means the length of the program divided by the number of panelists (everyone gets equal credit). For the remainder of the panel, panelists may claim only actual attendance time.

For example, if a program has two panelists and lasts four hours, each presenter (assuming equal speaking time) will receive a total of ten MCLE hours (eight hours for the speaking time (two hours times four) plus an additional two hours for "attendance time." If you leave the program after you speak, you will only get the speaker's credits. If you want the speaking hours divided up a certain way, please notify [NAME] in advance of the program. Remember to sign the MCLE Attendance Record.

Please have fun and we thank you again for your participation. We know it is a lot of work, but having well-trained associates is worth the effort we put in today. Please give [NAME] a call if you want to talk about your presentation or have any suggestions or comments.

Thank you.

PART III

Knowledge Management

CHAPTER 9

Knowledge Management: Harnessing Information and Expertise

"If you have knowledge, let others light their candles in it."
— Margaret Fuller

Knowledge management is one of the hottest topics in law firms these days. Using web-based technology to collect, organize, and access information, knowledge management lets lawyers harness information and expertise from within and outside the firm. Law firms' imaginations have been fired up by the seemingly infinite potential to make critical knowledge accessible to everyone in the firm anytime, anywhere. The main impetus for knowledge management is that it makes lawyers more efficient and effective. Through their computers, lawyers can be connected instantaneously to the information they need, the clients they serve, and the people with whom they work. With just a few mouse clicks, lawyers can access firm directories and calendars; find out which lawyers have certain expertise, experience, or clients; obtain CLE credit by reviewing a training program presented last month; and participate in a live meeting with clients in international offices. The resources they need to do their work are literally at their fingertips.

Law firms are also beginning to appreciate the power of knowledge management to promote lawyers' education and professional development by creating environments that are "rich in intellectual nutrients."[1] By connecting lawyers for learning and collaboration and delivering just-in-time training to the desktop, firms can spread knowledge instantly throughout the firm and integrate learning into daily legal practice. In today's hyper-competitive, knowledge-based economy, that kind of environment is a necessity for maintaining competitive advantage. The corporate world has embraced knowledge management fervently, with companies as diverse and DuPont, ChevronTexaco, General Electric, Ernst & Young, and

---

[1] Stephen V. Armstrong and Marc Lauritsen, "Working Smarter to Help Lawyers Work Smart: Linking Education and Information Technology," *Law Firm Governance*, Summer 1999, p. 56.

McKinsey asserting that knowledge management has given them a sustained competitive advantage in their respective industries.[2] ChevronTexaco, for example, estimates that two of its knowledge-sharing initiatives for project managers have each saved the company millions of dollars, and Ernst & Young determined that knowledge management increased its worldwide consulting revenues from $1.5 billion in 1995 to $2.7 billion in 1997.[3]

Knowledge management has its roots in information management. In its most basic form, knowledge management is a system for organizing and storing information, including lawyers' work product, so that that you or someone else can easily retrieve and reuse that information the next time it is needed. This simple type of knowledge management is certainly not new. Lawyers have always maintained files of the standard forms they have developed, and legal publishers have for decades produced books containing forms of agreements and pleadings with annotations about the proper use of each form. Law firms have long kept databases with information about their personnel, vendors, and clients. Case teams frequently prepare binders that contain descriptions of the pleadings, parties, issues, chronologies, and key documents that all team members need on a large piece of litigation.

Knowledge management is far more sophisticated than information management in that it applies lawyers' intelligence and experience to transform information into knowledge. Information is the raw data that goes into the system. That information is transformed into knowledge when the system interprets the data, provides a context for it, and organizes it so that users can apply it intelligently. By providing explanation and framework, knowledge management makes it easier for lawyers to evaluate the information they find and determine if and how to apply it in new situations. Like teaching and mentoring, knowledge management is a way to transfer knowledge, not just information.

Law is, of course, a knowledge-based profession, and a legal employer's most important assets are therefore intellectual. As an asset, knowledge has a unique characteristic. Unlike physical assets, which become depleted with use, knowledge can be stored, reused, shared, and expanded with use. It can be leveraged to inform and educate others without losing its value. Indeed, as people add to, modify, and enrich the firm's store of knowledge, they simultaneously benefit from it and

---

[2] Nancy M. Dixon, *Common Knowledge*, Boston, Harvard Business School Press, 2000; Chad Holliday, "Sustainable Growth, The DuPont Way," *Harvard Business Review*, September 2001, p. 129; Morten T. Hansen, Nitin Nohria, and Thomas Tierney, "What's Your Strategy for Managing Knowledge?" *Harvard Business Review*, March-April 1999, p. 106; www.mckinsey.com.

[3] "Chevron: Transferring Best Practices," *Training*, July 2001, p. 35; "What's Your Strategy for Managing Knowledge?" p. 110. This article also presents an example where one Ernst & Young team saved a full year of work by using the firm's knowledge management capabilities.

increase its value. Law firms realize that if knowledge is their most important asset and if it can be improved with use, then they should be capturing lawyers' knowledge and making it available throughout the firm. This is becoming more urgent as firms become global. Lawyers who are scattered all over the world possess important knowledge that could be useful to their co-workers everywhere. With access to the collective knowledge of the firm, these lawyers can add greater value for clients by being smarter, more responsive, and more agile. Marshalling and distributing that knowledge will give a firm a substantial competitive advantage.

The excitement over knowledge management has led to a passion for knowledge that rivals the ancient Gnostic belief that the path to true salvation was in the power of the mind over matter. As summarized in one study of knowledge management systems, "Organizations that are able to more effectively generate knowledge and capture and share learning enhance their strategic capabilities, achieve higher levels of technical effectiveness, and attain superior business performance."[4] Law firms are therefore beginning to collect information, acquire software programs, and utilize web-based technology to make knowledge easily accessible anytime, anywhere, to those who might need it.

How Does Knowledge Management Work?

Using browsers and Internet-based technology, knowledge management systems arrange, store, and retrieve information on the World Wide Web and on the firm's own web sites, intranets, and extranets. (Refer to Table 1 if you are unfamiliar with these terms.) Access is through a home page, and people navigate the system using a web-based browser. The information can be of any kind and in any format, and can include text, audio, video, and graphics. In addition, web-based knowledge management systems can provide countless features and advantages that paper-based systems cannot. (See sidebar on pages 312 and 313.)

Knowledge management links and integrates all the information repositories available on the web with additional information the firm chooses to obtain from and make available to its personnel, clients, and the public. External information can come from places like company web sites, specialized publications, CLE vendors, government databases, and every other information resource available on the web. Internal knowledge generated by the firm can be specific to a case, client, or department; it can be a record of prior transactions, a set of model documents, the

---

[4] *Strategies for the Knowledge Economy: From Rhetoric to Reality*, Korn/Ferry International in conjunction with The Center for Effective Organizations, Marshall School of Business, University of Southern California, Davos, Switzerland, 2000, p. 5.

> **TABLE 1. Terminology**
>
> - The **World Wide Web** is a publicly available global information system.
> - The **Internet** is the publicly available network over which web-based information is transported.
> - A firm's **web site** is its home on the web.
> - A firm's **intranet** is its private internal system for use by the firm's lawyers and staff.
> - A firm's **extranets** are private, secure web sites to which clients, co-counsel, and others can be given access through passwords.

description of a winning strategy or a list of practice tips for new associates. Examples of the internal information that can be integrated into the knowledge management system include:

- The firm's software programs (e.g., for case management, document drafting, document assembly, litigation support);
- Internally produced information repositories (e.g., archives, specialized databases, summaries of law in various jurisdictions);
- Documents of all kinds (e.g., research memos, standard forms, checklists);
- Training programs and tutorials;
- Firm publications;
- Firm marketing materials;
- Directories;
- Calendars; and
- Individual and group web pages designed by and for people in the firm.

In addition, firms can provide tools to facilitate communication and collaboration. The most common are virtual "chat rooms," where members of a team or individuals with a common interest can communicate online. This concept has been expanded to online "deal rooms" where lawyers and their clients can work together on documents and arrange business transactions through a dedicated web site. Some firms also host question-and-answer pages where clients can prepare

Advantages of Web-Based Knowledge Management Systems

- A vast array of information and resources can be accessed and linked.

- Data inside and outside the firm can be linked automatically. Clicking on a case citation, for example, can immediately bring that case up on the screen.

- Information can be enhanced with sound, video, graphics, and animation.

- Search engines can scour all the information available in the firm and on the web to find what lawyers need.

- Information can be presented in active and interactive formats. Individuals can ask and answer questions, complete and submit applications, generate reports, make decisions, and solve problems merely by following a series of prompts.

- Model documents and templates can be presented as standard forms with general applicability and, with modifications, as variations that can be used by particular groups to suit their specific needs. These forms can be annotated to demonstrate different kinds of applications or to form the basis of a tutorial. They can be linked with particular transactions, clients, training programs, applicable statutes, and textbooks.

- Information distribution can be controlled. Access to sensitive information and documents can be protected with passwords.

- Learning resources, including training programs and materials, are available to lawyers whenever they need or have time to use them. Learners can receive only the information they want or need; the instruction can be tailored to the learner's performance level and learning style; and the system can track any necessary administrative data (e.g., requirements, scores, completion, billing).

- Information sharing leads to greater innovation. When innovations occur, they can be made known to others who can make use of them right away and improve on them.

- Practice groups can have their own web pages to post knowledge specific to the group, contain chat rooms for teams, or present materials that colleagues can use for training and marketing purposes.

- Individuals can have personalized web pages on which they can post information they have developed or collected (e.g., "tips" for handling certain kinds of transactions).

- Individuals can set preferences on personal home pages for frequently used sites (like "My AOL" or "My Yahoo"). The system can continually and automatically look for information related to those preferences and notify the lawyer when new information is available. It can also track and remember an individual's prior searches, making the home page more "intelligent" every time it is used.

- Lawyers and clients can partner more easily. Clients can have direct access to their lawyers' files, bills, and educational materials; clients and lawyers can work together on documents at the same time; and lawyers can access brief banks and other resources available in clients' offices.

- Lawyers can work in real-time with groups and individuals located all over the world. They can draft documents with clients and attend depositions in other states without leaving their desks.

- Law firms in different states and countries engaged in similar kinds of cases can create and simultaneously access repositories of research, discovery, documents, experts, witnesses, and other relevant information.

- Web sites can be created for individual cases or transactions, and all co-counsel can coordinate efforts through a single web site. Pleadings and legal papers can be drafted in multiple locations, reviewed by the client, filed with the court, and served on all counsel electronically.

- Firms can meet corporate clients' need for consistency. Companies with many different outside law firms need to ensure that all their firms take consistent approaches to commonly recurring legal, regulatory, and administrative matters.

- Companies can easily communicate with all of their inside counsel and outside firms. By accessing clients' databases, pleadings, briefs, and documents, outside law firms can avoid inconsistencies that might compromise a client's position.

- Law firm mergers can be facilitated. The resources of the merging firms can be combined, thereby expanding the new firm's capabilities. The new firm's values and strategies can be widely disseminated.

their own legal documents or solve their own legal problems before talking with a lawyer. The potential power of such integrated knowledge management systems is stunning.

How Does Knowledge Management Benefit Lawyers and Firms?

The most obvious reason for gathering and distributing the firm's collective knowledge is that it makes practice far more efficient. Lawyers save time and effort in many ways:

- Easy access to previously used or created information (e.g., forms, procedures, research memos) eliminates duplicative work. Lawyers don't waste time "reinventing the wheel."

- Indexing, search engines, and communication links facilitate the retrieval of pertinent information.

- Lawyers can quickly identify and reach people with specific knowledge, expertise, experience, and contacts.

- Commonly recurring processes and procedures (e.g., due diligence, motion practice, administrative filings) can be described in detail, with explanations of the reasons for every step.

- Tools that quickly locate, sort, and rank relevant information accelerate decision making.

- Automated "news sorting" functions and "robots" can be employed to search the web and automatically inform lawyers about clients, industries, legislative developments, court decisions, and virtually any other type of news and developments. Automatic news alerts can keep lawyers and clients informed and up to date on the specific issues that interest them.

- Through extranets, lawyers, team members, clients, and co-counsel can work together effectively wherever they are, cutting down on the need for travel while allowing people to interact personally and directly.

Because lawyers waste less time and respond to client needs and inquiries more quickly and effectively, these efficiencies translate into better client service. Although some fear that too much efficiency may mean less billing and lower revenues, clients who are happy with cost-effective, responsive legal services are more likely to bring the firm repeat business and refer the firm to their colleagues.

Knowledge Management and Professional Development

Knowledge management can support every aspect of professional development. According to a 2001 survey of law firms,[5] firms use technology to support professional development through the following activities (listed in order of frequency):

1. Publish an in-house training calendar.
2. Collect and compile associate evaluations.
3. Store and index work product and model document files.
4. Publish a directory of in-house self-study resources.
5. Track work assignments.
6. Publish a calendar of external CLE courses.
7. Collect and compile upward evaluations.
8. Publish a directory of in-house experts.
9. Track progress toward development goals or milestones.

As this list shows, knowledge management supports professional development in many ways, including facilitating evaluations and tracking work assignments. Knowledge management can also help lawyers identify their learning needs and competency gaps by putting performance standards, partnership requirements, and evaluation criteria online. Software programs and templates can help lawyers create individual development plans and help practice groups develop business plans. Mentoring can also be promoted through online mentoring programs, materials, and chat rooms.

The use of knowledge management as a teaching tool is also growing rapidly. Technology is an expedient way to deliver training to busy lawyers. (The benefits, drawbacks, and implications of technology-based training are discussed in greater detail in Chapter 8.) How extensively knowledge management is used for training purposes is in large part determined by the firm's resources. Most firms can afford to provide access to online training through direct links to CLE vendors or by putting their own training programs online. But some large law firms are creating new types of learning resources by capturing and distributing the firm's knowledge

---

[5] Gaye Mara, "In-House Uses of Technology for Professional Development," *Professional Development Quarterly*, August 2001, p. 3.

specifically for training purposes. This is a far more complex and costly endeavor, but it does create customized learning tools for the firm's lawyers. Take, for example, the placement of standard license forms on the computer network. Many firms place these forms online. While this is valuable and helps lawyers save time, the forms alone are not educational. Associates need to learn which provisions to use for particular transactions. That requires intervention and interpretation. To add educational value to online forms, someone must annotate each form and each provision with an explanation of its implications, when to use and not to use it, and its relation to other provisions; the names and contact information for lawyers in the firm who have licensing expertise; the transactions in which lawyers in the firm have used the licenses; and hypertext links to transactions, lawyers, cases, articles, texts, statutes, and internal memoranda that are pertinent to the licenses. To do this requires a huge amount of time, work, and cooperation from lawyers experienced in using the licenses.

Obstacles to Knowledge Management

You might think that the major impediment to knowledge management is the limitation of current technology. This is not the case. Much of the necessary technology can be purchased off-the-shelf, downloaded from the Internet, or created by a firm. Many software programs now exist that permit even a small law firm to manage documents, information, and knowledge efficiently, and more information technology resources are being produced every day. Many knowledge management services (e.g., automated news sorting) are available to all law firms through outside vendors. So technology is not the problem. The real obstacle is lawyers' resistance. The value of a knowledge management system depends on what lawyers put into it and on how much they utilize it. To institute a knowledge management system, the greatest challenge is persuading lawyers to contribute to and use it.

The reasons that lawyers do not use knowledge management are practical, behavioral, and cultural.

■ Practical Obstacles

A comprehensive knowledge management system requires a lot of input from lawyers. Lawyers have to submit information and documents, record their wisdom and advice, and explain how they work and achieve results. This process is difficult and time consuming, and lawyers cannot always articulate the knowledge they are asked to contribute. That knowledge is both explicit and tacit. Explicit knowledge is visible; it is contained in books, documents, policies, manuals, photos, patents, databases, and countless other formats. Tacit knowledge is intangible and transitory. It includes unstated values, discussions among lawyers about case strategy, intuitive assessment of a potential new case, and the insights of a senior partner about how to frame an argument. About 80 percent of knowledge is tacit, making it extremely difficult to identify and organize. After all, how do you codify, much less manage, the thoughts in someone's head? Making tacit knowledge explicit requires people to reflect on and analyze what they know, how they do things, and why they do them that way. Firms are finding ways to help lawyers articulate and record their knowledge, but it requires lawyers to be willing to make time to reflect on, analyze, and write down their knowledge and experience.

Knowledge management also requires a dedicated staff to do the work. To have educational value, information must be transformed into knowledge so that lawyers can use it intelligently. People need to design and operate the technical features, figure out how knowledge is articulated and captured, and reconfigure the knowledge into an educational system. Turning documents, issues, and information into effective learning tools requires commentary, discussion of precedents, and links to additional resources. Consequently, knowledge management requires more than information technology (IT) specialists. It requires a multi-disciplinary team of specialists from many fields, including technology, library science, law, education, human resources, and professional development. Accordingly, firms are bringing together professionals from these diverse disciplines to study the way knowledge is created, transferred, and used; to find new approaches to codifying, organizing, and storing it; and to reinvent the way it is deployed to assist and educate lawyers.

Gathering and distributing the firm's collective knowledge is an extremely difficult, time-consuming, and expensive undertaking. Some large firms have a dozen or more people working on various aspects of knowledge management. Knowledge management systems take a long time to design and implement and even longer to show any recognizable returns on the firm's investment. That investment itself is never-ending. The knowledge base must constantly be updated and refreshed, as knowledge grows, standards change, or certain information loses its value (e.g., new statutes are adopted, policies are modified, patents expire).

■ Behavioral Obstacles

Successful knowledge management systems can only exist in an environment that fosters a desire for knowledge and ensures its continual creation, distribution, and application. People cannot be forced to contribute to or use knowledge management systems; they must do it voluntarily. This requires a willingness by lawyers to share what they know, i.e., the products of their experience and the practices, ideas, and documents that have worked well for them. Unfortunately, lawyers' habits and law firm environments work against this effort.

Some lawyers hoard knowledge. They are not inclined to share their "secrets of success" with others. They are highly individualistic and compete on the basis of what they know. They recognize that "knowledge is power" and prefer to use that power to benefit themselves. Compensation, influence, and advancement are determined competitively, and lawyers are rewarded on the basis of their individual expertise, client base, and ability to attract business. Their personal knowledge is therefore too precious to be shared with others. They jealously guard it, just as they guard their clients against poaching by other partners. If lawyers enjoy a competitive advantage by keeping client information, prized work product, and the lessons of experience to themselves, why should they share that information with their colleagues? Why relinquish control over something of such great value?

To make a knowledge management system work, lawyers must fervently believe in mustering the knowledge of the firm's lawyers for their collective benefit. If lawyers put their own interests above the firm's, lawyers will not support the system and a knowledge management initiative will be a waste of time and money. This is a real challenge in today's economic climate. Firms with lockstep compensation systems are more conducive to knowledge management because lawyers can contribute and share information without worrying about the effect on their income. Unfortunately, firms are moving away from lockstep to a more competitive system that rewards lawyers on the basis of their individual financial performance.

■ Cultural Obstacles

Knowledge management requires a strong learning-centered culture that values knowledge sharing. Some firms try to introduce knowledge management in order to change the culture, but the culture must be receptive to knowledge sharing in the first place. Partners who currently put security passwords on all the important documents they create will not change their behavior just because the firm implements a fancy knowledge management system. Similarly, if lawyers have no sense of loyalty and long-term commitment to the firm, they will not want to share their knowledge. Commitment to the organization is one the strongest predictors of knowledge sharing.[6] A firm with low attrition is more likely to implement knowledge management successfully.

---

[6] *Strategies for the Knowledge Economy: From Rhetoric to Reality*, p. 29.

Making Knowledge Management Work to Support Learning

In spite of these obstacles, law firms are finding innovative, cost-effective ways to use knowledge management to support lawyers' learning and development. Without knowledge management, firms will become dinosaurs. The speed, efficiency, collaboration, and education that knowledge management makes possible are essential for law firms to survive in today's world. Much of the technology needed for knowledge management is available at affordable prices, and new products and services are being developed all the time. The system can be modest or elaborate, depending on your firm's needs and resources, and you can purchase technology products and services or create your own.

However you approach it, instituting knowledge management in a law firm is a daunting project. The teaching and learning aspects are especially complicated. The following points will ease your efforts to build a learning support system with knowledge management tools and convince your firm's lawyers to use them.

■ 1. Relevance, Accessibility, and Ease of Input

Three principles govern the value and success of knowledge management — relevance, accessibility, and ease of input.

- **Relevance.** When deciding what to include for training purposes, be selective. Do not dump everything into your knowledge management system. The idea is to reduce information overload, not increase it. It is essential that potential items be screened for their relevance and value, and that only useful items be placed in the system.

- **Accessibility.** Make the process as simple to use as possible. Forget the bells and whistles that IT people love to include. Lawyers want effective but hassle-free tools. If the system is at all complicated, or if the searches take too much time, lawyers will not use it. Make searching easy by creating categories ("metatags") that identify themes and issues the way a lawyer would look for them. Use these categories for organizing all the materials you enter into the system. Arrange information by practice areas as well as specific topics.

    Accessibility also requires the system to be visually and esthetically pleasing. Consider using a graphic designer. Make sure that lawyers can input and retrieve information at all times and from almost any place, and that technical support, including a help desk, is available 24/7.

- **Ease of input.** The collection and input of knowledge must be as quick and easy as the searching. Lawyers' hoarding of knowledge may not really be a reluctance to share but rather a refusal to spend precious time writing down their contributions. Asking people to write down their thoughts for a database may simply be too nebulous and impersonal. Researchers have found that people who will not write down what they know are quite willing to share their knowledge when asked personally in a conversation,[7] and that they exchange knowledge in direct proportion to their level of face-to-face contact.[8] Interviewing lawyers personally and providing staff to input what lawyers show and tell them should increase the data you can accumulate for your knowledge management system. This will also facilitate knowledge input by reducing the time and work required of lawyers. Another work- and time-saver is automatic knowledge capture by a system that tracks the "Has anyone ever…" and "Does anyone know…" questions and answers that lawyers post on e-mail networks. The collected communications form a massive database of searchable information. Like a site for "frequently asked questions," lawyers can search the database for answers, discussions, and solutions contributed by others in the firm.

2. Agree on Learning Goals

The firm should identify a common purpose and reach consensus on specific learning goals. It should agree on the importance of using knowledge management to aid in achievement of those goals and on how knowledge management will assist in that endeavor. What do you hope to gain from a knowledge management system? How will you develop a learning/sharing culture with a sustained demand for knowledge? How can knowledge management help lawyers learn what they need to know for superior performance? Obtain commitments from departments and practice group leaders to support the project. One way they can manifest their support is by including knowledge management in their business plans.

---

[7] Dixon, *Common Knowledge*.
[8] Thomas H. Davenport, David W. DeLong, and Michael C. Beers, "Successful Knowledge Management Projects," *Sloan Management Review*, Winter 1998, pp. 43, 54.

3. Find a Champion

Appoint an influential firm leader to champion the project. You must have a guiding champion at the strategic level to set the effort in motion and sustain momentum during the long start-up process. Many law firms create a special role for the knowledge management project leader or director, similar to the "Chief Knowledge Officer" positions that now exist at many companies. By creating this role for a high-level manager, knowledge management becomes part of the firm's management structure and more supporters are enlisted.

4. Find the Right Personnel

An experienced lawyer, not an IT expert, should be in charge of the firm's knowledge management system. Knowledge management is about sharing knowledge of practical value to lawyers, and experienced lawyers are best able to identify and manage relevant content. They can make sure that the knowledge to which lawyers have access is valuable, useful, and understandable, no matter the source. Because they know how lawyers are taught to approach problems, they are better able to organize information so that system utilization is easy, quick, and worthwhile. Moreover, lawyers are more likely to accept knowledge management as an integral part of their practice when a lawyer heads up the effort. Lawyers may be wary of the system if they believe that IT personnel are making decisions about substantive content or that knowledge management is merely a new software application.

In addition, a comprehensive knowledge management initiative needs personnel with backgrounds in many areas besides technology and law: education, library science, training, and professional development. All of these individuals have expertise required to design, input, organize, run, and support the system, including the ability to evaluate commercial knowledge management products and services to determine which ones will suit lawyers' learning needs. Individuals who have expertise in multiple facets of knowledge management are highly sought after. This has led to the emergence of a specialized consulting field and the creation of alternative career paths for lawyers. A small but growing number of technically oriented lawyers with multi-disciplinary expertise are bringing their specialized talents to knowledge management projects as outside consultants. Within firms, full-time responsibility for knowledge management is being delegated to senior associates and partners. In some firms, lawyers hold the position for a fixed time period, while in others lawyers are leaving law practice to move permanently into knowledge management.

Knowledge management is also giving rise to the position of "Professional Support Lawyers" (PSLs). In creating these positions, American and Canadian firms are following the lead of English law firms, which typically employ cadres of PSLs to support their knowledge management efforts. These staff lawyers draft model precedents, collect and catalogue sample documents and research memoranda, keep lawyers up to date on legal and business developments, write articles, and develop training programs for lawyers and clients.

■ 5. Concentrate on Small Groups First

While some aspects of knowledge management are necessarily firm wide (e.g., directories, web-based training resources), efforts to create knowledge management systems that support learning and development should begin by focusing on one or two practice groups. Knowledge management systems for these groups can be organized around common problems, issues, practices, and activities. You can capitalize on lawyers' current knowledge sharing practices more readily because they are familiar with each other and share common practice and client concerns. Once you have a system up and running successfully in one practice group, it will also be easier to demonstrate the value of knowledge management to others in the firm and obtain their buy-in to knowledge management for their group.

■ 6. Identify Best Practices

Identify current competencies, effective performance, and best practices to build upon. Do not look for what is different or unusual, but determine what is common, what has produced outstanding results, and what experience might help someone practice more effectively. Your purpose is to use technological tools to build on and strengthen successful resources and practices. This means that lawyers must share what they know with each other so that the information in the system contains the best knowledge, experience, and practices that exist in the firm. Study their communication patterns, collaborative work processes, and document storing habits to learn how knowledge is currently shared in the firm. Observe how lawyers work, to whom they bring their questions, what kinds of questions are asked, and how they work with secretaries and staff.

Knowledge Management: Harnessing Information and Expertise

■ 7. Stimulate Usage

Decide how you will motivate lawyers to contribute to and use the system. Some lawyers will be eager to use knowledge management tools, but most will need to be prodded and persuaded. You will need deliberate, well-planned strategies to get lawyers to develop new habits and to overcome the obstacles to usage discussed earlier. Some specific measures, incentives, and rewards to consider are the following:

- Make knowledge management an integral part of every lawyer's workday. Start with your firm's home page. When people log on, give them something of immediate value. Let them see notices about upcoming training programs, solicit associates to staff new work assignments, post a tip for effective mentoring, announce a winning verdict, or link them to a news clip about a client.

- Change the compensation system to reward knowledge sharing.

- Create billing numbers so that lawyers can record time spent in knowledge management activities.

- Give people credit, recognition, and special rewards for their knowledge management efforts.

- Build knowledge sharing and development into job responsibilities at all levels and make it an expected part of the job. Make it a competency of effective practice and evaluate lawyers on their knowledge management activities.

- Use peer review to encourage use of knowledge management.

- Encourage informal "communities of practice," where people get together to discuss common interests about a discipline, industry, practice issue, or client.

- Create special roles for people to act as "knowledge sharing catalysts," spearheading the knowledge management effort. Give them prominence and visibility.

- Include knowledge management objectives in department and practice group business plans and link them to the firm's overall strategic plan. One UK-based international law firm, Hammond Suddards Edge, has done this very effectively. Referring to the fruits of knowledge management as "intelligence," the firm has identified specific objectives and success measures for "harvesting, storing, and managing intelligence" in every department. They designate the types of intelligence to be obtained and specify how the department will use the intelligence it gathers to enhance client service, communications, and marketing (e.g., to prepare client seminars and presentations).

- Lure people to the system. Some firms place instructional games on the system and award prizes to lawyers who play. One firm makes lawyers' compensation information available only on the firm's intranet. To find out what they are being paid, they must navigate the intranet. Seeing how easy it is to use the system has a positive impact on usage.

- Use contests and rewards as incentives. Some consulting companies encourage their consultants at the conclusion of each engagement to submit something they learned during that engagement. At the end of the year, the companies review all the submissions and give awards for the most valuable ones.

8. Demonstrate the System's Value

Show lawyers how the knowledge management system works, what it can do, and how it will benefit them personally. Seeing the value and importance of the system in action can convince lawyers to use it and reinforce a culture of learning in the firm. The system should be so simple to use that no training is necessary, but a hands-on demonstration is the best way to get lawyers interested in using the site. The firm's IT and professional development personnel can develop live and online demonstrations of the capabilities and use of the firm's technology-based resources.

9. Keep the System Current

Provide ongoing feedback and evaluation of the knowledge management system. Knowledge is fluid, constantly evolving, and always changing. Your system must be flexible, continually updated, and periodically upgraded. New knowledge must be integrated with existing related information. Obsolete or insignificant information and links should be weeded out.

■ 10. Maintain Perspective

Like online training, knowledge management is not a substitute for learning and communicating through face-to-face interaction. Lawyers still need to meet and work with others in person, especially when trying to develop new strategies, customize solutions for particular clients, or solve complex and unusual legal problems. Person-to-person knowledge sharing through brainstorming and conversations is essential to spark new ideas and generate creativity. Technology can facilitate communication and make learning more convenient, but it cannot supplant the on-the-job training and experience necessary to develop lawyers' skills, judgment, and proficiency.

PART IV

Budgeting

CHAPTER 10

Budgeting for a Professional Development Program

Firms rarely have sufficient funds for all the professional development programs they want or need. To obtain adequate funding for professional development efforts in your firm, your budget must be carefully conceived, well thought out, and tied to the firm's business goals. The budgeting process takes a great deal of time and requires predictions and estimates of future expenses that are hard to determine. Especially in times of uncertainty, budgets are subject to economic constraints that force choices among equally important but competing priorities. When firms slash expenses, training and development activities often bear the brunt because they do not generate revenues. Nonetheless, preparing a disciplined and thoughtful budget can highlight the positive impact of professional development on the firm's overall financial performance and justify the funds needed to protect important programs and to achieve the strategic goals of the firm.

When a firm allocates its money among departments and projects, its decisions have profound implications for the future direction of the firm. For this reason, a professional development budget should be viewed as "a planning tool, a communication tool, and an ongoing opportunity to strategize."[1] Preparing a budget makes you stand back and determine which professional development efforts are worthwhile, cost effective, and achieving intended results. You must demonstrate how professional development programs will help the firm reach its strategic goals and result in long-term profitability. Profitability in this sense is not defined as revenue production, but rather as an investment in the performance, recruitment, and retention of good lawyers. When your firm's lawyers are well trained and productive, the firm suffers less financial loss due to write-offs, has fewer dissatisfied clients, and faces a lower risk of malpractice liability. The importance of professional

---

[1] Stewart Whittingham, "Getting Beyond the Numbers: Budgeting for Professional Development," *NALP Bulletin*, October 2001, p. 12.

development for recruitment and retention of the best associates has been proven definitively. Retention alone justifies expenditures for a professional development program considering that the cost of replacing a lawyer is $250,000 and up.

To make professional development an integral and permanent part of firm management, it must be a fixed line item in the firm's budget. Major accounting and consulting firms spend 7 to 10 percent of annual revenues on training.[2] Surprisingly, however, many law firms do not even budget for professional development. In a survey conducted as background for this book, 25 percent of professional development directors who responded indicated that they did not have specific budgets for the firm's professional development activities.

The budgeting process must be thoughtfully planned and energetically coordinated. Depending on the size of the firm, preparing a budget may be a one-person activity or it may involve many people in different offices, departments, and practice groups. In a small firm, the professional development coordinator may prepare a single budget for all training and development activities. In a large, multi-office firm, the process can be very complicated. The head of professional development for the firm usually prepares the professional development budget for firm-wide activities. In addition, however, funds for specific training and development activities may be budgeted by various offices, departments, and practice groups. The professional development director must find and coordinate those budgeted items with the budgeted activities for the entire firm.

Budgeting and budget coordination can be made easier by using software programs, forms, and templates that standardize the budgeting process. These tools provide pre-set categories, guidelines, and restrictions that eliminate some of the guesswork inherent in the budgeting process and make it easier to track training and development activities. Software programs also track expenditures as they are made throughout the year and produce a variety of useful comparisons and reports. For example, you can obtain reports of utilization patterns in training courses, which can help you determine which training programs to keep and which to drop. Such data can also help you provide bottom-line justification for a program whose value is not widely appreciated.

---

[2] David H. Maister, *True Professionalism*, New York, The Free Press, 1997, p. 107; Austin G. Anderson and Arthur G. Greene, *The Effective Associate Training Program*, Chicago, The American Bar Association, 1999, p. 70.

The Budgeting Process

Before starting the budgeting process, the firm must decide who will budget for which activities. What should the firm-wide professional development director budget for, and what will be left to individual offices, departments, and practice groups? Will large department-specific programs (e.g., litigation training) be charged to the department or come within the overall firm budget? Will evaluations, mentoring, and training all be lumped together for budgeting purposes, or will each office or department have its own budget for these activities? How will outside CLE expenses be charged — to the firm or to specific practice groups? Whatever the firm decides, one person should coordinate all budget data in order to reduce redundancy, keep expenses under control, see that all desired development activities are provided for, and ensure that planned activities are in line with the firm's objectives. This process is best accomplished when all who are budgeting for professional development activities follow the same basic approach to budget preparation. That approach should follow this sequence:

- Establish overall professional development goals based on the strategic goals of the firm. The purpose of the budget is not merely to allocate money, but to make sure that the firm spends money most appropriately to achieve its business goals. You should be able to explain how professional development programs and initiatives will advance the firm's long-term interests.

- Outline a professional development plan that lists and prioritizes specific programs, projects, and activities designed to achieve the firm's goals.

- Determine the tasks, personnel, and resources required for planning and implementing these programs, projects, and activities.

- Determine the costs of the tasks, personnel, and resources required for each program, project, and activity.

With this information, you are ready to draft a budget. Preparing a professional development budget requires that you have a complete and well-planned professional development program for a set period of time. Even if you have a comprehensive plan that extends over several years, your budget should cover the period of the firm's budget, which is usually a year.

Begin by mapping out your professional development plan, month by month, for the upcoming year. (See Table 1.) Using a spreadsheet, list all of your proposed programs, projects, and activities for the year. For each activity, insert an estimate of expenses, not just for each program but also for each month. (See Table 2.)

Breaking down the total budget on a month-by-month basis allows for better cash flow management. This monthly breakdown lets the firm know what to budget for and informs the firm of the expenses it will likely incur at different times of the year. Monthly snapshots are especially useful if the firm has relatively stable and consistent program expenses during most of the year but a major expenditure during a one- or two-month period.

The process of developing a plan and setting priorities allows your goals to drive your budget rather than the other way around. Economic forces frequently lead to mid-term budget revisions. If your final budget is subsequently reduced, it is easier to make adjustments when you know what your priorities are. With documented and well-thought-out program goals, you are in a stronger position to negotiate smaller reductions. It is also easier to discard programs according to previously decided priorities than to try to fit your whole program into a smaller budget.

TABLE 1. Monthly Working Plan for Training Budget

JANUARY, 20_ _

Program title	Description	Link to firm goals	Length	Audience	No. attendees	Location	Cost	Priority
First-Year Litigation Training	Practice basics; 12 weekly breakfast seminars taught by firm lawyers; videoconference	Accelerate associate proficiency	1 hour	First-year Litigation Associates	20	All offices	$8,000 (video-conferencing, food)	Essential
First-Year Business Training	Practice basics; 9 weekly breakfast seminars taught by firm lawyers; videoconference	Accelerate associate proficiency	1 hour	First-year Business Associates	17	All offices	$6,500 (video-conferencing, food)	Essential
Avoiding Sexual Harassment	Video-based course materials; led by J. Jones of Labor Group	Risk management; ensure respectful workplace; MCLE compliance	2 hours	All lawyers	30/class	All offices	$2,500 (for instructor travel, food)	Essential
Stress Management	Outside yoga instructor (pilot program)	Lawyer well-being	1 hour	All lawyers	10/class, 1 class	Boston	$500 (instructor fee)	Wishful

TABLE 2. Monthly Operating Expense Worksheet

Description	Jan.	Feb.	Mar.	April	May	June	July	Aug.	Sept.	Oct.	Nov.	Dec.

1. Professional Development Department Administration

___ ___ ___ ___ ___ ___ ___ ___ ___ ___ ___ ___

Total: _____

Assumptions: This figure assumes the costs incurred by the Professional Development Department for travel to professional conferences and associated expenses. Also assumes the cost of travel and expenses related to a firm-wide needs assessment project involving the two Professional Development Managers.

2. First-Year Training Program

Litigation — weekly sessions:

___ ___ ___ ___ ___ ___ ___ ___ ___ ___ ___ ___

Business/Transactions — weekly sessions:

___ ___ ___ ___ ___ ___ ___ ___ ___ ___ ___ ___

Total: _____

Assumptions: This figure assumes the costs for these comprehensive programs. Weekly sessions for all first-year associates in all practice groups. Costs include videoconferencing and food.

3. Sexual Harassment Avoidance

___ ___ ___ ___ ___ ___ ___ ___ ___ ___ ___ ___

Total: _____

Assumptions: This program is an ongoing and essential part of the firm's risk management effort. Figure assumes costs of new, more current video materials, and of travel expenses for J. Jones to conduct training in all firm offices.

With your plan in hand, break down the costs of each program, project, and activity. Be as specific as you can. One of the trickiest parts of budgeting is forecasting expenses, especially for new projects that have no budget history. Your forecasts need not be exact, but they must be close. They must provide sufficient guidance for the firm to set aside enough money for all planned activities. To research the potential costs, you can obtain information from many sources, including:

- Expense histories of prior professional development efforts in the firm;
- Records from accounting or financial services personnel;
- Outside professional development consultants;
- Quotes solicited from outside vendors and providers; and
- Professional development counterparts in other firms.

Look for costs associated with program development, equipment, facility rental, fees for faculty and consultants, outside CLE costs, travel, and food. Some firms also budget for staff wages, benefits, and overhead, and for the value of lawyers' time. Table 3 breaks down each of these cost categories into specific potential components. Tracking and comparing these costs from year to year can be very helpful in planning future programs and budgets.

When you have cost estimates for all of the pieces of your budget, add them up. If your firm has given you a total budget figure beforehand, see if you can squeeze your program into it. Some firms begin by asking the professional development director for a budget proposal and then responding to it. In either case, if the firm gives you less money than you request, you have to make some tough decisions and careful choices. You can respond in many ways. Some tactics to consider are to:

- Negotiate for more money.
- Delete some programs. One way to do this is to assign priority rankings and costs to each program, project, or activity. List them on your spreadsheet in order of priority. The total budget amount you have been given is your cut-off point. Add up the costs of your proposed programs until you reach the cut-off point. Programs below that point are dropped.
- Modify programs to save as many as you can (e.g., change vendors, consider alternative facilities, reduce the number of days).
- Move a scheduled project to a different time of year, which may make more money available for it.

TABLE 3. Breakdown of Cost Categories for Budgeting

- Program development
    - Literature search
    - License fees for program materials
    - Copying charges
    - Course materials
    - Marketing
- Equipment purchase or rental
    - Software and hardware
    - Audiovisual equipment
    - Flipcharts, pointers, training aids
- Facilities
    - Rental fees
    - Resort and recreation costs
- Faculty and consultants
    - Fees and honoraria for outside faculty and consultants
    - Travel expenses for outside faculty and consultants
- Outside CLE
    - Registration fees
    - Service contracts with outside CLE providers
    - Software and hardware for online programs
- Travel
    - Transportation costs for firm lawyers
    - Hotel and meal costs
- Food and catering
    - In-house events
    - Off-site events
- Staff wages, benefits, and overhead*
- Lawyers' time*

---

* Few law firms include the costs of wages, benefits, and overhead costs for professional development staff and lost billings for lawyers, but this is something that should be checked with firm management and financial services.

After making all necessary adjustments, prepare the final budget for submission. Some of the items you might include to make the budget easier to follow and more likely to be approved are the following:

- An executive summary that sets forth program goals, budget assumptions, overall costs, time frames, and resources required.

- A chart, list, or calendar of events to present an overview of the program and its components.

- Narrative descriptions and explanations of any new or major projects that may be questioned.

- A comparison (narratives, tables, and/or graphs) between this budget and the previous year's budget.

- An explanation of how any concerns that arose under previous budgets have been remedied.

Hopefully, the budget will be approved as submitted. If it is not and further revisions are necessary, repeat the steps outlined above.

Special Budgeting Issues for the Professional Development Director

The professional development director is ultimately responsible for the program budget. Budgeting does not occur in a vacuum. There are political and financial considerations that affect the professional development program and the director's role in it. The amount of money devoted to professional development is not simply a result of the firm's economic condition, but is in large part determined by the director's political savvy and leadership.

A great deal of budgeting is political. In preparing a budget, make it a point to identify your most steadfast supporters and be sure they understand what you hope to accomplish. Give them all the information they need to become strong advocates for the professional development program. Expand your base of support by keeping people informed. Involve department and practice group leaders, and the individuals responsible for professional development throughout the firm, in the budgeting process. Solicit their suggestions and viewpoints. Keep these people informed during the year by sending monthly or quarterly financial reports that compare actual and budgeted expenses; hold periodic meetings with them. Such meetings can serve many purposes. Among other things, they:

- Keep people apprised of the various professional development activities throughout the firm.

- Permit an ongoing dialogue about goals, plans, and revisions.

- Promote exchange of information and strategies for supporting, integrating, and facilitating professional development efforts.

- Promote regular review and revisions of budget assumptions and forecasts.

- Enable people to make adjustments to programs or budgets if circumstances change.

- Update people on their own group's financial performance against the professional development budget.

- Help people identify and correct budget variances promptly.

Recognize that some people may have personal agendas or make faulty assumptions about the professional development program. Different offices, departments, and practice groups may want to budget for programs that overlap or conflict with the firm-wide training budget you are preparing. Using conflict management skills and calling on your supporters may be necessary to resolve these differences.

Anytime you deal with money, people may question your motives and your integrity. It is important that you understand this and that you handle the firm's money in a straightforward and transparent way. Your credibility is as much at stake in budgeting as in every other aspect of your work. Spend money wisely. Look for ways to economize on your programs. Run cost comparisons and determine whether your programs are being conducted as cost-effectively as possible. Just because last year's seven-day trial advocacy course was a big hit does not mean you need to repeat every aspect of it this year. Especially during economic downturns, you may be able to put on a program of equal quality for less money by eliminating or reducing some non-essential costs (e.g., holding a videoconference instead of having lawyers travel, using courtrooms instead of a resort facility for training sessions, catering dinner in the firm instead of going to a restaurant to celebrate a program's conclusion).

Do not inflate or pad a budget. Make your budget as accurate and reliable as possible. Budgeting is not an exact science, and occasionally you may under- or overestimate. Underestimating can lead to cuts in important activities or embarrassing mid-term requests for additional funds. Overestimating can make you look like a hero at first, but it may cause management to look at subsequent budgets with skepticism and lead to significant reductions in subsequent years.

If you need budgeting assistance, call on your firm's accounting or financial services personnel. They can educate you about many aspects of budgeting, which is especially valuable when you prepare your first budget. They can also help you in formatting and researching the budget, tracking expenses, and producing reports.

PART V

Coordinating Professional Development Efforts with Recruiting, Summer Programs, and Orientation

CHAPTER 11

Associate Recruiting and Summer Programs

Recruiting is not a professional development function, but the two activities are interrelated. Both recruiting and professional development play roles in identifying the characteristics of good lawyers for the firm; both help new hires become oriented and assimilated into the firm; and both play pivotal roles in the law firm's summer program. Recruiting looks for candidates who have the potential to succeed. Professional development tries to optimize that potential when lawyers come to the firm by giving them the training, tools, and experiences they need to achieve high levels of performance. Summer programs in particular lay the foundation for students' future development as practicing lawyers. This chapter addresses ways to weave professional development into your firm's recruitment and summer program efforts. For a comprehensive discussion of recruiting and summer programs, see Gayle P. Englert's *Leading the Legal Recruitment Team: A Recruitment Administrator's Handbook* (NALP, Washington, DC, 2001).

Recruiting and professional development personnel are concerned with attracting, developing, and retaining talented lawyers for the firm. They do their principal work at different points on a continuum, with some direct overlap. In many law firms, recruiting and professional development come under the same organizational umbrella. This pairing makes sense. In a small firm, both functions may be part of one department and headed by one person; in a large firm, they may be two separate functions headed by two administrators who report to the same director.

Law firms place a high priority on recruitment, believing that bringing associates with sterling credentials into the firm will give the firm a competitive advantage. That may be a start, but all firms in the same league are drawing from the same talent pool. The real way for a firm to distinguish itself is to turn the promising students it hires into exceptional lawyers, thereby "creating a proprietary talent pool through judicious developmental practices."[1] And the best way to do that is for the firm to emphasize professional development early for the students it recruits. Especially if your first-year associates come predominantly from your firm's summer program, that program must be coordinated with the professional development program and based on the same strategic goals.

Associate Recruiting

Associate recruitment and professional development overlap in two important areas: determining which candidates are the most likely to succeed in the firm and attracting those candidates to the firm through a first-rate professional development program. Both of these factors are also critical to retain the best associates once they have joined the firm.

Most lawyers believe that if they hire people with the "right stuff," those people will succeed in the firm. The question that gives them pause is how to ascertain and measure what the "right stuff" is. They mostly define it in terms of performance and achievement as reflected in résumés: schools, grades, law review, clerkships, and outstanding accomplishments in law, academia, business, community, political, or personal spheres. Increasingly, law firms are taking a more strategic approach to hiring by establishing hiring criteria. These criteria target the characteristics of lawyers needed to build and sustain the firm, and they make the recruiting process more precise and effective.

Firms begin targeted recruitment efforts by describing the skills and characteristics needed for success in the firm. The firm might ask the recruitment committee to be in charge of this effort, appoint a special firm-wide task force to do it, or have each practice group define its own criteria. References that assist in developing hiring criteria include the firm's competencies (see Chapter 7), strategic plan, and mission statement or statement of core values. Some firms use outside consultants to help them look critically at the people who have succeeded as associates and partners in the firm and the factors that have contributed to their success.

Once the criteria are determined, training should be provided in interviewing skills. All lawyers who interview candidates need a thorough understanding of the hiring criteria and must be able to apply them appropriately as they meet with candidates. It is important to note that, as with competencies, hiring criteria should not be so limited that interviewers seek only one type of person or personality. Your hiring criteria should accommodate today's diverse law student and lawyer populations. (See Chapters 7 and 13 for discussions of diversity considerations.)

---

[1] Morgan W. McCall, Jr., *High Flyers*, Harvard Business School Press, Boston, 1998, p. 136.

The second area of overlap between recruiting and professional development is the opportunity for growth and learning. Students and associates place great importance on the availability of training, mentoring, quality work assignments, and other aspects of professional development. Knowing this, recruiters and interviewers sometimes promise more to candidates than the firm is prepared to deliver. When associates discover that what the law firm actually provides differs substantially from what was promised, they often become disillusioned and leave.[2] It is essential that the firm's recruitment materials, including firm résumés, brochures, and web sites, accurately describe the professional development programs, activities, and opportunities that exist in the firm. One way to check for accuracy and consistency is to have your firm's recruiting materials reviewed by junior lawyers, the marketing department, and the lawyer or specialist in charge of professional development. These materials should then be used in skills training programs for interviewers; interviewers need to understand the importance of communicating a realistic picture of the firm. Recruitment and professional development personnel should collaborate in planning this training.

Summer Programs

The summer program serves as the principal vehicle for recruiting associates, especially in large and mid-size firms. Firms scrutinize students' work, behavior, and interaction over the summer and decide whether to offer them permanent jobs. But summer associates are also observing the firm to decide if the fit is good for them. Research has proven that opportunities for growth and development are a major priority for new lawyers, and a strong learning culture can be the deciding factor for a student weighing alternative job offers.[3] One of the primary things they look for is the quality of work, training, mentoring, and feedback available to them. These are all within the purview of the professional development program. Therefore, although recruiting, hiring committee, and/or summer program committee personnel run the summer program, professional development specialists should be partners in the effort.

It is quite amazing how much more lawyers will cooperate in professional development activities for summer associates than they will for the associates who are in the firm. Perhaps it is because they feel that to compete for the best law students they have to "prove" themselves, so they are on their best behavior.

---

[2] *Keeping the Keepers: Association Retention in Times of Attrition*, The NALP Foundation for Law Career Research and Education, 1998, p. 45.
[3] *Ibid.*

Perhaps it is because the summer program makes concentrated demands for a brief and finite time period. Whatever the reason, professional development personnel should try to harness the positive energy that lawyers put into the summer program and keep it going throughout the year.

The core elements of a summer program are set out in Table 1. Every one of these elements has a professional development aspect, which is discussed below. Some of these impact the development of students in the program; others affect the development of lawyers who work with summer associates.

TABLE 1. Elements of a Summer Program

1. Orientation
2. Work assignment process
3. Effective supervision
4. Feedback and evaluations
5. Learning
6. Personal attention
7. Social events
8. Program evaluation

Orientation

The purpose, format, and content of summer program orientations are similar to orientations for new associates. (See Chapter 12). The principal difference is that summer associates spend only a few weeks in the firm, so they must be oriented to the work and life of the firm in a compressed period of time. Firms should schedule at least one or two full days of orientation when summer associates arrive. Sessions to convey practical information or teach practice skills can be added during that initial orientation or at different times throughout the summer.

As with new associate orientations, orientation for summer associates should familiarize them with the culture, practice, personnel, and operations of the firm, and initiate the relationship-building process. Orientation should also explain the summer program and procedures, including how summer associates will receive work assignments, how their work will be evaluated, and when and how decisions will be made about permanent job offers. It should inform summer associates about how to work with their mentors, the technology and administrative support available to them, where to go if they need help with assignments or work management, and such operational details as timekeeping and expense reimbursement. The agenda should tell summer associates which training programs are available to them and the firm's expectations for their attendance at these programs.

Work Assignments

The heart of any summer program is the opportunity for law students to do real legal work that gives them a taste of what they can expect if they join your firm. Summer associates should have diverse work experience, be exposed to the variety of work the firm has to offer, and work with as many lawyers as possible, all within a few weeks' time. All of these factors allow students to make smarter career choices and get them started along a learning path.

The work experience should be as true to life as possible. One of the main reasons that associates leave law firms within the first year or two is their disappointment with the reality of practice.[4] Many new associates believe that their summer experience misled or misinformed them about the true conditions of practice in the firm. A realistic summer experience can prevent attrition later on. Giving summer associates a broad base of realistic experience enables the firm to better judge the summer associates' abilities and decide if the summer associates will be a good fit for the firm. The firm can observe how the summer associate handles different kinds of work challenges and interacts with lawyers, staff, and clients. Identifying students who would not make a good fit averts the extension of offers to individuals who are more likely to fail or leave.

Law firms give careful attention to procedures for assigning work to summer associates, but they do not always devote enough attention to monitoring the quality and mix of associates' work experience. All summer associates should have analytical and written work as well as assignments that give them a close-up look at what experienced lawyers in the firm do every day. Research and other writing-based assignments are important, but sitting in on a strategy session or participating in a document production or due diligence review makes the abstract notion of law practice more concrete and real. "Out-of-office" expeditions and "hands-on" assignments — e.g., attending client meetings, hearings, closings, or negotiations — are the most interesting and highly desirable work experiences for summer associates. These are the kinds of experiences that excite law students about practice

---

[4] *Keeping the Keepers.*

and interest them in the firm. Because many law students are interested in pro bono work, the firm should also include summer associates in pro bono activities, discuss the firm's policies about pro bono assignments, and give them an honest and realistic preview of what pro bono work they would be able to do if they join the firm.

Effective Supervision

Because lawyers are more willing to participate in summer programs, this is a terrific opportunity to teach them supervision skills. The skills are the same whether supervising summer associates, paralegals, or junior partners and carry over to all supervisory situations, not just the summer program. Supervisors have enormous influence on the experience of summer associates. Supervising lawyers control the kind of work experience, informal training, and feedback students receive. Their assessment of a student has considerable influence on whether or not a permanent position is offered.

Supervising lawyers must be familiar with the firm's hiring criteria and performance standards and able to apply them appropriately to summer associates. Recruitment and professional development personnel should distribute this information and work together in developing supervisory skills training. The training should include delegation and feedback skills and should be given to all lawyers who will act as supervisors during the summer program.

Feedback and Evaluations

Summer associates need to know right off the bat what kind of performance the firm expects. They need this information even more urgently than new associates since their time in the office is so short. In addition, summer associates are eager to know how well they meet the firm's expectations. For many summer associates, the summer program is their first introduction to a law firm environment, and it is completely different from the school and work environments they have known before. Law students are accustomed to being graded; without feedback, they have no way to tell how they measure up to the firm's standards or expectations. Students need this feedback quickly and frequently because they have little time in which to make changes and improvements. Feedback is important from the firm's perspective as well as for the student's development. The firm needs to see how the summer associate responds to feedback, learns what is necessary, and makes appropriate adjustments.

In addition to informal, everyday feedback, supervising lawyers should be expected to meet with the summer associate in person to go over each completed project, discuss the work, answer questions, and review the student's performance. Discussions during the feedback sessions should address both the summer associate's technical ability and professional and management skills (e.g., taking initiative, thinking and acting independently, work relationships with team members, responsiveness to supervisors and clients). Supervising lawyers should also complete an interim project evaluation form for submission to the summer program committee.

That committee or the recruitment director should use the information from these evaluation forms to give each summer associate at least one formal mid-summer review and an overall evaluation at the end of the summer. The mid-summer review is important to let summer associates know if their work is acceptable and where improvements are needed. It provides another opportunity for summer associates to ask questions and learn how they are doing, and gives those who are not doing well a chance to correct course while they still have time to prove themselves worthy of an offer.

The end-of-summer evaluations should assess summer associates' overall work abilities and whether they fit the culture and philosophy of the firm. Written evaluations should be obtained from the summer associates' principal supervisors, and should also be solicited from others who interacted with the summer associate and have something of value to contribute. The question of fit goes to behavior, attitude, interests, and personal characteristics beyond work product. A brilliant student who cannot get along with others may not be the best fit for a firm whose ethos is based on teamwork. An assessment of fit is made easier if the firm has clear hiring criteria based on specified core competencies and values.

The recruitment director, summer program committee, and/or the hiring committee should collect the written evaluations and compile a summary. They should prepare these summaries against a backdrop of the firm's hiring criteria. The hiring partner and/or members of the hiring or summer program committees should deliver the end-of-summer in-person reviews of summer associates. These reviews usually include an offer of employment or an explanation why an offer is not being extended.

Delivering feedback is difficult and requires training and tact, and the summer program presents a great opportunity to teach these skills to lawyers. Giving feedback and delivering reviews to summer associates is an excellent way for associates to learn and for partners to hone feedback and evaluation skills. Associates often supervise summer clerks, which means they have to give summer associates feedback. In many firms, associates also sit on summer program and hiring committees, and, in that capacity, they often participate in summer associate reviews. All lawyers who participate in delivering feedback informally or through formal reviews need to be taught to do so effectively and with great sensitivity. The professional development specialist should work with those in charge of the summer program to see that training is provided for these tasks.

Summer associates might be asked to evaluate their supervisors in upward reviews of partners and senior associates. (See Chapter 7.) Their ratings and comments should be maintained in the strictest confidence.

Learning

Law students enter summer programs not just to get a future job but also to learn about the practice of law. In addition to informal on-the-job learning, formal learning — through informational seminars, educational experiences, and training programs — should be an integral part of the summer program. Informational seminars present the firm's various practice areas and clients, and inform summer associates about their practice options if they join the firm as associates. Educational experiences, such as tours of a courthouse or attending a bar association conference, are events and activities that teach summer associates lessons about practice. These experiences may be tied to work assignments or scheduled as stand-alone events.

Training programs impart legal skills and knowledge or offer tips about how to make the most of the summer experience. Including summer associates in highly practical and interesting training programs demonstrates the firm's commitment to learning and ongoing professional development, which helps recruiting efforts. Summer associates should be invited to the firm's regular training seminars, and, if sufficient resources exist, special training programs can be designed just for them. Of particular interest and value to summer associates are programs that provide insights and advice about the practical issues of daily work life: how to manage time and workload, ask assigning lawyers for clarification and feedback, or work with a secretary. Associates in the firm can lead these seminars. Substantive legal topics and practice skills can be taught by associates and partners. These programs do not need to be complicated or elaborate. They can be low-budget, informal sessions: brown bag lunches, roundtable conferences, client presentations, or panel discussions led by lawyers from the firm. Firms with ample budgets may choose to do more in-depth training programs that require more planning, greater resources, and specially trained faculty (e.g., negotiation, legal writing, or deposition workshops).

In 2001, Howrey Simon Arnold & White LLP inaugurated an innovative and intense summer program. Called "Howrey Bootcamp," the program was designed to show summer associates the real work that lawyers in their firm do, which is primarily litigation. The program focused on trial advocacy training and lasted four weeks; in 2002, it was lengthened to five weeks. Each student spent the first three weeks in one of the firm's offices and then all students came together for two weeks at a training facility in Leesburg, Virginia. During the latter two-week period, the students attended courses in litigation related subjects (e.g., discovery, direct and cross-examination) and engaged in numerous litigation exercises based on a case study that the firm developed. Faculty consisted of partners from the firm, and for each team of three summer associates a partner or senior associate acted as a full-time coach, staying at the training facility and working closely with the summer associates throughout the two weeks. Although the time frame was brief, the intensity of the work experience allowed summer associates to learn a great deal about the firm and trial practice, and allowed firm lawyers to get to know a small group of summer associates very well. This training-based program will benefit the firm when some of these students join the firm as associates because they will begin with a solid understanding of the firm's trial practice.

Personal Attention

Summer associates need personalized attention from one or more lawyers in the firm who can help socialize them, offer career advice, serve as a confidante, monitor work assignments, or perform a variety of other functions. You might call them advisers, buddies, or mentors; the title matters far less than the function, which is to provide each summer associate with at least one person who offers personal guidance and support. These people play many different roles depending on the nature and purpose of the program, but primarily they provide a line of communication and assistance for any problems, questions, or issues that arise for summer associates.

Many firms establish mentoring programs to provide this individualized attention. As with other mentoring programs, it is essential that participants know the summer mentoring program's purpose and goals and fully understand what they are expected to do to achieve these objectives. The firm should provide clear guidelines and instructions to mentors about their responsibilities in the summer program. See Chapter 6 for a detailed discussion of mentoring program goals and guidelines.

The degree of structure and complexity of a summer mentoring program depends on the size of the firm, the size of the summer associate class, and the purpose of the program. Smaller firms with just a few summer associates may assign one mentor, while larger firms may assign two or three. The most important consideration is that at least one of the mentors be a peer, relatively speaking. Junior associates who have recently been through the summer program themselves are especially good in this mentoring role because they understand what summer associates are going through. More experienced lawyers can also be valuable mentors. Having a partner act as a mentor to a summer associate can make a powerful impression on a student and demonstrate that the firm seriously cares about connecting with future lawyers.

Mentors get to know summer associates very well and can be instrumental both in addressing the development of the summer associate and in furthering the firm's recruiting efforts. Summer associates may assume that their mentors are confidantes and divulge information about their personal problems and insecurities. Issues about confidentiality should be addressed clearly at the outset of the summer program so that all participants understand if mentors will disclose this information to the hiring committee or if confidentiality will be maintained. If a firm wants to offer confidential counseling, it might be better to utilize alternative approaches. Instead of having mentors act as confidantes, the firm can use an ombudsperson or designate certain partners or associates for this purpose.

Social Events

Part of professional development is forming professional relationships. A summer program's social agenda provides summer associates a chance to form personal relationships and observe the social culture of the firm. Firms should provide a mix of social events, combining casual, low-key activities in small groups with larger organized events. Many social events can be built around learning experiences, such as a dinner and discussion of trial skills following a field trip to the courthouse to watch a trial. Many firms combine their yearly lawyer retreats with the summer program. This allows the entire firm to be together in a relaxed setting, lets summer associates meet more people, and gives them a better sense of what the firm is like.

Set aside some time for summer associates to get know each other. The first time to do this is during orientation. Some firms hold special social events just for summer associates, such as lunches, evenings out on the town, or an off-site retreat.

Press coverage of law firm summer programs tends to give disproportionate attention to elaborate social events and excursions. Many summer associates have come to feel entitled to three-day river rafting trips and all-expense paid weekends at elegant resorts. Firms that desire and can afford spectacular perks should have them, but they are not essential to a successful summer program. What really matters is the quality of the social interaction, not the expense or elegance of the activity. Casual social events are often the most fun; participants feel more comfortable, relaxed, and spontaneous. An outing to a local museum or an evening at a comedy club can be as effective and more enjoyable than a weekend at a fancy golf resort or a formal dinner party in a hotel ballroom. They are also much less expensive, an important consideration when law firms tighten their belts.

Program Evaluation

The professional development aspects of the summer program should be evaluated and the findings should be shared with the firm's professional development specialist. Through exit interviews or surveys, departing summer associates should give feedback to recruiting and hiring personnel about what works and what doesn't in the summer program. In addition, lawyers, recruiting personnel, and other summer program participants should be asked to assess the effectiveness of the summer program. These assessments can help the firm's recruitment, hiring, and professional development personnel improve the summer program each year and support the firm's ongoing professional development efforts for lawyers.

CHAPTER 12

Orientation Programs

Orientation programs introduce lawyers to a firm's culture, values, practice, and work expectations. They welcome new lawyers; introduce them to firm policies, practices, and people; start integrating them into the firm; and get them off to a good start. It is important to distinguish at the outset between the *orientation programs* that some firms conduct and the *administrative orientation* that all lawyers go through when they join a new firm. *Orientation programs* involve organized presentations, classes, and discussions and are conducted for groups of lawyers. The lawyers in question may be new associates, lateral associates, lateral partners, or a combination of these groups. *Administrative orientation* is simply taking care of employment-related paperwork, introducing the new lawyer to people in the firm, and imparting practical information about the firm's systems and operations. Administrative orientation is usually done individually as each lawyer arrives, although with a large number of arrivals it may be done in a group. This chapter deals principally with formal orientation programs because they initiate the firm's broader professional development program. Administrative orientation is discussed briefly in the sidebar on the following page.

The strategic purpose of a law firm orientation program is to begin preparing new and lateral associates for practice and ultimately for partnership, and to lay the groundwork for new and lateral partners to succeed as partners in your firm. Orientation programs set new and lateral associates off in the right direction by providing information and instruction that introduces them to the firm and to practice. Associates are educated about the firm's expectations for performance and development, and made more knowledgeable about their practice groups and the firm. Orientation programs can also advertise the training and development resources available in the firm and provide substantive training in various aspects of practice.

For partners, orientation begins lateral partners' acculturation into the firm and the integration of their practices and clients with those of the firm. Orientation is also valuable for new partners elevated to partnership from within the firm,

Administrative Orientation

Virtually all firms conduct administrative orientations, which are basically a transfer of information. When new lawyers arrive at the firm, they are told about office policies, compensation, employment benefits, billing procedures, and other operational and administrative issues. New lawyers spend hours completing forms, getting identification cards and pass codes, learning to use the telephone and find the mail room, touring the office, meeting people on their floor, and settling into their new offices. Training in how to use the computer, telephone, and other technology and communication systems is usually conducted in the lawyer's first few days in the office. This administrative orientation is usually conducted individually, but much of it can be done in a group if many new lawyers start at the same time. For classes of new entry-level associates or summer associates, portions of the administrative orientation may be incorporated into the formal orientation program.

Someone in the firm from the recruiting department or hiring committee should be responsible for seeing that everything is in place when new lawyers arrive. A checklist for new hires ensures that everything is covered and makes the job easier for the person responsible. The checklist should include everything the lawyer needs to get started. This is important so new lawyers get the right impression. It gives them confidence that the firm is a well-run organization that has prepared for their arrival and wants them to feel at home. In addition to such obvious points as having a fully equipped office and functioning technology, the checklist should include having an assigned "buddy" to provide a personal contact in the new lawyer's practice group and at least one work assignment to get the lawyer started immediately. The checklist should also include notifying the firm's lawyers and staff about the new lawyer's background, experience, and practice area. Including a photograph of each new lawyer on a new arrival memo or e-mail notice is a nice extra touch. This allows people in the firm to recognize new lawyers and welcome them in a more personalized way.

although their orientation is of a different sort. The new partners need to be prepared to take on the identity, role, and responsibilities of partnership. This preparation should begin when they are senior associates in anticipation of being promoted to partnership — a time when they are particularly receptive to learning. A formal orientation program for newly elevated partners can ease their transition into the complex new role they are assuming. The Appendix following this chapter contains agendas for Shook, Hardy & Bacon LLP's "Becoming a Partner" program for associates within two years of partnership consideration (Appendix 12-A) and Pillsbury Winthrop LLP's orientation program for new and recent lateral partners (Appendix 12-B).

Orientation is the starting point for retaining talented lawyers. An effective orientation program should leave newcomers excited about being at the firm, motivated to get to work, and confident and ready to practice and succeed. Bringing lawyers together and having them meet their new colleagues in the firm initiates the process of building personal relationships and integrating lawyers into the firm's culture and social life. Lawyers who are carefully oriented to both the firm and their work stay longer and reach full productivity sooner than others. In contrast, the lack of solid relationships with others in the firm is one of the main reasons that lawyers leave law firms. This is true for lateral partners as well as for associates. Lateral partners who are not successfully integrated into the firm are likely to move yet again. Orientation for lateral partners increases the likelihood they will stay and succeed in your firm.

Most firms focus on the administrative details of orientation. In small firms with only one or two new lawyers joining at a time, the administrative orientation may be the only organized orientation process. But large firms with a lot of new lawyers usually hold additional orientation events to commence professional development efforts for new associates and facilitate the development process for lateral lawyers and new partners. These formal orientation programs range from short and highly focused, to lengthy with an extensive curriculum. Their purpose is to give lawyers the tools and information they need to become contributing and productive participants in the life and practice of the firm. An orientation program shows them who and what the firm is, lets them get a closer look at the organization they have joined, and proves that their decision to join the firm was a wise one.

Content and Format of Orientation Programs

The content of an orientation program depends on your audience, on what you want to accomplish, and on how much time you have. In designing the orientation program, keep your audience needs in mind. It is most important to anticipate and address the pressing questions that these lawyers will want to have answered. New associates in particular need basic information to put them at ease and ready to get to work. It is also important in designing the program to get input from partners and firm leaders about what they believe should be covered.

Much of the information to be covered in orientation can be placed on the firm's computer network. Many firms use electronic and web-based media (e.g., videotapes, CDs, intranets) to present basic information about the firm, its practice areas, and its lawyers. Online tutorials about the firm's technology resources can supplement basic training on use of the computer system by educating newcomers about the firm's various technological capabilities and how to use them. You can also use these media to transmit the firm's cultural and practice expectations, such as the firm's approach to client service, business development, and billing practices. By putting manuals and handouts online, you can make them available to all lawyers for future reference. This is a convenient way to convey information, especially when lawyers are joining the firm at different times during the year. These resources are not, however, an adequate means of integrating newcomers into the firm and making them feel a part of the firm community. That aspect of orientation is critical and requires in-person contact and social activities.

New Associate Orientation

Orientation is a time of excitement and anticipation for new associates. As smart and confident as they are, the first few days at the firm can be pretty scary. For most new associates, joining a law firm is their first real job. Even if they were in your summer program, that was a short-term gig. Becoming a regular associate is — hopefully — a more permanent engagement. New associates are under considerable pressure to perform quickly but know very little about how to actually get things done. They now shoulder work responsibilities that have serious, real-life consequences. Many have to supervise people for the first time. Orientation gives new associates the basic, practical information and advice they need to enter practice in your firm.

How do you know what to include in your firm's orientation program? Start by finding out what is most worthwhile and important for new associates to know. Survey partners, second-year associates, and lateral associates who arrived during the last year about what they feel is important to include in the program. You might also ask secretaries and paralegals what they think new associates should know. All of these groups have points of view that are different, valid, and important. The more groups you include in your survey, the broader your perspective will be about what new lawyers need to learn. Send out an open-ended survey (e.g., "What do you wish you had been told in your first few weeks at the firm?") or a survey that lists ideas and asks respondents to rank them. One professional development director found that partners wanted orientation to include legal writing, timekeeping, billing, and ethics, while associates wanted "nuts and bolts" information about how to get things done: how to open a file, how to work with a secretary or paralegal, how to get work assignments. Faced with these differences, the program designers had to set priorities and be selective. They decided to tailor the orientation program to the associates' recommendations, adding a session on timekeeping and billing. The other topics suggested by the partners, legal writing and ethics, were not included in the initial orientation but were scheduled as future training seminars.

Orientation programs for new associates should cover at least five basic elements:

1. **Introduction:** Welcome to the firm; firm culture; vision and direction for the future; firm practice areas and clients.

2. **Practice:** Transition to practice (or for laterals, to practice in this firm); what the firm expects from them, what new lawyers should expect; working with secretaries, paralegals, and teams; how work is assigned; professional conduct; evaluations; professional development; confidentiality; risk management; pro bono work; partnership and alternative career paths.

3. **Resources:** Support available for practice; where and how to get questions answered; mentoring and training; technology; marketing; library.

4. **Operations and administration:** How the firm operates, how to get things done; office systems, including timekeeping and billing; accounting and financial services.

5. **People:** Who's who in the firm; socializing with others, especially other new lawyers.

Some of these subjects may be covered during individual administrative orientations, especially for associates who arrive weeks before the orientation program is held. In addition to these five elements, some issues are office and practice group–specific. Firms should design a core orientation program that covers the topics pertinent to all new lawyers, and leave offices and practice groups free to add supplemental orientation sessions for their particular constituencies. Supplemental sessions can be held during the time when all lawyers are together for the core orientation, or they can be held at a later time in individual offices. Attendance at the orientation program should be mandatory for new associates.

Topics that are appropriate for a new associate orientation program include those listed in Table 1. These topics can also be the subjects of weekly or monthly seminars separate from the orientation program. One essential part of any orientation program is a personal greeting by the chair or managing partner of the firm. This firm leader should meet with the new lawyers to welcome them and to convey the firm's vision, values, and direction.

One of the most popular sessions for new associates is an open discussion by and for associates. Partners are barred from these sessions. New associates ask questions about practice and life in the firm, and experienced associates offer answers. Another worthwhile session is a free-form discussion led by one or more firm leaders (e.g., the managing partner, executive committee members). In both types of sessions, panelists or presenters give new associates insights and advice about the issues that are on new lawyers' minds.

Typical new associate orientation programs range from one day to two weeks. Some firms use the initial orientation program merely as an introduction to the operation of the firm, with little substantive legal content. At the other extreme, some law firms hold intensive "boot camps" for one or two weeks that include training on legal topics; tips and advice about practice, time, and work management; legal writing; ethics; and a host of other selected subjects.

Many firms use orientation to kick off the firm's associate training program, but training is not integral to the orientation process. Most training sessions can be held separately in the course of your associate training program over the following weeks or months. There are some exceptions, however. Training in how to use the firm's technology should take place within the first few days of a lawyer's arrival at the firm, whether as part of structured presentations or on an individual basis. While technology training is urgent and cannot wait, there is no urgency to begin training in substantive law, practice skills, and management skills during orientation. Another exception may be educating new associates about conflicts of interest, risk management, and rules of ethics. Check with your firm's risk management partner to determine if your malpractice carrier requires or recommends that any particular subjects be covered with new lawyers upon arrival.

If your firm intends to include substantive training for new associates during orientation, it is best to teach basic concepts and principles of several topics and/or teach only a few subjects intensively. Intensive training on too many different topics can become overwhelming, especially for associates who do not have the experiential context to make the learning meaningful. When too much is presented at once, it becomes a blur. Some subjects are better taught after associates have experience to which they can relate classroom training. In-depth programs on many complex subjects are better taught after orientation. Teach the subjects with the greatest

TABLE 1. Potential Topics to Include in New Associate Orientation Programs

Background and Transition
- Firm history, culture, and clients
- Firm structure, management, and administration
- Practice groups in the firm
- Identification/introduction of key administrative and management personnel
- The nuts and bolts of law practice
- The differences between law school and law practice
- The unwritten rules of practice

Managing Work and Self
- Working with secretaries, paralegals, and teams
- How to open and manage files
- Time management
- Dealing with clients and client expectations
- Partner expectations and how to meet them
- How to deal with work overload and competing demands
- Working with supervisors
- Work-life balance
- Stress management

Operations and Policies
- How to get things done in the firm
- Law firm economics
- Risk management practices
- Work assignments and staffing procedures
- Compensation
- Expense reimbursement procedures
- Timekeeping procedures
- Calendar system
- Billing practices and expectations
- How practice group rotation works
- Deciding on an area of specialization
- How the mentoring system operates
- Technology available in the firm, including the firm's intranet
- How to use the firm's technology
- Training expectations, programs, and resources
- CLE and professional development

(continued)

(Table 1 continued)

- Business development expectations and techniques
- Performance evaluation standards and processes
- Policies and procedures for pro bono work
- Library resources

Professionalism
- Ethics and professional responsibility
- Professional conduct
- Confidentiality
- Avoiding malpractice claims
- What it means to be a good firm citizen

Topics for Training Seminars
- Substantive law topics
- Management skills
- Legal writing
- Diversity
- Communication styles
- Presentation skills
- Business development

importance and immediacy at the orientation, and schedule others over the following weeks or months.

Orientation for Laterals

Orientation programs for lateral associates and partners differ from those for new associates. Laterals are experienced lawyers, so the program content does not need to dwell on issues that new lawyers need to know. However, orientations for laterals should contain the same principal elements as new associate orientations.

The firm must ensure that laterals understand the reasons they were hired and their anticipated role in the firm and in their practice groups. Orientation programs can be a time to clarify the firm's expectations about how the lateral lawyer will fit into the firm's overall practice. These issues should have been fully discussed during the recruitment period, but further elucidation can take place during orientation sessions.

Orientation can educate lateral lawyers about the kinds of behaviors and work habits that are expected in the firm. Lateral lawyers who come from corporate, government, or public interest jobs may be new to law firm practice. They are skilled in practice but need to learn how to operate in a law firm environment. Some lawyers may have to change the way they work to accommodate the firm's culture and procedures. As experienced lawyers, laterals have established habits and patterns that have served them well in other workplaces. However, your culture may not tolerate behaviors that are acceptable elsewhere. In an illustrative case, a lateral sixth-year associate came from a firm that was extremely hierarchical and authoritarian. She was accustomed to issuing directives to secretaries, paralegals, and junior associates, who treated her deferentially. Her new firm was egalitarian, collaborative, and team oriented. The new lawyer's demanding, arrogant manner created considerable conflict with team members, and many of them soon refused to work with her. An orientation program that educated lateral lawyers about such cultural norms could have alerted this lateral associate that she needed to adjust her work style and habits.

The firm can further facilitate integration with a standard short-term transition plan for laterals that includes involving the lateral in firm training programs, committees, business development activities, and social events. A mentor or professional development specialist should work with the lateral and keep track of his or her progress. Inviting laterals to participate in training programs is a good way to orient and integrate experienced lawyers who are new to the firm. It is also a good idea to ask laterals to draft a longer-term development plan (as discussed in Chapter 7) shortly after arriving.

■ Lateral Associates

Lateral associates have to adapt to a different workplace and learn how to maneuver in their new environment. Orientation gives them the practical information they need to make a successful transition to practice and to your firm. Lateral associates should receive individual orientation when they arrive and they should be invited to attend new associate orientations as well. If the firm has a large number of lateral associates, the firm might schedule separate sessions for laterals during the new associate orientation program, or hold an orientation just for laterals. Many of the topics listed in Table 1 for new associates would also be appropriate in an orientation program geared to lateral associates.

Orientation for lateral associates requires some special preparation and groundwork. It is important to assess lateral associates' skills, knowledge, and experience before or when they arrive so that they can be placed in appropriate roles on work teams. The orientation process can give lateral associates insights about how they compare to associates in their new firm and how they measure up to the firm's performance standards and expectations.

Two other considerations in orienting and integrating lateral associates are their work assignments and their involvement in training programs. New work assignments are especially important for lateral lawyers because they are eager to meet the challenges of a new job. Unlike new associates, laterals are experienced, able, and ready to go to work as soon as they arrive. There should be at least one assignment waiting for them when they get to the firm. This not only gets them up and running, it also gives the firm an early opportunity to assess their capabilities. Associates may have had markedly different work experience in their former firms than lawyers at the same seniority level in your firm. You cannot rely on seniority level as a gauge of experience or ability. A third-year lateral associate may have had far more or far less sophisticated training and experience than a third-year lawyer in your firm. Observing the lateral associate carefully during the first few weeks at the firm can give you an indication of where the lateral associate stands.

If the firm has ongoing training for associates, lateral associates should be encouraged to attend those programs. Laterals may be more selective depending on their skill and experience levels, but attending the firm's training seminars has several benefits. It can teach them content that they need, teach them the firm's approach to issues and practices, and accelerate their acculturation. The firm can expedite their learning by giving them access to the firm's past training programs and materials through videotapes, hard copies, or online.

■ Lateral Partners

Orientation for lateral partners is completely different than for new and lateral associates. The objective is the same: to facilitate their entry into the firm. But the approach is far more individualized and on a higher plane. Integrating the practices and clients of the lateral partner and the firm is instrumental, and most firms begin to take care of this process during the "courting" period before the new partner arrives. But business integration is not the only orientation concern. Research shows that lateral partners are most satisfied with their new firms when they are effectively integrated into the partnership and culture, not just the business of the firm.[1]

Orienting lateral partners requires special orientation events that focus on familiarizing the new partner with the firm and how it operates, absorbing the new

---

[1] Major, Hagen & Africa, *Lateral Partner Satisfaction: Who Has It, How They Got It, and How to Enhance It,* April 1997.

partner into the life of the firm, and educating and exciting members of the firm about what the lateral partner can do for them.[2] Orientation for lateral partners involves marketing as well as learning. It is as much about informing existing partners of the laterals' talents and expertise as it is about teaching laterals what their new firm is like. Existing partners must accept the lateral partner as a peer, and the orientation process is a vehicle for creating rapport, building trust, and forming strong bonds with others in the firm.

An effective way to accomplish these orientation objectives is in an off-site event where existing and lateral partners can socialize and discuss their respective clients, practices, and business plans. Over a day or a weekend, they can learn who can offer support to their current clients, explore opportunities for collaboration with other partners, and explore how they can cross-sell services to one another's clients. While much of this occurs informally, the event should include at least one session where existing and lateral partners formally exchange information about their clients, expertise, practices, and business plans.

A good way to welcome a high-profile new partner into the firm is a reception to which the firm's clients and the new partner's clients are invited. This introduces the partner to the firm's clients and creates a nice occasion for casual interaction with former, current, and potential clients. Other ways to orient new partners and integrate them into the life of the firm include the following:

- Ensure that new partners know how to access the staff, marketing, and administrative help they need to support their practice.

- Hold lunches every month or two just for lateral partners, or for lateral partners and small groups of lawyers in the office.

- Involve the new partner in a major matter for an existing client.

- Involve the partner on a committee or in some aspect of firm governance.

- Have the new partner tour the other firm offices.

- Invite the new partner to speak at a partnership, firm, or practice group meeting.

- Ask the lateral partner to participate in a team presentation or educational seminar to existing or potential clients.

---

[2] Nina J. Hamberg, "A Blueprint for Marketing Lateral Partners," *Law Practice Management*, March 1997.

- Invite lateral partners to participate in training programs as faculty. This allows them to communicate their expertise to the firm, gives them exposure to other lawyers, and identifies them as part of the firm's professional development team.

Orientation for Newly Elevated Partners

Most firms do not provide orientation for associates who are elevated to partnership — but they should. These new partners need a different kind of orientation, however. Unlike orientations for associates and lateral partners who are new to the firm, newly elevated partners know the firm through years of personal experience. What they do not know is what their movement into the partnership means and how it will change their professional and personal lives. Orientation explains the implications of partnership and gets them ready for the new challenges that await them.

Becoming a partner involves more than a shift in status from employee to owner. It is a rite of passage that entails a new way of thinking about practice and about the firm. Law firms that provide an orientation for new partners tend to concentrate on the financial consequences of partnership. But partnership involves many changes and new responsibilities besides financial ones. New partners need to appreciate the professional, business, interpersonal, and personal ramifications of becoming a partner. With this knowledge, they can become more productive and effective more quickly. The sooner they begin to think and manage like a partner, the more they can contribute to the business and profitability of the firm. Orientation should prepare new partners for these changes.

The financial aspects of becoming a partner are indeed important and need to be covered in orientation. New partners need to be educated about what partners have to plan and pay for, including insurance, taxes, capital contributions, and retirement. They need to learn cash flow management and fiscal discipline. New partners are often shocked to learn about the finances of their firm and about how their income will be affected. They have difficulty dealing with the shift from salary, bonus, and paid benefits to irregular cash distributions and the uncertainties and liabilities of ownership. Becoming a partner requires them to pay for many benefits for the first time and to buy into the firm. For some new partners, this results in a decline in income.

Orientation should also address the professional, business, interpersonal, and personal implications of becoming a partner. (See Table 2.) New partners need to understand how the transition from associate to partner changes their roles and responsibilities in the firm, especially regarding client management and business

TABLE 2. Orientation Topics for Newly Elevated Partners

1. **Partnership agreement and its implications**
2. **Firm's strategic plan and direction**
3. **Firm economics and finances**
    a. How the business operates
    b. Reading financial reports
    c. Practice, client, and matter profitability
    d. Costs of attrition
    e. Legal marketplace and trends
4. **Firm governance**
    a. Firm structure, including all offices
    b. Officers and directors
    c. Firm leadership (managing partners, chair of firm, department and practice group chairs)
        i. Role and authority
        ii. Selection
    d. Policies and decision-making
    e. Committees
    f. Partnership meetings
    g. Firm administration and operations
        i. Departments
        ii. Directors, managers, and administrators
        iii. Risk management procedures and requirements
5. **Financial aspects of partnership**
    a. Compensation
        i. Draws and distributions
        ii. Origination credit
        iii. Allocation process
        iv. Benefits (insurance, pensions, and retirement planning)
        v. Taxes
    b. Capital contribution
    c. Debt and personal guarantees
    d. Firm investments

(continued)

(Table 2 continued)
- e. Charitable contributions
- f. Collections

6. **Management responsibilities**
    - a. Professional conduct
    - b. Practice management
        - i. Specialization
        - ii. Project management
        - iii. Managing teams
    - c. Fiduciary responsibilities
    - d. Client management
    - e. Use of technology
    - f. Evaluations (including peer, upward, and 360° reviews)
    - g. Mentoring and training
        - i. Responsibility as a role model
        - ii. Responsibility as a mentor
        - iii. Acting as faculty in firm programs

7. **Leadership**
    - a. Motivating and inspiring others
    - b. Developing leadership skills
    - c. Assuming leadership roles and responsibilities
    - d. Willingness to be led
    - e. Expectations
    - f. Compensation for leadership activities

8. **Clients and business development**
    - a. Existing firm clients
    - b. Client service expectations
    - c. Client teams and industry groups
    - d. My clients or firm clients?
    - e. Building a practice: Expectations for new partners
        - i. Business development activities
        - ii. Cross-selling
        - iii. RFPs
        - iv. Personal marketing plans
        - v. Resources and support available in the firm

> **9. Good citizenship**
>   a. In firm
>   b. In community
>   c. Pro bono policies and expectations
>
> **10. Personal life**
>   a. Making time for family, friends, outside interests
>   b. Finding mentors for yourself
>   c. Self-awareness
>   d. Coaching (availability)
>   e. Managing self

development. The way new partners handle these activities will have a significant impact on their continued professional success and financial rewards. They need to know what is expected of them, what support the firm will provide, and how they can acquire and polish the skills they need to be successful in these areas. New partners also need to understand the firm's expectations concerning their participation in governance and administration, recruiting, mentoring, and training, including the impact of these non-billable activities on their careers and their compensation. And they must be conscious of their new responsibilities as role models to the associates whose ranks they have just left.

Partnership also transforms relationships with colleagues in the firm. Relationships with both partners and associates take on a different cast. New partners are often disillusioned by power plays, political intrigues, and conflict among partners. No longer employees, new partners must compete for a fair share of clients, work, and profits. Even their former mentors now treat them like competitors. In addition, new partners are surprised to learn that associates no longer consider them friends. Instead, as "partners," they have gone over to the other side of the "we/they" relationship. Associates trust them less because these new partners are now their bosses with power over their future. New partners are disconcerted, confused, and sometimes hurt by all of these new political and interpersonal realities.

Becoming a partner adds new stresses on lawyers' personal lives. Ownership and management responsibilities are added to their already intense practice demands. For the years leading up to partnership, they have worked very hard and sacrificed much of their personal time. Becoming a partner increases the demands on their time even more. Combined with their new business and management responsibilities and the change in the way their colleagues view and treat them, these pressures can be traumatic and take a toll on their personal lives.

Organizing an Orientation Program

In addition to deciding the program content, organizing an orientation program requires consideration of four issues:

- Timing and frequency,
- Personnel,
- Location, and
- Social events.

Timing and Frequency

The timing and frequency of orientation programs differ depending on the groups of lawyers being oriented.

- **New Associates**

Orientation programs for new associates must be timed to coincide with their arrival. The administrative orientation should occur as soon as the associate arrives at the firm, although some orientation materials and information can be provided in advance through the mail, via e-mail, or by providing access to the firm's intranet. For instance, many firms give new associates firm handbooks, employment forms, first-year training schedules, and mentor assignments two to four weeks before they begin work. The formal orientation program should also take place immediately or as soon after arrival as practicable. In order to maximize the benefits for all new associates and limit effort and expense, it is best to have all of the new associates present for a single orientation. However, with recruiting and lateral hiring going on year-round, new associates may stagger in over several months or episodically throughout the year. This makes scheduling this orientation program very difficult.

To deal with this problem, firms with large numbers of new associates increasingly require associates to begin on the same day in August or September, on one of two or three designated starting dates during the fall, or on or before a certain date. When the firm's policy does not require all associates to arrive by a relatively early date in the fall, the firm faces a dilemma: it either has to put on an orientation that comes too late for early arrivals or hold more than one orientation, which increases cost, consumes more time, and thwarts the social purpose of orientation. As a result, many firms without a fixed starting date require that new associates attend orientation even if they have not yet begun to work at the firm. These firms usually pay the expenses of associates who must travel to the orientation even if they are not yet on the firm's payroll.

■ Lateral Lawyers

All lateral lawyers need to be formally welcomed and oriented to the firm when they arrive. Lateral associates and partners generally join the firm one at a time or in smaller groups than new associates. Firms that do a lot of lateral hiring may have new lawyers arriving throughout the year. To deal with the ongoing need for orientation as laterals arrive, law firms are conveying more and more orientation material through electronic programming. This allows the firm to present orientation information to new lawyers whenever needed. From time to time, the firm facilitates live sessions, inviting all recent lateral arrivals to discuss their experience and ask questions. They also hold special social events for lateral lawyers as they arrive or whenever the numbers of new arrivals reach a critical mass.

■ Newly Elevated Partners

Most firms name new partners once a year. A formal orientation for new partners should be held shortly after partnership decisions are announced or within the first three months thereafter.

Personnel

The recruitment director, often together with training or professional development personnel, usually organizes the orientation program for new and lateral associates. Committees that deal with hiring, summer programs, and associate affairs often participate in planning the program.

Presentation of orientation programs for new and lateral associates can involve a large cast of characters, depending on what the firm wants to accomplish. The firm's managing partner and hiring partner should officially extend the firm's welcome. This is best done in person, but large firms (especially if they have repeated orientation sessions) may use videoconferencing or even a videotaped presentation if necessary. For most orientation topics, lawyers or personnel from the firm can serve as faculty (e.g., a librarian talking about research, or a panel consisting of a secretary, a paralegal, and an associate discussing how they work together). If the firm includes substantive legal programming during orientation, the firm's own experts should act as faculty. This shows associates the resources and talent available to them in the firm. Other personnel who might participate in the orientation program include:

- **Partners.** Partners should play a prominent role in the orientation program. When partners — especially distinguished partners — act as faculty, the message to associates is that the firm cares enough to send its leaders to meet with them. It educates associates about who these partners are and what they do. It allows the partners to do some internal marketing, interest associates in what they do, and possibly attract associates to their practice groups. Participating in the orientation also gives partners some idea of what the new associates are like and what they are thinking about.

- **Managers, directors, and key administrators.** Orientation is a good time to introduce new associates to the managers, directors, and key administrators in the firm. In many firms, these introductions occur during the administrative orientation. Alternatively, firms may build the introductions into the developmental orientation program. Presenters may include managers, directors, or administrators of accounting/financial services, professional development, human resources, office services, technology and information services, legal personnel (including paralegals), marketing, the library, the mailroom, and word processing. Each person should make a brief presentation to describe what they do, how they can help associates, and how they can be reached.

- **Department and practice group leaders.** Department and practice group leaders can describe their practices and clients.

- **Recruiting personnel.** Individuals involved in recruiting and hiring know the new lawyers, and their familiar faces may be comforting to anxious newcomers. It may be advantageous to give them a prominent role in planning and running the orientation program. Recruiters can be particularly good at addressing issues of transition to practice, either alone or with members of the hiring or associates committees.

- **Committee representatives.** Representatives of key firm committees can discuss what their committees do, describe interesting past or current projects, and explain if and how associates can participate in their committees.

- **Staff.** Paralegals, secretaries, and other professional and support staff can provide practical advice about working in the firm and explain how legal teams work together. They give new lawyers information and insights on how they expect to be treated and how they can make life easier for associates — if treated well.

- **Ombudsperson.** If the firm has an ombudsperson, that individual should explain the purpose of the position and what kind of assistance is offered.

- **Outside faculty.** Outside speakers or faculty can provide training on management topics or specific skills (e.g., time management, legal writing, business development). Guest speakers, including clients, law school professors, or judges, add interest to the program and highlight the firm's business, outside connections, or place in the community.

Practice group or department chairs are responsible for organizing orientation for lateral partners who join their groups. They may delegate the actual programming to recruiting, professional development, and/or marketing department personnel. Department and practice group leaders (though not necessarily the chairs) should also help plan sessions on practice group–specific topics for these lateral partners.

Orientation for new partners elevated from within the firm involves information about the firm and preparation for the partner's new role. While the managing partner and professional development specialist should plan this program, they may seek assistance from outside consultants regarding the latter component.

Location

Law firms with only one office or few associates may choose to hold their orientation programs on-site. This is convenient for all involved and keeps costs relatively low. However, on-site programs should include a dinner or social event outside the office so that participants can relax, have fun, and interact more casually.

For large multi-office firms, deciding on the location for an orientation program raises complex issues. It involves all the usual difficulties of putting on an orientation program, plus the additional logistical problems of travel schedules and accommodations for lawyers from different states and possibly different countries. Many international firms fly all of their new associates to a central location for orientation. New lawyers generally welcome the chance to visit the firm's other offices, but those who must travel long distances lose a day or more from work due to travel time and jet lag. Firms with a robust "home office" culture and facilities that can accommodate large groups may want to hold all orientations in the main office. Firms that have a "decentralized" structure and de-emphasize the dominance of any particular offices may prefer to hold each orientation at a different location. These firms might consider alternating East and West Coast offices, bringing everyone to a smaller office, or holding regional orientations for groups of offices. Some firms hold two or more simultaneous orientations in different regional locations. They combine live on-site programming with a few videoconference sessions for the group as a whole.

Orientation programs that require lawyers to travel are expensive, and the decisions about where to hold them often rest on financial concerns. Air travel, hotel lodging, and facility costs add up quickly. Law firms are inclined to favor bringing everyone to the city where most lawyers are located so that fewer have to travel. However, there may be cost advantages to using a smaller venue where total costs will be cheaper. Look into these options before making a decision.

Many large firms have sufficient space and large enough conference rooms in their offices to accommodate all new lawyers and faculty for an orientation program. This is convenient and cost effective. However, large firms may find it preferable to reserve a training or resort facility instead. Using these facilities makes it easier for participants to concentrate on the program and harder for them to be called away. Such facilities have professional staff and technical resources that relieve orientation planners of many of the anxieties and logistical details that go into complex programming. Using an outside facility and its resources may also present more options for recreation, social events, and casual interaction.

Social Events

Orientation is the first step in fostering collegiality and a sense of affiliation, and every orientation should have a social component. Orientation program agendas should give new arrivals time to get to know each other and their colleagues. The social aspects of orientation programs are very important for the firm as well as for the new lawyers. Associates who go through orientation together begin to identify with the firm and see themselves as part of the law firm community. Personal relationships start to form, which connect lawyers to the firm and promote retention. Most new associates decide whether to stay or leave a firm within the first six to twelve months. Failure to form personal connections during orientation can delay their assimilation into the firm and even lead to early departures.

When a group of lateral lawyers joins the firm together, the social component of orientation plays a critical role in assimilating the group into the firm. Occasionally firms acquire a small law firm or hire a team of lawyers from another firm. If these laterals view themselves as an independent unit, feel isolated, or have trouble adjusting to their new work environment, the lawyers may fail to bond with the new firm. It is therefore vital that the lawyers in the group begin to identify with the new firm right away and become integrated into the new firm's culture and practice. Social events during a group's first few months at the firm support and hasten this process.

Orientation-related social events need not be elaborate or expensive, nor do they need to be part of a formal orientation program. The first social event should be a "first day lunch" with two or three lawyers from the firm. Socialization is fostered when new lawyers have a chance to talk casually with each other and with their new colleagues in the firm. This may just be some free "play time" together and a chance to have fun. If you hold a large social event or welcoming reception during the orientation program, it is a good idea to invite people whom new lawyers already know (e.g., assigned mentors or buddies, hiring committee members, and summer associates committee members). In addition to the social events held during orientation, various kinds of social events for new lawyers should be scheduled throughout the year.

One particularly valuable orientation activity is an immersion experience to promote team-building and social bonding. These unique experiences range from outdoor "ropes course" programs to cooking classes, but all involve extensive social interaction among participants. They are usually led by outside trainers or facilitators and take place off-site.

APPENDIX 12-A

Shook, Hardy & Bacon LLP

Becoming a Partner — Part I

Note: This is a 90-minute program followed by lunch.

I. **The Ownership Vision**
   A. Change Is Not Overnight
   B. Criteria for Partnership
   C. Governance
      1. Firm wide
      2. Office level
      3. Practice group level

II. **Rainmaking**
   A. Partner Role
   B. Preparation for Role

III. **Managing Money/The Firm's and Yours**
   A. Firm
      1. Time
      2. Bills
      3. Collections
      4. Write-offs
   B. Personal Finances
      1. Insurance
      2. Taxes
      3. Pension and profit sharing
      4. Buy-in for equity partners
      5. Personal guarantees

IV. **The New Partner View**
   A. Transition
   B. Finance
   C. Leadership

V. **Questions and Answers**

Becoming a Partner — Part II

Note: Part II takes place one week after Part I.
Like Part I, it is a 90-minute program followed by lunch.

I. What Is the LLP Anyway, and How Does It Work?
   A. Two Classes of Partners
   B. Partnership Meetings
   C. Capital
   D. Partnership Agreement

II. The View from the Executive Committee (the Vision for the Firm)

III. Process of Recommendations and Approvals
   A. Associates Committee
   B. Divisions and Sections
   C. City Offices
   D. Executive Committee

IV. Myths and Realities
   A. Number of Partners Now and in the Future
      1. Income partners
      2. Equity partners
   B. Years to Partner
      1. Associates
      2. Laterals
      3. Of Counsel On-Track
      4. Years to Equity Partner
   C. Compensation Process: How Does It Work?

V. The Move from Associate to Partner
   A. Changes from Junior to Senior Associate — Getting Ready
   B. Reviewing Options Other than Partnership — It's Your Choice, Too
   C. Things I Wish They Had Told Me

VI. Questions and Answers

APPENDIX 12-B

Pillsbury Winthrop LLP

Orientation — New and Lateral Partners

Lunch and Introduction

I. Practice Focus: Building the Firm's Future

- Firm-wide plans to build and expand the Firm's high-value practice areas.
- How individual partners can develop market opportunities in their own practices that will increase the Firm's national and international recognition and ability to attract high-value work.

II. Obligation to Partners and Others: Becoming the "Best People to Work With"

- Teamwork: Meeting a commitment to other partners; interacting with and supervising associates and staff.
- What makes associates and staff want to work with certain partners? (and how NOT to develop a reputation as a partner for whom no one wants to work).
- What attributes did you value in partners you worked for when you were an associate?
- What about a partner's management style made coming to work an energizing experience (or not) for both associates and staff?
- The importance of mentoring and feedback and how to make it a part of your daily interaction with associates and staff. A new partner will speak briefly about the success of the NY mentoring program.
- Sharing responsibility for Firm administration.

III. The Law Firm as a Business: Processes and Profitability

- Firm finances: current and projections.
- Compensation Committee, compensation process; Full Commitment Plan.
- Partners' responsibilities as fiduciaries.
- Taking an ownership interest in the Firm and becoming a decision-maker.
- Increasing your profitability.
- Billing practices, allocation of resources and managing profitability.
- Giving/splitting managing, origination, and billing credit to/with associates/senior attorneys.

IV. "What I Know Now, I Wish I Knew Then"

- Recent new partners share what they have learned as partners and about the Firm — compensation process, team work, business development, how to deal with senior partners as a partner (how has it changed), serving as role models; becoming an owner.

V. Obligation to Yourself and to Your Career

- Managing your career.
- Planning your career development path; managing and growing a practice.
- Setting increased levels of professional goals.
- Adapting to practice and market changes.
- Balancing client, administrative, and personal commitments.
- Establishing a role in the external legal community.

VI. Obligation to Client Service — Meeting Client Needs and Expectations

- Partner obligations to clients: Client expectations of partners; managing and meeting client expectations; dealing with client demands.
- Providing the best client service: The art of "selling" your product; understanding client needs; increasing sensitivity to client "politics."
- Utilizing marketing and practice development personnel to support client service.

VII. Conclusion: "Now Go Do It!"

- Successfully integrating the many hats of a PW partner.

PART VI

Special Issues Related to Professional Development

CHAPTER 13

Women and Minority Lawyers

Law firms must pay special attention to professional development and advancement of women and lawyers of color. Firms frequently institute diversity initiatives designed to increase their numbers of women and racial minority lawyers, and sometimes these efforts are effective. Many bar associations and other legal organizations have published goals, guidelines, and model programs for increasing diversity, and for the most part the profession has taken its responsibility to increase diversity seriously.[1] Although the desire may be genuine, the results so far are meager. Women now constitute almost 30 percent of lawyers but only 15.6 percent of law firm partners[2] and 9 percent of General Counsel positions in Fortune 500 companies.[3] African-American and Hispanic lawyers together represented only 7 percent of lawyers in 1998, a smaller percentage than in all professions except dentistry and natural science.[4] In 2000, only about 10 percent of all lawyers, 3 percent of law firm partners, and 2.8 percent of Fortune 500 General Counsel were lawyers of color.[5]

The most common way that law firms tackle this problem is to increase recruitment efforts. However, even law firms that do well in recruiting women and minority lawyers have trouble retaining them for very long. The average annual attrition rate for women associates (15.7 percent) is higher than for men (14.3 percent), and minority men and women have the highest annual departure rates among all associates (21 percent and 19 percent, respectively).[6] The reasons for this high attrition are numerous and can only be reversed by redefining the culture of the legal workplace. Implementing a comprehensive professional development

---

[1] See references listed at the end of this chapter.
[2] NALP 2000-2001 *National Directory of Legal Employers*.
[3] ABA, "A Snapshot of Women in the Law in the Year 2000."
[4] ABA Commission on Racial and Ethnic Diversity in the Profession, "Lawyer Diversity Reaches a Plateau," *ABA Journal*, January 2002, p. 31.
[5] *Bar None*, p. 5. Part of the increase in the percentage of minority lawyers between 1998 and 2000 is attributed to the inclusion of Asians and Native Americans in the year 2000 statistics.
[6] *Beyond the Bidding Wars,* The NALP Foundation, Washington, DC, 2000.

program is one strategy that will advance law firms' retention of women and minority lawyers. As discussed throughout this book, the primary professional development systems — training, work assignments, evaluations, and mentoring — are important for the professional well-being and success of all lawyers. But they are even more important for women and minority lawyers, who are more easily marginalized in the traditional mainstream law firm culture.

Diversity Training

Diversity training for all lawyers is now a mainstay of law firm training programs. Many law firms offer diversity training because it is the "right" thing to do, but they also do it for important business reasons: to increase teamwork, promote workplace harmony, prepare lawyers for international assignments, teach lawyers skills needed to exploit a global marketplace, or protect the firm against harassment, discrimination, and lawsuits. Effective diversity training does not focus exclusively on women and lawyers of color; it also covers other aspects of diversity, including sexual orientation, religious beliefs, disabilities, and even political views and generational differences.

Diversity training is important, but law firms should not rely on training alone to advance diversity. Training courses raise awareness and offer advice on transcending differences, but these courses can only go so far. They must be bolstered by real cultural support, starting with the firm's leadership. True diversity can only flourish in a culture that respects differences and does not let those differences stand in the way of a person's success. Many of the obstacles to diversity are subtle and even unconscious. Training can make people more sensitive to these biases and barriers, but it cannot eliminate them. That takes a more comprehensive organizational intervention.

Training for Practice Development

To promote the professional development of women and minority lawyers, the firm should offer courses designed to enhance lawyers' professional skills and practice development. The firm should provide these programs for all lawyers, not just women and minorities, but lawyers in these groups may benefit the most from them. These courses should cover the skills and practices necessary for professional advancement, such as communication, client relations, business development, networking, and working with mentors. Lawyers need to be taught how to maximize their performance, enhance the value of their contributions to the firm, and facilitate their participation in all aspects of professional life. Lawyers who are unfamiliar or uncomfortable in the majority culture may want specialized courses, such as more intensive orientation programs, assertiveness training, or lessons in how to deal with uncomfortable situations. If individual lawyers have particular needs, coaching may be a good alternative to training.

Work Assignments

A structured system for work assignments is especially helpful for women and minority lawyers. A structured system finds appropriate developmental assignments for associates and monitors their work experience and progress. In contrast, a laissez faire approach to work assignments puts women and minority lawyers at a disadvantage. The lack of structure in the laissez faire model means that personal relationships and subjective judgments have inordinate influence over the way work is distributed in the firm. Since women and minority lawyers are often excluded from the informal networks through which work assignments flow, they are more easily overlooked when new assignments become available. A structured system protects them by seeing that work is equitably and appropriately assigned.

Evaluations

The use of benchmarks, competencies, and well-designed performance evaluations can protect women and minority lawyers against bias and discrimination. When law firms rely on "subjective standards of excellence" to evaluate associates and make promotion decisions, it is easy for them to perpetuate stereotypes and prejudicial attitudes. The clearer and more objective the standards are, the more equitable the evaluations will be. When promotion decisions are based on objective rather than subjective assessments, individuals from non-traditional backgrounds are more likely to be judged on their merit and performance.

A formal evaluation system also ensures that women and minorities receive regular feedback. For many women and minority lawyers, informal feedback is either sugar coated or non-existent. Because of lawyers' discomfort or uncertainty about what is "safe" or "acceptable" for them to say to women and minorities, they avoid saying anything critical of these lawyers' performance. Formal evaluations, based on clear criteria, can correct this situation and give these lawyers constructive and meaningful feedback. Using performance standards and evaluations to create individual development plans encourages lawyers to identify and maximize their strengths, and to address their development needs. In this way, development planning can provide valuable career guidance and direction for women and minority lawyers.

Upward and 360° evaluations can also produce important feedback for partners and senior associates about their supervision of and interactions with women and minority lawyers. This information can contribute significantly to changing both the behaviors of individuals and the culture of the firm.

Mentoring

Mentoring is a proven modality for promoting the advancement of women and lawyers of color. Advancement in law firms depends in large part on personal relationships, informal networks, client contacts, and an appreciation of law firm politics. Women and minority lawyers have a more difficult time in all these arenas, and mentors can help them overcome these difficulties. Law firms must make special efforts to provide mentors for these lawyers, through both structured mentoring programs and personal outreach by partners. Partners must make the time and effort to get to know the women and lawyers of color in their firms, regardless of whether they are mentors in a formal program or on an informal basis. Only when partners know these lawyers well, can they offer meaningful career advice, advocate for these lawyers, and champion their progress.

Culture Change

Professional development systems can promote diversity by ensuring fairness, offering support, and encouraging all lawyers to achieve their potential. But to sweep away the subtle inequities and barriers to advancement, the legal workplace must become more hospitable to lawyers who do not fit the traditional law firm model. This requires a colossal initiative to change law firm culture. To begin the process, diversity must be seen as a high-priority strategic initiative that is integral to the business success of the firm. Firms must acknowledge the salutary contributions that diverse perspectives and approaches bring to an organization's strategies, operations, and practices.[7] Firm leadership must vigorously promote diversity and be accountable for their results. Law firms that embark on this course often dedicate full-time diversity directors to guide the effort.

One area where law firm culture causes particular concern is the conflict between work and personal life. The conventional career path in most law firms requires an oppressive time commitment that persists throughout a lawyer's career. Although it is hard to achieve work-life balance in many workplace environments,

---

[7] David A. Thomas and Robin J. Ely, "Making Differences Matter: A New Paradigm for Managing Diversity," *Harvard Business Review*, September-October 1996.

working in a law firm is especially harsh on lawyers' personal lives. Most lawyers in private practice now bill close to 2,000 hours a year (and more in large firms), which means at least 60-hour workweeks.[8] Work-life conflict due to these time pressures is a major reason that lawyers look outside law firms for employment.[9] And, while these pressures affect all lawyers, they have a disproportionately negative impact on women.[10] Firms that are interested in changing their work culture can find many concrete, practical recommendations to accommodate alternative schedules and career paths for their lawyers.[11]

Useful References on Diversity and Work-Life Balance:

Ida O. Abbott, *The Lawyer's Guide to Mentoring*, (NALP Washington, DC) 2000.
Bar Association of San Francisco, "Fifty Firms Commit to No Glass Ceiling for Women," May 16, 2002. (www.sfbar.org)
Bar None: Report to the President of the United States on the Status of People of Color and Pro Bono Services in the Legal Profession, Lawyers for One America, San Francisco, CA, 2000.
Creating Pathways to Diversity and *Diversity Best Practices Handbook*, Minority Corporate Counsel Association, Washington, DC, 2000.
Diversity in the Executive Suite: Creating Successful Career Paths and Strategies, Korn/Ferry International and Columbia Business School, 1998.
Facing the Grail: Confronting the Cost of Work-Family Imbalance, Boston Bar Association, 1999.
Sylvia Ann Hewlett, *Creating a Life: Professional Women and the Quest for Children*, Talk Miramax Books, New York, 2002.
Manual of Model Policies and Programs to Achieve Equality of Opportunity in the Legal Profession, The Bar Association of San Francisco, 1994.
Goals and Timetables for Minority Hiring and Advancement (1996), and *1999 Interim Report* (1999), The Bar Association of San Francisco.
Deborah Graham, *Second to None*, ABA (expected publication date 2002).
Deborah L. Rhode, *Balanced Lives: Changing the Culture of Legal Practice*, American Bar Association Commission on Women in the Profession, 2001.
David A. Thomas, John J. Gabarro, *Breaking Through: The Making of Minority Executives in Corporate America*, Harvard Business School Press, Boston, 1999.
Joan Williams, Cynthia Thomas Calvert, *Balanced Hours: Effective Part-Time Policies for Washington Law Firms*, The Project for Attorney Retention Final Report, May 2001.
Women in the Law: Making the Case, Catalyst, New York, 2001.

---

[8] Rhode, "Balanced Lives."
[9] *Ibid.*; "Facing the Grail."
[10] Sylvia Ann Hewlett, *Creating a Life: Professional Women and the Quest for Children*, Talk Miramax Books, New York, 2002; Rhode; "Facing the Grail"; "Women in Law: Making the Case."
[11] See, e.g., "Facing the Grail"; Williams and Calvert; "Women in Law: Making the Case."

CHAPTER 14

Associate Participation on Committees

Committees serve more than a management function: they are proving grounds for professional and leadership development. Committees provide effective means for lawyers to participate in firm governance and policy making, learn about the operation and priorities of the firm, practice leadership roles, and gain visibility and prominence. Committees give lawyers important insights into firm politics and involve them in firm management. Associates report that being placed on important committees and working groups demonstrates the firm's confidence in them as future firm members, and that inclusion in firm management enhances their work satisfaction and retention.[1] Conversely, associates cite the lack of communication between associates and firm management as a major source of dissatisfaction.[2] Still another important reason to include associates on firm committees is that it fosters the development of personal relationships with fellow committee members, strengthening ties to the firm.

The number and composition of committees vary according to the firm's culture and management style, and the differences among firms cover a wide spectrum. On one end are firms with a tight hierarchical management structure that have few committees and limit membership on those committees to partners; they tend to share little information with associates, although the managing partner may present an annual "state of the firm" address to associates. On the other end are egalitarian, decentralized firms that have many committees with broad participation; they tend to share substantial information about firm policies and finances with associates. The firms with the most open membership policies include associates on all committees except the committee that deals with partner compensation. (See Table 1.) Although many firms find that governance by committees is cumbersome and

---

[1] *Beyond the Bidding Wars*, The NALP Foundation for Law Career Research and Education, 2000, p. 67; *Perceptions of Partnership*, The NALP Foundation, 1999, p. 109.
[2] *Keeping the Keepers*, The NALP Foundation, 1998, pp. 38, 78.

slows decision-making, committee participation is an effective mechanism for furthering associate development.

Serving on committees enhances learning, leadership, and retention. By their participation, associates who excel at teamwork have an opportunity to shine. For those lawyers whose strengths are in fields other than teamwork, committee participation is an effective way to learn and practice the professional skills needed to succeed in a work environment: collaboration, listening, consensus building, trust building, interpersonal conflict management, meeting management, and effective communication. These are all critical skills that are not taught in law school or in most law firms. Yet they are vital to getting work done with other people.

Associates who work on important committees become part of firm management; in that sense, they become invested in the firm through the work that their committees do. They and their peers feel that they have a voice in firm management, making the firm seem less secretive and more responsive to associates' concerns. Working on committees also develops leadership potential. Many firms report that their leaders are principally lawyers who have played significant roles on firm committees. An associate who co-chairs the summer program committee can receive

---

TABLE 1. Committees on Which Law Firm Associates Serve*

- Alumni Relations
- Associates
- Associate Compensation
- Associate Evaluations
- Associate Liaison
- Building/Facilities
- Career Enhancement
- Client Development
- Diversity
- Ethics
- Finance
- Foreign Interns
- Gender
- Hiring
- Legal Personnel
- Library
- Management
- Marketing
- Mentoring
- Office Operations
- "One Firm"
- Paralegal
- Policy
- Practice Curriculum
- Pro Bono
- Professional Development
- Professional Responsibility
- Quality of Life
- Recruitment
- Space Planning
- Summer Program
- Technology
- Training
- Women's Issues

* Based on a 2001 survey of law firm members of the Professional Development Consortium.

plaudits that significantly enhance his or her prospects for advancement to partnership. Working together on a project with experienced partners, junior lawyers intimately observe business and leadership in action, learn from watching role models, and find influential mentors. They learn how to make decisions, manage issues, and solve real firm problems.

Some firms give associates significant responsibilities, such as running summer programs, supervising associate evaluations and reviews, and making partnership recommendations. Giving associates such key management responsibilities means that the firm is willing to share with them the vital information that impacts their careers. It also sends a clear signal that the partners respect their intelligence and ability, and want them to be meaningful participants in the firm. In addition, serving on a committee enables associates to meet lawyers in other practice areas and to create relationships outside the normal sphere of practice.

In most committees, associates are full members with the same responsibilities as partners. Some firms have associates as ex officio committee members who participate only to hear and convey information but without a vote or authority. Few firms allow associates to chair committees other than an associates committee comprised exclusively of associates, but some firms do permit associates to serve as co-chairs or chairs.

Firms that intend to open membership on key committees to associates need to think through the ramifications. One consideration is that committee work can require a substantial commitment of non-chargeable time that may negatively impact the associate's compensation and advancement. Associates will resist participating unless the firm reassures them that participation is valued, expected, and will not affect them detrimentally.

Another consideration is that placing associates on certain committees will give them access to sensitive information about the firm. This is not an issue on committees that deal with matters like the library or technology, but it may be a problem on the firm's executive committee or associate compensation committee. Therefore, the firm needs to be willing to have that information distributed to associates. Unfortunately, what occasionally happens is that firms appoint associates to executive, policy, or other key management committees but ask them to leave during discussions of sensitive topics or to withhold what they learn from their fellow associates. Either scenario places the associate in an untenable position. The former causes discomfort and awkwardness and, by excluding the associate, contradicts the message of openness and inclusion that committee membership implies. The latter causes the associate to become alienated and distrusted by peers, whom the associate is ostensibly representing on the committee. To avoid either situation, the exact role of the associate on such committees must be defined in advance and explained to everyone in the firm. If the associates are to be genuinely included in firm management, then they should play a full role on the committee. If, however, they are only to be conduits for transmitting information between associates and management, then they should be invited only for specific items on the agenda.

Associate Committees

Most firms have at least one committee that addresses issues affecting associates. This is usually a committee *on* associates, which decides firm policies that impact or concern associates (e.g., evaluations, part-time work, parenting leave). Some firms also have a committee *of* associates, which raises associate-generated issues for presentation to the firm's decision-makers. Committees *on* associates may include associate members but more often do not; committees *of* associates may include partner members but more often do not. Both types of committees frequently include or meet regularly with the managing partner, executive director or office administrator, professional development director, or ombudsperson. They may also have a member who acts as a liaison between partners and associates.

If a firm is going to have associates serve on any committees, these associate-related committees are the most appropriate ones for them to join. In addition to the benefits of committee participation generally, these committees have the most direct impact on associates' lives in the firm. Having associates participate in these committees is beneficial to the firm as well. Associate representatives are the firm's primary source of information about associates' needs and concerns. They present new ideas and fresh perspectives on timeworn policies and practices. As liaisons between associates and the firm, they can distribute management proposals, explain management's intentions, and promote new plans to associates.

Associate Selection for Firm Committees

Membership selection methods vary among firms and among committees within firms. Some of the selection methods include:

- Appointment by the managing partner.
- Appointment by the management committee.
- Appointment by committee chairs.
- Election by associates.
- Election by all lawyers.
- Volunteering.

The criteria used to select associate representatives also vary. Some associates may be at-large representatives, without any more specific constituency, while many firms choose associate committee members to represent specific classes (e.g., a representative for first- and second-year associates), offices, departments, practice groups, or floors (e.g., one associate committee member from each floor in the office). Firms that strongly encourage associate participation in committees can create membership opportunities, make membership voluntary, and permit any associate who wants to participate to do so. For example, Fried, Frank, Harris, Shriver & Jacobson has an Associates' Committee comprised of the Managing Partner, Executive Director of the Office of Associate Affairs, and three associates. The Associates' Committee has several subcommittees (called "portfolios") that involve numerous associates in different issues related to work and professional development, including substantive training and orientation, policies and compensation, and management training. Membership on these portfolios is open to any associate who wishes to participate.

CHAPTER 15

Career Guidance

Lawyers face career choices throughout their professional lives and need to make smart decisions about them. To take control of their careers, lawyers have to appreciate their goals and ambitions, set priorities, and take actions that will work to their advantage. Sometimes they need guidance to help them manage their careers. While law firms are not responsible for providing professional career counseling, they can give lawyers much of the assistance they need through the firm's professional development program.

Lawyers today realize that they have to be proactive in managing their careers. They understand that legal employers do not promise permanent, long-term work arrangements, as the recent recession has painfully shown. Without such guarantees, and with many opportunities available to them, lawyers recognize that they have to be "employable." For associates, that means having sufficient training and experience to move to the next job. For partners, it means having a book of business that is professionally and financially stable and rewarding for themselves, valuable to the firm, and portable in case they have to move to another firm. Although most firms balk at the notion that they should provide training and development for lawyers who will leave them, it is a fact of life in today's world that some lawyers will indeed leave, and that they will leave even earlier if their employers do not meet their professional development needs. By helping lawyers make wise career decisions, law firms can benefit from lawyers' proficiency and dedication while they are at the firm and from their referrals and goodwill if they leave.

The need for career guidance starts in law firms when lawyers enter practice and continues through retirement. Some of the career issues that lawyers face include:

- Specialization.
- Partnership preparation.
- Alternatives to partnership.

- Involvement in bar, community, public service activities.
- Full-time or part-time practice.
- Work-life conflict.
- Retraining.
- New employment opportunities.
- Outplacement.
- Retirement.

Career guidance is most readily provided in a culture that focuses on professional development. The way to create this kind of environment is to start emphasizing the growth and development of your lawyers early in their careers — as early, in fact, as the summer program. Law students and first-year associates who set priorities, goals, and career directions will become more astute and satisfied lawyers. These neophytes should begin to think about and decide what kind of work, practice, and life they want to have. They should consider the challenges that excite them and those they would rather avoid. Once they know their priorities, they can set short-term and long-term goals and design a career track. The purpose is not to set a plan in stone, but for associates to have a clear sense of purpose and direction. When new opportunities come their way inside or outside the firm, they are prepared to make better decisions and smarter choices.

The firm can assist associates by giving them information about available career options. Benchmarks, competencies, and partnership criteria lay out a lawyer's standard career path in the firm. If the firm offers non-traditional or alternative career paths (e.g., part-time partnerships, managerial positions in professional development or knowledge management), the firm should let associates know about them.

This process of determining priorities, goals, and career direction is as valuable for experienced lawyers as it is for new associates. New partners, for example, can become more effective more quickly if they are purposeful in choosing their work and clients. Rather than accept assignments arbitrarily, they should design the type of practice they want by making work decisions that are in line with their priorities and goals. When they are proactive, new partners waste less time on insignificant work and extraneous business development and spend more time on activities calculated to advance their interests and those of the firm. Similarly, for lawyers who are thinking about leaving practice or suffering mid-career angst, career guidance can provide a smooth transition rather than an abrupt and stressful change. This is vitally important for the firm, not just the individual lawyer. When lawyers leave, it permits the orderly and uninterrupted move of clients and ongoing matters to new responsible lawyers. Lawyers with mid-career crises may need some time to take a fresh look at their priorities and goals. With support and guidance from the firm, many of these valuable lawyers will not leave. They may be able to reinvigorate their practice and stay in the firm by accepting new and different responsibilities, changing the pace of their work, or retraining for a different practice area.

Of course, retraining is not limited to troubled mid-career lawyers. It is an important management tool for law firms, especially during times of economic downturns. For lawyers in practice areas suffering a work slowdown, retraining may serve the firm's needs as well as the lawyer's. Retraining retains talented and productive members of the firm, allows the firm to reallocate and redistribute work, and enables the firm to open new practice areas or expand busy ones. Retraining requires that the lawyer be motivated to change (rather than forced to do so), and it necessitates adjustments of time and money. The firm should give the lawyer sufficient time to make the transition. Depending on the practice area involved, this may take anywhere from six months to two years or even more, especially if the lawyer is a partner who must rebuild a practice. During this transition period, the lawyer may have to accept a decrease in compensation.

Career guidance can also assist the firm in retaining partners who are approaching retirement. The high number of baby boomers in law firms means that many firms will face the prospect of losing a large number of key partners to retirement within a short period of time. Firms should prepare for this by helping partners in their forties and fifties plan for retirement in ways that will lessen the impact on the firm when they leave. Phased retirement, part-time work options, and enticing work incentives can be used to keep senior lawyers in the firm longer. Firms can retain the talents of these partners even after they stop practicing law by inviting them to assume responsibilities for teaching, mentoring, and pro bono projects on a full-time or part-time basis. This keeps retired lawyers connected to the firm community and promotes the development of the younger lawyers they teach. It also allows retiring partners to continue making contributions that are personally satisfying to them and advantageous for the firm.

Firms that choose to provide career guidance for their lawyers can do so in many ways. They can assign someone in recruiting or professional development to deal with lawyers' career concerns, or they may offer professional counseling to lawyers by hiring a career counselor or contracting with an outside counseling service. Whoever provides this career support, it should be integrated with the firm's professional development systems. In particular, mentors and supervisors can work with individual lawyers to keep their careers on the right track. Using competencies, performance reviews, and development plans, as discussed in Chapter 7, they can help lawyers determine how best to use their strengths and interests to fulfill their personal and professional aspirations.

CHAPTER 16

Succession Planning

Law firms must make a concerted effort to identify, retain, and groom their leaders of tomorrow. Law firms secure their future through succession planning. By choosing and preparing the lawyers who will succeed current leaders, firms can ensure that they will have leaders who will sustain the firm's excellence and carry it into the future. As law firms become larger and more businesslike, they can no longer "tag" new leaders at the last moment, when current leaders leave, retire, or die. Instead of waiting passively, firms need to be proactive in determining the kind of leaders they will need. Then, through careful and ongoing succession planning, they can select the lawyers who will be those leaders and prepare them for leadership roles.

To undertake succession planning, the firm must answer four questions:

1. **What are the firm's future leadership needs?**
2. **What competencies are needed to be a leader in the firm?**
3. **Who has the skills and talents to move into leadership roles?**
4. **What is the best way to train and prepare future leaders?**

Determining future leadership needs requires understanding the firm's future intentions and direction, and anticipating vacancies in leadership positions. These steps will help the firm identify where and when leadership will be needed. If the firm plans to undertake new strategic initiatives, such as opening new offices or starting new practice areas, lawyers will need to be lined up to lead these efforts. In addition, calculating when current leaders' terms expire and forecasting retirements and attrition over the next one to three years, will tell your firm when and how many new leaders will be needed. Of course, not everything can be planned for; some internal and external forces are beyond the firm's control. But analyzing upcoming needs and putting a succession plan into place will enable the firm to cope more effectively when unexpected events occur.

One of the things the firm's current leaders should look at is the age distribution of the firm's partners. Because of the demographics of the profession, many firms have a disproportionate number of lawyers who are in their late forties and early fifties. Unlike earlier generations, many of these lawyers will retire before reaching their sixties. This makes it imperative for the firm to take steps to keep productive lawyers on board and try to stagger their departures so that a leadership vacuum does not occur. The succession planning process should identify the partners who may be contemplating retirement within the next few years. The firm should then work with these lawyers to plan for a smooth and orderly transition of leadership.[1]

Once future leadership needs are identified, professional development systems can help your firm address the last three questions.

■ 1. Leadership Competencies

Leadership is a collection of practices and behaviors that arouse the talents and energies of people to do their best and achieve common goals.[2] Leadership includes a constellation of attributes, skills, and practices that include trust, excellent "people" skills, high professional standards, confidence, a willingness to take risks, and a sense of humor. The literature suggests dozens of ways of looking at leadership and a multitude of characteristics associated with leadership. Different law firms emphasize different characteristics. Some firms prize risk-taking while others place greater importance on steadiness. Each law firm must decide its own definition of leadership and the competencies it seeks in its leaders. In addition to current leadership competencies, the firm should determine any special skills and talents that will be needed by leaders in the future. Consider the firm's strategic plan; upcoming challenges inside the firm and in the legal marketplace; and factors critical to the firm's success. Your firm can determine the specific competencies and qualities of firm leaders when it establishes its benchmarks and competencies for purposes of the evaluation process. Alternatively, the firm can engage a consultant to conduct an analysis of the competencies that will be needed to lead your firm.

■ 2. Identifying Lawyers with Leadership Skills and Talents

Professional development systems can help your firm identify prospective leaders. Through observation, you can identify lawyers with leadership potential

---

[1] See, e.g., Ronald M. Martin, "Saving the Boomers," *Law Practice Management*, April 2001, p. 36.
[2] Ida Abbott, "Can Lawyers Learn to Lead?" *Developing Legal Talent: Best Practices in Professional Development for Law Firms*, Washington, DC, NALP, 2001, pp. 38, 41.

during work assignments, committee activities, special projects, and client interactions. Another way to identify leadership talent is through the performance evaluation process, especially 360° reviews. Once your firm has identified a pool of potential future leaders, you should prepare them to assume leadership roles. Some of these lawyers may be groomed for specific leadership positions, while others can be slated for leadership positions and activities as they open up. Most leadership positions will go to partners, but firms should also give special attention to associates. A few firms cultivate their most promising associates by promoting them after four or five years of practice to a special senior associate status, and by giving them extra training and support in leadership, management, and client development. Firms may not want to give such obvious preferential treatment to high potential associates because it can lead to morale problems among those who are not selected. Some firms also fear any gestures that might be misinterpreted as a promise of partnership. Nonetheless, firms must somehow let their best associates know they are considered prime partnership and leadership candidates.

■ 3. Leadership Training and Preparation

Once the firm identifies prospective leaders, each one should have a personal leadership development plan. Find out through personal interviews what these lawyers perceive their development needs to be with respect to leadership. Determine their leadership experience and current stage of leadership development by reviewing their performance evaluations and work histories. Next, compare this information against the future leadership needs of the firm (which you have previously identified) and note any gaps. The development plan for each prospective leader should focus on those gaps. The plan should provide resources, training, and experiences that will help these lawyers develop their full leadership capabilities. One way to embark on leadership development planning is to ask current law firm leaders what experiences and training were most beneficial for them.

Leadership development plans should be tailored to the individual. There are many approaches and techniques to consider in drafting a plan. Here are some ideas:

- ■ Assign current leaders as mentors to teach and support prospective leaders. Linking prospects to experienced firm leaders or partners who will soon retire enables new leaders to learn from their predecessors.

- ■ Draw up individual development plans that identify competencies needing reinforcement or improvement. Provide specific leadership coaching, experience, and training to address those competencies.

- Assign special work assignments, committees, task forces, and projects that will give future leaders a chance to practice leadership skills and show what they can do.

- Give special assignments that provide high visibility with clients, broaden client experience, and strengthen client relationships.

- Provide in-house training in leadership skills.

- Send prospects to outside leadership training programs.

- Include leadership development strategies in new partner orientation programs.

- Hire executive coaches for prospects to help them become more effective leaders.

- Encourage prospects to participate in community activities to increase their reputation and visibility in the community, meet potential clients, and practice leadership skills.

CHAPTER 17

The Role of the Ombudsperson

A recent development in some law firms is the designation of one person to act as an "ombudsperson." This person serves as an in-house neutral who investigates and tries to resolve work-related complaints and disputes through counseling, mediation, or recommendations to management. The role derives from the Scandinavian model of a respected, independent public official who investigates citizens' complaints and criticizes government agencies.[1] As the position has evolved in the United States, however, ombudspersons are typically employed by the organizations they monitor, although they are outside the usual chain of command and report directly to the chief executive.

A law firm ombudsperson mediates, communicates, and alleviates associate matters and concerns, but the specific roles of ombudspersons vary from firm to firm. The person may serve as a bridge for communication between the associates and the firm or merely as a conduit for associates to communicate their views, ideas, and complaints to firm management. Neutrality is generally considered essential, so that the ombudsperson is not perceived as a representative of either associates or management and maintains the trust of both. Nonetheless, in some law firms, the ombudsperson actually serves as an advocate for associates on policy and practice issues when those issues are too contentious for individual associates to speak up. Some ombudspersons also arrange outplacement and conduct exit interviews.

Law firm ombudspersons frequently act as confidantes to associates. Because they maintain strict confidentiality regarding associate communications, the ombudsperson is someone "safe" to whom associates can take their most sensitive and personal work concerns and problems. Consequently, the ombudsperson hears all

---

[1] Linda R. Singer, *Settling Disputes: Conflict Resolution in Business, Families, and the Legal System*, Westview Press, Boulder, CO, 1990.

kinds of concerns, from the trivial and mundane to those that can make or break associates' careers.

Firms that have ombudspersons find that they offer substantial benefits to associates and to the firm:

- Associates' feel that their concerns are heard and acted upon through the ombudsperson's access to firm management and/or participation in firm management decisions.

- Misperceptions and miscommunications between associates and partners are more readily cleared up.

- Problems between associates and supervisors on work and performance issues can be promptly investigated, mediated, and resolved.

- Associates' productivity, work satisfaction, and retention are enhanced.

- Ombudspersons serve as additional counselors for associates on such issues as specialization, career decisions, and work relationships.

- Ombudspersons can give the firm early warnings of trouble brewing and take steps to resolve them.

In many ways, a law firm ombudsperson acts as a "super mentor," offering help and guidance to associates. The ombudsperson can supplement the mentoring program or, if the firm has no formal mentoring program, serve as the associates' source of support and assistance. If an associate seeks assistance for a problem, the ombudsperson can help the associate work out a plan to address the problem, intervene on behalf of the associate, or act as an intermediary between the parties. In firms whose mentoring programs permit mentors to supervise associates on client matters, an ombudsperson can serve as the associates' confidante. When associates cannot get along with a mentor who is also their supervisor, they can go to the ombudsperson for confidential advice and help.

Law firm ombudspersons are usually partners or personnel in recruiting or professional development. The position is not full-time but rather an additional role for someone in the firm who is respected and trusted by both associates and partners. Ombudspersons must be selected very carefully. On a personal level, the individual must possess tact, sensitivity, patience, and excellent interpersonal skills, and hold the trust, credibility, and loyalty of the firm's lawyers and staff. On an institutional level, the ombudsperson must have access to and influence with associates and partners, as well as authority to intervene when necessary to resolve associate issues expeditiously. In addition, in order to provide advice and guidance regarding work and career concerns, the ombudsperson must have thorough knowledge of the professional development resources and systems available within the firm.

Because the most important ingredient is trust, the ombudsperson must be autonomous. If associates view the person as a powerless administrator or a management "mole," the ombudsperson will be ineffective. The role of the ombudsperson must therefore be very clearly explained to and accepted by the firm, and championed by the firm's leadership and its associates through their recognized leaders.

PART VII

Professional Development in Corporate and Government Settings

CHAPTER 18

Corporate Law Departments

Just like law firms, corporate law departments must provide learning and development opportunities for their lawyers. In-house lawyers have the same need for continual learning and support to stay at the top of their game. Corporations face the same competitive pressures as law firms in recruiting, developing, and retaining first-rate lawyers. But corporate law departments face different issues and conditions as well:

- Lawyers have one client — the corporation.

- Opportunities for advancement within the law department are generally more limited than within a law firm, but multiple career options in law and business are open to the corporation's lawyers.

- Corporations hire few inexperienced lawyers.

- The corporate work environment generally features more peer support and less internal competition.

- Lawyers have no billable hour requirements.

- There is no need for rainmaking.

These features, among others, impact professional development in corporate law departments. Because of the similarities and in spite of the differences between the private and corporate settings, corporate law departments must address each component of professional development to meet the unique learning and development needs of their in-house lawyers. These professional development components include:

- Career advancement and development.

- Orientation.

- Work Assignments.

- Evaluations.
- Mentoring.
- Training.

Given the special issues and conditions in corporate law departments, let's look at how corporations can foster their lawyers' professional development in each of these areas.

Career Advancement and Development

The distinguishing feature of corporate law departments is that they have only one client — the corporation. This can be exciting and challenging as well as frustrating and limiting. Depending on the size of the department and the nature of the company, lawyers may be able to try out many different practice areas or choose to become expert in a few. In many law departments, especially small ones, in-house lawyers have to handle every legal matter that comes in, which means they enjoy constant variety, opportunities for new learning, and a lot of independence. This makes work interesting and requires them to be jacks-of-all-trades. However, it is difficult for lawyers in small departments to develop specialties. Specialization is more common in larger departments.

Another distinction from private practice is the availability of multiple career options within the corporation. While there is little upward mobility in most corporate law departments, diverse career paths are open to in-house lawyers within the company. The limitation on advancement within the law department is that few executive slots exist at the top. Corporations have only one General Counsel and few Associate or Assistant General Counsel positions, so lawyers seeking executive-level jobs must wait a long time for an opening. Lawyers who have no ambition to advance up the corporate ladder are content to remain technical specialists without executive responsibilities. Those lawyers who do seek advancement can move higher in the department through several intermediate steps. Each step carries a different title, new responsibilities, and, sometimes, higher compensation, but the path usually stops short of the top slots.

Alternatively, lawyers can move out of the law department into the business side of the company. These lawyers enjoy substantial and unique opportunities for career development, corporate advancement, and leadership. Corporations are filled with high-ranking business executives who started out in the law department. Branching out into the business arena offers lawyers significant new professional challenges and rewards. They learn to apply their legal skills and training in new ways to help the corporation build and sustain a successful business. Lawyers can be found in many corporate departments, including marketing, regulatory affairs, human resources, securities, mergers and acquisitions, industrial relations, and public relations.

In large corporations, lawyers are frequently able to move from one specialty to another within the law department and from one business unit to another within the company. Many firms permit and even encourage lawyers to spend time in company offices in other locations in the United States or abroad. Some corporations make national or international experience a requirement for advancement.

Many law firm lawyers change practice areas when they become in-house counsel. It is easier for litigators to move into business than it is for business or transactional lawyers to move into litigation. Many litigation skills (e.g., framing legal arguments, questioning witnesses) carry over to any area of legal practice or business. Litigators are able to apply those skills to new fields of practice when they join corporate law departments, whereas moving into litigation requires intensive training in new practice skills. Moreover, the substantive knowledge lawyers acquire in representing litigants often prepares them effectively for handling their new in-house practice. For example, a lawyer who litigated software licensing issues in a firm has knowledge and experience that can easily be applied to commercial contracting or intellectual property work.

Orientation

Orientation for new law school graduates must prepare them for law practice in general and for practice in the corporation. Since most lawyers hired by business entities have previous legal experience, their arrival in the law department is similar to the arrival of lateral lawyers at a law firm. The same orientation considerations discussed in Chapter 12 apply to in-house lawyers. Lawyers who join a corporate law department need orientation to the new company as well as the new department. They need to learn many things: what the company does; who's who in company; corporate policies; the way the company processes work; the company's style in dealing with business partners, clients, and competitors; where to go to get needed information; who needs to review or approve an agreement; and countless other bits of information that will enable them to work and succeed in the corporation. Because the corporate business environment changes frequently, lawyers need to be updated constantly on changes in corporate policies, processes, personnel, structures, products, and the industry in general. Lawyers who have been stationed in international offices need to be re-oriented when they return to the states.

Lateral lawyers who have never worked in-house before need to learn about the corporate environment from square one. These lawyers need to learn skills and approaches that are not emphasized in other work settings. They have to develop an intimate understanding of the corporation's business and start thinking in terms of bottom line instead of billable hours. Lawyers with a background in business may catch on quickly to the way in-house lawyers approach client problems. But lawyers who come from law firms or government may have to adjust to a significantly different way of thinking.

Corporations need both administrative and formal orientations for new lawyers. Orientation should cover the values, structure, systems, operations, procedures, and personnel of both the law department and the company. New counsel need to understand at the outset both how the law department functions and how it relates to the rest of the company. Orientation may take place in one or two days, but in large corporations the orientation process may go on for several months. In addition to the initial orientation, companies can conduct seminars and multi-day conferences to educate their new lawyers on business, management, and legal topics. Many orientation materials can be provided online. The corporation's human resources department usually oversees general orientation to the company for all new employees, including lawyers. Law department managers should work with human resource personnel to organize and conduct additional department-specific orientation programs for lawyers.

Work Assignments

Work is not assigned in law departments the way it is in law firms. When legal work comes in, it "finds its owner" — that is, it flows logically to the person most qualified to do it. If that person is swamped, he or she seeks assistance from someone else in the law department. In a small department, the qualified lawyer is usually a generalist. In larger law departments, lawyers are divided into areas of functional expertise (i.e., patents, tax, litigation, securities) and new projects may be screened, assigned, and monitored by department managers. In small and large departments, in-house counsel tend to work independently; case or transaction teams that do exist are leanly staffed.

The law department should encourage lawyers to be involved in the business of the corporation. It is very important for the corporation's business people to view lawyers as respected contributors to the business. Lawyers should be members of business teams, committees, and task forces that are exploring new markets, developing corporate strategies, or addressing other business matters that have legal implications but may not be seen as legal issues. These assignments give lawyers a chance to learn more about the operation and business of the company, work directly with the company's business people, achieve visibility in other departments, appreciate new business perspectives, and develop internal networks that contribute to advancement.

Law departments must take care that their lawyers are receiving work that is interesting, challenging, and requires them to stretch their abilities. Although in-house lawyers usually handle diverse problems, they can easily fall into the same trap as private lawyers who become skillful at one thing, resulting in consistent but unexceptional performance. Lack of new challenges can also lead to boredom and dissatisfaction, especially if in-house lawyers believe that more interesting work is being sent to outside counsel. To help lawyers stay motivated and keep their legal skills sharp, law departments can encourage their lawyers to actively partner with outside counsel by participating directly in discovery, trials, and deals.

Stretch assignments are another way for lawyers to stay sharp, stay motivated, and develop new capabilities. It is well established that extremely challenging assignments are one of the most effective ways that executives develop leadership skills.[1] Corporations often take individuals they consider to have high potential and place them in difficult projects or situations in which they have to learn quickly and perform well under pressure (e.g., to turn around a failing business unit). Stretch assignments need not be severe, so long as they push the lawyer to expand beyond his or her comfort zone. Successful performance in a stretch assignment results in new learning, high visibility with senior management, and enhanced professional development, and opens up new doors to advancement within the company.

Evaluations

Most corporate law departments conduct performance evaluations of lawyers in their department. Corporate structure and formal human resource procedures usually ensure that performance evaluations of in-house counsel are done regularly and based on clearly articulated standards. In many of these departments, lawyers are evaluated by all the people with whom they work: paralegals, clients, and other lawyers. Evaluation of in-house lawyers requires clear descriptions of lawyers' job responsibilities, identified competencies, and criteria for advancement, and the evaluations should be tied to those competencies and criteria. In most companies, the General Counsel sets the basic criteria for advancement and promotion, but the lawyers in the department, often with assistance from human resources personnel,

---

[1] Morgan W. McCall, Jr., Michael M. Lombardo, and Ann M. Morrison, *The Lessons of Experience: How Successful Executives Develop on the Job*, Lexington Books, New York, 1988.

usually develop the appropriate standards and competencies for in-house lawyers. Lawyers are evaluated on core competencies specific to lawyers, as well as those that apply to all company employees, such as team cooperation and responsiveness.

Evaluations can be used for more than annual performance reviews. For example, the Colgate-Palmolive Company law department has established a comprehensive approach to career development that uses competency-based evaluations, together with individual development plans, to create succession planning profiles. These profiles combine information from each lawyer's evaluation (past performance and activities) and development plan (future goals and aspirations) into a one-page record — a succession planning profile — that the organization uses when new positions or work opportunities come up. The profiles are on a database that can be searched for particular entries (e.g., background, performance, language). Using this data, managers can match individuals with assignments that best suit their professional development needs and goals.

Corporate law departments that do not currently conduct evaluations or do not base evaluations on performance standards should review the discussion of evaluations in Chapter 7, which provides guidelines that can be adapted to the corporate environment.

Mentoring

Legal departments tend to be collegial, and lawyers routinely mentor and teach each other. In-house counsel frequently work alone, with only one lawyer assigned to cases and transactions. When lawyers need help, they call on their colleagues in the department to share expertise, talk over problems and strategies, and lend support and assistance. One reason they routinely teach each other is that they are all working for the same client and the same objective — to make the business succeed. Another reason is that they do not have billable hour requirements hanging over their heads. This means that their compensation is not negatively affected if they spend time mentoring and teaching others.

In-house lawyers in very small legal departments do not have an adequate number of departmental colleagues who can teach them. They face many of the same issues as their counterparts in solo and small private law firms. As the sole source of legal advice for the company, they have to learn quickly, use resources wisely, and think creatively. But they often lack informal, day-to-day interaction with professional colleagues that facilitates learning the skills and knowledge needed to excel in their jobs. The isolation of these lawyers also limits the availability of mentors, especially mentors who understand their career concerns.

Whether in small or large law departments, in-house lawyers must seek their own mentors. While peers can provide worthwhile information and assistance, lawyers also need mentors who can help them advance their careers. These mentors may be within the law department, from another corporate group, or from outside the company. Managers often act as mentors. They have the responsibility for developing the lawyers they supervise, and they help those lawyers set goals, find high-visibility assignments to showcase their skills, and advocate for their promotion. But if managers do not take on this role, then in-house lawyers need to find individuals from other parts of the company who will act as their mentors. Even if lawyers have good mentors inside the company, outside mentors can provide useful and objective insights and perspectives about career issues. Outside mentors are especially advisable for lawyers in very small law departments.

Corporations sponsor many types of formal mentoring programs for "high-potential" employees. Managers identify personnel who show high potential for moving into management and leadership positions. These high-potential individuals are matched with mentors who are senior managers and executives in the company. Some of these programs target women and minorities, but many are not limited to any particular group. These programs present superb career advancement opportunities and in-house lawyers should take advantage of them.

For law departments that wish to be more systematic about mentoring for in-house counsel, the discussion in Chapter 6 of mentoring and mentoring programs provides instruction and guidance. The corporation's human resource department may be able to provide information about mentoring opportunities and programs for lawyers inside and outside the company. (See sidebar on the opposite page.)

Training

Many corporations provide training through in-house or outside programs. Because they hire experienced lawyers, they provide little training in basic legal knowledge or practice skills. But even experienced lawyers need training about the business, culture, philosophy, and systems of the company, as well as its legal issues and practices. Law departments also need to provide the training necessary for in-house lawyers to keep their knowledge and skills up to date, although the degree of training is less than it would be for brand new lawyers.

The extent of formal training is related in large part to the size of the company, the size of the law department, and the General Counsel's philosophy about training. The typical corporate legal department has only about ten lawyers,[2] and

> ## Outside Mentoring and Coaching Services
>
> It is becoming common in corporations today to provide mentoring and coaching for lawyers by contracting with outside providers. Companies do this either by enrolling lawyers in outside mentoring programs or retaining professional coaches to work with lawyers inside the company. Outside mentoring programs, especially for women, are available in many communities. These programs pair up selected lawyers with a mentor from another company for a one-year period. Typically, the mentoring experience is further augmented by workshops, networking events, and presentations that focus on career advancement strategies.
>
> Internal services are offered through professional coaches who work one-on-one, in confidence, with in-house lawyers. Corporations that provide such services usually hope to improve lawyers' work performance and satisfaction. Performance improvement may be remedial, but more often it is intended to help executives become as effective as possible. A secondary goal is to have outside coaches give the company feedback that can lead to institutional improvements in management, development, promotion, or retention. While this feedback is important to the company, the outside coach must be able to guarantee the lawyer complete confidentiality. Feedback to the company must be presented in terms of general findings and patterns; individual lawyer communications must be safeguarded. When contracting for outside mentoring or coaching services, it is therefore imperative that the corporation and the provider have a very clear agreement about objectives, roles, responsibilities, and most importantly, confidentiality.

even in a large law department, there are only a few lawyers in any particular legal specialty. It is not cost-effective to conduct specialized training for small groups of lawyers in many different fields. In addition, because law departments are considered cost centers rather than profit centers, corporations allocate relatively few resources to lawyer training. Law departments therefore limit the amount of formal training they do in-house. Nonetheless, when the General Counsel firmly believes

---

[2] "In-House Counsel: Good Value to Corporations Worldwide," *Legal Management*, March-April, 2002, p.14.

in the importance of continuing education for lawyers, law departments usually obtain the resources needed for training. (See sidebar.)

When a law department conducts its own formal in-house training, lawyers in the department generally design the programs.[3] The most common approach is to integrate training into regularly scheduled law department meetings (e.g., by setting aside time to discuss new legal developments). The training faculty usually consists of lawyers or business people in the corporation, corporate trainers, human resource personnel, or outside faculty. Most training subjects relate to legal knowledge, practice skills, and technology, but in-house lawyers also need training in other areas, such as client relations and management skills. Courses in these subjects should be tailored to the corporate workplace.

---

3 A law department initiating or reassessing lawyer training should conduct a needs analysis and draft a training plan, as discussed in Chapter 8.

Training Program at Oracle Corporation

One corporation whose law department conducts extensive in-house training is Oracle Corporation, which has 45 lawyers in the United States and more than 100 lawyers worldwide. For their U.S.-based lawyers, the law department holds monthly training sessions that lawyers attend in person or by teleconference. Program topics are far ranging and cover legal, management, and business issues. Given the rapid changes in the software industry, these seminars help in-house counsel stay up to speed on company products and policies, current and potential legal issues, and the software industry in general. In addition to lawyers, employees from accounting, contracting, sales, and other aspects of the company's business are invited to attend these training sessions. The training programs integrate lawyers into the business of the company and make business people comfortable with the law department and its counsel. Every year or two, Oracle also holds a global conference, bringing lawyers from all of its offices worldwide to one location. These gatherings are devoted to a legal topic that has international importance for the company's business (e.g., privacy). Speakers from within and outside the company address various aspects of the topic in great depth. Although this kind of conference is an elaborate undertaking, the law department finds that this investment in its lawyers' professional development is worth the effort.

Because they serve only one client, in-house lawyers do not have to develop their own client base or worry about "rainmaking." Nonetheless, in-house lawyers' efficacy and career advancement depend on their delivery of quality client service. They must be highly sensitive and responsive to corporate needs. Even more than lawyers in private firms, in-house lawyers are expected to counsel and prevent legal problems, and solve them creatively and cost-effectively when they arise.

Good management skills are also a necessity for in-house lawyers. Inside the law department, they must know how to manage and coach the people they supervise and mentor, and they also have to be effective managers of outside counsel. In-house lawyers have to educate outside counsel about the company's operations and expectations. They also have to instruct and supervise outside counsel effectively, and monitor the legal work that outside lawyers do. The management skills necessary for this role do not come naturally to many lawyers, so the corporation should offer its lawyers appropriate training in this area. At Turner Broadcasting Systems in Atlanta, for example, all lawyers receive management and supervisory skills training in programs presented by the company's Professional Development Center.

Few law departments offer all the training their lawyers need. To provide this training, they can turn to other departments within the corporation, use outside resources, and utilize knowledge management technologies. These three approaches include the following measures:

Corporate Training Resources

- Utilize the training resources and programs available in other corporate departments (e.g., human resources).
- Invite corporation lawyers, business people, and experts to make presentations at law department meetings.
- Use company-developed or purchased tutorials and training programs.

Outside Resources

- Pay for lawyers to attend pertinent CLE programs and conferences sponsored by outside vendors or clients.
- Sponsor lawyers to join professional associations and networks that provide learning conferences and resources.

- Send lawyers to private law firms' training programs as guests.
- Invite law firms to present training programs for the law department.

Knowledge Management Technologies

- Put legal policy manuals online to explain the company's legal policies and practices.
- Create a knowledge portal intranet with links to outside training resources, including outside law firms' web pages and extranets.
- Make use of computer-based mentoring and training.
- Provide access to training in other locations through videoconferencing, teleconferencing, and webcasting.
- Set up chat rooms to promote information sharing and collaboration.
- Collect briefs, documents, and information from past and current cases and transactions into online brief banks and information repositories.

CHAPTER 19

Lawyers in the Public Sector

Lawyers who work for government agencies have the same need for professional development as those in private law firms and corporate law departments. However, the public sector has economic, bureaucratic, and political constraints that make professional development systems hard to implement and maintain. Because there are so many different local, state, and federal agencies, each with its own approach to professional development, it is difficult to generalize about what is available to government lawyers. Some observations can be made, however.

Government lawyers are not paid as well as their private sector counterparts with comparable expertise and responsibilities. The government therefore entices lawyers with other perks, including exciting work, decent work-life conditions, job stability, and fulfilling career opportunities.[1] At the United States Department of Justice, for example, many lawyers are motivated by "the desire to personally manage cases, get front-line litigation experience, and make a difference."[2] In many government law departments, the work is indeed challenging and interesting, and work conditions are generally felt to be conducive to having a personal life. The absence of billable hours, partnership pressures, and business development demands creates a work environment that is cooperative, collegial, and for many lawyers more appealing than private practice.

One thing that holds true is that most government lawyers get a high volume of work experience right away. The work is usually high quality and often cutting-edge. Government agencies and departments usually have no excess capacity; even new lawyers are given a great deal of responsibility very quickly. Most learning happens on the job with the aid of supervisors and informal mentors. Few offices have structured mentoring programs, although interest in mentoring appears to be growing.

---

[1] Jennifer Myers, "The Lure of Uncle Sam," *Legal Times*, July 30, 2002.
[2] Rena Cervoni and Jeanne Svikhart, "Demystifying the Process: An Insider's Look at DOJ's Recruitment of Lateral Attorneys," *NALP Bulletin*, January 2001, p. 1.

There are, however, downsides to government work. Career paths can be blocked because, as in corporate law departments, there are few openings at the highest levels. The job security that makes government work attractive also keeps some government lawyers in their positions beyond their peak effectiveness. Because of caps on promotion and compensation, senior lawyers often make no more money than the lawyers they manage. This environment may stymie ambitious lawyers.

Another shortcoming is that the quality and amount of training for government lawyers is inconsistent. Although lawyers in many government agencies receive training in substantive law and in skills directly applicable to their work, the amount of formal training available to government lawyers is to a large degree determined by the commitment and power of the elected individual at the top. Elections often result in leadership changes, shifting priorities, and loss of continuity. Elected officials who control the budgets of government law offices rarely view training for lawyers as a budget priority. The need to cut costs, or at least keep costs under control before the next election, results in a short-term focus, not the long-term view that professional development requires.

In many government agencies, training is ad hoc rather than systematic. Typically, one or more lawyers who are interested in training conduct programs that interest them, or where they see a particular need. Faculty consist of lawyers in the office or from another government agency who are selected for their subject matter expertise. Little regard is given to teaching ability or effective program design. Training may continue so long as these interested lawyers are in the office, but it often ceases if they leave.

Recognizing the value and importance of internal professional development efforts, government entities are beginning to dedicate more extensive resources to in-house training for their lawyers. The attractiveness of government work is greatly enhanced by structured opportunities for professional growth and development. In a competitive job market where public entities cannot come close to matching the salaries available in the private sector, training and development initiatives are highly attractive benefits. Like law firms, government employers have found that training their lawyers in-house produces many significant advantages. (See Chapter 8.)

One unique advantage of training in government practice is that it facilitates greater alignment between policies and practice. Public sector lawyers operate within the context and constraints of public policies regarding substantive law and procedure. Personnel dedicated to lawyer training and development can help formulate, screen, and broadcast policies and practices, and then teach lawyers what they need to know to carry them out.

Because of all these benefits, many government law offices are making lawyers' training and development a priority and are devoting substantial resources to it. Two states that have undertaken extensive professional development initiatives for government lawyers are New Jersey and Massachusetts.

In 2000, the New Jersey Attorney General established the Attorney General's Advocacy Institute to provide training for public sector lawyers. (www.njadvocacy-institute.com). Within its first year and a half, more than 1,900 lawyers participated in its programs. The Advocacy Institute presents lectures, seminars, and skills training workshops that address the learning needs of lawyers in different legal divisions. Some programs have general application while others are highly specialized. The Advocacy Institute places special emphasis on the quality of its programming. It sets high standards for course content and teaching, carefully screens and evaluates trainers, and provides training for instructors in teaching and presentation skills. Program faculty include in-house government lawyers, outside trainers, and prominent private lawyers who are recognized experts in their fields. In conjunction with every training program, the Advocacy Institute prepares extensive practice guides that include procedures, pointers, forms, and best practices. An intranet is being developed that will allow the Advocacy Institute to place program materials, practice guides, brief banks, and training resources online. Recognizing its fiscal responsibilities as a public sector training entity, the Advocacy Institute calculates and tracks the expenses per lawyer of each proposed program to determine the cost-effectiveness of conducting programs as opposed to sending lawyers to outside courses.

In Massachusetts, a Senior Counsel in the Attorney General's Office oversees several professional development activities through "Tom Reilly's AG Institute." The AG Institute conducts a large number of training courses in substantive law, skills, management, writing, and legal procedure; presents orientation programs for new lawyers; and sponsors brown bag lunches and other short programs for lawyers to discuss current cases and legal issues, including ethics issues. In addition to training, the Attorney General's Office promotes lawyers' professional development through evaluation and mentoring. All lawyers except those in the highest positions are evaluated every year. The evaluation process includes setting and monitoring individual performance goals. Informal peer mentoring is common, and under the directorship of the AG Institute, there is also a formal writing mentor program and a new manager's mentoring program.

At the federal level, there are many training and development opportunities and resources for lawyers. The Department of Justice (DOJ) is the largest legal employer in the world, with almost 9,000 lawyers throughout the nation.[3] There are 38 separate organizations within the DOJ, each with multiple sections, and they all operate independently with respect to professional development activities. Because the DOJ has lawyers working in virtually every substantive area of law, practicing in the federal government offers expansive practice opportunities. Positions in many agencies and departments are highly competitive and working for the DOJ is a prized credential. DOJ employment can therefore serve as "a very effective career development tool."[4]

One section of the DOJ with a high commitment to training is the Tax Division. The Tax Division has one client, the Internal Revenue Service, which mandates consistency in application of federal civil and criminal tax laws. The Division has many separate, specialized agencies, each of which handles lawyer training and development independently. In order to ensure that all federal tax lawyers have the skills, knowledge, and understanding that they need to apply the tax laws consistently, the Tax Division has an Office of Training, headed by a Director who is a tax lawyer. The Director supervises three full-time staff and two students. This Office conducts an extensive training program for all Tax Division personnel with an array of courses and workshops that range from basic subjects and procedures to highly esoteric topics.

An important training resource available to all government lawyers is the Federal Office of Legal Education (OLE), which develops and conducts legal education and training for lawyers in the Department of Justice and other departments in the Executive Branch.[5] The OLE sponsors the National Advocacy Center (NAC) in Columbia, South Carolina, operated by the Department of Justice's Executive Office for United States Attorneys. Courses cover a wide range of federal practice subjects and issues, civil and administrative law, trial and appellate advocacy, and management skills. Experienced federal trial and appellate lawyers teach the courses, which include basic and advanced programs, as well as special courses for experienced lawyers who are new to government practice. Courses are held throughout the year at the NAC and many are available on video and audiotape. Some courses are broadcast live by satellite to U.S. Attorneys offices around the country. The National Bankruptcy Training Institute is also located at the NAC, and the National District Attorneys Association conducts programs there for state and local prosecutors.

---

[3] "Where the Government Jobs Are," *Legal Times*, July 2002.
[4] Linda Cinciotta, "Professional and Career Development in the Federal Government," http://www.usdoj.gov/oarm/pdq.htm.
[5] The Office of Legal Education web site is http://www.usdoj.gov/usao/eousa/ole.html.

Ida O. Abbott, Esq., is a leading authority on lawyers' professional development, having almost 30 years' experience as both a lawyer and consultant. Her firm, Ida Abbott Consulting, advises law firms and organizations worldwide on all aspects of lawyer development, performance, management, and retention, and on the career advancement of women. Ida has served as a San Francisco Superior Court judge pro tem, held leadership positions in the Bar Association of San Francisco and the State Bar of California, and is a founding member of the Professional Development Consortium (PDC).

For more information on her expertise and services, visit her web site at **www.IdaAbbott.com** or contact her at **IdaAbbott@aol.com**.

Ida is the author of two other best selling books, *The Lawyers' Guide to Mentoring* and *Developing Legal Talent*. She also wrote the popular booklets, *Being an Effective Mentor: 101 Practical Strategies for Success*, and *Working with a Mentor: 50 Practical Suggestions for Success*. All of these publications are available from NALP.

NALP is a nonprofit alliance of ABA-accredited law schools and legal employers. Founded in 1971 as the National Association for Law Placement, NALP is committed to the mission of providing preeminent leadership and expertise in legal career planning, recruitment and hiring, employment, and professional development worldwide.

To order *The Lawyer's Guide to Mentoring* or *Developing Legal Talent* by Ida Abbott or the mentoring booklets mentioned above, or to learn about other resources available from NALP, visit:

www.nalp.org

Index

360° evaluations/reviews, 184, 201, 219-221, 225, 381, 394

ABA, 17-18n, 21-22n, 30, 152n, 155n, 185n, 204n, 228n, 242, 250, 267, 271n, 378, 382
    MacCrate Report, 31, 204n, 242n
    Model Rules, 30
ABA Center for Continuing Legal Education, 267
ABA Center for Professional Responsibility, 271n
ABA Commission on Billable Hours, 17-18n, 152n, 155n
ABA Commission on Racial and Ethnic Diversity, 378
ABA Commission on Women in the Profession, 185n, 382
ABA Model Rules, 30
Abbott, Ida O., 111, 154n, 163n, 185n, 259n, 382, 393n
Abrahams, Sharon M., 285n
Ackoff, Russell L., 111
ACLEA — see Association for Continuing Legal Education
Adult learning, 92-95
    environment, 104-110
    formal learning, 103-104
    informal learning, 101-104
    Knowles, Malcolm, 92-93
    Kolb's Learning Model, 93
Affiliates, The, 145
African-American lawyers, 378
AG Institute, 413
AILTO, 259, 267, 271
ALA — see Association of Legal Administrators
ALI-ABA, 9, 259, 267
Alliances, 84
Alston & Bird LLP, 214
Alternative career paths, 321
Am Law 200, 24
Aman, Catherine, 32

American Bar Association, 17-18n, 21-22n, 30, 152n, 155n, 185n, 204n, 228n, 242, 250, 267, 271n, 378, 382
American Bar Association Pro Bono Project, 152n
American Law Institute, The, 278n
American Lawyer, The, 119n
American Society for Training and Development, 251, 267
Anderson, Austin G., 204n, 242n, 329n
Argyris, Chris, 94n, 111
Armstrong, Stephen V., 15n, 26n, 308n
Assessing professional development programs, 50-51
Association for Continuing Legal Education, 250-251, 267
Association of Legal Administrators, 73, 204n, 242n, 267
ASTD — see American Society for Training and Development
Attorney General's Advocacy Institute, 413
Axelrod, Beth, 185n

Bar Association of San Francisco, 382
Beers, Michael C., 320n
Behaviors, 101
    changing, 101
Benchmarks, 116, 189-190, 192-193, 204-205, 207, 236, 239-240, 393
    diversity issues, 380
    tiers, 192
Benefits of professional development, 24-32
    CLE compliance, 32
    client relationships, 30
    liability, protection from, 31
    professional responsibility, 30
    professional satisfaction, 29
    profitability, 26
    promotion, 28
    recruitment, 27
    retention, 28
    succession planning, 31
Billable hour targets, 18
Billable hours, 17, 135, 139, 174
Billable hour requirements, 18
Bingham McCutchen LLP, 133n, 137
Blackwell Sanders Peper Martin LLP, 190n, 191
Borden Ladner Gervais LLP, 27

Brag memos, 215
Bransford, John D., 98n
Braverman, Paul, 24n
Brown, Ann L., 98n
Budgeting, 327-337
    budgeting process, 330-335
    justifying costs, 328-329
    small firm, 329
    special issues, 335-337
Business goals and strategy, 14-15, 37, 43, 236
Business objectives, 15

Calvert, Cynthia Thomas, 382
Career benchmarks — see Benchmarks
Career counseling, 388
Career guidance, 388-391
Catalyst, 22n, 154n, 382
    Women in the Law: Making the Case, 22, 154, 156
Center for Law Firm Management, 234
Certification, lack of, 73
Certified Legal Manager (CLM), 73
Cervoni, Rena, 411n
Changes in attitudes about legal careers, 23-24
Changes in law practice, 17-19
    less career certainty, 19
    less loyalty and cohesion, 19
    more pressure at work, 17-18
    more speed, less down time, 18
    more work, less opportunity to learn, 18
Changes in the industry, 19-23
    growth and consolidation, 20
    tight labor market, 21-23
Changing behaviors, 101, 216-219
Chat rooms, 311
ChevronTexaco, 225, 308-309
Chitwood, Stephen R., 204n, 242n
Churchill, Winston, 129, 153
Cinciotta, Linda, 414n
CLE, 32, 65, 71, 86, 237-238, 241, 247-250, 267, 270, 273-274, 276, 283, 286, 288, 299-301, 315, 409
    choosing providers, 299-301
    firms as accredited providers, 278-281
    mandatory, 284
    online, 254-256
    tracking, 32, 67, 69, 71, 237-238, 255-256, 274, 279-281

CLE tracking, 32, 67, 69, 71, 237-238, 255-256, 274, 279-281
Client contact, 124
Client surveys, 240
Coaching, 165, 258, 407
    in corporate law departments, 407
Cocking, Rodney R., 98n
Cognitive knowledge, 96-98
Colgate-Palmolive Company, 194-195, 405
Columbia Business School, 382
Committees, 58, 82, 367-368
    associate, 386-387
    associate participation on, 383-387
    associates, 86
    professional development, 65-66, 87
Communication, 58-59
Compensation, 108, 125
Competencies — see Core competencies
Components of professional development, 33-35, 56
Cooley Godward LLP, 285, 303-306
Core competencies, 45, 189-190, 194-195, 205-207, 236, 239-240, 393
    diversity issues, 380
Corporate law department, 194, 225, 359, 400-410
    career advancement and development, 401-402
    coaching, 407
    evaluations, 404-405
    knowledge management, 410
    mentoring, 405-407
    orientation, 402-403
    positions, 401
    training, 406-410
    work assignments, 403-404
Corporate Pro Bono Project, The, 152n
Course design, 257-261
    audience needs, 257
    developing an agenda, 259, 261
    securing resources, 261
    setting learning objectives, 257-258
    teaching methods, 259-260
Cross-staffing, 140
Culture, 185, 378, 389
    diversity issues, 381-382
Culture, firm, 44
Cusumano, Michael A., 277n

Davenport, Thomas H., 320n
Deal rooms, 311
DeLong, David W., 320n
Department of Justice, 413-414
Designing a professional development program, 36-61
    Force Field Analysis, 52-53
    SLOT analysis, 53-54
District Attorneys, 149
Diversity issues, 378-382
    culture, 381-382
    evaluations, 380
    mentoring, 381
    training, 379
    work assignments, 380
Diversity training, 233, 379
Dixon, Nancy M., 309n, 320n
Dorsey & Whitney LLP, 81, 175
DuPont, 308-309

E-learning, 251
Ely, Robin J., 381n
Emerson, Ralph Waldo, 154
Emotional intelligence, 100-101
Englert, Gayle P., 340
Ernst & Young, 308-309
Evaluation summary, 212
Evaluations, 71, 138, 166, 182-230, 239
    see also *Performance standards*
    360-degree reviews, 184, 195, 201, 219-220, 221, 225
    anonymity, 213-214
    appeals process, 227
    associates, 45, 199, 221
    benchmarks, 192 (*see also* Benchmarks)
    client evaluations, 221
    corporate law departments, 404-405
    delivering, 216-217, 224
    development goals, 229-230
    development plans, 218-219
    development-oriented, 197-199
    diversity issues, 380
    evaluators' selection, 223
    follow-up, 225-227
    frequency, 225
    initiating a system, 228
    level system, 190-191
    lockstep system, 190-191
    maximizing participation, 226
    new program roll-out, 224-225
    partners, 200-202, 219, 221
    peer reviews, 184, 219-220
    performance standards, 186-189, 191, 202-205
    personnel and resources, 227-228
    pre-partnership review, 222
    procedures, 208-227
    purpose, 196-201
    questionnaires, 209-210
    self-assessments, 215
    Special Counsel, 222
    summer programs, 345-347
    training to deliver, receive, 217
    upward reviews, 45, 184, 201, 213, 217, 219-221, 226
Evaluators, 223
Exit interviews, 240, 350
Experience-based learning, 94
Extranets, 251, 310-311

Faculty, 262-270, 302
    guidelines, 303-306
    in-house, 262-266
    outside, 266-270
    training, 264-266
"Families," 133
Farella Braun + Martel LLP, 110
Federal Office of Legal Education (OLE), 414
Feedback, 109, 129, 182-185, 215
    summer programs, 345-347
Fenwick & West LLP, 138
Firm culture, 44
Fitch, Valerie, 272n
Force field analysis, 52-53
Formal learning, 103-104
Fried, Frank, Harris, Shriver & Jacobson, 81, 387
Fuller, Margaret, 308

Gabarro, John J., 382
Galvin, Tammy, 251n
General Counsel positions, 401
General Electric, 308
Generational differences, 16
Goal setting, 107

Goals, strategic, 37, 43
Goleman, Daniel, 100n, 111
Gottlieb, Anita F., 204n, 242n
Government settings, 359, 411-414
　　training, 412-414
Graham, Deborah, 382
Greene, Arthur G., 204n, 242n, 329n
Group mentoring, 160-161

Hale and Dorr LLP, 291-293
Hallowell, Edward M., 254
Hamberg, Nina J., 361n
Hammond Suddards Edge, 323
Handfield-Jones, Helen, 185n
Hansen, Morten T., 309n
Heller Ehrman White & McAuliffe, 299n
Hewlett, Sylvia Ann, 382
Hispanic lawyers, 378
Holliday, Chad, 309n
Holton, Elwood F., 93n, 111
Horvath, Joseph A., 92n, 111
Howard Rice Nemerovski Canady Falk & Rabkin, 290
Howrey Simon Arnold & White LLP, 347
Human resource management, 139
Human resources department, 80, 82

Informal learning, 101-104
Informal mentoring, 156
Intellectual capital, 91
Interdisciplinary groups, 147
Internal alliances, 84
Internet, 251, 311
Intranets, 59-61, 203, 251, 310-311

Job descriptions, 88-90
Jones, Thomas, 30n
Jordan-Evans, Sharon, 119n
Juli, Krista, 299n

Know-how, 97
Know-what, 96
Know-why, 97
Knowledge
　　cognitive, 96-98
　　practical, 96-98
　　understanding, 96-97
Knowledge management, 307-325
　　and professional development, 315-316
　　automatic knowledge capture, 320
　　benefits, 314
　　in corporate law departments, 410
　　obstacles, 316-318
　　personnel, 321
　　PSLs, 322
　　supporting learning, 319-325
　　web-based systems, 312-313
Knowles, Malcolm, 92-93, 111
Kolb's Learning Model, 93
Kolb, David, 93, 111
　　learning model, 93
Korn/Ferry International, 310n, 382
Kram, K. E., 157n
Kritzer, Herbert M., 20-21n

Laissez faire, 131, 380
Landwell Legal Services, 20n
Lardent, Esther F., 150n
Latham & Watkins, 147, 294-298
Lauritsen, Marc, 308n
Lawyer integration, 71
Layoffs, 140
Leadership training, 394-395
Learning, continuous, 106
Learning culture, 103
Learning environment, 104-110
Learning goals, 320
Learning objectives, 257-258
Learning outcomes, 118
Learning resources, 109
Learning styles, 95
Learning theory, 91-111
Legal careers, 23
Leishman, Tim, 27n
Letalik, Norman, 27
"Level System," 190-191
Lewin, Karl, 52

Lex Mundi, 150
Librarians, 86
LL.M. degree programs, 283
"Loaner" program, 149-150
Lockstep system, 17, 190-191
Lombardo, Michael M., 126n, 404n
Loyola University School of Law, 271

MacCrate Report, 31, 204n, 242n
Magliozzi, Sandra, 299n
Maister, David H., 30n, 230, 185n, 329n
Major, Hagen & Africa, 360n
Mara, Evelyn Gaye, 204n, 242n, 257n, 315n
Marketing, 85
Markides, Constantinos C., 277n
Marshall School of Business, 310n
Martin, Ronald M., 393n
Mayson, Stephen, 234
McCall, Morgan W., Jr., 104n, 111, 126n, 341n, 404n
McCollam, Douglas, 20n
McCutchen Doyle Brown & Enersen LLP, 133, 137
McKinsey & Company, 115, 232n, 309
McMeekin, Chris, 104n
Mentor, natural, 161
Mentoring, 108, 154-181
    as business imperative, 163
    benefits, 154-157
    career functions, 157
    and coaching, 165
    diversity issues, 381
    group, 160-161
    in corporate law departments, 405-407
    informal, 156-158
    long-distance, 172
    performance-based, 164
    psychosocial functions, 157
    recognition, 159
    resources, 159
    responsibilities, 166
    skills, 175-176
    small firms, 161
    summer programs, 348-349
    training curriculum, 181
    training in, 175-176
    upward, 160
    women and minority associates, 156

Mentoring agreements, 167, 180
Mentoring programs, 156, 160-175
    checklist for establishing, 177-179
    confidentiality, 168-169
    criteria for participation, 167
    duration of relationship, 167
    elements, 163
    financial support, 169
    guidelines, 167-169
    incentives for participation, 174
    leadership commitment, 163
    objectives, 164-165
    program coordinator, 169-170
    recruiting mentors, 172
    scope of relationship, 168
    selection and matching process, 170-172
    time commitment, 168
Mentors as supervisors, 173
Merit system, 17
Metatags, 319
Michaels, Ed, 185n
Miller, Katya, 299n
Minority Corporate Counsel Association, 382
Minority lawyers, 378-382
Model Rules of Professional Conduct, 30
Morgan, Miller & Blair, 161
Morris, Kathy M., 15n
Morrisey, George L., 53n
Morrison & Foerster LLP, 81, 169, 299n
Morrison, Ann M., 126, 404n
Myers, Jennifer, 22n, 411n

NALP, 154n, 159n, 185n, 228n, 267, 277n, 340, 378n, 382, 411n
    Beyond the Nuts and Bolts, 228
NALP Foundation, The, 21n, 22n, 23n, 25n, 29n, 154n, 344n, 378n, 383n
    Beyond the Bidding Wars, 22n, 29n, 378n, 383n
    Keeping the Keepers, 22n, 25n, 154n, 344n, 383n
    The Lateral Lawyer, 21n, 22n, 23n, 25n
    Perceptions of Partnership, 23n, 114n, 154n, 156n, 383n
National Advocacy Center (NAC), 414
National Bankruptcy Training Institute, The, 414
National District Attorneys Association, 414

National Institute for Trial Advocacy, 149, 259, 271
Native Americans, 378n
New York University School of Law, 271
NITA — *see* National Institute for Trial Advocacy
Nixon Peabody LLP, 211
Nohria, Nitin, 309n

Objectives, 15-16
Ombudsperson, 369, 396-398
Online training, 354
ORACLE, 238, 281
Oracle Corporation, 408
Orientation programs, 242, 351-375
    administrative, 351-352
    associate, 358
    content and format, 353-366
    in corporate law departments, 402-403
    lateral associates, 359-360
    lateral partners, 360-362, 375
    laterals, 358-359, 367
    location, 369-370
    new associate, 354-358, 366
    newly elevated partners, 362-367, 372-375
    personnel, 367-369
    purpose, 351-353
    social events, 370-371
    summer programs, 343-344
    timing and frequency, 366-367
Outside providers, 407

Pacific Rim Advisory Council, 150
Palazzo, Dottie, 280n
Paralegals, 86
Partner development, 72
Partner of the Year Award, 175
PDC — *see* Professional Development Consortium
Pearlman, Laura, 119n
Peer reviews, 184, 220
Performance standards, 186-189, 191, 202-208
    benchmarks, 189-190, 192-193, 204-205, 207
    core competencies, 189-190, 194-195, 205-207
    diversity issues, 380
Pillsbury Winthrop LLP, 353, 374-375
    lateral partners, 374

PLI — *see* Practising Law Institute
"Pods," 133
Polak, Werner L., 26n
"Pools," 133, 137
Post-graduate training, lack of, 96
Practical knowledge, 97-98
Practice environment, 17
Practice group assignments — rotation systems, 146-148
Practice groups, 145-148
    assignments, 146
    changing, 148
    interdisciplinary, 147
    new associate assignments, 146
    SIGs, 147
Practising Law Institute, 252
Pro bono, 150, 152-153
Pro Bono Institute, The, 152n
Productivity, 135-137
Professional development committee, 65-66, 87
Professional Development Consortium, 9, 267, 384n
Professional Development Institute, 9
Professional Development Quarterly, 200n, 251n, 253n, 280n, 315n
Professional development specialists, 66-90
    finding, 76-79
    qualifications, 73-76
    reporting relationships, 79-83
    responsibilities, 66-73
    titles, 66-67
Professional judgment, 99-100
Professional support lawyers, 322
Project for Attorney Retention, The, 382
Proskauer Rose LLP, 107
PSLs, 322
Public Defenders, 149
Public interest, 359
Public sector, 411-414

Question-and-answer web pages for clients, 311

Recruiting, 85, 240, 340-350
Resistance to change, 17
Retention, 71-72
Rewards, 108
Rhode, Deborah L., 382
Risk-taking, 109
ROE, 277-278
ROK, 277-278

Sabbaticals, 110
Sasser, W. Earl, 30n
Schon, Donald, 94n
Schroeder, Jim, 20n
Secondment, 149
Severson & Werson, 289
Shadowing, 107
Shearman & Sterling, 150
Shook, Hardy & Bacon LLP, 353, 372-373
SIGs, 147
Simpson, Liz, 277n
Singer, Linda R., 396n
Sloan, Peter B., 190n
SLOT analysis, 53-54
Small firms, 14, 20, 39, 41, 64-65, 73, 130-132, 142, 161, 211, 221, 232, 244, 246, 282, 289, 316, 329, 340, 348, 353, 405-406
Special Counsel, 222
Spherion Corporation, 23-25
Stark, Edward C., 111
Sternberg, Robert J., 92n, 111
Strategic plan, 240, 393
Strategic vision, 14-15
Strategy, developing, 38, 41-54
    information gathering, 41-46
Strategy, leading, 38-41
    decision-making responsibility, 40
    information-gathering responsibilities, 39-40
    oversight, 39
"Stretch" assignments, 126, 128-129
Succession planning, 31-32, 392-395, 405
Summer programs, 340, 342-344
    elements, 343
    evaluations and feedback, 345-347
    learning, 347-348
    mentoring, 348-349
    orientation, 343-344
    social events, 349
    supervision, 345
    work assignments, 344-345
Supervising lawyers, 120-122, 125
    summer programs, 345-346
Svikhart, Jeanne, 411n
Swanson, Richard, 93n, 111
SWOT analysis, 53n

Tacit knowledge, 92
Teaching methods, 259-260
Thelen Reid & Priest LLP, 288, 299
Thomas, David A., 154n, 156n, 381n, 382
Thomas, Lewis, 104
Tierney, Thomas, 309n
Tiers, 192
Time management, 233
Tom Reilly's AG Institute, 413
Torres, Sandra, 269n
Training, 231-306
    see also CLE
    administrative support, 274
    client relations/development, 244
    communications, 244
    costs, 275
    course design, 257-261
    curriculum, 289-298
    curriculum considerations, 242-247
    designing a plan, 241
    diversity issues, 233, 379-380
    e-training vs. classroom, 254-255
    encouraging participation, 285-287
    evaluating, 275-278
    faculty, 262-270, 302-306
    follow-up, 258
    in corporate law departments, 406-410
    in government settings, 412-414
    in-house vs. outside CLE, 247-251
    including clients, 287-288
    interdisciplinary, 243
    management, 243
    mandatory vs. voluntary, 284
    materials, 270-272
    multi-office firms, 281-284
    needs analysis, 235-241
    online, 254-255, 315
    orientation, 242

(Training, continued)
    practice skills, 242
    professionalism, 244
    setting priorities, 240-241
    sites, 273
    small firms, 244, 246
    substantive law, 242
    technology, 244, 251-256, 275
    time frame, 247
    time management, 233
    timing of, 272-273
    topics, 245, 302
    use of copyrighted materials, 271
    writing, 233

Training and Development, 119n
Training partners, 64-65
Turner Broadcasting Systems, 409

U.S. Attorneys, 414
University of Pennsylvania, 271
Upward mentoring, 160
Upward evaluations/reviews, 184, 200n, 213, 217, 219-221, 226, 381
    summer programs, 347

Videoconferencing, 253, 367

Wallace, Jean E., 154n
Web site, 310-311
Web-based training, 251
Webcast, 252-253
Welch, Jack, 31
White, Christine, 253n
Whittingham, Stewart, 277n, 328n
Wiley Rein & Fielding LLP, 165

Williams, Joan, 382
Wilmer, Cutler & Pickering, 81
Women lawyers, 378-382
Work allocation systems, 131, 136, 380
    see also Work assignments
    laissez faire, 380
    traffic signal system, 136
    vs. laissez faire, 131
Work assignments, 107, 114-129, 131-133, 135-145, 147-153, 166
    administrative support, 144
    allocating, 130-135
    allocation system, 143-144
    allocation system components, 140-142
    assignment broker systems, 132-134
    developmental, 116-124, 126-129, 136-139
    diversity issues, 380
    "families," 133
    free market systems, 134-135
    human resource management, 139
    in corporate law departments, 403-404
    learning outcomes, 118
    monitoring, 135-139
    "pods," 133
    "pools," 133, 137
    practice group, 145-146, 148
    pro bono, 150, 152-153
    productivity, 135-137
    progress, 137-139
    "stretch" assignments, 126, 128-129
    summer programs, 344-345
    workload disparity, 139
    written procedures, 141-142
Work-life balance, 357, 381-382, 389, 411
World Wide Web, 251, 310-311
Writing classes, 233